CO-AVN-605

UNIVERSITY OF WINNIPEG
LIBRARY
DISCARDED
515 Portage Avenue
Winnipeg, Manitoba R3B 2E9

Literary Theory and Structure

PN
85
. B72

Literary Theory and Structure

Essays in Honor of William K. Wimsatt

edited by Frank Brady, John Palmer,

and Martin Price

Yale University Press · New Haven and London

1973

Copyright © 1973 by Yale University.
All rights reserved. This book may not be
reproduced, in whole or in part, in any form
(except by reviewers for the public press),
without written permission from the publishers.
Library of Congress catalog card number: 72-91311
International standard book number: 0-300-01603-4

Designed by John O. C. McCrillis
and set in Baskerville type.
Printed in the United States of America by
The Vail-Ballou Press, Binghamton, New York.

Published in Great Britain, Europe, and Africa by
Yale University Press, Ltd., London.
Distributed in Canada by McGill-Queen's University
Press, Montreal; in Latin America by Kaiman & Polon,
Inc., New York City; in Australasia and Southeast
Asia by John Wiley & Sons Australasia Pty. Ltd.,
Sydney; in India by UBS Publishers' Distributors Pvt.,
Ltd., Delhi; in Japan by John Weatherhill, Inc., Tokyo.

Contents

Preface

The authors and editors of the essays here presented have come together in this undertaking to honor William K. Wimsatt, Jr., on his sixty-fifth birthday. Some of the participants have had the benefit of his stimulating companionship as a teaching colleague at Yale University; all of them know the warmth of his friendship and his generosity as a colleague in the realm of letters. The list of eligible contributors compiled on such a basis—scholars who over the past four decades have been taught or influenced or otherwise kindly treated by William K. Wimsatt—could of course have been indefinitely extended. The group who have here made their public acknowledgment are therefore to be regarded simply as representative of the larger number whose papers would have been gratefully received for this collection if problems of time and space had not intervened.

"Literary Theory and Structure," the general theme under which the essays of this collection were prepared, was chosen both for its promise as a subject deserving further critical discussion and for its appropriateness in terms of the occasion. No reader of this volume will need to be instructed on the commanding (and in some instances, for our time at least, decisive) role played by the contributions of William K. Wimsatt in this area of criticism. As will be seen, the theme has been interpreted here with some measure of freedom—sufficient, it is hoped, to offer the reader a generous variety of engagement but not so broad as to put aside the sense of a community of discourse. As widely as they range, however, and appropriately representative as they all are of various strata of the Wimsatt lode, they by no means reflect all the multi-faceted richness of the whole. So many civilized interests, pursued with such zest and such consistency of intellectual and moral commitment over so long a time and adding up to so large a body of

vii

enduring accomplishment, could not even be touched upon in their entirety in a collection having to be kept within manageable limits.

Whatever the reverences usually attending so senior an anniversary, seldom could an occasion of this sort have had less of a valedictory significance. It is for contributors and editors alike the happiest of its aspects that it honors a man who makes his large way through the world with undiminished powers to learn and to instruct, and ever enlarging powers to inspire affection and respect.

Theory

Synchrony and Diachrony: A Plea for the Use in Literary Studies of Saussure's Concepts and Terminology

FREDERICK A. POTTLE

During the greater part of my adult life, I have been trying to work a satisfactory way through the problem of time in the study of literature; particularly, to clarify my notions concerning "criticism" (or "evaluation") and "history of literature." In order to do my job as a teacher of English literature, I was in daily need of such distinctions, but for many years I had a discouraging feeling that my organizing principles lacked clarity and logical coherence. From the time that the New Criticism appeared, I felt that it ignored or slighted a necessary dimension of literary studies, but my definitions of the lack and of the dimension never satisfied me long.[1] I belatedly found in Ferdinand de Saussure a model for the radical analysis I was attempting to make, and as Saussure, though very well known to linguists, is a scholar who still remains practically unknown to teachers of English literature, I shall devote this essay to an exposition of his central principle and a translation of that principle into forms that teachers of literature can use.

Ferdinand de Saussure was not a teacher of literature; rather, he was a teacher of language in and for itself, a philologist, a linguist. A Swiss educated in Switzerland and Germany, he was variously Instructor in the École des Hautes Études, Paris (1881–91), Professor of Indo-European Linguistics and Sanskrit at Geneva (1901–13), finally also Professor of General Linguistics at Geneva (1907–13). In the last-named capacity, he laid the theoretical foundations for a science of general linguistics in lectures which were never published and of which no comprehensive manuscripts have ever been found. His *Course in General Linguistics,* like Aristotle's *Poetics,* was reconstructed from student notes, and, like Aristotle's *Poetics,* is bumpy and difficult reading. His great contribution to linguistic theory was to make a radical distinction between what he called the static or synchronic approach to language and the evolutionary or diachronic approach. Before I state this distinction abstractly, let me embody it in an illustration of my own.

Wade Baskin, translator of the English edition of Saussure's *Course,*[2] says in his Introduction that Saussure's "unique insight into the phenomenon of language brought to fruition the best of contemporary thinking." If I had found that use of the word "fruition" in a student's paper in the earlier years of my teaching, I should flatly have told the student that it was incorrect. "The word 'fruition,' " I should have said, "has nothing to do with the word 'fruit'; it means 'enjoyment.' It was taken into English from French in the fourteenth century, its ultimate original, Latin *fruitiōnem,* being a noun of action from *fruī,* 'to enjoy.' Down to about 1885, as is shown by the *Oxford English Dictionary,* it was consistently used in its etymological sense. The beautiful Epiphany collect of the *Book of Common Prayer* petitions 'that we, who know thee now by faith, may after this life have the fruition of thy glorious Godhead.' Suckling and Cowley wrote poems entitled *Against Fruition,* and Waller answered Suckling; all three only too clearly meant not procreation but sexual enjoyment. Milton meant sexual enjoyment when he contrasted to wedded love

> the bought smile
> Of Harlots, loveless, joyless, unindeard,
> Casual fruition.[3]

The prayers of Milton's Adam and Eve before the Fall, said Dr. Johnson, consisted of little more than admiration and gratitude. 'Fruition left them nothing to ask, and Innocence left them nothing to fear'; that is, 'They were already enjoying everything they desired, and all their enjoyments were innocent.' [4] But from late in the nineteenth century, undoubtedly because knowledge of Latin was becoming rare among literate speakers of English, 'fruition' was assumed to have as its stem the accidentally identical 'fruit,' and 'fruition' acquired the meaning 'a coming into fruit, a fulfilment.' A careful speaker will avoid that usage as a barbarism."

So in 1930, but though I shall never use the word so myself, I no longer challenge the usage in others. Indeed, the most I had a right to say to my supposed student forty years ago would have been, "Do you consider that usage respectable? Has 'fruition' been used in that sense by enough respected speakers of English to assure its status?" For any one who has given the matter proper thought knows that the meanings of words are not fixed by their etymologies and are not fixed by the ways they have been used in the past. "Fruition" is by no means the only English word that has shifted its meaning through folk (that is, historically uninformed) etymology. "Demean" = "lower in dignity, debase" does not derive historically from "mean" = "inferior, base"; its historical connection is with "demeanor" "behavior" and it derives from French *demener*. The sense "lower in dignity, debase" did not become common till the eighteenth century, and probably arose from misinterpretation of passages like Shakespeare's "Now out of doubt Antipholus is mad, / Else would he neuer so demeane himselfe." [5] And the fact that meanings of words become old-fashioned or obsolete is so well known as to require no illustration. The sole authority for good usage in language at a given moment in history is the prevailing usage of respected speakers of the language at that moment. But, if the usage of the past is no absolute rule for the usage of the present, the converse is equally true. A teacher who assigned the present-day meaning of "fruition" to texts by Suckling or Waller or Milton or Cowley or Johnson would seriously misread his author.

Saussure seldom dealt with semantics, but he provides many grammatical examples of the distinction. In modern English, with relatively few exceptions, the plural of nouns is formed by adding -*s* or -*es* to the singular, but Old English, like Latin, preserved several classes of nouns, and formed the plural with various endings, of which -*as* was only the most common. In a very early period of the language, the modern English word "foot" was *fōt* and the plural was * *fōti*. By the operation of two general sound changes which had nothing to do with meaning, * *fōti* became *fēt* (Modern English "feet"). *Fōt* in Old English of the historical period, we would now say, belongs to a small class of "umlaut plurals" (Modern English "foot" : "feet"; "tooth" : "teeth"; "goose" : "geese") which form their plurals, not by a suffix, but by internal change of a vowel. From the evolutionary (diachronical) point of view, however, that was not at all what happened. The change of vowel was not a mechanism for indicating plurality. It was something that happened to *every* stressed *ō* in the language when an *i* followed in the next syllable; the change affected nouns, verbs, adjectives, and adverbs indiscriminately. From the diachronical point of view * *fōti,* through fortuitous sound change, simply *lost* its sign for the plural. Umlaut plural did *not* evolve phonologically out of plurals in *i*. It was a brand new psychological creation by speakers of the language: when * *fōti* lost its *i,* they *read plural signification into* the alteration of the vowel. For *any* difference between forms, even if it is fortuitous, even if it is a difference between something and nothing, can be taken advantage of and *made* to "signal the distinction between singular and plural: *fōt* : *fēt* is no better for this purpose than *fōt* : * *fōti*. In each state the mind infiltrated a given substance and breathed life into it." [6]

Accordingly, Saussure insisted on the necessity of distinguishing absolutely between the study of states of a language (e.g. Twentieth-century English Grammar) and the evolution of a language in time (e.g. Old and Middle English Grammar). Though he frequently spoke of static linguistics and evolutionary linguistics, he preferred the terms "synchronic" and "diachronic": "Everything that relates to the static side of our science is synchronic; everything that has to do with evolution is diachronic." [7] Further, he continues, not only are the two approaches distinct, they cannot be blended operationally. If one is studying a language-state, one "must discard all knowledge of everything that produced it. . . . The diachronic facts are not related to the static facts which they produced. They belong to a different class. . . . The diachronic perspective deals with phenomena that are unrelated to systems although they do condition them." [8] A state of language corresponds to a state in a game of chess. A person who sees a chess-board after several moves have been made can play the game out just as well as a spectator who has seen the game from the beginning. The way the state came about makes absolutely no difference to the playing of the game.[9]

Saussure believed that economic science, by its radical prag-matic division of the discipline into political economy and eco-nomic history, showed the same inner necessity as language-study of holding synchrony and diachrony apart. In other learnings where time is or may be a factor—astronomy, geology, law, polit-ical history—he saw no embarrassment in a mingling of modes.[10] What shall we say of synchrony and diachrony in the study of liter-ature?

It has been contended that the separation in that province also must be absolute: "Every poem is anonymous; and between the materials of a poem and the poem itself the difference is ab-solute." [11] In my own fairly extensive experience I have not found this to be true. Some of the many attempts I have made to enlist diachrony (sources, influences, biography) in aid of the reading of poems as poems seem to me to have elicited synchronic value in a clean and efficient manner.[12] But I have to add that in my teach-ing I have found myself steadily working towards a separation of the modes. I now think that I was mistaken about the direction of much of my ancillary diachronics: I was getting values all right but the values were diachronic values, better obtained by apply-ing that mode pure. The connection between diachrony and syn-chrony in the study of literature is real but it is a subtle and diffi-cult connection which requires awareness and much practice if it is to be effectively exploited. What Saussure did for me was to show in a thoroughly convincing manner that two approaches to language, both of which he and I considered necessary, were *dif-ferent;* was it not probable, then, that these two approaches as applied to literature were different too? And it seemed to me so important to establish this fact of difference that for some time

I have resolutely separated them in my teaching and have tried to get my students in their exercises to do the same. It is essential in this business to know exactly what you are doing; and the best way to train yourself in that knowledge is to practice the modes pure.

The synchronical mode should surely take precedence at any level of instruction. One does not primarily read poems as documents for constructing a history of literature. On the first time round, nothing is gained by reading poets in the order of their birth-dates, nor by reading an author's poems in the order in which he wrote them, nor by reading his entire poetical works. The teacher's rule for making assignments should be simply to select from each poet the poems which his last year's students found most congenial. Each poem is like Saussure's chess-game: it doesn't matter how the pieces got that way. Antiquarian annotation should be strictly confined to what is needed for playing the game out, to things like glossing words that have become archaic or have significantly changed their meanings. Annotation should always turn in towards the poem; any annotation that insists on turning out to other things should be saved for later. The most illuminating figure for synchrony is that of a landscape perspective, a figure of which Saussure was as fond as the New Critics are. We stand here at a given spot and look towards the horizon. What we see depends on our position. What we see is what we see: we cannot include in our panorama any elements of the landscape that are out of the line of our vision. And what we see is a unity. We know of course that some of the objects we see are near enough so that we could touch them and others are miles away, that near objects are distinct and distant objects hazy, but there is no gulf fixed anywhere between the here and the there, the foreground and the distance. We feel the same way about the whole sweep. In the literary application of the figure, space becomes time. We view literature as a state. Standing in contemporary literature we accept as much of the literature of the past as is accessible to us from that point of view, and we apply exactly the same standards of judgment to it that we apply to contemporary literature. We have become very much aware of this method in the last forty years: it is commonly called "evaluation" or "criticism."

I deplore and wish to change this terminology, for it assumes, either expressly or by implication, that diachronic study of literature is *not* criticism. The synchronic and the diachronic modes differ radically, but not because one of them is critical and the other something else. Diachronic study of literature deals with values as evolving and changing in time; what is now narrowly called criticism deals with values in a state, with static value. Synchrony based in the present may be thought to be more original than diachrony, for values in the present are in process of being defined, and the synchronic practitioner has a chance of making the definitions himself, whereas (it may be argued) the values of the past have long since been defined and the diachronic practitioner needs only to describe, to select. But it is not true either that the values of the past have all been defined in the past, or that selection is always made easier by the passage of time. All selection implies discrimination, and that is precisely criticism. We acknowledge it by the terms (fortunately still with us) of "critical edition" and "textual criticism."

"History of literature" is also an ambiguous term, for, as we have seen, history may be either synchronic or diachronic. Historians are by no means confined to process; they can give us the static depiction of particular periods (The Era of Prohibition, The Age of the Antonines) as well as chronicles of the rise and fall of empires. In political history, Saussure pointed out, the two modes can be blended without embarrassment, and they have been so blended, so that one has to classify historians by preponderance of mode. History down to the eighteenth century seems to have been pretty much synchronical. We are particularly aware of this in medieval history with its obtrusive anachronisms; writers then, we say, "lacked the historical sense." A remark like Chaucer's "There is no newe gyse that it nas old," [13] occurring in a tale in which Greeks of the age of Theseus are costumed as European knights of the fourteenth century, or like that of the Fool in *Lear,* "This prophecy Merlin shall make; for I live before his time," [14] should however warn us that earlier writers were not

so much unaware of the differences between ages as uninterested
in them. Voltaire, Hume, and Gibbon ought probably to be
classified as synchronic historians. The twentieth-century reader
(if I am a fair specimen) is charmed by Gibbon's elegantly off-
color detail, but puzzled and bored by his way of telling a story.
In fact, Gibbon seems to wish to avoid the imputation of telling
a story: he writes as though the story were already well known
and he were alluding to it or commenting on it. Everything in
Gibbon is referred to the present; he gives us a telescope but still
confronts us with a perspective panorama. Johnson's *Lives of the
Poets* (to give an example from history of literature) is a massive
example of synchronical theory applied to encyclopedic subject-
matter. Johnson loved antiquarian research but got angry whenever it was suggested that the past had done something better than
the present was doing it. He stands, like Gibbon, on an
eighteenth-century plateau up to which he is quite confident that
the ages of barbarism were toiling.

Central to the diachronical mode in history stands the commanding figure of a novelist: Sir Walter Scott, but Scott had
very interesting English predecessors. Samuel Richardson wrote
no historical novels, but he is nevertheless the most intensely
diachronical of English writers. Lovelace's driving passion is not
lust: he is consumed by a twofold passion for stratagem and for
recording the progress of his stratagem, as he himself says, by
"writing to the moment." [15] That is, though necessarily writing
after the events, he gives each scene its own particularity and
uniqueness, as though that moment was all the time there was.
The other characters in *Clarissa* do not theorize about history as
he does, but their writing is no less "to the moment." The
epistolary form is probably the best that could have been devised
for this exuberantly diachronical view of life. Sterne's *Tristram
Shandy,* for all its clowning, is a serious assault on the central
diachronical paradox: if an accomplished writer set himself to
recapture his past in detail, giving each period the feeling it had
while it was being lived, he would never get beyond his boyhood,
for it takes much longer to write a continuous record of life in
that mode than it does to live it. James Boswell, surely influenced

by Sterne and probably more deeply influenced by Richardson, began in 1762 to keep a vast diachronical journal, writing, like Lovelace, "to the moment," and very rarely lapsing into the perspective mode. Like *Tristram Shandy*, and for the same reason, his work is fragmentary. Robertson's *History of America*, a brilliant, now unfortunately neglected, work, is political history in the diachronical mode. Unlike Voltaire and Hume and Gibbon, Robertson tells a story, tells it with suspense and color, which means that he is not collapsing time and that he lives through each portion of the story for its own sake. But it was undoubtedly Walter Scott who revolutionized the Western mode, implanting in the minds of all Europeans so engrossing a diachronical sense that for a century people tended to assume as a matter of course that diachronical history was the only kind there was.

We are back again to synchrony now, and synchrony of a very pure and self-conscious sort. It took me a long time to see that F. R. Leavis's *Revaluation* and *The Great Tradition* were in any proper sense history of literature. Brought up and steeped in the diachronical mode, I could not feel any writing to be historical if, as it seemed to me, it made discontinuous selection from the past to buttress a present-day thesis. Tradition for me was the whole motley legacy of past events and sayings that people of former ages had thought important enough to record. A "tradition" in the English novel that excluded Fielding and Scott seemed to me both arrogant and absurd. But though one may find Leavis's particular perspectives harsh and narrow, one has to grant the legitimacy of his method. Perspective from a viewpoint entails exclusions; from some viewpoints, very large exclusions. A selective state is still a state. "In static linguistics, as in most sciences, no course of reasoning is possible without the usual simplification of data." [16]

From the time that modern linguistics came into existence down to the twentieth century, it was completely dominated by diachrony. Traditional graduate study in English developed in Germany out of historical philology and pretty much reproduced its methods. In the days before 1930, it was assumed as a matter of course that graduate study in English should be based on diachronic philology (Gothic, Old English, Old Norse, Old French), that English literature should be studied in the diachronic mode, that the literature studied should be at least fifty years old, and a fortiori that scholarly journals should confine themselves to diachronic philology and diachronic history of literature. Forty years ago diachrony began to retreat, and the retreat has ended in a rout. The old requirements of historical philology have been quite abandoned. History of literature of the diachronic sort is rapidly disappearing from the university curriculum. *PMLA* now regularly prints articles indistinguishable from those in *The Kenyon Review*.

On the face of it there does not seem to have been any need of so radical a revolution. The leaders of the old school—to make what I am saying quite concrete, let me quote two past presidents of the Modern Language Association, Albert S. Cook and Karl Young—by no means disparaged synchronic criticism. I have heard both Cook and Young aver repeatedly and sincerely that sound criticism was the goal of all scholarship. Only, they thought that criticism, like teaching, was an art that could not be taught directly, and that graduate instruction should aim at giving students the historical learning that would enable them to be *good* critics.

Many students in my day (I fancy from the very beginning of the system) felt the purely linguistic aspects of graduate study in English to be irrelevant to their needs and disliked and resented them accordingly, but I cannot remember that there was then any significant revolt from diachrony in history of literature. However, two years after I entered the Yale Graduate School, *The Wasteland* appeared, a new period in English literature was inaugurated, and those who shared the new sensibility felt an overriding need to work out immediately the specifications of this new literature, and to revalue the writings of the past with relation to it. For this they felt diachronic history of literature to be totally unhelpful. It was unhelpful because its facts were different from the facts of "evaluation" or synchrony.

This is of course only a partial description of a small part of a vast general reorientation which in the present state of our knowledge is as inexplicable as the Great Consonant Shift or the march of the lemmings. When the New Criticism began to revolutionize our teaching of English literature at Yale, I warned my friends in the department of history that they had better prepare for similar commotions in their own discipline. They smiled at me, but it turned out as I predicted. Narrative (that is, diachronic) history is now confidently derided by leaders in the field as trivial, and the going kind of history considers not the whole past but the "useful" or "relevant" past.[17] Sheer synchrony. The sciences have followed or are following suit. In geology, diachronical study is out and geophysics is in. The hottest area in biology is molecular biology.

Whether by taking thought we can significantly alter a situation like this is certainly doubtful. The mind of man—in science no less than in the arts—has perhaps always shown a preference for passionate rather than balanced commitments. We make enormous advances in one direction at a time, contemptuously neglecting other areas that in the long run prove just as exciting and valuable. Perhaps the current is too strong for us to make headway against, but we are not condemned to roll down it sedate and darkling. We need to realize what we are doing, we need to consider thoughtfully whether it would not be better if our endeavors were more judicious, and—unless we are practical determinists, which very few human beings really are—we should try to achieve the better even if the effect of our endeavors seems to be inconsiderable. We can at least criticize.

It may be objected that this is only a plea for setting the clock back, but it is not. Diachrony is not just another name for Romanticism. The Romantic sensibility undoubtedly found the evolutionary mode more congenial than the static, and the greatest practitioners of diachrony have been Romantics. The approach to languages in terms of their descent and affiliations, with strong emphasis on the earlier periods, was their forte: they invented historical philology no less than the historical novel. Franz Bopp and Jacob Grimm linked arms with Walter Scott. But it is the great error of our time to assume that the diachronical mode in criticism was merely the philosophy of an era, was always mistaken, and is now happily dead, just as it was the error of forty years ago to assume that evaluation properly looked for its standards only to the classics of past ages, and that the synchronical mode, as ignobly unlearned and facile, had no place in professional instruction. The two modes correspond to two ineradicable needs of human nature and will always persist. We want to know the past as it relates to the present; we want to know the past for its own sake. We do not really set up utility as our justification for either endeavor. I explore the past for the same reason that Mallory gave for climbing Everest: it's there. There may be utility in climbing Everest, but nobody would ever have risked his life on the venture because he thought he was performing a useful act. The man who did it did it because climbing Everest satisfied a powerful craving, because he enjoyed it.

Granting this, it might still be the case that the two modes have eternally to be party affairs, Republicans and Democrats, ins and outs. Perhaps we have always to live in a polemical atmosphere, saying things about our opponents and their platforms that we only half believe because an election is always coming up. Perhaps literature by its very nature is so passionate a thing that one cannot be reasonable about it. If I thought that were true, I should long since have chucked the whole childish business and looked about for a more grown-up way of making a living. I advocate a judicial rather than a partisan stance, and an education that makes students aware of both modes, practically and theoretically, that tries to train them out of an exclusive and savage (basically fearful) dedication to either. Of course I do not expect that many of them in their professional careers will contribute original knowledge to both areas. Fields of personal research are as often as not determined by sheer academic accident, and when they are not, a man has a right to choose how he will invest the time he saves for exploring and writing. But I see no reason why all academics, by a judicious use of other people's books, should not be able to maintain the balance that strikes me as desirable. The sort of well-trained student I have in mind would on the one hand not have flaunted the linguistic illiteracy that characterized far too many of the academic reviews of the last Merriam-Webster Dictionary, and on the other hand would have been incapable of the dogmatic historicism that prevailed in academic criticism fifty years ago. There is no doubt that an active possession of both modes, though it would reduce the intensity of much academic writing, would temper and enrich it. As I have said, the synchronical mode surely offers the right *approach* to literature. In a Freshman course or an elective taken by non-majors, it may be wise not to enlarge on that mode at all. But the moment the question of higher learning enters—that is, in courses designed for majors and graduate students—the diachronic method should also be introduced, because it is, if not half of, at least an indispensable element in, learned as opposed to naïve criticism. And it should not be confined to a merely ancillary or annotative role, to turning up meanings and structures for a synchronical reading to use. The study of literature no doubt begins with the reading of poems as poems, with getting the same kind of gratification out of Dryden and Wordsworth that one gets out of Yeats and Eliot, but an educated or learned study of literature cannot stop there. The mark of a truly humane education is to be able to accept one's own age gratefully and confidently while maintaining towards it the wariness that one ought always to maintain towards any considerable source of power. Our own age is the only age we can ever live in, and it is silly to spend our brief hour fearing and disparaging it. Yet our age is certainly a limited age, and it is the mark of humane education to be aware of its limitations. I do not maintain and never have maintained that poems should be judged only by the standards of their authors or of the times in which they were written. I do maintain that a thoughtful attempt to reconstruct such judgments is a check on the provinciality and arrogance of our own time. A truly humane education uses academic studies for whatever power they have to bring the drives of human nature into conscious and fruitful harmony.

"Linguistics," says Saussure, "having accorded too large a place to history, will turn back to the static viewpoint of traditional grammar but in a new spirit and with other procedures, and the historical method will have contributed to this rejuvenation;

the historical method will in turn give a better understanding of language-states. . . . One must sense the opposition between the two classes of facts to draw out all its consequences. . . .
Each language in practice forms a unit of study, and we are induced by force of circumstances to consider it alternately from
the historical and static viewpoints." [18] I heartily endorse that
program. In teaching it presents no practical problems at all. Instead of the old method of beginning the study of Wordsworth
with *Lyrical Ballads* (or Wordsworth's even earlier work), one begins with *The Ruined Cottage,* goes on to *Michael* and *The Old
Cumberland Beggar,* to *Resolution and Independence,* to selected
lyrics, to *Lines Written above Tintern Abbey,* to *Ode, Intimations
of Immortality,* to *The Prelude* (selections for undergraduates, the
whole poem for graduate students). No biography (except of
course as *The Prelude* is biography), no talk about the originality
of *Lyrical Ballads,* no discussion of the famous Preface, just successive attempts to read and evaluate the poems. *Then* a chronological survey of *Guilt and Sorrow* (graduate students would add
An Evening Walk and *Descriptive Sketches*), *Lyrical Ballads* with
the Preface, *Peter Bell,* the patriotic sonnets, *Ode to Duty,* and
Elegiac Stanzas Suggested by a Picture of Peele Castle. The avowed
attempt would be to construct a chapter of diachronical history
of English literature.

But how does one do that? The welter in existing history of
literature, as René Wellek has repeatedly pointed out,[19] bears
testimony to the general naïveté of the literary mind with regard
to the principles of historiography. There has never been much
attempt to work out a theory for the history of literature that will
differentiate it from political or economic or intellectual history,
and the existing studies often combine assumptions that appear
to be unrelated if not conflicting. Judging from the existing
specimens, history of literature may deal with biography of
authors, with the illustration of social or national history or of
Geistegeschichte, with literary sources and influences, with the
invention and development of formal devices, with the emergence
and proliferation of genres. Our standard textbook histories consist for the most part of brief biographies of authors followed

by individual "appreciations" or critiques, the norms of judgment being the author's own, though generally with some historical qualification, express or implied. In all these varied activities it is hard to discern any common factor except the chronological: the authors are all writing with an awareness that the matter they are dealing with is not only separated from us by time but that it evolved in time.

This should not surprise us if we have ever seriously attempted to work out a general definition for diachronical history as such. Any one who tries it with no special axe to grind is bound to come out with something as simple and capacious as Oakeshott's conclusion, "History is the way in which we conceive the world *sub specie praeteritorum:* its differentia is the attempt to organize the whole world of experience in the shape of past events." [20] Any kind of writing that recognizes, in Carlyle's phrase, that something *was* [21] is diachronical history. And since people find it necessary to invoke what *was* in endlessly different ways, there have been and are going to be lots and lots of kinds of history. Who fifty years ago could have predicted that political history was going to turn so enthusiastically to quantification and prosopography? History, like literature, exists for man and not man for history. History, like literature, responds to the needs, to the *historical* needs, of human sensibilities. Theory as to what history ought to be at any given present time is always going to be just as passionate and just as dogmatic as the theory of what poetry ought to be, or painting ought to be.

Saussure had his chess-game, I am fond of the figure of a string of beads. If you want a synchronical view, look at the string end on; if you want a diachronical view, stretch it across your field of vision. A figure of beads does some violence to experience, for experience while we are experiencing it has more the qualities of a stream. But in order to think about the past, we seem to have to divide it into identifiable portions: ages, periods, reigns, schools. The diachronical view emphasizes the uniqueness of these units, the differences between them. Especially it is aware of the irreversibility of time. When one of those periods was unfolding, that was all the time there was. English literature of the Age of

Johnson had a rich perspective, but that perspective did not include Wordsworth, Scott, Dickens, Tennyson, Yeats. There *is* an impassable gulf fixed between us and any period of past time. The diachronical historian is very much interested in these former perspectives, which of course seemed just as extensive to the people who experienced them directly as ours do to us. What did English literature seem like in 1798? Or, to revert to the landscape figure, what kind of view could I get if I were on that blue hill over there? Let us suppose that for some reason not hard to invent I could not walk or be carried to the hill. I could still inquire whether anybody had ever taken a photograph from it, and if I in fact turned up such a photograph, I would have a sort of answer to my question. The photograph would not by any means be the same thing, or as good as, direct personal vision, but it would do. The scrupulous and thoughtful historian knows that he cannot literally place himself in any period of past time. What he does do is to use with as much imagination as he possesses photographs made in the past by photographers of varying degrees of competence. He calls them documents.

The diachronical mode in the nineteenth century took over many of its working concepts from the natural science that was then so triumphantly emerging: not only geneticism but determinism and positivism. I sometimes wonder if the present revolt from diachrony is not basically a revolt from determinism. Even those who believe that Divine Providence may be directing the events of human history hesitate to point out the signs of that intention in any detail. Diachrony seems to show men and empires swept helplessly along in a meaningless flood. No matter how coherent and logically impressive diachronic systems may be, humanists may be refusing to operate them if they seem to contain no element of human freedom. Here Saussure's analysis is wonderfully assuring. Languages are systems of meaning. The great diachronic sound changes, though they are almost certainly psychological in origin, appear to have no regard whatever for meaning. Nothing could be more inexorable and total than the way in which, during a definite period of time, they transform a language, destroying and corrupting significant elements in its system. When * fōti became fēt, that noun lost its sign for the plural. What could speakers of English do? They were by no means helpless, but their choices were historically limited. One thing they could *not* do was to hang on to or restore * fōti. Because of the active existence of fēt, it would probably have been impracticable to give fot by analogy the ending of another class: * fōtas (Modern English "foots"). What they *did* do, by sheer free will, was to declare fēt a quite satisfactory plural. If, in human affairs, diachrony is deterministic, synchrony is not: "[Sound] changes are wholly unintentional while the synchronic fact is always significant." [22] The choices of synchrony are conditioned or limited by diachrony, but there are choices enough.

I find it rewarding to write diachronical history of literature under the successive heads of Climate of Opinion, Sensibility, and Idiom. A climate of opinion generates a sensibility which generates an idiom. Of course that is over-simplified, like the chemistry texts I studied fifty years ago which represented most chemical reactions as moving only from the left-hand side of the equation to the right. Sensibility works back on climate of opinion to accelerate its drift; idiom reacts on both sensibility and climate of opinion. But as a clarifying diagram, Climate of Opinion → Sensibility → Idiom will do. Climate of opinion is the sort of thing Basil Willey presents in his extremely useful "background" studies. The mechanical philosophy of the seventeenth century with its central metaphor of a clock-universe generated a historical sensibility which constructed the experienced world in terms of transcendency, regularities, norms, checks and balances, centripetal force, subordination of parts, intellect over feeling, essence over experience. The heroic couplet of Dryden and Pope —a free choice among many possibilities—was the consummate expression—the idiom—of the historical sensibility we call neo-classical. The developing revolutionary climate of opinion of the eighteenth century which we call Romanticism substituted an organism for a clock as its universe-metaphor and generated a sensibility which constructed the experienced world in terms of immanence, diversities, expansion, centrifugal force, worth of the individual, nationalism, emotion over intellect, experience over essence. The consummate idiom of this sensibility was enounced in English by Samuel Taylor Coleridge and presented most massively by William Wordsworth. This is only a harsh brief outline, omitting nearly all the concretions which would give life to such a study. A history of literature of this sort would combine *Geistesgeschichte,* biography, psychology, and formalism; the investigation of idiom would be explicitly related to diction, imagery, and metrical devices. Many authors would be cited, and each would be studied as much for his divergence from the central pattern—his historical uniqueness—as for his conformities. A particularly interesting problem, for example, would be posed by James Thomson. Is he really enouncing a new idiom or is he just Pope in a Miltonic key? The matter throughout would be under strong chronological tension. In this kind of history of literature it matters, or may matter, very much which of two poems was written first. One would watch with real suspense the log-jam of an inarticulate new sensibility building up, the awkward efforts to break the jam by writers who see what needs to be done but cannot quite accomplish it, and would attempt to transmit a sense of the headlong fury of the drive when some destined original genius pulls the tangled and stagnant words into a pattern that will enable them to leap and dance on the surging current of sensibility. Think how *fast* Romantic idiom moved between 1795 and 1815; think accordingly what historic importance attaches to Coleridge's *Eolian Harp* (1795). Such study is surely neither trivial nor irrelevant.

NOTES

1. I should like to have the present essay regarded as an extension and in some respects a revision of the ideas expressed in "The New Critics and the Historical Method," *Yale Review,* 43 (1953), 14–23.

2. Ferdinand de Saussure, *Course in General Linguistics,* trans. Wade Baskin, Philosophical Library (New York, 1959), p. xi.

3. *Paradise Lost* IV.765–67.

4. *Lives of the Poets,* "Milton" (I, 174 in G. B. Hill's ed., Oxford, 1905).

5. See O.E.D. The lines from Shakespeare are *Comedy of Errors* IV.iii.82–83.

6. Saussure, trans. Baskin, pp. 83–85. See also p. 159.

7. Ibid., p. 81.

8. Ibid., pp. 81, 83, 85.

9. Ibid., pp. 88–89.

10. Ibid., p. 79.

11. This dictum was reported to me many years ago as having been made at a meeting of the Modern Language Association.

12. For example, in "The Eye and the Object in the Poetry of Wordsworth," *Wordsworth Centenary Studies,* ed. G. T. Dunklin (Princeton, 1951), pp. 25–31.

13. *Knight's Tale,* line 2125 of F. N. Robinson's text of *The Canterbury Tales, Complete Works of Chaucer* (Boston, 1933 and later).

14. *King Lear* iii.ii.95.

15. *Clarissa, or The History of a Young Lady,* vol. 4, letter 58 of the 3d ed. (1750–51) and editions adhering to it. Shakespeare Head ed. (Oxford, 1930), iv, 385.

16. Saussure, trans. Baskin, p. 102.

17. For examples, see *Daedalus,* Winter 1971 ("Historical Studies Today").

18. Saussure, trans. Baskin, pp. 82–83, 99. "Historical" of course means "diachronical," and "history" means "diachronical history."

19. For example in Chapter xix of *Theory of Literature,* by René Wellek and Austin Warren (New York, 1942 and later), and in "The Impasse of Literary History," review of *Theory of American Literature,* by H. M. Jones, and *Literary History of the United States,* by R. E. Spiller and others, *Kenyon Review,* 11 (1949), 500–06.

20. The formulation quoted is actually by R. G. Collingwood, *The Idea of History* (New York, 1946 and later), p. 152.

21. "Boswell's *Life of Johnson,*" in *Critical and Miscellaneous Essays* (this essay originally published in 1832).

22. Saussure, trans. Baskin, p. 85.

The Concept of Literature

MONROE C. BEARDSLEY

The uses of the term "literature" are varied, their differences subtle, their lines of connection tangled. We have to deal, evidently, with a cluster of concepts, rather than one. Yet my title is not a misnomer. For an enterprise of conceptual analysis may be constructive as well as descriptive, and I would like not only to sort out some of the current concepts, sharpen distinctions, and trace logical relationships, but also—if possible—to work toward a recommendation. It is often easy to frame a definition that seems sound on the surface, only to find that its adoption brings disturbing gaps or redundancies into our conceptual scheme or requires unacceptable adjustments in other definitions that belong to the same system. On the other hand, it sometimes turns out that alternative sets of concepts are basically equivalent and equally convenient, because they mark, in different terms, the same useful or even indispensable distinctions.

I should confess at the start that in pondering the question, What is literature?, I can't promise to avoid questions of philosophical aesthetics. Those who are concerned with "defending the domain of poetry and poetics from the encircling (if friendly) arm of the general aesthetician," as W. K. Wimsatt has done,[1] may charge me with overprotectiveness. But the marking out of such domains, the rectification of boundaries and the establishment of clear titles, are themselves aesthetic tasks.

One of the less probematic remarks that can be made about the term "literature" is that it is a collective name for literary *works*. True, critics sometimes speak of a "literary quality," and even of degrees of such a quality, and this usage deserves study. But more usually, and intelligibly, "literature" marks off a species of the genus of discourses—i.e. written or spoken pieces of natural language. A discourse is either a literary work or it is not a literary work—or it is a borderline case that balks at classification (which is why we may be tempted to say that it has "literary quality," perhaps meaning that it has some claim, though not a decisive claim, to be called a literary work).

Suppose we agree that literature is the class of literary works. What then? It depends on how much stress we lay on "work." If we make it a mere substitute for "discourse," we get what might be called a *language concept* of literature, and our problem is to discover the marks by which literary discourses are distinguished from nonliterary discourses. If, on the other hand, we take "literary work" as an abbreviation for "literary work of art," we get an *art concept* of literature, and a quite different task confronts us.

The second interpretation may seem the more natural, so let us explore its consequences at once. It entails that we do not know what literature is until we know what art is—i.e. what makes something a work of art, whether verbal or visual or musical. We can tell whether something is a discourse, say a piece of English prose, without knowing anything of its origin; but we cannot tell whether something is a work of art without knowing anything of its origin. For whatever else may be said about this most disputed concept, surely a work of art is at least an artifact, something produced intentionally, and perhaps more specifically with an aesthetic intention. Whatever forms and qualities an object—say, a piece of stone—may feature, we would ordinarily say, I think, that if it can be shown to have acquired those forms and qualities independently of any human acts or purposes, it is not a work of art.

What are we to say, then, of such objects as computer poems? The IBM 7094-7040 DCS at the Yale Computer Center has turned out such stanzas as this:

> The landscape of your clay mitigates me.
> Coldly,

By your recognizable shape,
I am wronged.

Is this a literary work (or part of one)? Two answers are open to
us. First, we might say that it is indeed literature, but not a literary work of art (since computers have no intentions); it is a
literary discourse, and classifiable as such in virtue of certain
forms and qualities. Thus we cut the logical link between "literature" and "literary work," and must proceed to define the
former independently of the latter. We might go on to say that
what we have here is indeed a poem, but not all poems are
literary works: a poem is a literary work only if it has been composed by a human poet.

If we take the second terminological path, we do not necessarily
deny that "The landscape of your clay" is literature. That depends
on how broadly we conceive "compose." We can take the computer as poet; then its work is not, strictly, composed, for no
intentions occur. Or we can take the programmer, Professor
Marie Borroff, as the poet, and regard the computer as only a
rather elaborate mechanism used in composition; then the results
can be called literary works of art. This involves some strain on
our usual language, since the programmer's instructions, in
SNOBOL 3, furnished the computer only with some abstract
syntactic constraints plus a vocabulary from which to make random selections. Thus it was intended that an adverb would appear in a certain slot, but not that it would be "coldly." Yet we
might say that the work as a whole was composed, since it did
not come into being by accident, and certain features were determined by a human will. And since the final product is a result
of Professor Borroff's selection from the various printouts, and
also of her arrangement of the text into lines, there may be quite
enough design involved to warrant our applying the term "literary
work of art."

Thus the art concept of literature may be stretched enough to
cover computer poems. It excludes those as yet wholly imaginary
masterpieces randomly typed out by assiduous chimpanzees (who
have so far done much better in painting than in poetry); of these
we may want to say, first, that as long as they remain nonexistent,

the problem of classifying them does not arise; and, second, that if they begin to appear, no harm will be done by refusing to call them literature. In the same way, if a chimpanzee happened to put two sticks together that formed the letter *T*, we would want to say that he did not make a *T* on purpose, even if he crossed the sticks on purpose. Yet suppose we gradually reduced the role of the programmer in the productions of IBM 7094-7040 DCS, leaving it more and more to its own devices. The odds against its coming up with "The landscape of your clay" would become enormously greater, of course, yet they would not reach impossibility. And if the same discourse were produced entirely, or almost entirely, by chance, we would still call it a poem, just as we called the chimpanzee's stick-work a *T*. It would not be in a very different category from so-called automatic writing, or a passage dictated in a trance.

There is a point, then, in trying to separate the objective from the psychological elements in our concept of a poem, and of literature in general. We can use two concepts, and both seem to be in operation. The art concept is genetic, since it includes an essential reference to what the maker intended to do, and thought of himself as doing, in creating the discourse. The discourse concept is nongenetic; it is confined to linguistically discernible features. There seems to be a historical development from one to the other. Before detailed and systematic study of the language of literature, it is natural to identify literature by its source or manner of production. It is what a poet sings or what is offered on certain occasions or (later) printed with certain indicators of its kind. But as our understanding increases, the concept becomes less dependent on genetic considerations. We can recognize a poem under all sorts of conditions, without knowing how it came to be written. The broadening of the range of contemporary poetry, and the arrival of the computer, have helped bring us to this freedom.

If we admit the theoretical possibility that one may aim, and try, to compose a literary work and fail—and that one may compose, or cause to be composed, a literary work without aiming to—then we have detached our concept of literature from our concept of its genesis, even if we concede that all the literary works that are of interest to us, or are likely to be of interest to us, are discourses in whose composition human beings have had a hand. So we can ask for an analysis of the concept of literature, understood in this objective fashion: what goes into the class, what is excluded, and how we tell the difference.

One way of marking off a class of literary discourses from other discourses is provided by what I have called the "semantic definition" of "literature": literature consists of those discourses a substantial portion of whose meaning is implicit (or secondary) meaning.[2] This thoroughly nongenetic definition depends on an account of implicit meaning, which was given in terms of the concepts of connotation and suggestion, and of which various species were noted. It is designed to distinguish poems among verses and literary essays among discursive writings. Thus it aims to capture what may be called the *extended* concept of literature, the sense in which the term is applied to some works of history, sermons, speeches, letters—to Bacon's essays and Cicero's orations and parts of the Old Testament.

This proposal has been thoroughly and forcefully criticized by Colin A. Lyas. Though conceding that it accords with what "some critics are prone to do," [3] Lyas holds that it fails to match the usage of more typical, or sounder, critics, and violates a basic condition that must be satisfied by any acceptable definition of "literature." He makes a number of good points, and throws light on the entire enterprise. Some of his objections bear most heavily on the unfortunate, and indefensible, manner in which the original proposal was framed: "A literary work is a discourse in which an important part of the meaning is implicit." The qualifier "important" was certainly misleading, though not so misleading in its context as in this isolated sentence. Since there are obvious difficulties in speaking of amounts of meaning, the definition was designed to flaunt its vagueness, which it did all too well. But it does make sense (as Lyas apparently agrees) to say of two discourses that one carries a greater part of its meaning by way of the connotations of its words, the implications of its syntax, the thematic reverberations of its objects and acts.

Lyas has two main lines of argument against the semantic

definition. I shall return to the second one later. The first is that the presence of substantial implicit meaning in a discourse is neither a necessary nor a sufficient condition of its being a literary work.

That substantial implicit meaning is not *necessary* is a familiar contention. Famous examples like "The Red Wheelbarrow" crop up as interesting borderline cases, of which we could say that anyone who claims that they are indeed literary works (however minimal) is committed to showing that noteworthy meaning is implicitly present. Lyas offers what *"might* be an example" from Brecht:

> When in the white sickroom of the Charite
> I awoke towards morning
> And heard the blackbird, I knew
> Better. For quite a time
> I had no longer been afraid of death. Considering
> That nothing could be amiss with me, provided
> I myself was missing. Now
> I succeeded in being glad about
> The singing of all blackbirds, even after me.[4]

But when he adds, "Here there does not seem to me to be any more implicit meaning than one could expect to find in any piece of discourse," [5] I wonder whether the notion of implicit meaning has been communicated. What are we doing as we come to realize that in this poem the blackbird is not a bird of ill omen but the bringer of a new sense of life, if not discovering implicit meaning? And how is the central paradox of the poem—the inseparability of fearing death and affirming life—presented, except implicitly? "The singing of blackbirds" is not just the singing of blackbirds. Substantial implicit meaning seems to be at least one thing that is (by contrast) missing from, say:

> When I awoke at Lankenau Hospital at 6:00 A.M.,
> And found the nurse giving me another injection,
> I asked her at what time breakfast would be served.

Of course, I do not deny that these lines could be embedded in a context in which they would take on a greater significance, but by themselves they do not make a poem, and not literature.

Lyas's argument that substantial implicit meaning in a discourse is not *sufficient* to make it literature consists largely in
selecting various types of implicit meaning and showing that
none of them, taken individually, is found only in literature. This
is true, but it doesn't touch the proposed definition. What does
touch it is his contention that implicit meaning can be "a large
part" of ordinary discourse.[6] It is true that much of our verbal
interchange, beyond the most elementary level, abounds in hints,
innuendoes, suppressed premises and conclusions, etc. But I think
we have a rough sense of a norm in the relationship between what
is conveyed implicitly and what is conveyed explicitly. We recognize discourse that strains toward the side of extra-explicitness as
technical and specialized to the needs of a science or a profession;
we recognize discourse that leans toward richness in implicit
meaning, hypersemantic discourse, as taking on a rather different
character. In a business letter there may be implicit promises, hints
of personality traits, threats, even wit, but the main information
is given in the lines, not between them. A joke, on the other hand,
offers very little on its primary level, compared to the point that
makes it funny. A metaphor has no literal significance at all, taken
as a whole; all of its relevant meaning is implicit. And in a lyric
poem, if we can distinguish, say, what the solitary reaper *is* from
what she conjures up in the mind of her observer, we find a great
deal more of the latter.

It may also be useful to introduce a certain flexibility into the
account by acknowledging that norms may be relative to genre.
For example, when we read a large number of historical writings,
we may form the notion of a norm for this group of discourses,
compared to which we would then say that some books on the
Civil War, some biographies of Napoleon, are literature, others
not. But this norm may be somewhat different from those that
hold for discourses on, say, ecology or gastronomy or philosophy.

No doubt these are loose ways of speaking, perhaps too loose to
be useful. Since the difference between any two discourses in this
respect is a matter of degree, the spectrum practically continuous,
and the difficulty of making precise discriminations considerable,
some will feel that it is better not to try to introduce the terms
that purport to mark a difference in kind. We could speak of

degrees of literariness, or intensity of literary quality, as a comparative property, according to the semantic criterion—but not of literary or nonliterary discourses. Yet having gone so far, we may also find it convenient—and sufficiently in accord with at least one strand of familiar usage—to call those discourses that have a marked degree of literariness, decidedly above the norm, literature *tout court*.

Thus I am persuaded that a case can still be made for regarding the possession of an above-normal proportion of implicit meaning as a sufficient condition of being a literary discourse—though not of being a very good one. It is another segment of its border that leaves me least satisfied about this domain. The definition will cover a great deal of prose fiction, including those novels and short stories that are most worthy of attention from a literary point of view. But it will not cover all prose fiction. If we seek a definition that will provide this service—and there are reasons for thinking we should—then we shall have to look further.

A fresh way of regarding literary discourses has emerged in recent years. In involves a concept first advanced by J. L. Austin and later developed by William Alston, John B. Searle, and others.[7] I shall use the term "utterance" as an abbreviation for "act of producing, in speech or writing, a sequence of characters that belong to a language." When an utterance occurs under certain conditions, it may also be an "illocutionary act." For example, if a person with certain qualifications utters certain words on a certain sort of ceremonial occasion, while placing one hand on the Bible, he is taking an oath of office. A mere utterance has semantic and syntactic, and even stylistic, properties. What makes it an illocutionary act is that it conforms to a set of linguistic rules that specify the conditions required for that sort of act to be performed: rules about the nature of the speaker, the hearer, the situation. An utterance does not count as a warning if the event warned against is regarded as desirable by the warnee ("I warn you that you will be kindly treated"); it does not count as a command or request if the act referred to has already been performed ("Please call me yesterday"). Rules of this kind specify the *constitutive conditions* of the illocutionary act. Other rules specify its *purported conditions:* for example, a warning purports that the speaker wishes the hearer to escape the impending harm; if the speaker does not wish this, his warning is insincere, but it is no less a warning, provided the constitutive conditions are satisfied. Again, a request purports that the speaker desires the act requested to be performed, but an insincere request is still a request.

To decide whether an utterance is the performance of an illocutionary act, one inquires whether the constitutive conditions are satisfied; if they are, one can go on to inquire whether the purported conditions are also satisfied. These questions are not always easy to answer, and sometimes they cannot be answered decisively, in which case we have a form of ambiguity—as when, for example, a person in a position of authority asks that something be done, and it is not clear whether he is giving an order or making an unofficial request. If a prescribed form of words is available ("That is an order"), the ambiguity is resolved. Sometimes we are in doubt whether someone is expressing his own opinion or merely passing on, without endorsement, the opinion of another. Sometimes we are quite certain that no illocutionary act has been performed at all: if an actor on the stage utters the constitutional words, "I do solemnly swear that I will faithfully execute the Office of the President of the United States," he is not taking an oath of office, but imitating the taking of an oath of office. He is engaged in make-believe.

While I was working on a series of lectures a few years ago, it occurred to me that the speaker in a poem can be said, on one level of analysis, to be performing a series of illocutionary acts, though in such a way as to fashion them into a single compound act.[8] He pleads, cajoles, deplores, regrets, blesses, curses, beseeches, prays, commemorates, elegizes, resolves, resigns himself. But if we take the speaker to be a fictional entity, then of course these are not genuine illocutionary acts, but make-believe. So I suggested that a poem might be characterized, or even defined, as the imitation of a compound illocutionary act.[9]

"Imitation" must be taken here in what might be called its

"depicting" rather than "portrayal" sense.[10] That is, the act imitated need not be anything that has ever occurred; one can imitate a Cookie Monster gobbling cookies, though there is no such thing. This is an old discomfort in the term. In its unguarded use it tends to commit the imitation theorist to too much, so that we want to reply that Prufrock is not imitated but invented or created. It may be safer to call the poem an "imitation illocutionary act"; it may be safest to avoid the term completely and stick to "make-believe."

Two other writers have arrived independently at very similar views. Marcia Eaton adopts the doctrine of illocutionary acts but adds that

an author frequently performs what I call translocutionary acts, whereby he attributes or transfers illocutions to dramatic speakers or protagonists. (When Hamlet says, "Get thee to a nunnery," a command is being made, not by Shakespeare, but by a dramatic speaker, viz., Hamlet.) [11]

The concept of "translocutionary act" is not very clearly formulated, but the basic idea seems sound. When Shakespeare wrote down that bit of dialogue for Hamlet, he wasn't exactly "attributing" an illocutionary act to Hamlet, as when a view is attributed to "high government sources." But, to take a plainer case, we could say, in Eaton's terms, that Browning performs translocutionary acts in uttering words that purport to be those of a bishop ordering a tomb or a duke justifying his murder of his wife.

Eaton evidently, and correctly, does not regard a translocutionary act as a kind of illocutionary act. To report an illocutionary act ("The President asked for the public's cooperation during the freeze") is to perform an illocutionary act. To tell a tale ("The Gingerbread Man said, 'You can't catch me.' ") is not to perform an illocutionary act. It is playing with words, rather than working with them. Of course, by telling the tale we may give a child pleasure, but giving pleasure is not an illocutionary act—it is what Austin called a "perlocutionary act," i.e. obtaining results by means of language.

The application of illocutionary-act theory to the definition of literature has been most carefully worked out by Richard Ohmann, whose proposal is stated in these words:

A literary work is a discourse whose sentences lack the illocutionary forces that would normally attach to them. Its illocutionary force is mimetic. By "mimetic," I mean purportedly imitative. Specifically, a literary work *purportedly imitates* (or reports) a series of speech acts, which in fact have no other existence.[12]

He argues that in all literary works, not only in poems, the constitutive conditions for performing a complete and genuine illocutionary act are not met, so that the utterance is, in Austin's term, "infelicitous"; yet some of the ingredients are there, so that the reader can fill in the imaginary world in which the fictional speaker performs his fictional illocutionary act. To consider one sort of factor (not discussed by Ohmann), an illocutionary act is not completed until there is what Austin calls "uptake"—e.g. X has not warned Y unless Y hears the warning and takes it to be such. When a poem is addressed to a skylark, a waterfowl, a field mouse, a dead athlete, spring, autumn, the west wind, the moon, or Brooklyn Bridge, no uptake is conceivable, and the utterance fails to be an illocutionary act. This is one of the plainest forms of infelicity, but there are many others.

I think it is a mistake to say that in a literary work the "illocutionary force is mimetic," if this means that performing an imitation illocutionary act is performing a kind of illocutionary act (pretending to fall down stairs, or acting out the fall, is not falling down stairs), or to speak of "the illocutionary act of writing a literary work." [13] What we have in, say, Shelley's poem, is a complete verbal utterance that would, given certain conditions (e.g. that a skylark were present, that it could understand English), actually be an illocutionary act.

This proposal seems to me illuminating, and I believe that it in fact provides a sufficient condition for a discourse to be a literary work, though not necessarily a good one (as Ohmann notes). But when proposed as a *necessary* condition, it is open to some objections, which we must consider briefly.

First, as Ohmann explicitly says, the illocutionary-act definition of "literature" will not serve for what I have called the extended concept, which takes in some essays, sermons, etc. The preacher, the polemicist, the philosopher, the historian, is not making-believe, but actually exhorting, pleading, praising, putting down, attacking, arguing, narrating. Ohmann's definition, he says, is designed to mark out the class of "imaginative literature," as distinguished from *belles lettres:* it includes fiction, but not non-fiction. It states the necessary and sufficient conditions for what we may call the *central* concept of literature (poetry and prose fiction). Surely the Ohmann proposal marks an important distinction. And if we follow his lead, we are not debarred from literary criticism of *The Stones of Venice, Of Holy Dying,* "A Free Man's Worship," and "Aes Triplex," even if they are not literary works.[14] On the other hand, if we prefer to cling to the extended concept of literature, we can do so by combining the two definitions we have been discussing. A literary work (in the extended sense) would then be any discourse that is *either* an imitation (compound) illocutionary act *or* distinctly above the norm in its ratio of implicit to explicit meaning.

But does the illocutionary-act definition state a necessary condition for literature, even in the central sense? It seems that one can perform an illocutionary act with a poem. Ohmann's example is Elizabeth Barrett Browning. Surely there are circumstances under which her sending or giving "How do I love thee?" to Robert constitutes a declaration of love. Ohmann's solution is to say that at the time of presentation, the poem was no longer a literary work. I would rather try to distinguish the act of writing the poem (the original utterance) from the act of using it in some way; after all, any woman could perform the same illocutionary act by presenting someone with Elizabeth's poem. It is the act of composing that issues in the poem, and this act, we might argue, is not an illocutionary act—for one thing, because there is no uptake, but also because the process of formalizing a sentiment in verse and rhyme, giving it artistic shape, implies a degree of detachment from the illocutionary role, even if the sentiment is sincerely felt. Then to present the poem is to do something else with it; but to use a literary work for any purpose, as political propaganda, advertising, or inspiration to worship, does not take away its literary status.

I doubt, however, that we can cope in this way with all of the difficult examples. "Avenge O Lord thy slaughter'd saints" responds to an event and, I suppose, automatically secures uptake. There is Kipling and there is Housman on the Golden Jubilee. Is it really plausible to say that in "Adonais," in "English Bards and Scotch Reviewers," in "Pied Beauty," in "Ode to the Confederate Dead," there is only make-believe? Is there no illocutionary action in Allen Ginsberg's "America" (1956)?

> America when will we end the human war?
> Go fuck yourself with your atom bomb.

Well, perhaps this last is not the best example. When the speaker says, later on,

> America free Tom Mooney
> America save the Spanish Loyalists
> America Sacco & Vanzetti must not die,

we note some infelicities in these imperatives. Perhaps they help to make the whole poem fall short of being an illocutionary act. But not all poems have this feature. When we think of poems read at antiwar gatherings or published in *The Nation*—or even in *Novy Mir,* if Yevgeny F. Markin's two poems of December 1971, "Weightlessness" and "The White Buoy," were really defenses of Alexandr I. Solzhenitsyn—it becomes harder to separate the act of composing from the act of presenting. It is not obvious that any of the conditions for a full illocutionary act are lacking. So perhaps such poems must be placed outside the central class of literary works, though (since they are clearly poems) well within the extended class—an argument for the extended concept of literature.

The only way I can see to avoid this conclusion is to argue, along the lines suggested earlier, that the very possession of certain formal features or other internal marks is in itself a withdrawal of illocutionary force. But though I have tried to defend this position,[15] I am no longer convinced that it can be maintained.

I would make a provisional stop at this point—though conscious that a great many questions remain hanging in the air—if it were not for the challenge presented by Colin Lyas's second objection to the semantic definition of literature—an objection that bears as heavily on the illocutionary-act definition. "Literature," he says, is an "approval term." To apply it to a discourse is to praise, and (more particularly) to praise aesthetically. From this assumption, Lyas draws two conclusions. First, he says that no definition of "literature" is acceptable unless the properties cited in its definiens are such as to "lead us to a favorable evaluation of any work exemplifying the quality in question." [16] This eliminates the semantic definition, apparently, since mere possession of substantial implicit meaning is not in itself an aesthetic merit, and not all aesthetic merits in literature are dependent on substantial implicit meaning. Second, he says that *any* property that is an aesthetic merit in a discourse can be regarded as a criterion of literature—that is, it helps justify our calling that discourse literature. Lyas cites perhaps a score of such properties, among them compactness, sophistication, simplicity, charm, elegance, thrillingness, being well constructed, perceptiveness, sensitivity, psychological penetration, suspense, irony.[17]

This normative concept of literature—the concept of literature as aesthetically praiseworthy discourses—is a recurrent one. Lyas has stated it well, but he hasn't really defended it: he simply "draw[s] attention to the fact" that "literature" is a normative term.[18] His omission is understandable, since we do not really know how to show that a term is or is not normative, per se or in a certain use. The question is much in dispute among philosophers. We can throw light on a particular case by tracing logical connections with other terms. For example, when we want to make an adverse judgment of such a discourse as *Peyton Place,* we may feel a little uneasy about saying that it is "poor literature," and want to say instead that it is "poor as literature" or "poor, considered as literature"—which suggests that we sense an honorific element in the term's meaning. On the other hand, we may find ourselves drawn toward accepting a logical connection between the concept of literature and the concept of literary

genres—not that all literature belongs to a genre, but that anything that belongs to a genre is literature. We have a need for a
concept of literature for which this principle holds, and I believe
we sometimes rely on one. Now we can certainly speak of poor
poems and bad poems, in some sense or other, and if (by the
genre principle) every poem is a literary work, then "literary
work," it would seem, is not honorific. From this argument the
alternative conclusion could be drawn that literature is not after
all simply the class of literary works—since one of these terms
is normative, the other not. But if we reject this escape, then my
argument has some weight, I think, against the claim that "literature" is inherently normative.[19] Of course the sentence "X is
literature!" can be used to perform the illocutionary act of praising, with the help of a suitable context or tone of voice. But so
can a great many other sentences of a similar logical form whose
nouns would not be thought to qualify as normative: "cheesecake," "snow," "a dog," "a bed." As long as we admit the literal
possibility of bad cheesecake, "cheesecake" has no built-in approval.

Although I believe that "literature" has not been proved to be
a normative term, in its usual applications, Lyas's argument suggests an interesting point. For it still remains to be shown why any
particular way of drawing lines among discourses is to be recommended. And this is especially true of the tentative suggestion
that "literary discourse" might be defined as "discourse that is
either an imitation illocutionary act or distinctly above the norm
in its ratio of implicit to explicit meaning." Unless we can demonstrate some connection between the two concepts included in
this disjunctive predicate, the definition will seem as arbitrary
and capricious as would a definition of "broose" as "anything that
is either a broom or a moose."

What I wish to suggest, by way of conclusion, although without anything like an adequate defense, is that there is indeed an
underlying relationship between (1) being an imitation illocutionary act and (2) being distinctly above the norm in ratio of
implicit to explicit meaning. Though these two properties signify
very different sources of literature, or of the literary impulse, their

convergence is no accident, and it is understandable why they may belong together in a disjunctive definition of "literature." Both are forms of verbal play that set a discourse notable apart from pragmatic functions—one by deficiency of illocutionary force, the other by excess of semantic display. Both help to make a discourse self-centered and opaque, an object of attention in its own right. Though perhaps not all of the characteristics regarded as aesthetically praiseworthy by Lyas (and I am dubious about some of them) depend specifically on absence of illocutionary force or presence of substantial implicit meaning, nevertheless, it may be that the peculiar value of literature *qua* literature is favored and promoted by both of these properties. It is among discourses marked off from the ordinary run either by withdrawal from the illocutionary sphere or exploitation of linguistic resources that aesthetic goodness is most likely to be found. So it makes sense to mark out the class of literature as that class within which *good* literary discourses are most hopefully to be sought.

NOTES

1. See "The Domain of Criticism," in *Aesthetic Inquiry: Essays on Art Criticism and the Philosophy of Art,* ed. Monroe Beardsley and Herbert Schueller (Belmont, Calif., 1967), p. 26.

2. See *Aesthetics: Problems in the Philosophy of Criticism* (New York, 1958), pp. 126–28.

3. "The Semantic Definition of Literature," *Journal of Philosophy,* 66 (1969), 90.

4. Ibid., pp. 91–92.

5. Ibid., p. 92.

6. Ibid., pp. 89, 90. Richard Ohmann has raised the same objection in "Speech Acts and the Definition of Literature," *Philosophy and Rhetoric,* 4 (1971), 6–7.

7. J. L. Austin, *How to Do Things with Words* (Cambridge, Mass., 1962); William P. Alston, *Philosophy of Language* (Englewood Cliffs, N.J., 1964); John R. Searle, *Speech Acts* (Cambridge, 1969).

8. I had forgotten Austin's suggestion that poetry is one of the "etiolations" of language (see pp. 22, 92*n*) and his remark (p. 104) that "Walt Whitman does not seriously incite the eagle of liberty to soar."

9. See *The Possibility of Criticism* (Detroit, 1970), pp. 57–61.

10. For these terms, as applied to visual representation, see *Aesthetics,* pp. 269–78.

11. "Art, Artifacts, and Intentions," *American Philosophical Quarterly*, 6 (1969), 167; cf. Eaton's "Good and Correct Interpretations of Literature," *Journal of Aesthetics and Art Criticism*, 29 (Winter, 1970), 226–33.

12. "Speech Acts," p. 14; cf. Ohmann's "Speech, Action, and Style," in *Literary Style: A Symposium*, ed. Seymour Chatman (London and New York, 1971).

13. Ibid., p. 13.

14. An interesting borderline case is classical oratory of the epidictic genre, discussed by Chaim Perelman and L. Olbrechts-Tyteca, *The New Rhetoric*, trans. John Wilkinson and Purcell Weaver (Notre Dame, 1969), pp. 47–51. Since it was abstracted from legal and political contexts, it "seemed to have more connection with literature than with argumentation" (p. 48). But Perelman and Olbrechts-Tyteca are no doubt correct in concluding that "epidictic oratory forms a central part of the art of persuasion" (p. 49), in that it serves to "increase the intensity of adherence to certain values" (p. 51). This is its *perlocutionary* force, which, however, depends on its being genuine argument, rather than make-believe argument.

15. See *The Possibility of Criticism*, pp. 58–61, and the discussion of fiction in *Aesthetics*, pp. 411–14, 420–23.

16. Lyas, p. 83.

17. Ibid., pp. 82, 86, 92, 93, 95.

18. Ibid., p. 83.

19. Ohmann recognizes a "non-honorific sense" of the term, "which is a common one in actual use" (see "Speech Acts," p. 1).

UNIVERSITY OF WINNIPEG
LIBRARY
515 Portage Avenue
Winnipeg, Manitoba R3B 2E9
DISCARDED

Some Aims of Criticism

E. D. HIRSCH, JR.

The Literary Study of Literature

The dominant movement in literary criticism since the 1940s is probably best called "intrinsic criticism." In discoursing upon it, I shall occasionally use the more familiar term "New Criticism," but only on the understanding that the reference is to an international movement of very broad scope, and not to Anglo-American manifestations alone. The guiding principle of the movement, which arose in academic circles in the 1920s and 1930s, was not formalism, or close analysis, or stylistics, but rather the programmatic idea that literature should be described and estimated in its own intrinsic categories. Many present-day reactions against formalism do not really attack this central conception, but propose the substitution or addition of broader intrinsic categories like recurrent myths, period styles, genre-traits, and modes, which define other aspects of the world of literature. The original and powerful programmatic idea—that literature should be dealt with as literature and not some other thing—still remains the dominant though not the only guiding principle for the teaching and criticism of literature.

The underlying unity and broad influence of the movement can be seen in the continuing force of its insistence on literary categories. One of the objections it brought against older forms of literary study was that literature lost its essential character when viewed as a mere effect of historical influences. Literary works, it was insisted, are not mere historical documents. Their historical dimension can be understood properly only when historical forces are described in literary categories—particularly those pertaining to the traditions of literary art. The same principle—translation into literary categories—must be applied to all the other dimensions of literature, moral, political, psychological, and social, in order to achieve appropriate results.

An account of the psychological dimension of literature that won few adherents but was nevertheless highly characteristic of the new program is found in a stimulating early work of I. A. Richards, *Principles of Literary Criticism* (1924). Psychologically, the most beneficial literature, in Richards's view, is the kind that harmonizes a large number of disparate and conflicting psychic impulses. Thus, a formal or purely literary criterion of excellence, similar to the kind proposed by Coleridge, is altogether concordant with Richards's psychological criterion. Literature that is formally rich and complex, and brings into unity a great many opposite and discordant elements achieves excellence both as literature and as therapy.[1] Since the two kinds of criteria coincide, the psychological values of literature can be accommodated to literary categories.

This pattern of accommodation is very widespread and is particularly interesting in its application to the moral dimension of literature. Writers like F. R. Leavis and Yvor Winters, though different in their preferences, were alike in correlating the qualities of an author's moral vision with the qualities of his style. Excellence of moral vision does not guarantee literary excellence, but the reverse does hold: literary excellence implies and requires moral wisdom, while inadequate moral conceptions will exclude an author from the highest achievements of literary art.[2] While these critics are essentially moralists of literature, they feel required to transform moral into literary judgments, thereby treating literature as literature.

In the work of W. K. Wimsatt, the principle is developed more subtly and cogently. Artistic complexity implies and reflects the moral complexity of actual life. Good literature, which is, for Wimsatt as for Richards, complex literature, will tend on the whole to have a positive moral tendency—even an immoral play like *Antony and Cleopatra*. By a structural correspondence, the moral issue can be accommodated to literary categories.[3] And

Wayne Booth, proclaiming his loyalty to the principles of Chicago that Wimsatt deplored,[4] follows a very similar pattern of accommodation. If an author does not implicitly take an ethical stance, and if that stance is not one we can respect, then his devices will not effectively work upon us. His work must be judged unsuccessful under purely literary canons.[5]

The intrinsic movement is sometimes attacked for not attending to the external implications of literature, and recently Frederick Crews has condemned the criticism of Northrop Frye for this sin of omission.[6] I think it was sound of Crews to argue that Frye's work is not a departure from but belongs to the very center of intrinsic criticism. But to the complaint that he has ignored society Frye has replied with some justice that he has had in view scarcely anything else.[7] Under Frye's conception, the informing myths of literature are not just recurrent structures of poetry, drama, and fiction, but also universal constructs of the human imagination, and thus constitutive not only of literature but of society as well. For Frye (as for Shelley, whom no one would accuse of not attending to society) both social institutions and literary works are built in the smithy of the human imagination. The internal characteristics of literature reflect social and ethical implications through a system of genetically based correspondences, so that to describe the one is to describe the other. The social is *aufgehoben* in the literary.[8] The structure of this accommodation is very similar to that of Richards, Leavis, Winters, Wimsatt, and Booth.

This characteristic strategy of New Criticism can be seen as an attempt to overcome the traditional disjunction between the artistic qualities of literature (*dulce*) and its instrumental effects (*utile*). The attempt is best understood not as disinterested speculation but as part of the general program to understand literature from within. Frye hoped to make criticism a science, and for him, as for earlier theorists of New Criticism, this meant the development of categories and classifications peculiarly appropriate to the subject.[9] Such an aim would explain the common assertion of a pre-established harmony between the external effects of literature and its internal traits, allowing the former to be accommodated to the latter. For if the psychological, moral, or social effects of literature, important though they may be, are described in alien psychological, moral, or social categories, and judged according to the alien criteria of those fields, then literature becomes a mere instrument, just as for history it had been a mere document.

Even if the accommodation of external effects to literary categories should be judged logically inadmissible, the main thrust of New Criticism would be scarcely affected, for the focus of the movement has not been on the external effects of literature. Indeed, New Criticism can reasonably argue that these effects vary so greatly from one context to another that the whole unmanageable question is better left alone. While I would by no means accept such an a priori dismissal of this important subject, I do think we must concede that the intrinsic criticism of literature has been and still remains our most powerful programmatic idea.

For many years now, the very power of the idea, and its persistence, have generated protests against what has seemed an overly hermetic conception of literary criticism.[10] Academic critics have been asked to show more concern for historical and biographical contexts, for the social relevance of literature, and for our present cultural and psychological needs. Individual critics have followed these injunctions, some of them long before the pleas were made, and many teachers of literature, including some figures of importance in New Criticism, have been sympathetic to the pleas and protests. But the calls have not been answered on a big scale because so far they have not been followed by counterproposals that can compete with New Criticism in intellectual stature or practical effectiveness.

On a practical level, for example, these counterproposals do not imply educational goals sufficiently definite to form the basis of textbooks and teaching guides like *Understanding Poetry* and its counterparts in Britain and Europe. That is at the least a failure in strategy, for under our present institutions, the main consumers of literary criticism are students fulfilling course requirements and teachers setting them. It cannot be expected that some new theory of criticism will take hold if it does not reach beyond scholarly and journalistic writing to embrace the concrete goals of classroom teaching. It is permanently to the credit of New Criticism that it transformed and improved the teaching of literature. A new theoretical proposal that does not promise similarly to invigorate teaching will fail to interest those who will alone determine the success or failure of any fresh critical movement.

But the practical success of New Criticism was not based merely upon its power to generate teaching guides and classroom methods. Teachers would not have embraced its methods if they had not found in the intellectual claims of New Criticism an appeal quite separate from that of its pedagogical usefulness. Intrinsic criticism claimed to be an intellectual and theoretical advance over older forms of historical, biographical, and philological study, and that claim was accepted. The New Criticism thereby had a purely intellectual success greater than anything to be hoped for by those who attack it on the grounds that it has grown boring and can no longer meet the ideological and psychological requirements of the young. Those are not trivial objections, and they will certainly prove fatal in the end to the dominance of intrinsic criticism. Nevertheless, they are not in themselves theoretical objections which give promise of an intellectual advance.

Admittedly, the power of boredom over intellectual fashions must never be underestimated, but its positive, generative capacities are not great. When the spokesmen for New Criticism pressed their case against Old Philology, they did not claim preferment merely as agents of a new *Zeitgeist* arrived on the scene when the old and stale ideas had completed their historical mission. Their argument was of quite a different sort. In essence it said that the Old Philology had been misguided from the start; that its naive methods and aims were quite inappropriate to its subject matter; and that the whole discipline of literary study should be put on a new and permanently valid footing, with methods, aims, and assumptions truly appropriate to literature. This claim of inherent theoretical superiority was on many counts valid, and in the end, the methodological and theoretical superiority of New

Criticism must be considered the main reason for its practical success inside the classroom and beyond.

Yet the current disaffections have more than temporary implications. They indicate, I believe, a flaw in the central, universally shared principle of intrinsic criticism, or at least in the assumptions on which the principle has been applied. Although the primary reason for the success of New Criticism has been its superiority to the methods it replaced, there is still room to doubt its claim of unique superiority as based on its specially appropriate and intrinsic character. The "literary study of literature" has a privileged ring to it, like "the proper study of mankind is man." [11] But what lies behind tautological formulations like the injunction to consider a poem as a poem? This methodological banner cry has not been extended to other fields—to the study of history as history, or the study of medicine as medicine. This does not mean that for literary study the formulation was meretricious or meaningless; one can only object that the meaning has not been made explicit. The Popean injunction to study literature as literature lends the program an apparently privileged status, but what the formulation in fact proposed was the study of literature as art.

This implication of the program was hardly covert. Nobody made a secret of it. Most of the major theoretical expositions (by Walzel, Richards, Crane, Wellek, Wimsatt, Staiger, Frye, and others) explicitly defined literature as art or accepted the definition as an assumption too obvious to belabor. It is difficult to remember whether Ingarden's book of 1931 was called *Das literarische Kunstwerk* and Kayser's of 1948 *Das sprachliche Kunstwerk*, or vice versa. It hardly matters, since either would serve as the title for a German version of several works originally composed in English. Even theorists who focused their attention on subjects broader than the individual literary work of art assumed, as their guiding principle, that the proper study of the critic is literature-as-art.

Is this a valid assumption? Is the study of literature as art uniquely appropriate to its subject matter, and therefore, by inherent right, the proper governing principle of criticism? In my own mind, that is the big question, and I shall try to deal with it in what follows, but first it must be said that the implicit claim of privilege by New Criticism is unquestionably justified on one point. If one goal of inquiry is to discover and define the artistic traits and values of literature, then the study of literature as art is privileged for that inquiry. It must be said further that the pursuit of this inquiry with energy and intelligence over the past four decades has advanced our understanding of literature as art beyond anything accomplished along those lines in previous times. The rhetorical analyses of Antiquity, of the Middle Ages, and the Renaissance—periods when rhetoric stood at the center of education as it no longer does—seem to me mechanical and un-informative when set alongside the best works of New Criticism. And, on the theoretical side, poetics has been advanced beyond anything achieved by Aristotle or anyone else. It is unlikely that so much would have been accomplished if New Criticism had not conceived its mission to be uniquely privileged. Whether or not that conception is valid, the accomplishments remain.

The Idea of Literature

The axiom that literature-as-literature equals literature-as-art implies that the distinctive and essential feature of literature, marking it off from other forms of language, is its artistic char-acter. Although this essentialistic doctrine is rarely stated in blunt nakedness, it is a necessary assumption of intrinsic criticism, and is the main implication to be drawn from phrases like "the liter-ary work of art," "literature as literature," "poem as poem." When these implications are formulated explicitly, they run like this: Literary criticism should conform to the essential nature of its subject. The essence of literature is art. It follows that aesthetic inquiry is essentialistic and thus privileged.

Tolstoy, playing the role of the little boy who gazed on the naked emperor, would ask, "What is art? Does art have an es-sence?" The learned despisers of aesthetics like Tolstoy are not always fair-minded in their dismissals, and in any case the ques-tion "What is literature-as-art?" may not depend for its answer on exercises in general aesthetics. When Tolstoy objected that most works on aesthetics paid no attention to the question "What is Art?" but expended their energy on the fruitless question "What is Beauty?", the objection was unfair.[12] The very concept of art in Tolstoy's sense, which is the dominant modern sense, did not have broad currency before the last half of the nineteenth century. Some of the theorists Tolstoy chastises would not have clearly understood his question. It is probably best to set general aesthetics aside, and approach the issue in a restricted way by asking more narrowly whether literature has an artistic essence that can sanction a privileged form of criticism.

In some modern theoretical discussions this problem is avoided by focusing attention on poetry and the poem—the traditional subjects of poetics. But the principles set forth in such theories are meant to apply with various degrees of adequacy to other forms of literary art, such as novels. Similarly, other specialized theories of particular genres can bypass the question "What is literature?" by limiting the reference to those genres alone. Nevertheless, the big question about literature is always implicit in these theoretical exercises because the artistic character of poems and the other genres remains always at the center. More- over, the subsumption of these diverse genres under literature is the unquestioned basis of the institutionalized discipline to which these discussions contribute. Certain nonliterary genres are ex- cluded; as yet, no professor of literature has busied himself with a theoretical discussion of statutory codes.[13] The notion that there is a valid category, literature, distinct from other kinds of writing which do not qualify, is a ubiquitous and, in many respects, as I wish to concede from the start, valid idea.

The idea is, however, surprisingly recent in its correlation with a single word. Although "literature" occurs very early in English, it did not normally refer even to a corpus of works be- fore the nineteenth century. The only meaning given in any edi- tion of Johnson's *Dictionary* is: that which a person has read, his literature, his learning.[14] I find no example of the word in its present, aesthetic connotation before the 1850s. When De Quincey contrasted the literature of knowledge and the literature of power, he was moving in his second category toward the current meaning, but the category of literature per se was still quite undifferentiated.[15] Nor can I find the modern usage in Hazlitt or in Coleridge, whose *Biographia Literaria* is a history of his reading, thinking, and writing that gives as much weight to philosophers as to poets, and to his own journalistic and philosophical work as to his poetry. Coleridge conveys the modern sense of "literature" by the phrase "polite letters," sometimes by "poetry." [16] Similarly, when Hazlitt writes of "American Literature," the essay which uses that phrase in its title focuses on the sermons and moral tracts of Dr. Channing.[17]

The French, apparently, began to restrict the sense of the word before the English or Americans. Some uncertain examples of such restriction for *littérature* can be found in the late eighteenth century, particularly in Voltaire, who wished to exclude merely technical manuals from the honorific classification.[18] Diderot and his colleagues, besides urging the study of ancient authors under "Littérature," correlate the term with "les Sciences proprement dites." [19] Thus, before the nineteenth century in France, *littérature* had by no means captured the semantic field of *belles lettres,* though the English use of "literature" late in the nineteenth century was probably, as with many words of aesthetic orientation, an adoption from a more precocious French usage.

In itself, this kind of historical semantics has little significance for the theoretical question I have posed, and no great reliance can be placed even on the precision of the historical inferences themselves, which need the support of more detailed researches. Nevertheless, some pertinent inferences can be drawn. We can surmise, for instance, that although an idea corresponding to the modern sense of "literature" may have existed before the later nineteenth century, indeed certainly did exist under formulations like "polite letters," the unitary force of the conception was not very central or even very natural to earlier cultures. Strong evidence, including that accumulated in controlled experiments, exists to support the view that unitary words tend to replace phrases only when a new interest or importance is attached to the concept represented by the phrase.[20] The implication is that sometime in the later nineteenth century, but not before, phrases like "polite letters" no longer suited the new importance and prominence of the unitary conception that still attaches to the word "literature."

Why did the unity of the conception appear so tardily to the minds of men? Probably for the reasons which delayed the modern sense of "art," and which hindered the emergence of "science" in its current acceptation. I believe it is reasonable to guess that in English the modern senses of "literature," "science," and "art" are all inventions of the Victorians. Certainly, they were the first to require these interrelated conceptions, while the props of revealed religion grew ever weaker as foundations for their spiritual world. "Art" and "literature" are secularized conceptions which embrace writers of the most divergent religious and ethical persuasions within a unified humanistic orientation. That is a plausible inference to be drawn from the preoccupations and linguistic traits of a writer like Matthew Arnold, who as Wellek points out, is also one of those to whom we owe the exaltation of the word "criticism," along with the word "culture." [21]

The rather late origins of the unitary sense of "literature" do not impair the validity of the concept. What the relative modernity of the word helps explain is why no definition of "literature" can embrace the current meaning through a grouping of traditional genres. A definition adequate to the modern meaning seems to require the modern category of "art." For instance, the following might be thought to cover the dominant present usage: "Literature comprises any linguistic work, written or oral, which has significant aesthetic qualities." Our modern usage can no longer be restricted as to genre, nor can it be limited to works having significant aesthetic intentions, since many works belonging to literature did not intend a predominantly aesthetic appeal. That is readily seen in a book like Moulton's *The Bible as Literature,* or in standard courses that begin with the Bible (as literature), move on to Homer and Greek tragedy, through Shakespeare and Dickens to T. S. Eliot.[22] Nobody misunderstands the title of Moulton's book, and few protest the formulation of immensely heterogeneous syllabi for literary courses. The only definition adequate to our sense of literature is one that avoids terms im-

plying common independent traits. Our definition must therefore be further amended: "Literature comprises any linguistic
work, written or oral, which has significant aesthetic qualities
when viewed from an aesthetic perspective." The further qualification is required to bring otherwise subordinate aesthetic qualities
to the center of attention. The modern concept of literature implies a modern, aesthetic mode of perception. Literature cannot be
defined adequately without taking that mode of perception into
account.

If that is indeed the only kind of definition adequate to our
present usage of "literature," then the question about the privileged nature of aesthetic criticism appears in a new light. Because
an aesthetic approach inheres in the very concept of literature, it
appears to be indeed intrinsic. The difficulty is that the concept
of literature is not itself a privileged category for the works it
embraces. Since literary works were not always conceived under
a predominantly aesthetic mode, we cannot assume that a stress
on aesthetic categories corresponds to the essential nature of individual literary works. Other categories, including instrumental,
ethical, and religious ones, may be more correspondent to their
individual emphases and intentions. An intrinsic critic might
reply, "Yes, that is all very well, but we want to know these works
as literature." To which no objection can be raised except to observe that such a pursuit is not necessarily intrinsic, and that
whether the inquiry is specially appropriate to the nature of a
work depends, ad hoc, on the individual case. We can accept the
classification "literature" as valid, but not as privileged, and it
follows that we must say exactly the same for the literary study
of literature. It is valid, but not privileged.

I have argued elsewhere the general point that no critical
approach to a wide multiplicity of works can possibly be privileged or intrinsic.[23] The only activity attendant upon criticism
that has a privileged character is the construction of meaning,
which is no necessary part of criticism. One must, of course,
understand a linguistic work in some degree before discussing it,
but one's understanding need not be the main subject of one's
criticism. And even understanding (i.e. the construction of origi-

nal meaning) as contrasted with misunderstanding has only an ethical and not an ontological claim to privilege. It is well known that criticism based on misunderstanding can be valuable and even valid in some respects. The most one can say for aesthetic criticism is that it is intrinsic to the concept of literature, which is not itself an intrinsic concept. Aesthetic criticism must therefor relinquish its principal claim.

We should go further. In one respect aesthetic criticism has been distortive. By claiming to be intrinsic to the nature of literature, it implies that the nature of literature is aesthetic. But, in fact, literature has no independent essence, aesthetic or otherwise. It is an arbitrary classification of linguistic works which do not exhibit common distinctive traits, and which cannot be defined as an Aristotelian species. Aesthetic categories are intrinsic to aesthetic *inquiries,* but not to the nature of literary works. Exactly the same can be said of ethical and psychological categories, or any critical categories whatever. They are intrinsic only to the inquiries for which they are appropriate. The idea of literature is not an essentialistic idea, and no critical approach can, without distortion, make essentialistic claims upon literature. The methods and aims of criticism must be justified on other grounds.

The Aims of Criticism

Those aims are ultimately general and abstract, but it is pertinent to look first at a practical side of our present situation. I ventured the sociological prediction that no critical program will succeed in the present day unless it generates practical aims and procedures that apply to the classroom. This may seem doubtful in view of the current instinct of students to believe that more truth and value are found in underground studies than in those pursued within institutions. But the teacher's instinct of self-preservation has gradually made the content of established courses resemble ever more closely whatever can be discovered underground. Literary study is at present astonishingly heterogeneous. In some American universities little remains that the underground can call its own. I am not referring just to courses that stress or include pornography, but to the whole range of subject matters and their mixtures, historical-modal, generic-thematical, modal-generical, historic-thematical, covering, for instance, "The Literature of Fantasy," "Women in Literature," "The Black Man in Literature," "Patristic Elements in Anglo-Saxon Literature." The aesthetic mode of perception can no longer be considered the governing mode, and the only vestige that remains of its former potency is the continued cheerful use of the word "literature" in the titles of these courses. This may be a mere concession to academic propriety, without further significance, and probably no critical program could bring conceptual order to this multeity, which has far outstripped all current descriptions of modern literary criticism. Perhaps conceptual order should not be the aim. But the present realities can hardly be ignored. In contemplating the function of criticism at the present time, necessity as well as duty direct the mind to the aims of literary education.

The current pedagogical expansion of literature suggests we may be gradually returning to a more venerable, undifferentiated usage under which "literature" covers everything worth preserving in written form, whether or not it has artistic merit. If so, the process is entirely natural. The domain of literature was quite heterogeneous even under the aesthetic dispensation, and when that approach began to seem one-sided, it was natural to extend the capacious domain by including works of value that have little aesthetic appeal. The best that is thought and said is not always said well, even if it ought to be, and the aims of humanistic education do not necessarily coincide with traditional academic boundary lines. Humane studies have a natural tendency to be imperialistic. The study of history has constantly encroached upon literary and philosophical subjects, especially in the vigorous fields of intellectual and cultural history. To the extent that philosophy has kept within narrow confines in recent years, it has withered as a vigorous subject of instruction in the humanities. On the other hand, and quite regardless of interdepartmental courtesies, even the most imperialistic subject needs a center. It needs predominant emphases determined by its educational missions, and these need to be defined in some relation to other humane studies. We need to know where we fit in, and what we ought specially to do.

The academic success of New Criticism was enhanced because it seemed to supply a center for literary study. Just as its intrinsic claims argued its centrality, so did its battle cry "autonomy" support the natural, centripetal impulse of the discipline. Autonomy was asserted for the literary subject matter and for literary methods. The discipline thereby defined itself over against other disciplines, and was able to defend its territorial rights and independence.[24] This center has proved to be unstable, not just through the natural imperialism of humanistic subjects, which resists the centripetal impulse, but also through the inadequacy of "autonomy" and its corollaries for defining the special missions of literary education. The literary work of art can be sealed off for contemplation, or confined to the "world of literature," but it is a philosophical mistake to argue that this procedure is sanctioned by the special ontological status of literature, or that the methods of literary study are different in principle from other kinds of inquiry. This philosophical difficulty shows itself on a practical level in the contortions that are required when you attempt to accommodate all the important traits and values of literature within purely literary categories.

The difficulty is venerable and undoubtedly permanent. The central example in the history of criticism has been the unresolved tension, going back to Plato at least, between technical and instrumental excellence in poetry. Aristotle's implication that good tragedy, being purgative, is good for the state, is not a sufficient answer (whether or not it was so intended) to the more general problem Plato raised. A work can be technically (artistically) good, yet have bad, indifferent, or good effects. A work can be technically bad, yet have good, indifferent, or bad effects. What teaches may not please; what pleases may not instruct.[25] The pansynergist Coleridge gave priority to pleasure over instruction in the domain of poetry, which, he said, teaches *through* pleasure, but not even Coleridge claimed instructiveness for all poetry that pleases. In recent days the old tension has manifested itself as the literary excellence of literature versus its relevance.

This tension has never been successfully resolved in the realm of theory, though many impressive attempts have been recorded. And yet, it is another fact in the history of criticism that technical and instrumental judgments are woven both together in the work of the most honored and durable practical critics. The best critics have not been categorical purists. If you judge under instrumental categories, according to the probable effects of literature, you will judge like Plato. If you restrict yourself cogently and rigorously to aesthetic categories, you will theorize like de Gourmont. If you judge literature as art, your criticism will benefit if somewhere along the line you make a logical or categorical mistake. Only the critic who uses both categories and embraces both kinds of value does justice to the aims of literary education, and by extension, the aims of criticism. Intrinsic theory has encouraged the belief that aesthetic categories can implicitly embrace instrumental values, a mistake which has led to a one-sided emphasis on the technical aspects of literature and a neglect of straightforward ethical judgments. What we need is not a theoretical synthesis, which is impossible, but a restoration of balance in theory as well as practice.

But the road of excess leads to counterexcesses. Instead of a restoration of balance we could be in for a moralistic, not to say self-righteous, rebellion against aestheticism that would be less serviceable to humane education than the one-sided aestheticism it replaced. The technical, aesthetic kind of literary study at least opens up a world not explored in other humane subjects, whereas the ideological touchstones that are now applied to literature (racism, male chauvinism, etc.) are also applied without restriction to history, social studies, and some of the natural sciences. Within this universal revisionism, literary study has no special contribution to make. A dizzy oscillation from extreme Aristotelianism to extreme Platonism is not a restoration of balance.

As the patron saint of literary education, my candidate is Matthew Arnold, whose contraries Sweetness and Light seem specially appropriate for describing the recurrent tensions of literary criticism. Arnold saw that neither the aesthetic nor the moralistic attitude to life and literature can be reduced to its contrary. He also perceived that the function of criticism is determined by the needs of the present time, not by some eternal formulation. Yet he was not an historical relativist. The aims of criticism change with history only because the deeper principle of balance is absolute and therefore requires different applications at different times. This absolute principle of balance is the antique norm of human fulfillment—the classical ideal of harmony under which all the conflicting appetences of life are nourished, with none subjected to the tyrannical domination of another. Thus, for Arnold, neither an aesthetic nor an instrumental conception of literature can alone suffice. Pursued with provincial excess, both kinds of criticism restrict the range of values in literature, and betray the heterogeneity of its nature and our own.

This classical ideal of balance, governing culture, education, and criticism is at bottom an ethical ideal; indeed, it is the ground principle of the *Nicomachean Ethics*. In my opinion Arnold is profoundly right to set the aims of criticism on foundations that can be described ultimately in ethical terms. Indeed, the chief justification for aesthetic contemplation and a moral holiday is ultimately an ethical justification. The foundation of literary criticism, including the scholarly and scientific study of literature, cannot be the special nature of the subject matter, since literature has no special nature. The foundation for the aims of criticism is the answer given to the ethical question "What are the special contributions that criticism and literary education can make at the present time?"

We need to keep our *special* obligations in view, for the general goals of fullness and balance hold for all humanistic culture, just as the admonition to know the best that is thought and said transcends any single field of learning. Our special contribution is not restricted to aesthetic concerns. We seem now to be relinquishing our overemphasis on the artistic aspect of literature, and I have tried to show the theoretical justification for our doing so. That hardly means we should entirely abandon the aesthetic approach; it means only that we should keep it in bounds and resist its essentialistic claims. The soundest justification for aesthetic inquiries in literary education is that they pertain to one side of human nature and should be pursued somewhere. If departments of literature do not pursue them, probably nobody else will.

The same defense can be offered for keeping poetry and prose fiction as our central subject matter, along with the writings of Kierkegaard, Eldridge Cleaver, Plato, and other sages in the continuum of literature. Poetry and fiction are worth studying, and if we don't keep them alive in humanistic education, nobody else will. That is the only justification we need. We do not need to claim a false ontological or elitist status for these writings, or attempt any but heuristic definitions of their nature. The approach we take to them should be determined by the needs of the time, and the needs of the inquiry we have chosen to pursue, not by the presumptuous claims of any special method.

Under our present institutions, the aims of literary criticism coincide largely with the aims of literary education. But not entirely. One very special obligation of departments of literature is the advancement of literacy—the refinement, up to the highest level, of reading and writing. If you take away the theoretical scaffolding that supported the aesthetic bias of New Criticism, you would still be left with its honorable emphasis on the improvement of reading. For I. A. Richards, one of the founding fathers, this high conception of literacy was central.[26] That is another residue we must not lose. In fact, we should stress it more, especially writing.

But in the end it would be misleading to suggest that any aim of criticism or of literary study has more than a contingent claim upon us. No form of criticism is inherently privileged. If this conclusion removes some external props from our ethical decisions, the consolation is that the props have not been sturdy and reliable. Another consolation is that literature, like criticism, is more capacious and, in its untrammeled diversity, more important than any aesthetic conception of literature has made it out to be.

NOTES

1. I. A. Richards, *Principles of Literary Criticism,* 2d ed. (1926), pp. 201–02, 204: "This reconciliation, this appeasement, is common to much good and to much bad poetry alike. But the value of it depends upon the level of organization at which it takes place, upon whether the reconciled impulses are adequate or inadequate." "We have to ask in applying the test what the responses in question are, and in the case of poetry they are so varied, so representative of all the activities of life, that actual universal preference on the part of those who have tried both kinds fairly is the same (on our view) as superiority of the one over the other. Keats, by universal qualified opinion, is a more efficient poet than Wilcox, and that is the same thing as saying that his works are more valuable."

2. The following three passages by Winters are from *Primitivism and Decadence* (1937), as reprinted in *In Defense of Reason* (New York, 1947) on pp. 22, 24, and 28 respectively: "The rather limp versification of Mr. Eliot and of Mr. MacLeish is inseparable from the spiritual limpness that one feels behind the poems." "Literary history is packed with sickening biographies. But it is worth noting that the poetry of such a man, say, as Rochester (who in this is typical of his age) displays a mastery of an extremely narrow range of experience." "It should be observed again how the moral discipline is involved in the literary discipline, how it becomes, at times, almost a matter of living philology."

These two passages from Leavis are in the Penguin edition of *The Great Tradition* (London, 1962), pp. 12 and 17 respectively: "There can't be subtlety of organization without richer matter to organize, and subtler interests than Fielding has to offer. He is credited with range and variety. . . . But we haven't to read a very large proportion of *Tom Jones* in order to discover the limits of the essential interests it has to offer us. Fielding's attitudes and his concern with human nature are simple." "When we examine the formal perfection of *Emma,* we find that it can be appreciated only in terms of the moral preoccupations that characterize the novelist's peculiar interest in life. Those who suppose it to be an 'aesthetic matter,' a beauty of 'composition' that is combined miraculously with 'truth to life,' can give no adequate reason for the view that *Emma* is a great novel, and no intelligent account of its perfection of form."

3. See *The Verbal Icon: Studies in the Meaning of Poetry* (Lexington, Ky., 1954). "The moral value in any given situation, what is right, is abstract; it is known by rule and conscience. By necessity it excludes. Neither a right nor a wrong choice, however, excludes the awareness of many values, some interrelated and supporting, some rival, some sacrificed by a choice, some in some situations held in ironic balance or entering into unresolved tensions" (p. 98). "A poem, even a great poem, may fall short of being moral. . . . It is yet true that poems as empirically discovered and tested do tend within their limits and given the peculiar *données* or presuppositions of each, to point toward the higher integration of dogma" (p. 100). Wimsatt adheres to a system of values in which "poetic is distinguished from moral and both are understood in relation to the master ideas of evil as negation or not-being, a gap in order, and of good as positive, or being—in the natural order the *designed complexity* of what is most truly one or most has being" (p. 100; my italics).

4. Booth calls a big essay by McKeon "the fullest statement of the critical pluralism on which this book is based." *The Rhetoric of Fiction* (Chicago, 1961), p. 403.

5. *The Rhetoric of Fiction*, p. 138: "We may exhort ourselves to read tolerantly, we may quote Coleridge on the willing suspension of disbelief until we think ourselves totally suspended in a relativistic universe, and still we will find many books which postulate readers we refuse to become, books that depend on 'beliefs' or 'attitudes' . . . which we cannot adopt even hypothetically as our own." And on p. 378: "Impersonal narration has raised moral difficulties too often for us to dismiss moral questions as irrelevant to technique."

6. "Though first-rate critics like Wilson, Empson, Trilling, and Burke have not hesitated to make 'extraliterary' sense of literature, the idea that we positively ought to do so is conceived as a threat to scholarly balance. The critic already knows what he is doing and will be all right if he can just keep himself from being overly drawn toward either what Frye has called 'the myth of concern' or the 'myth of detachment' " (in "Anaesthetic Criticism: I," *The New York Review of Books*, 26 Feb. 1970, p. 33). It has been said that Frye is more concerned with criticism as criticism than literature as literature. But criticism is an autonomous enterprise only under an intrinsic conception of literature that limits itself to certain kinds of writings or to certain special traits in writing. Otherwise Frye's theory of criticism would belong simply to psychology and anthropology, which it indeed does, willy-nilly, when it claims to make true, large-scale statements about the human mind.

7. "And as some of those who write about me are still asserting that I ignore the social reference of literary criticism, the sub-title calls the attention of those who read me to the fact that I have written about practically nothing else." *The Stubborn Structure: Essays on Criticism and Society* (London, 1970), p. x.

8. The following passages are from *Anatomy of Criticism* (Princeton, 1957). pp. 115, 119, and 122 respectively: "The archetypal view of literature shows us literature as a total form and literary experience as a part of the continuum of life, in which one of the poet's functions is to visualize the goals of human work. As soon as we add this approach to the other three, literature becomes an ethical instrument, and we pass beyond Kierkegaard's 'Either / Or' dilemma between aesthetic idolatry and ethical freedom, without any temptation to dispose of the arts in the process. Hence the importance, after accepting the validity of this view of literature, of rejecting the external goals of morality, beauty, and truth. The fact that they are external makes them ultimately idolatrous, and so demonic." "When we pass into anagogy, nature becomes, not the container, but the thing contained, and the archetypal universal symbols, the city, the garden, the quest, the marriage, are no longer desirable forms that man constructs inside nature, but are themselves the forms of nature. Nature is now inside the mind of an infinite man who builds his cities out of the Milky Way." "The anagogic view of criticism thus leads to the conception of literature as existing in its own universe, no longer a commentary on life or reality, but containing life and reality in a system of verbal relationships."

9. *Anatomy*, p. 7: "If criticism exists, it must be an examination of literature in terms of a conceptual framework derivable from an inductive survey of the literary field."

10. See, for instance, Walter Sutton, *Modern American Criticism* (Englewood Cliffs, N.J., 1963), p. 289: "The most obvious need of critical theory today is the integration of aesthetic or formalist and social or historical considerations. Literature and criticism are social functions. . . . The critic and scholar will increasingly realize that he is socially engaged in all his activities. It is his obligation to keep criticism open to new ideas and values so that it may continue to provide fresh knowledge of an ever-expanding world of interrelated literary and social experience." The most trenchant statement I know of is in Robert Weimann, *"New Criticism" und die Entwicklung Bürgerlicher Literaturwissenschaft* (Halle, 1962), p. 131: "Die neukritische Grundanschauung vom Kunstwerk als einem in sich ruhenden Phänomen leugnet ja jede Beziehung zwischen Werk und Realität. Sie verwirft dreierlei: die historische Wirklichkeit, damit aber zugleich das Publikum und schliesslich auch den Künstler als Bezugspunkte der Dichtung. Dementsprechend ist auch ihre Frontstellung eine dreifache: sie wendet sich gegen das Aristotelische Prinzip der *mimesis* oder Nachahmung, gegen das Horazsche Prinzip *aut prodesse aut delectare* und schliesslich gegen die letzte von der Romantik geduldete und geförderte ausserästhetische Bestimmung—die biographische Beziehung zum Schöpfer des Werkes. Sie negiert also die abbildende-verallgemeinernde, die didaktischeunterhaltende, und die Ausdrucksfunktion der Kunst. Sie verwirft damit die Kunstanfassung der grössten Dichter der Vergangenheit."

11. Out of countless examples, take Leavis: "Literature will yield to the sociologist, or anyone else, what it has to give only if it is approached as literature." *The Common Pursuit* (London, 1952), p. 193.

12. See especially chaps. 3 and 4 of *What Is Art?*

13. The principles of R. S. Crane, based on the formal requirements of *any* genre, can be so extended. Yet this would still remain a formal, technical approach, and thus "aesthetic" in the broad sense of the term. Moreover one can apply stylistic and other categories used in other forms of intrinsic criticism to any utterance, literary or nonliterary, with useful and appropriate results.

14. The first definition in the *OED* runs as follows: "Acquaintance with 'letters' or books; polite or humane learning; literary culture. Now *rare* and *obsolescent*. (The only sense in Johnson and Todd 1818.)"

15. See *The Collected Writings of Thomas de Quincey*, ed. David Masson, 14 vols. (Edinburgh, 1890), x, 46: "The word *literature* is a perpetual source of confusion, because it is used in two senses, and those senses liable to be confused with each other. In a philosophical use of the word, Literature is the direct and adequate antithesis of Books of Knowledge. But in popular use it is a mere term of convenience for expressing inclusively the total books of a language" (from "Letters to a Young Man etc.," 1823). He took up the attempt again in 1847 (xi, 53): "What is it that we mean by *literature?* Popularly, and amongst the thoughtless, it is held to include everything that is printed in a book. . . . Not only is much that takes a station in books not literature; but inversely much that really *is* literature never reaches a station in books. The weekly sermons of Christendom, that vast pulpit literature which acts so extensively upon the popular mind—to warn, to uphold, to renew, to comfort, to alarm—does not attain the sanctuary of libraries in the ten-thousandth part of its extent." (To this de Quincey ap-

pends a note excluding the "Blue Books" of Parliamentary statistics from the honorary classification.)

16. *Biographia Literaria,* ed. Shawcross, 2 vols. (Oxford, 1907), I, 26: "Now it is no less remarkable than true with how little examination works of polite literature are commonly pursued." And on p. 159: "But woefully will that man find himself mistaken who imagines that the profession of literature or (to speak more plainly) the *trade* of authorship, besets its members with fewer or with less insidious temptations than the church, the law, or the different branches of commerce."

17. See *The Complete Works of William Hazlitt in Twenty-One Volumes, Vol. 16: Contributions to the Edinburgh Review,* ed. P. P. Howe (London, 1933), pp. 318–37. The title is "American Literature—Dr. Channing." It is a review of *Sermons and Tracts* (1829) and ranks Channing with Irving, Cooper, and Brown.

18. Voltaire's view is similar to de Quincey's of 1847: "Le mot ouvrage de la littérature ne convient point à un livre qui enseigne l'architecture ou la musique, les fortifications, la castramétation, etc.; c'est un ouvrage technique." Quoted by Paul Robert under "littérature" in *Dictionnaire alphabétique et analogique de la langue française: les mots et les associations d'idées,* 6 vols. (Paris, 1966), IV, 124–25.

19. "Terme général, qui désigne l'erudition, la connaissance des Belles Lettres, & des matieres qui y ont rapport. Voyez le mot LETTRES, où en faisant leur éloge on a démontré leur intime union avec les Sciences proprement dites." Vol. 9 of *Encyclopédie ou dictionnaire raisonné des sciences des arts et des metiers* (Neuchâtel, 1765).

20. Roger Brown, *Words and Things* (Glencoe, Ill., 1958), pp. 229–53.

21. René Wellek, *Concepts of Criticism,* ed. S. G. Nichols (New Haven, 1963), p. 31: "While in France Sainte-Beuve re-established the supremacy of the critic as a public figure and in England Matthew Arnold made criticism the key to modern culture and the salvation of England, in Germany criticism lost status drastically."

22. Richard Green Moulton, *The Bible as Literature* (London, 1899). This began as a university syllabus, published in 1891, under the title *Syllabus: The Literary Study of the Bible.*

23. "Privileged Criteria in Literary Evaluation," in *Yearbook of Comparative Criticism, Vol. 2: Problems of Literary Evaluation,* ed. Joseph Strelka (University Park, Pa., 1969), pp. 22–23.

24. This is a recurring topos or archetype of intrinsic criticism. As late as 1957 Frye was stating: "It is clear that the absence of systematic criticism has created a power vacuum, and all the neighboring disciplines have moved in" (*Anatomy,* p. 12).

25. These pronouncements, which follow Plato's views in the *Laws,* are subjects for further study rather than self-evident truths. The subjects have not been carefully studied. Even after you have won provisional agreement about the nature of a good or bad effect, you will still need to find out empirically, in a

given cultural situation, what the *predominant* effect of a work (or a fashion) actually is. Students of literature need not leave this empirical work to others; it falls under the "literary study of literature" just as much as aesthetic inquiries do. "Minor" works of art like Mrs. Sherwood's *The Fairchild Family* are said to have twisted influential minds of a whole age, not because the books were technically bad, but precisely because they were technically (artistically) effective and thereby all the more pernicious. In the absence of careful empirical studies of effects, we are well advised to follow Plato and not prejudge the issue with a middle category "art" that magically fuses the technically effective and the morally good.

26. And by him continually restated. See *Speculative Instruments* (London, 1955), "Responsibilities in the Teaching of English," pp. 91–106.

Words, Language, and Form

MARIE BORROFF

The "language" of literature is often discussed in criticism, but
rarely defined: many implicitly different concepts of language
are revealed by a comparative examination of the statements
made about, and especially the terms used to describe, what is
uniformly called "language." We may find a broad opposition
between language and content, or reality, or truth—as when language is called "ornate" or "transparent" or "artificial"; thus
Maynard Mack says of *King Lear* that it "uses for the most part
the barest bones of language to point at experiences that lie beyond the scope of language." [1] Language may be described in
terms borrowed from human character or behavior, as when it is
said to be "austere" or "pompous" or "exuberant"; thus David
Lodge identifies in the fiction of Jane Austen a "vocabulary of
discrimination . . . which asserts the prime importance . . . of
exercising the faculty of judgment." [2] Still other descriptions are
couched in terms of language *qua* language—of facts or phenomena that can be pointed to, even counted, on the printed page;
but here too there is diversity in the aspect or aspects of "language" selected for discussion or analysis. The focus may be on
diction, or on functional varieties of language (i.e. levels on a
scale of formality), or figures of speech, or patterns or devices of
sound; it may be on syntax, narrowly or broadly defined—on
forms of the verb, proportions of the parts of speech, or clauses
or sentences viewed as like or unlike in pattern, or as alternative
realizations of the "deep structures" posited by transformational
grammar.[3] Richard Ohmann has recently argued for the importance of considering literary language as sequences of verbal acts,

having such forms, above and beyond the "act" of uttering of a sequence of words per se, as assertion, denial, exhortation, and so on.[4] Many other illustrations of this diversity in the meaning of "language" could be cited, and what is true of language itself applies even more emphatically to language as an aspect of style.[5] My purpose in what follows is not to put forward one "correct" definition, either of language or of style, but rather to suggest some distinctions that may prove useful in setting different critical concepts of language in one array, in complementary rather than antagonistic relationship. I hope these distinctions may finally afford a new approach to the old and vexed problem of the "form-content" dualism as bearing on the theory of stylistic analysis.

A preliminary distinction must be made between two kinds of critical enterprise bearing on language however defined, one concentrating upon a single passage in the context of a literary work, or perhaps a short poem in its entirety, the other seeking to identify recurrent features or aspects of form. The first is concerned with what is individual or expressively distinctive, the second with what is typical or characteristic, whether the "typical" be found in a genre, a period, an author, or even a work. Now no one would deny that these two sorts of enterprise are necessarily related in that the identification of "recurrences" presupposes the recognition of individual "occurrences." But there may be a more profound relationship than this: a passage chosen for intensive analysis because of its particular significance, its "saliency" in the context of an author's writings, may reveal a set of interacting features characteristic of many other passages as well. What is studied as unique may prove emblematic.

To insist on the relationship between the intrinsic significance of the language of a passage and the recurrence of identifiable features of language is to insist, as I should wish to do, on the relationship between what is formal in language and what is dynamic, between the visible expressive means and the invisible expressive thrust. A formal feature both is and does something. Insofar as the forms assumed by language draw themselves to our attention, they signalize what they express, tacitly claiming for it an importance making it worthy of our close attention. The critic of literary language must finally examine this claim, else he runs the risk of seeming to place some of the most memorable verse and prose in our tradition on a par with the Story of Jack a Nory.

As a first step on the theoretical footbridge connecting the formal with the dynamic aspects of language, we must consider the nature of meaning, and in so doing we must begin with the meanings of single words, the primary building blocks of all semantic structures. Here it is necessary to reinvoke the classic concept of an ideational disjunction between words and things. Such a theory affirms that words do not, in any useful sense of meaning, "mean" things; rather, they mean categories, which are ideas, in application to things.[6] For the purposes of such a theory of language, the word *meaning* is restricted to the denotation of categories. The word-thing relationship, in which meaning may, but need not, serve as an intermediary, will here be called reference; the things to which words are related will be called *subjects of reference*—collectively, *subject matter*. The distinction between meaning and reference is too obvious to require extended discussion. It may be demonstrated by such a simple exercise as citing pairs of words, different in meaning in the narrow sense, which might be used to describe or call attention to the same subject, action, or attribute: *man, doctor,* with reference to the same person; *go, drive,* with reference to the same trip; *vivid, scarlet,* with reference to the same color; *heavy, overweight,* or *gross,* with reference to the same poundage; *agree, shake hands,* with reference to the same outcome of negotiations. As an apt designator for words in their denotative-referential capacity, serving to hold this aspect of language separate for purposes of analysis, I propose the word *term*.

But once meaning has been distinguished from reference, it is immediately necessary to put the two together again. Comprehension of the status of a word as a term, i.e. of its denotative meaning, depends on our perception of, or assumption concerning, a subject to which it refers. It has been said that no one can understand the word *cheese* unless he has a nonlinguistic acquaintance with cheese. The observation applies a fortiori to those words, and they are legion, having two or more different meanings. A speaker who knows all the dictionary definitions of a word must still know to what it is being applied in order to know which definition is operative. The word *doctor* means one thing with reference to the early Christian writers, another when we are ill; the word *eye* means one thing in a hurricane forecast, another in an ophthalmologist's waiting room. And so on. In that the word *doctor* has two denotative values with reference to two different subjects, it may be said to function in the language as two different terms. Pairs of words like *doctor* and *ophthalmologist* differ as terms in application to a single subject. Given that a word functions as a term only in reference to a known or assumed subject, the possibility of synonymy in language becomes easier to envisage. Two terms may be synonymous—may denote the same category—in the same verbal or situational context (*doctor* and *physician, ophthalmologist* and *eye doctor*), though two words are never or rarely synonymous in the sense of having the same full range of denotative values.

Comparing synonymous terms, we encounter striking and important expressive differences, including those usually treated under the heading of diction. *Doctor* and *physician* illustrate such a difference, as do *eye doctor* and *ophthalmologist;* or, more startlingly, *headshrinker,* or its reduction *shrink,* and *psychoanalyst;* or, again, *doctor* and *healer* (in, say, the phrase "the healer's art"), or *doctor* and *leech.* Here we have to do, as I should like to put it, with comparisons not between words as terms but between words as words, that is, between words considered as linguistic "counters" without regard to meaning. *Physician* and *ophthalmologist* are more learned or formal, as words, than *doctor* and *eye doctor; headshrinker* and *shrink* are more colloquial than *psychoanalyst; healer* is more literary and high-flown than *doctor; leech* is an archaism. These attributes derive not so much from the relation between a given word and the subjects of reference to which it has been applied as from the sorts of occasion with which the word is associated. The "occasion" of using language is here defined in terms of level of formality as well as other circumstances. A man may read an essay to some friends and then converse informally with those same friends; the language he uses in doing these two things will differ in accordance with the difference between the two "occasions" in this sense. Learned or formal status derives from use exclusively or chiefly in formal contexts—i.e. in finished verbal structures directed toward an impersonal "public." Colloquial status derives from use exclusively or chiefly in the casual, "person-to-person" language of everyday. Archaic status derives from cessation of use, or, in some classes of archaisms, from cessation of use on everyday occasions with continued use, or at least preservation, in literary works.

If we consider the range of values a word may have as a term together with its qualities as a word, it is evident that the latter tend to vary with the former. *Leech* is an archaism as a term referring to a man as a member of a particular profession, but not as a term in marine zoology. *Shrink* is a slang word as a noun referring to a man belonging to a certain profession, but not as a verb referring to an alteration in size. More important, the quality of any word as a word changes when it is used creatively as a metaphor, i.e. when one of its values as a term undergoes an intelligible transmutation in a different sphere of reference. A word so used has an enhanced vividness if only because it is startling in its new context. An established metaphor, on the other hand, has qualities as a word deriving from the contexts with which it has been associated; the word *physician* in the sense of "one who can heal love-sickness," as used by Chaucer, belongs to the poetic diction of his time.

We may sum up by saying that the expressive value of a word in context, as defined so far, consists of its denotational significance as a term and its qualities as a word, including not only such aspects of its status as have been discussed above, but its phonetic shape and the degree of stress it receives in the sentence. A third dimension of the expressive value of a given word, its relevant associations with other subjects of reference and kinds of occasion, is of immense importance for the language of poetry, and will be reintroduced in connection with the analyses of particular passages below.

Language consists not of words as items but of words syntacti-

cally connected in statements, questions, pleas, apostrophes, and
so on, which in turn are linked in patterns of reiteration, exposition, argument, description, narrative, and the like. If we
consider the part played by syntactic structures in conferring expressive values upon words in sequence, it becomes apparent
that these structures play a double role, having conceptual aspects
analogous to denotative meanings, and qualitative or stylistic aspects analogous to the qualities of words as words. Conceptually,
syntactic structures superimpose on the meanings of single
words a complex of elaborative meanings expressing such relationships as agency, time, and attribution, as also do function words,
e.g. the conjunctions and prepositions, which are not "terms" as
here defined. Consider the following sentence: "The doctor saw
him this morning and told me not to worry." Here a set of conceptual relationships among the terms *doctor, see, morning,* etc.,
is signified by syntax and function words; these relationships
would be altered if the sentence were changed to "He saw the doctor this morning and told me not to worry." But another sort of
syntactic change, to "The doctor, having seen him this morning,
told me not to worry," not only tightens slightly the signified
logical connection between the actions of seeing and telling, but
gives the first part of the sentence a more formal ring. In fact,
there is now an awkwardness resulting from a strain between the
formal quality of the participial construction and the everyday
diction and grammar of the rest of the sentence. "The doctor,
having seen the patient this morning, reports that his condition
is good," would be more all of a piece. This wording sounds like
an official announcement or news bulletin rather than a statement made in informal talk. Space does not allow detailed consideration of this point, but it is clear that there is a "diction" of
syntactic structures, deriving from use on different kinds of occasion as do the qualities of individual words, and differing from
the conceptual values of syntax in the same way that the values
of words as words differ from the values of words as terms.

Any term differs from any other (synonyms aside) as one denoted idea differs from another denoted idea: the term *chalk*
differs from the term *cheese* as do chalk and cheese themselves.

But there are certain respects in which terms signifying different ideas may nonetheless be alike, and these general characteristics of terms are clearly in some sense characteristics of "language." *Doctor* and *ophthalmologist* differ from each other as do *cheese* and *cheddar,* or *book* and *text,* or *implement* and *scalpel,* and the members of these pairs resemble each other in that the first is comparatively general, the second specific. "They agreed on the bagain" and "They shook hands on the bargain" signify the same event in different language, i.e. in different terms; here the difference is between abstract and concrete—the event in the latter formulation, we may say, is expressed *in terms of* physical action. So too with "He assented" and "He nodded his head," or "He took a newspaper and paid for it" and "He took a newspaper and put a dime down on the counter." Two other kinds of terms, qualitative and sensory, may be mentioned briefly. Qualitative terms introduce an explicit component of emotion or judgment above and beyond the factual content of language; sensory terms denote particular aspects of sensory experience such as colors, textures, odors. The statement "The doctor deftly drew a sample of blood" contains a qualitative term of praise which might be replaced by objective language, as in "The doctor drew a sample of blood quickly and without causing the patient pain." A reference to "The white-coated doctor, smelling faintly of disinfectant" is elaborated in terms of sensory experience.

It should be noted that the different meanings of a single word may have different characteristics as terms. A concrete term will, if used with frequency, tend to develop one or more metaphorical terms that are abstract, e.g. *eye* in the phrase "the mind's eye" or "with an eye to." This process is reversed when an abstract term takes on a concrete meaning, e.g. *transmission* (in an automobile), *notions* (in a department store). *Fair* is a qualitative term of praise (and a poetic word) in the meaning 'lovely'; it is a qualitative term of disapproval (but not a poetic word) in the meaning 'mediocre'; it is a comparatively objective term in a weather report.

It follows from what has been said that the language of a passage may be analyzed from two theoretically distinct points of view. It presents itself on the one hand as a series of terms, each having in context its own primary or "operative" meaning, upon which a set of elaborative meanings has been imposed by syntactic structures. Aside from their meanings per se, these terms will have characteristics of a general nature, such as specificity, concreteness, qualitativeness, and so on, which may be salient in particular passages or recurrent as features. To analyze language in this sense is to direct attention toward what is shared between a given passage and a literal translation of that passage in a language having a grammatical system much like that of the original—a passage in English translated, say, into French, German, or another modern language of Indo-European descent. But a passage also presents itself as a series of words having qualities as words above and beyond their characteristics as terms—words that are common, formal, colloquial, rare, archaic, and so on. And, as was indicated earlier, any word may have a range of additional values as a term (and hence of qualities as a word) relevant to the content of a given passage; such relevance is especially probable in the richly expressive language of poetry. All metaphors and ambiguities, to name only two generally recognized features of poetic language, involve at least two values of the metaphorical or ambiguous word in question as a term.

To analyze the shared aspects of an original and a literal translation in a closely related language is to concern oneself with the ideas signified by syntactically related words and the subject matter to which those ideas are applied. Such an analysis represents one abstractive step away from the language of the text in all its particularity. Another way of demonstrating this is to consider the resources of synonymy afforded by a given language. A writer's use of, say, *begin* rather than *commence,* or *doctor* rather than *physician,* or *repose* rather than *rest,* may be thought of as concretizing, giving phonetic shape to, the idea signified by both words of any of the pairs. The relationship between choice of terminology and choice of words need not be thought of as involving a succession in time, though one may occasionally be conscious, as a speaker or writer, of hesitating between synonyms at the brink of utterance. I shall have more to say on this point below.

To see how these distinctions might be applied to an actual passage of poetry, let us consider the following stanza, which occurs toward the end of Robert Lowell's "The Drinker":

> The cheese wilts in the rat-trap,
> the milk turns to junket in the cornflakes bowl,
> car keys and razor blades
> shine in an ashtray.

The difficulties involved in translating this passage into French or German would, I take it, be largely cross-cultural, depending on whether there were words having the same meanings as *junket* and *cornflakes* in French or German.[7] (Such difficulties would be a symptom of Lowell's characteristic use of terminology, as described below.) But even if other terms had to be substituted in translating these two words, much of the effect of the original would be retained. That is, the significance of the details themselves, in the context of the poem, would be preserved. Most obviously, these details portray the condition of the drinker's home: rats, or suspected rats, that have not been caught; unwashed dishes; tabletop clutter. The cheese and milk which objectify this condition in their moldly and curdled state are esthetically distasteful. Razor blades lying in an ashtray together with car keys threaten with cut fingers anyone who might reach for the keys; latently, they suggest violence, perhaps even suicide.

Examined for characteristics of terminology, aside from signified items of content, the passage proves to be built largely of concrete terms many of which are also highly specific, as shown by a comparison with other equally concrete terms which might have been used to refer to the same things—*rat-trap, junket, cornflakes, car keys,* rather than *trap, curdles* (for "turns to junket"), *cereal, keys.* This penchant for concrete specificity shows itself elsewhere in the poem, e.g. in *Bourbon, plastic tumbler, alka seltzer, parking meter, forsythia,* and is in fact a feature of Lowell's descriptive style, a feature which can, by and large, be reproduced in translation. Also reproducible in French or German is a significant feature of the syntax of the passage: the cheese, milk, car keys and razor blades are imagined as agents performing actions (compare "There is sour milk in the cornflakes bowl," etc.), and these actions are imagined as in process (compare "The milk has turned to junket," etc.). *Shine* is more active in the semantic sense, though not in the grammatical sense, than, say, *lie*. All this in turn points to another aspect of the significance of the listed details: they imply the passage of time. The changes taking place in the house contrast implicitly with the trapped plight of the drinker, held as if by a barbed hook on a tight line in his "galvanized" despair.

The concluding stanza follows.

> Is he killing time? Out on the street,
> two cops on horseback clop through the April rain
> to check the parking meter violations—
> their oilskins yellow as forsythia.

This concluding image is significant in that it involves functionaries of the law, associated (though not on the parking meter level) with standards of right action against which individual conduct is measured. Infractions of law are being noted, and penalties duly exacted, but these are superficial, contrasting radically with the degradation in which the drinker is foundering unobserved. Parking meter violations also involve the passage of time and imply a relationship between an undesirable "stasis" and the inexorable process of change. But the cars which have been left at the meters are at least in use; the drinker's car keys lie in the ashtray. Spring rain and seasonally blooming bushes are stereotypes of promise and hope—subverted ironically here, of course, as also are the festive associations of the metaphorically signified champagne, invoked to describe the fizzing of an anti-hangover remedy. These aspects of the significance of the stanza could be reproduced in a close translation; any difficulties of the translated version for the foreign reader would again be cross-cultural, driving from a possible lack of words for, or familiarity with, parking meters and policemen's yellow rain-gear.

But the final stanza presents other difficulties that are not cultural in nature. There are one or two problems of diction—*cop* is colloquial in comparison with *policeman,* as is "killing time" in comparison with "wasting time" or "whiling time away." Elsewhere in the poem there are words of opposite quality: *beseeching, ponderous, euphoric*. A range of values of diction is characteristic of Lowell's verbal style, and a translator would be bound to attempt to get an equivalent range while preserving the original meanings. More important are certain expressive values in the stanza which depend on the range of meaning of two words: *violation* and *kill*. *Violation* is used in English with reference not only to traffic laws but to the moral code in its more solemn aspects; this relevant sense enhances the ironic disparity between the depth of the drinker's *accidia* and the pettiness of the wrongdoing which is being punished on the city streets. Of key significance is the expression "killing time," which harks back to the opening of the poem: "The man is killing time—there's nothing else." The literal meaning of *kill* hovers behind both occurrences of the expression, and there is a sinister implication in the fact that the question "Is he killing time?" immediately follows the reference to razor blades. The real point of the question, as worded, is that the man is not, in fact, "killing time" in the sense of nullifying its effects. Time is passing, turning cheese to mold, souring milk, and causing meters to expire. Time is, in fact, killing the man. The loss of this thematic implication in the substitution of a different way of putting the idea would do serious harm to the poem.

A similarly striking example of a fusion of the expressive value of words as terms with the values of relevant associations may be found in the concluding stanza of Lowell's "For the Union Dead."

> The Aquarium is gone. Everywhere,
> giant finned cars nose forward like fish;
> a savage servility
> slides by on grease.

Here, both the descriptive detail itself and the terminology in which it is expressed are linked to the preceding stanzas with an intricacy it is impossible to treat adequately here. The Aquarium is the initial subject of the speaker's thoughts in the poem, remembered from childhood visits, associated still with a wistful longing for "the dark downward and vegetating kingdom / of the fish and reptile." Such a "dark downward kingdom," but without the redeeming innocence of the animal realm, manifests itself in present-day Boston, where St. Gaudens's bronze Civil War relief, portraying the negro infantry who gave their lives in the battle to free the slaves, shakes from the vibrations of the bulldozer excavating a huge underground parking garage. The two concluding lines link an abstract term with a verb and prepositional phrase signifying physical action; *servility* thus takes on a quasi-concrete metaphorical meaning comparable to the concrete sense of *monstrosity*. *Savage* and *servility* are also terms of contradictory meanings, so that their juxtaposition has the additional force of an oxymoron.

In the wording of these lines, *savage, servility,* and *grease* all have a range of associations evoked in the context of the poem as a whole. *Savage* as a noun can mean 'primitive man'; it thus suggests the stereotype of the jungle-inhabiting African, looked down upon yet enslaved by white Americans, and brings out by ironic contrast the heroism of the descendants of Africans commemorated by the bronze relief. *Servility* means both a contemptible 'slavishness' of behavior and a state of 'enslavement,' alike applicable to the Boston of the speaker's vision, where a monument to men who died to free slaves is now only an irritating reminder of past ideals, sticking "like a fishbone in the city's throat." *Grease* means "motor lubricant," as in the phrases "grease job" and "grease monkey"; in such expressions as "slick as grease" it implies a somewhat questionable ease and speed; in the phrase "to grease someone's palm" it refers to bribery. The related adjective *greasy*, in application to persons, is a qualitative term of contempt.

We must now return to the question raised at the beginning of this essay: that of the content-form dualism and its value in the analysis of style. If one considers a passage partly as a series of significant descriptive details, partly as a syntactically ordered series of terms having particular meanings and general characteristics, and partly as a series of words having certain values as words and certain relevant associations, where is form and where is content? Where, in fact, is "language"?

An answer to the first question has already been given in part. The analysis of words as terms, it was argued, differs from the analysis of the same words as words, each having its unique range of associations, by one degree of abstraction from the actuality of a text. But once this is recognized, we can then see that the summarized descriptive content of a passage—say, the sour milk, cheese, keys and razor blades in Lowell's "The Drinker"—differs in the same way from the actual series of terms having syntactic form in which this content is embodied. That is, the analysis of descriptive content represents one further abstrative step from the text than is represented by the analysis of words as terms. And descriptive content itself has its significance in relation to the plot or conception of the poem—in this instance, the moral and marital plight of the drinker. Curdled milk in a bowl of cornflakes might, in a setting in real life, have an entirely different dramatic significance, or no particular significance at all. It is because it does have significance in the plot of this poem, we assume, that it "materialized" in the mind of the composing poet.

One must conclude that there exists a range of levels at which a critic may engage the poetic text, from the most concrete and particular to the most abstract and general. Though I hold no brief for any set number or nomenclature, I have found it useful for theoretical purposes to identify four levels: *verbalization, formulation, development,* and *conception.* Of these, the first two represent complementary aspects of the language of the text; the last two are related as the articulation and ordering of the plot of a poem in "chapters" is related to the plot itself. (One aspect of development in "The Drinker," for example, is the fact that the poem ends with a description of policemen outside the house checking parking meters.) The level of formulation is the level of terminology and of grammatical structure in its conceptual aspects; a good deal of specimen analysis on this level has been presented above. The level of verbalization includes not only diction and the range of relevant associations of particular words, as discussed above, but phonetic and metrical features and the stylistic aspects of grammatical structure. Development, formulation, and verbalization may be viewed as related both to con-

ception or "plot" and to each other as a set of formative levels,
such that not one, but a number of different form-content relationships may be analyzed in a poem, depending upon what is
held constant as a "given" and what is discussed in relation to it
as a dramatically significant rendering or realization. Thus development is "form" in relation to conception as "content";
formulation is "form" in relation to either conception or development; verbalization is "form" in relation to conception, formulation, or development. And conception itself is "form" in relation
to its sources in the poet's mind and experience, the literary conventions he inherits, and the expressive potentialities of the
language of his time.[8] It is obvious that, in practice, criticism
tends to operate on more than one level, picking out what is especially significant in one of these relationships at one moment,
in another at another.

I have deliberately spoken of "levels" rather than of "phases"
or "stages," in order to avoid any implication of a succession in
time, of purporting to describe in chronological order the mental
activities of the creating poet. In the actual process of composition, we know, the formulation of a detail may give rise to the
conception of a poem; the choice of a rhyme-sound which must
be embodied in particular words may suggest a descriptive detail,
or influence level of diction. Are such sequences exceptional,
however? Surely in all purposeful activity, a generalized impulse
to act precedes the manner of the action. One is inevitably reminded of the "levels" analyzed in transformational grammar,
where abstract "deep structures" are "rewritten" in successively
more concrete versions, the culminating step being the substitution
of a string of actual words for a full set of grammatical (but not
terminological) designations. Whether the levels posited either
for that grammatical model or this poetic one represent an actual
sequence in time remains doubtful, and can perhaps never be
known.[9] The value of the models for analytical purposes is independent of, or at least prior to the revelation of, their "truth" in
terms of neuropsychological events.

Much has been said in the discussion of particular passages in
this essay about "significance" at various levels, but the question

of *what* is signified in poems has not been raised. It will be apparent that I consider significance in poetry to be dramatic, so that an account of it must involve a step from the realm of linguistic fact—what is there on the page—to the realm of experience, the arena in which emotions, states of mind and body, ethical qualities, and the recognizable individuality of human beings, all interact, portrayed by means of a single sequence of words in which all aspects of form are simultaneously realized. The significance of any form-content relationship is an arrow, or, better still, a vector or line of force to which the reader responds by grasping its directive import.[10] In poetic language of the order of Lowell's these lines of force work on all formative levels to strengthen, enrich, complicate, or qualify each other, so that a revelation concerning any one of them furthers our understanding of the others. What we as readers of poetry understand and respond to in Lowell's "The Drinker" and "For the Union Dead" is a man whose awareness is bound up with moral insight and simultaneously with suffering, a man whose consciousness has a distinctive quality one recognizes as Lowell's as one recognizes the "eye" of a gifted photographer in a photograph. Even an aspect of language as seemingly mechanical as the presence of specific concrete terms is dramatically significant in relation to this consciousness: such terms imply a clarity and intensity in the speaker's perception of the identities of things which is almost painful, which has about it something of the obsessive.

What, then, of "language"? In taking the step from the realm of linguistic fact to the existential arena portrayed by language, one need not, indeed should not, set the facts aside. It remains relevant that Lowell's "language" is concrete and specific in a precise, measurable way; that his range of diction is wide; that he signalizes certain details by using verbs denoting actions in the present where other verbs in another tense might have been used. These are only a few of the factual statements that one might wish to make about particular passages or recurrent features in the language of Lowell. But it is equally true, though not equally factual, to say that Lowell's language is vivid, highly charged, mordant, agonized, obsessive. These are statements, properly speaking, about the man portrayed by language rather than language itself. Both sorts of statement are relevant to the power and purpose of poetry; each will carry more conviction, and represent a more adequate knowledge of the created work, in conjunction with the other.

NOTES

1. *King Lear in Our Time* (Berkeley: University of California Press, 1965), p. 99.

2. *Language of Fiction: Essays in Criticism and Verbal Analysis of the English Novel* (London: Routledge, 1966), p. 99.

3. A classic example is W. K. Wimsatt, Jr.'s *The Prose Style of Samuel Johnson,* first published in 1941, successive chapters of which are entitled "Parallelism," "Antithesis," and "Diction"; a chapter on "Other Qualities" includes discussions of sentence-length, imagery, inversion, and chiasmus. Alan Sinfield's *The Language of Tennyson's "In Memoriam"* (Oxford, 1971) includes two chapters on diction, two on syntax, two on imagery and one each on sound and rhythm. Space forbids more than a minimum of additional citations, but cf. Stanley Greenfield, "Grammar and Meaning in Poetry," *PMLA,* 82 (1967), 377–87; Seymour Chatman, "Milton's Participial Style," *PMLA,* 83 (1968), 1386–99; M. A. K. Halliday, "Linguistic Function and Literary Style: An Inquiry into the Language of William Golding's *The Inheritors,"* in *Literary Style: A Symposium,* ed. Seymour Chatman (New York: Oxford University Press, 1971), pp. 330–65; and my own "Robert Frost's New Testament: Language and the Poem," *Modern Philology,* 69 (August 1971), 36–56.

4. "Speech, Action, and Style," in *Literary Style: A Symposium,* pp. 241–54.

5. General surveys of the problem of defining style in relation to language may be found in Seymour Chatman, "The Semantics of Style," *Social Science Information,* 6 (1967), 77–99, and Graham Hough, *Style and Stylistics* (London: Routledge, 1969). Hough's book includes brief critical discussions of the work of a number of recent theorists and practitioners of stylistic criticism; there is an annotated bibliography. See also *Literary Style: A Symposium,* passim, which is of interest partly for the accounts of the debates among the participants following the presentation of each essay.

6. See Sir Alan Gardiner, *The Theory of Speech and Language* (Oxford: Clarendon Press, 1951), chap. 1; Roger Brown, *Words and Things* (Glencoe, Illinois: The Free Press, 1958), "Introduction," pp. 7–16, and chap. 3, "Reference and Meaning," pp. 82–109; Mortimer Adler, *The Difference of Man and the Difference It Makes* (New York: Holt, Rinehart and Winston, 1967), chaps. 8–11.

7. Such translations may in fact exist, but I have not been able to locate them.

8. Roland Barthes, in "Style and Its Image" (*Literary Style,* ed. Chatman, pp. 3–10), playfully suggests that discourse is "a construction of layers" like an onion rather than "a species of fruit with a kernel," as the old form-content analysis had it; these "layers (or levels, or systems)" are related finally only to each other

(p. 10). The multi-level theory of form and content presented here, however, envisages a final level which is not related as form to anything else: the sources or preconditions of the shaping act of the poet.

9. Shortly after writing the above, I came upon these relevant remarks by T. S. Eliot in a letter to Lytton Strachey dated June 1, 1919: "Whether one writes a piece of work well or not seems to me a process of crystallisation—the good sentence, the good word, is only the final stage in the process. One can groan enough over the choice of a word, but there is something much more important to groan over first" (quoted in *Lytton Strachey, A Critical Biography*, II: *The Years of Achievement*, by Michael Holroyd [New York, Holt, Rinehart and Winston, 1968], p. 364).

10. R. A. Sayce, in "The Definition of the Term Style" (*Proceedings of the Third Congress of the International Comparative Literature Association*, The Hague, 1962, pp. 156–66), notes that "a reader of Tolstoy, . . . who knows no Russian, clearly grasps much in the way of plot, character, description and so on, and equally clearly loses something. . . . As long as some sort of equivalent can be achieved in different languages, the absolute identity of form and content can hardly be maintained" (p. 161). In my terms, this reader enters the Tolstoy novel at the level of formulation; the significant relations between this and other more abstractive levels of its form are thus accessible to him.

Poetry and the Poem: The Structure of Poetic Content

THOMAS McFARLAND

Our use of the terms "poetry" and "poem" involves a paradox. On the one hand, we customarily invoke the words as referring quite interchangeably to the same artistic activity; and on the other we sense in them a certain difference in semantic overtone. The word "poetry" suggests something unbounded, a current of awareness and feeling only adventitiously caught in words, while "poem" suggests something closed and delimited, a verbal artifact.

"Poetry," in the former signification, represents a conception that might justly be called Platonic (although I use the adjective not at all in Ransom's sense). In Plato's approval, as expressed in the *Phaedrus,* of a poetry that is at once a mania and a philosophical glimpse of ultimate reality, we see a tendency to supplant the notion of "poem" as artifact with that of "poetry" as current of feeling:

There is a third form of possession or madness, of which the muses are the source. This seizes a tender, virgin soul and stimulates it to rapt passionate expression, especially in lyric poetry. . . . But if any man come to the gates of poetry without the madness of the Muses, persuaded that skill alone will make him a good poet, then shall he and his works of sanity with him be brought to nought by the poetry of madness. [245A]

The same sense of enraptured flow, by which poetry is precisely not delimited artifact but a momentary participation in an unlimited current of feeling, is emphasized in the *Ion:*

As the worshipping Corybantes are not in their senses when they dance, so the lyric poets are not in their senses when they make these lovely lyric poems. No, when once they launch into harmony and rhythm, they are seized with the Bacchic transport . . . as the bacchants, when possessed, draw milk and honey from the rivers, but not when in their senses. So the spirit of the lyric poet works, according to their own report. For the poets tell us, don't they, that the melodies they bring us are gathered from rills that run with honey, out of glens and gardens of the Muses, and they bring them as the bees do honey, flying like the bees. And what they say is true, for a poet is a light and winged thing, and holy, and never able to compose until he has become inspired, and is beside himself, and reason is no longer in him. [534A–B]

Poetry, in this understanding, boasts an extraordinarily distinguished lineage of practitioners and guardians. It is, to cite a single instance, what Shelley pays homage to in his *Defence:*

Poetry, in a general sense, may be defined to be "the expression of the imagination": and poetry is connate with the origin of man. Man is an instrument over which a series of external and internal impressions are driven, like the alternations of an ever-changing wind over an Aeolian lyre, which moves it by their motion to ever-changing melody. . . . In the infancy of society every author is necessarily a poet, because language itself is poetry; and to be a poet is to apprehend the true and the beautiful. . . . A poet participates in the eternal, the infinite, and the one.

But in such formulations the conception of "poem" is devalued; the hardness of outline that we associate with artifact is blurred and veiled.

The conception of poetic act as "poem"—that is, as artifact—is, however, nearly as ancient and quite as distinguished in its partisans, as is that of poetic act as "poetry." It is implied in Aristotle's insistence that poetry, whether tragic or of other kind, should involve the idea of "a whole," with "a beginning, middle and end" (*Poetics* 1450^{b}25–30; 1459^{a}15–20). And all those aspects of the poet's utterance that we associate with the notion of craftsmanship, as opposed to that of a divine current of inspiration, tend toward the same understanding. Thus Du Bellay argues that it is not enough to allege that poets are simply born: whoever wants poetic immortality must remain long in his chamber, must "sweat and tremble repeatedly," must endure "hunger, thirst, and long vigils"; for it is on these wings that "the writings of men mount up to the sky." [1] Again, Ben Jonson praises Shakespeare for his "well torned, and true-filed lines," and says that he "Who casts to write a liuing line, must sweat, / . . . and strike the second heat / Vpon the *Muses* anuile." It is in this tradition that Pope can complain that "Ev'n copious Dryden wanted, or forgot, / The last and greatest art, the art to blot." It is in this tradition, too, that T. S. Eliot speaks of "the intolerable wrestle / With words and meanings." And in his *Discoveries* Jonson, asking "How differs a poeme from what wee call poesy," concludes that "*A Poeme* . . . is the worke of the Poet; the end, and fruit of his labour, and studye." All such attitudes tend toward an emphasis on the poem as artifact, as consciously formed verbal structure. This is the "art" that in the Renaissance and the seventeenth century was so frequently differentiated from "nature," or the unconscious product of inspiration.

The divergence in conception between unconsciously or carelessly voiced "Platonic" poetry and carefully wrought "Aristotelian" poem is further indicated by the simultaneous currency, in both antiquity and the Renaissance, of the dual conception of the poet as reflected in the Greek *poietes,* on the one hand, and the Latin *vates* on the other. "What is a poet?" asks Jonson. "A *Poet* is that which by the Greeks is called . . . ὁ ποιητής, a maker, or a fainer . . . according to *Aristotle* from the word ποιεῖν, which signifies to make or fain." Sidney, however, notes that "Among the Romans a Poet was called *Vates*, which is as much as a Diviner, Fore-seer, or Prophet." *Poietes,* in other words, refers to the maker of "Aristotelian" poems; *vates* to the communicant of "Platonic" poetry.

To view the matter from another perspective, we see evidence of the difference between "poetry" and "poem" in Poe's well-known insistence that "a long poem does not exist." It is, indeed, the recognition of this difference, together with an unwillingness to credit it, that underlies Poe's whole contention:

a poem deserves its title only inasmuch as it excites, by elevating the soul. The value of the poem is in the ratio of this elevating excitement.

. . . That degree of excitement which would entitle a poem to be so called at all, cannot be sustained throughout a composition of any great length. . . . *Paradise Lost* . . . in fact, is to be regarded as poetical, only when, losing sight of that vital requisite in all works of Art, Unity, we view it merely as a series of minor poems. . . . After a passage of what we feel to be true poetry, there follows, inevitably, a passage of platitude which no critical pre-judgment can force us to admire.

But obviously, long poems *do* exist. Long poems, that is, as verbal artifacts. What might not exist are long, seamless flows of "poetry." In short, Poe expects "poem" to mean "poetry"—the Platonic current. His phrase "elevating the soul" indicates this bias, as does the still more significant phrase "true poetry."

Coleridge, on the other hand, observes and reports the same facts as Poe does but interprets them in a different awareness. For Coleridge, the conception of "poem" is not dictated absolutely by the conception of "poetry." Like Poe, he observes that poetry and poem are not always identical; unlike Poe, he accepts rather than suppresses the resulting postulation of two entities:

whatever *specific* import we attach to the word, poetry, there will be found involved in it, as a necessary consequence, that a poem of any length neither can be, or ought to be, all poetry. Yet if an harmonious whole is to be produced, the remaining parts must be preserved *in keeping* with the poetry; and this can be no otherwise effected than by such a studied selection and artificial arrangement, as will partake of *one,* though not a *peculiar* property of poetry.

Actually, the dual existence of "poetry" and "poem" is an omnipresent reality in poetic practice, and our recognition of it can shed light on certain aesthetic problems. For instance, it is a common practice for a poet, even a major one, to neglect "poetry" in order to serve the structure of "poem." Take, for a single example, Wordsworth's fine sonnet, the first part of which runs as follows:

> The world is too much with us; late and soon,
> Getting and spending, we lay waste our powers:
> Little we see in Nature that is ours;
> We have given our hearts away, a sordid boon!

Here the phrase "late and soon" adds little or nothing to the poetic statement. The poetry would mean the same if it simply ran, "The world is too much with us: / Getting and spending we lay waste our powers." The redundant "late and soon" is there because of the demands of the "poem," that is, it satisfies the requirements of the metrical pattern adopted in the sonnet. Likewise, the dubious phrase "a sordid boon," which though not redundant is clumsily archaic, and which is justified mainly as the rhyme to "soon," serves the need of the "poem" more than that of the "poetry."

On the other hand, one frequently encounters instances where diminished concern with the "poem" occurs alongside heightened concern for the "poetry." An example is "Kubla Khan." Here the "poem" is a broken form, but the "poetry" is dipped from the high Platonic stream. Indeed, as Elizabeth Schneider has pointed out, the concluding lines are drawn directly from the *Ion:*

> Weave a circle round him thrice,
> And close your eyes with holy dread,
> For he on honey-dew hath fed,
> And drunk the milk of Paradise.

This intensification of "poetry," however, is set against a denigration of "poem": at this very moment the poetic whole is simply denied, for the "poem" ends, uncompleted. So Coleridge seems in this instance to elevate the conception of *vates* at the expense of that of *poietes.*

To be sure, poetry as the artifact of a *poietes* and poetry as the vision of a *vates* were not, and are not, emphases that ought necessarily exclude one another; indeed, the interchangeability of the words "poem" and "poetry" in ordinary use, as well as repeated statements of poets and theorists, demonstrate that the optimum situation would be one in which the two terms coincide. Shelley, to cite an instance, fuses emotional "Platonic" flow and perdurable "Aristotelian" artifact in his ideal of a "great poem":

A great poem is a fountain for ever overflowing with the waters of wisdom and delight; and after one person and age has exhausted all its divine effluence which their peculiar relations enable them to share, another and yet another succeeds, and new relations are ever developed, the source of an unforeseen and an unconceived delight.

In actual practice, however, the two conceptions coincide less often than one might expect. A whole class of poetic phenomena, grouped by Addison under the rubric "false wit"—that is, Herbert's "Easter Wings" or, as Addison says, "Poems cast into the Figures of *Eggs, Axes* or *Altars*" (*Spectator* 62)—testifies to the tendency of some poets to lay disproportionate stress on the conception of "poem." Although few actually claim that the poem as it appears on the page is the "real" poem (Wellek's essay, "The Mode of Existence of a Literary Work of Art," provides the classic argument against such a fallacy), the analogical thrust of "poem" as the product of a maker seems to extend toward a certain preoccupation with the literally visual object. Cummings's eccentricities about capitalization, or José García Villa's comma poems both attest this preoccupation. One of the best poets to whom such matters have been important is Stefan George, who designed his own typefaces and subscribed to a mystique of the poem's appearance on the page.

George's poetry, even aside from such a mystique, exhibits a strong sense of the artifact, a sense that is accentuated by a characteristically static subject matter. An example will suffice for demonstration:

> Komm in den totgesagten park und schau:
> Der schimmer ferner lächelnder gestade,
> Der reinen wolken unverhofftes blau
> Erhellt die weiher und die bunten pfade.
>
> Dort nimm das tiefe gelb, das weiche grau
> Von birken und von buchs, der wind ist lau,
> Die späten rosen welkten noch nicht ganz,
> Erlese küsse sie und flicht den kranz,
>
> Vergiss auch diese letzten astern nicht,
> Den purpur um die ranken wilder reben
> Und auch was übrig blieb von grünem leben
> Verwinde leicht im herbstlichen gesicht.
>
> Come to the park they say is dead, and view
> The shimmer of the smiling shores beyond,

The stainless clouds with unexpected blue
Diffuse a light on motley path and pond.

The tender grey, the burning yellow seize
Of birch and boxwood, mellow is the breeze.
Not wholly do the tardy roses wane,
So kiss and gather them and wreathe the chain

The purple on the twists of wilding vine,
The last of asters you shall not forget,
And what of living verdure lingers yet,
Around the autumn vision lightly twine.

Here both Platonic frenzy and Platonic current are absent; the
lapidary precision of diction, meter, and pattern is complemented
by near neutrality of emotion. The poetry is muted; the poem is
strong—almost palpably "there."

Indeed, the similarity of this emotionally neutralized poem to
Robert Penn Warren's prime example of "pure" poetry (in his
essay, "Pure and Impure Poetry") suggests that possibly his example is not one of "pure poetry" so much as one of "pure poem,"
and that its limitations are less the lack of the strengthening alloy
of impurity than simply a lack of poetry. Warren takes as his example Tennyson's lines,

> Now sleeps the crimson petal, now the white;
> Nor waves the cypress in the palace walk;
> Nor winks the gold fin in the porphyry font:
> The firefly wakens: waken thou with me.

The stillness of the emotional current, alongside the heightened
sense of artifice, seems to indicate that the lines are pure poem;
as is also the tendency in such traditions as *haiku*.

Many poems diminish poetry in quite another way. I have in
mind particularly certain aspects of the poetic practice of Dryden,
Pope, and their contemporaries, where the epigrammatic compression, tightly reined couplets, and extraordinary attention to
"numbers" emphasize the idea of poem, while the poetry is
evacuated, as it were, to such a degree that Arnold called these
writers "not classics of our poetry" but "classics of our prose."
Think, for instance, of Dryden's "Religio Laici," which begins,

> Dim as the borrow'd beams of moon and stars
> To lonely, weary, wand'ring travelers
> Is Reason to the soul

and ends, nearly nine hundred lines later, with the statement

> And this unpolish'd, rugged verse, I chose
> As fittest for discourse, and nearest prose;
> For while from sacred truth I do not swerve,
> Tom Sternhold's, or Tom Sha———ll's rhymes will serve.

Yet despite Arnold's dictum, and despite Dryden's own admission of the interchangeability of verse and prose in this instance, "Religio Laici" is, one thinks, clearly a poem. It is prosaic but not prose. For a poem, though we often use the term to indicate the full coincidence of artifice and poetry, can contain a minimum of poetry and maintain itself simply by artifice. That is to say, a poem in one sense is simply anything that first of all looks like other poems, and secondly is claimed to be a poem by its author or someone else. As Coleridge says:

If a man chooses to call every composition a poem, which is rhyme, or measure, or both, I must leave his opinion uncontroverted. The distinction is at least competent to characterize the writer's intention.

But if the definition sought for be that of a *legitimate* poem, I answer, it must be one, the parts of which mutually support and explain each other; all in their proportion harmonizing with, and supporting the purpose and known influences of metrical arrangement.

By the first part of Coleridge's standard, "Religio Laici" is indubitably a poem, and by the second, it is, if not quite so indubitably, still a respectable candidate for the title. For Coleridge, quite significantly, does not in this definition insist that a poem must be characterized by poetry.

Much the same claim could be made for Pope's "Essay on Man." We find it a more significant poem than "Religio Laici," probably because its technical proficiency is greater, its argument more subtle, and its leaven of poetry somewhat more evident (e.g. "die of a rose in aromatic pain"). But, like Dryden's poem, it is an artifice for prosaic, not poetic awareness. "This I might have done in prose," writes Pope in a foreword prefixed to all editions from

1734 on, "but I chose verse, and even rhyme, for two reasons. The one will appear obvious; that principles, maxims, or precepts so written, both strike the reader more strongly at first, and are more easily retained by him afterwards: The other may seem odd, but is true, I found I could express them more *shortly* this way than in prose itself."

It should be observed that such prosaic poems are not bad poems. If "poem" and "poetry" were in our common understanding actually synonymous, then the absence of poetry would make it necessary either to say "Religio Laici" was no poem at all, or at best a bad poem. But few of us think of the work in that way; and almost no one, I believe, would seriously maintain that "An Essay on Man" is bad as an expression of verbal art. Whatever its aesthetic genre may be, its quality is not "bad." Even Arnold concedes such efforts the status of "classic." His own "Rugby Chapel," on the other hand, provides an example of what we call the bad poem: its verbal artifice is strained, its measure uncertain, and its diction false.[2] Arnold's emotion about his father rings counterfeit (perhaps because he himself was unaware of its ambivalence), and its shrillness is especially evident in the use of archaic second-personal forms. In the following lines from "Rugby Chapel" the badness verges on the ludicrous; the tongue-twisting "Sternly repressest the bad!" and "reviv'st, Succorest!" represent a bathos that Pope would have treasured:

> Still thou upraisest with zeal
> The humble good from the ground,
> Sternly repressest the bad!
> Still, like a trumpet, doth rouse
> Those who with half-open eyes
> Tread the border-land dim
> 'Twixt vice and virtue; reviv'st,
> Succorest!—this was thy work,
> This was thy life upon earth.

And yet even "Rugby Chapel" is a poem, though an inadequate one. It is not a strong poem with a minimum of poetry, as is "An Essay on Man," but a weak poem with an abundance of false poetry. It is not, however, any more than Pope's work, a piece of prose.

Still, one must concede that the distinction between poetry and prose is in fact an important aesthetic problem. And it is a problem that further reveals the existence of a fundamental difference between poetry and the poem. Poetry, if sufficiently weak, can fade into prose (even though the actual line of demarcation, like that between the state of sleep and the state of being awake, is in the event elusive). The poem, on the other hand, never fades by badness into prose. As we see in the instance of "Rugby Chapel," it simply becomes increasingly a bad poem. The writings of Robert W. Service and Edgar Guest are bad poems, not prose. Doggerel of the "Roses are red / Violets are blue" type constitutes a poem. Nonsense verse such as "Jabberwocky" is a poem. The result of party games where each of several guests supplies a line in a predetermined meter and rhyme scheme is a poem. Even a poem composed to be a deliberate fraud will still be a poem. For pattern and figure in language are of themselves sufficient to maintain the conception of "poem."

The boundary between the poetic and the prosaic becomes difficult to define only when we speak of "poetry" versus prose rather than "poem" versus prose. Most of us feel instinctively that certain impassioned prose is really poetry; and that certain attempts at poetry never leave the realm of prose, particularly those attempts that are not protected by the artifice of "poem." We recall T. S. Eliot's observation, in "The Music of Poetry," that "a great deal of bad prose has been written under the name of free verse. . . . But only a bad poet could welcome free verse as a liberation from form." The fact, however, that fine things have been written in free verse, as well as the fact that certain prose seems to qualify as poetry, indicates that verse form alone is not crucial. Coleridge notes that "The writings of PLATO, and Bishop TAYLOR, and the 'Theoria Sacra' of BURNET, furnish undeniable proofs that poetry of the highest kind may exist without metre"; and Shelley says that

The distinction between poets and prose writers is a vulgar error. . . . Plato was essentially a poet—the truth and splendour of his imagery, and the melody of his language, is the most intense that it is possible to conceive.

If the distinction between verse and prose is not necessary to the conception of "poetry," neither is the conception of beginning, middle, and end—that is, of completed form. The most obvious examples are supplied by Shakespearean tragedy, where parts of the language are in verse that is not poetic, where other parts are not in verse at all, and where the incidence of "poetry" does not occur in the context of "poem." It occurs rather in the psychological context of dramatic situation. One doubts whether greater poetry exists than Lear's speech:

> No, no, no, no! Come, let's away to prison;
> We two alone will sing like birds i' th' cage.
> When thou dost ask me blessing, I'll kneel down
> And ask of thee forgiveness. So we'll live,
> And pray, and sing, and tell old tales, and laugh
> At gilded butterflies, and hear poor rogues
> Talk of court news; and we'll talk with them too,
> Who loses and who wins; who's in, who's out;
> And take upon's the mystery of things
> As if we were God's spies; and we'll wear out,
> In a wall'd prison, packs and sects of great ones,
> That ebb and flow by th' moon.

There is no question here of free verse; the language is at once patterned and figured. And yet the speech is not a poem, that is, it is not something complete in itself as an artifact. It could not be taken out of its dramatic context and retain its full power. It is not even part of a poem, for though the whole play is doubtless a literary artifact, it is (despite the efforts of some Shakespearean critics to maintain the contrary) not a poem—not even a greatly extended poem. It is a play. The completed form in which Lear's speech resides is an existential configuration: a symbolic representation of human interaction. The "poetry" relates to the currents of this interaction, not to the artifice of "poem" as such.

We can see this distinction still more plainly by comparing two other Shakespearean passages, similar in statement but different in context. The first is his sonnet 66:

> Tir'd with all these, for restful death I cry:
> As, to behold desert a beggar born,
> And needy nothing trimm'd in jollity,
> And purest faith unhappily forsworn,
> And gilded honour shamefully misplac'd,
> And maiden virtue rudely strumpeted,
> And right perfection wrongfully disgrac'd,
> And strength by limping sway disabled,
> And art made tongue-tied by authority,
> And folly, doctor-like, controlling skill,
> And simple truth miscall'd simplicity,
> And captive good attending captain ill:
> >   Tir'd with all these, from these would I be gone,
> >   Save that, to die, I leave my love alone.

The second is a portion of Hamlet's "To be or not to be" speech:

> For in that sleep of death what dreams may come,
> When we have shuffl'd off this mortal coil,
> Must give us pause. There's the respect
> That makes calamity of so long life.
> For who would bear the whips and scorns of time,
> The oppressor's wrong, the proud man's contumely,
> The pangs of dispriz'd love, the law's delay,
> The insolence of office, and the spurns
> That patient merit of the unworthy takes,
> When he himself might his quietus make
> With a bare bodkin?

The passages are strikingly similar: each is in verse, each expresses a sense of gloom about existence, each lists a catalogue of generally experienced woes, each asserts that life is not worth living "except for." Both passages are unarguably what we call poetry. Yet the first passage is also a poem; the second one is not. The first needs no context (other than that supplied by the reader's own past) outside the confines of the sonnet form. The second calls not only upon the general experience of the reader, but also upon a knowledge of Hamlet's situation.

The import of such and similar examples becomes increasingly clear. Although we often use "poetry" and "poem" to mean the same thing ("verse" is perhaps the best name for this congruence), at other times we use the words as though they refer to matters that can exist separately from one another. At still other times we use them as coinciding, but only in the sense that the former is "in" the latter. In this usage, we seem to think of the poem as a kind of receptable for the poetry. Such variations indicate, I believe, that in the living use of language there is constantly recognized and maintained an undefined, but indispensable, distinction between the ideal identity and possible separability of poetic form and poetic content.

"Poetry," I suggest, often means that which corresponds to our intuitive sense of the content of a poetic act; and "poem," that which corresponds to our perception of its form.

I have been at pains to point out the unavoidability and constant recurrence of our sense of the difference between "poetry" and "poem," for to speak of significant distinctions between "content" and "form" requires the strongest kind of empirical foundation. The best established traditions of modern critical and aesthetic thought run counter to such dichotomies. We can see this in the change, which occurred some twenty odd years ago, in the teaching of poetry in our schools. Before the advent of the New Criticism, it was customary to teach the beauty of poetry, and especially to isolate individual passages as representative of that beauty. The procedure perhaps expressed itself with greatest prestige in Arnold's conception of "touchstones": brief poetic statements taken to represent absolute poetry. The poem as such tended to be neglected, beyond classifying it as a sonnet, or as written in Spenserian stanzas. But after the rise of New Criticism (which was more a pedagogic than a theoretically novel revolution), the emphasis changed from the beauty of isolated "poetry" to the perception of the unity of the "poem." The poem was read as a whole, without a content separable from that whole; individual lines were read not as "poetic" but as coherent with the whole. In this perspective, the critical judgment changed from evaluation of "beauty" to judgment of coherence: a poem was declared to be "successful" or not, depending mainly on whether it was a perceptible whole into which all images and statements fitted. The most influential single figure in this pedagogic revolution, Cleanth Brooks, accordingly asserted as "articles of faith" the facts that *"in a successful work, form and content cannot be separated,"* and that *"form is meaning."* [3]

To be sure, some modern theorists have clung to distinctions of form and content.[4] Yvor Winters boldly announces, for instance, an "absolutist" theory of literature, in which the poem is "good in so far as it makes a defensible rational statement about a given human experience." [5] And Richards's useful differentiation of "vehicle" and "tenor," as, too, Ransom's discrimination of "structure" and "texture," seem to be covert dichotomies of form and content. Yet by and large modern critics and theorists usually reject any essential distinction between form and content.[6] As Wellek and Austin Warren's formidable and pedagogically influential *Theory of Literature* puts it:

"Content" and "form" are terms used in too widely different senses for them to be, merely juxtaposed, helpful; indeed, even after careful definition, they too simply dichotomize the work of art.[7]

And even now, when New Criticism as a movement has passed into history, the most sophisticated theoretical attitudes continue to reject any attempt to define a significantly separable content in poetic form. As Samuel R. Levin, for instance, has recently said:

In my view it is those linguistic properties in a poem which induce the responses of unity, novelty, compression, etc. that go to make up poetic form. Comprehended in this view of poetic form are of course also the conventions—rhyme, meter, etc.—since they also conduce to the responses in question. When seen in this way, we can understand why form is so fundamental to poetry. On this view it is the content of a poem, what can be paraphrased of it, that is superficial; all the rest is form.[8]

Such an attitude reflects the important and still growing effect of a movement somewhat similar to New Criticism but theoretically more satisfying: that is, the linguistically oriented formalist tradition stemming from the allied schools of Russian Formalism and Prague Structuralism.

The leading idea of these schools was to see a poem in its relation to language as such. Most language is either not expressed at all (remaining potential expression, or in Saussure's term, *langue*) or, if expressed, is forgotten after it has served its purpose of communication. A poem, however, tends to be special—to be an artifact, an autonomous linguistic structure—and hence not to be used up in the act of communication. The way it prevents itself from being used up is by certain kinds of linguistic emphasis that both assert its difference from ordinary language and indicate its unity as an artifact. Such emphasis is supplied by rhyme, meter, assonance, consonance, unexpected words and combinations of words: in short, by all those features we usually find in a poem.

Thus Paul Valéry, writing from the standpoint of the poet rather than that of the linguist, sees the poem as radically different from ordinary language:

the language I use to express my design, my desire, my command, my opinion; this language, when it has served its purpose, evaporates almost as it is heard. I have given it forth to perish, to be radically transformed into something else in your mind; and I shall know that I was *understood* by the remarkable fact that my speech no longer exists: it has been completely replaced by its *meaning*. . . .

The poem, on the other hand, does not die for having lived: it is expressly designed to be born again from its ashes and to become endlessly what it has just been. Poetry can be recognized by this property, that it tends to get itself reproduced in its own form: it stimulates us to reconstruct it identically.[9]

This same distinction, though nowhere so pointedly expressed, had repeatedly been urged by the formalist theoreticians. As Havránek said, nonpoetic language is characterized by "automatization":

By *automatization* we . . . mean such a use of the devices of the language . . . that the expression itself does not attract any attention; the communication occurs, and is received, as conventional in linguistic form and is to be "understood" by virtue of the linguistic system.[10]

Poetic language, conversely, is made special by a process called "foregrounding," which Havránek defines as follows:

By *foregrounding*, on the other hand, we mean the use of the devices of the language in such a way that this use itself attracts attention and is perceived as uncommon, as deprived of automatization, as deautomatized, such as a live poetic metaphor (as opposed to a lexicalized one, which is automatized).[11]

Foregrounding is thus the central means by which language becomes poetic. Jan Mukařovský pointed out that

Poetic language cannot be called a brand of the standard. . . . The function of poetic language consists in the maximum of foregrounding of the utterance. Foregrounding is the opposite of automatization, that is, the deautomatization of an act; the more an act is automatized, the less it is consciously executed; the more it is foregrounded, the more completely conscious does it become. . . . In poetic language foregrounding achieves maximum intensity to the extent . . . of being used for its own sake; it is not used in the services of communication, but in order to place in the foreground the act of expression.[12]

It is noteworthy that the kind of poetic language of which Mukařovský speaks does not lead to "Platonic" poetry; rather, his emphasis on the fact that the more language is foregrounded "the more completely conscious does it become" identifies "Aristotelian" poem as the goal of that language.

The distinctions urged by these exponents of Prague Structuralism confirm earlier insights of Russian Formalism. Victor Shklovsky had in 1917 used the term "defamiliarization" to indicate what the Structuralists called "foregrounding":

Habitualization devours works, clothes, furniture, one's wife, and the fear of war. . . . And art exists that one may recover the sensation of life; it exists to make one feel things, to make the stone *stony*. . . . The technique of art is to make objects "unfamiliar," to make forms difficult. . . .

In studying poetic speech in its phonetic and lexical structure as well as in its characteristic distribution of words and in the characteristic thought structures compounded from the words, we find everywhere the artistic trademark—that is, we find material obviously created to remove the automatism of perception; the author's purpose is to create the vision which results from that deautomatized perception. . . . The language of poetry is, then, a difficult, roughened, impeded language.[13]

It is obvious, even from such brief quotations from their writings, that the formalist theoreticians and their sympathizers, by stressing the specialness of the poem as against the unspecialness of ordinary language (we use the word "prosaic" simply to mean the commonplace and unmemorable), have afforded a compelling insight into the nature of poetic language and of the linguistic work of art. Many kinds of problems are resolved by this insight. For a single instance, the theoretical problem of how some poems can be written in meter and rhyme, but others in meter only (the paradox of Milton saying that rhyme is "no necessary adjunct or true ornament of poem or good verse," even though our most naive intuition identifies rhyme as the first requirement of a poem), immediately disappears. For rhyme and meter, whatever their tactical differences, are here revealed as being merely variations of the same thing: that is, as forms of foregrounding that by their nature as repetition indicate both the specialness and the unity of the linguistic statement (and it is interesting to reflect that from a compositional standpoint, the construction of meter and that of rhyme demand from the poet much the same kind of labor).

Despite the cogency of formalist analysis, however, I disagree with an important implication of that tradition: I deny that poetic "content" inheres in the linguistic code. It does not seem to me that a poetic act can be described as merely an activation of language, no matter how sophisticated that activation might be. Nor do I accept Brooks's similar contention that *"form is meaning."* Although Boris Eichenbaum writes that "poetic form . . . is not contrasted with anything outside itself—with a 'content' which has been laboriously set inside this 'form'—but is understood as the genuine content of poetic speech," [14] and although Mukařovský says that "in a work of poetry . . . there is no fixed border, nor, in a certain sense, any essential difference, between the language and the subject matter," [15] I do not believe that such views account for the whole truth of poetic act. I maintain that there is indeed "essential difference" between the language and subject matter in the poetic act, that there is indeed content "set inside this 'form.' " The essential difference is the difference between poem and poetry; the content inside the form is the poetry within the poem.

In short, I hold that the formalist position accounts for poetic language, but not for the full poetic act. Or, stated another way, it is my contention that though linguistic manipulation can generate a poem, it cannot generate poetry as such.

In order to make this contention more clear, and to try to describe what a complete poetic act really is, I propose to conceive of the "ishness" under the Greek word ὀυσία, which is a term of distinguished philosophical lineage.[16] The *ousia,* or "isness," can then be conceived under three Latin terms, each of which is a synonym for the Greek word; specifically, I propose considering the poem (that is, the form) as poetic *substantia,* and the poetry (or poetic content) under the twin terms of *ens* and *essentia.* By doing so I hope to muffle any debilitating overtones that might reside in the words "form" and "content," where through long carelessness one tends to think of form as something like a stanza pattern, and of content as some kind of hortatory message. By using synonyms rather than widely different words, I hope to indicate the sense of the indispensability of "form" and "content" in the full poetic act. And by using three terms instead of "form" and "content" I hope to be able to talk of certain complexities not rewardingly designated by the single word "content."

By *substantia* I mean not only stanza form, not only meter and rhyme, not only the semantic references of the words in the poem, not only the sense of beginning and end, but also the statement of the poem. For instance, in Edwin Arlington Robinson's "Mr. Flood's Party," the *substantia* would consist not only of the seven stanzas of eight lines each, and of the rhyme pattern *a b c b,* but of the story of the old man who gives himself a lonely drunken party; not only of whatever visual sense is implied by the invocation of "harvest moon," but of whatever literary complex of associations is summoned up by the image of "Roland's ghost winding a silent horn." In brief, *substantia* includes not only the words and their patterns but also their meanings. Under this term I would place almost everything that formalist theory has to say about poetry.

The *ens* is a characteristic scarcely accounted for by formalist theory. The *ens* is the interanimation of the sense of self in the poetic statement with the perspective of the outer world; it is the fusion of mind and nature. Alternate phrasings might be the sense of "I am" interpenetrating the sense of "it is"; or the subject revealing itself in the object, the object in the subject.[17] "A Poet's *Heart & Intellect*," says Coleridge, "should be *combined, intimately* combined & *unified,* with the great appearances in Nature." "To end this eternal conflict between our Self and the World," says Hölderlin, "to re-establish the peace above all peace, which passeth all understanding, to unite ourselves with Nature, into one infinite entity, that is the aim of all our aspirations."

The *ens* is the same for all art whatever, although the manner of its realization may vary almost infinitely. Where the poetic *substantia* is remarkably different from the sculptural *substantia,* the poetic *ens* and the sculptural *ens* are alike. It is in its *ens* that poetic act most strongly connects itself with other art forms. As Wayne Shumaker says:

The task of art is to *ingest* whatever can be learned objectively about the world of the non-I and then to *give out* an image which will accord not only with nonhuman truths . . . but also with the forms of universal human feelings.[18]

The statement could describe either the *David* of Michaelangelo, where stone is given human shape, or Frost's "Stopping by Woods on a Snowy Evening."

Ens is embodied in such a statement as "Eternal smiles his emptiness betray, / As shallow streams run dimpling all the way," or in that where an observer says of wild swans that "Their hearts have not grown old." Any interfusion of an aspect of the nonhuman world with a human emotion or awareness is poetic *ens.* In "Mr. Flood's Party" we see *ens* in these words:

> Then, as a mother lays her sleeping child
> Down tenderly, fearing it may awake,
> He set the jug down slowly at his feet
> With trembling care, knowing that most things break:

Leavis's famous attack on Shelley, that his most serious fault is a "weak grasp upon the actual," is a judgment of that poet's deficiency in poetic *ens.* When Wordsworth observes that "there is not a single image from Nature in the whole body" of Dryden's work, the reproach refers to Dryden's lack of *ens* (which, indeed, is part of the reason for Arnold's feeling—he says so in his essay on Gray—that Dryden is not a poet). What Robert Langbaum has described as a characteristic of Romantic poetry is in fact a characteristic of poetry as such:

The romantic lyric or poetry of experience . . . is both subjective and objective. The poet talks about himself by talking about an object; and he talks about an object by talking about himself.[19]

Indeed, as Coleridge says very simply, "in every work of art there is a reconcilement of the external with the internal."

Much of the flocking of imagery and metaphor to poetry, whereby one might note "How like a winter hath my absence been / From thee," clusters in the area of poetic *ens*. When Byron says that "I live not in myself, but I become / Portion of that around me; and to me / High mountains are a feeling," the statement both describes and embodies poetic *ens*. And as is apparent from such examples, the ways in which the intermixing of subject and object can occur in *ens* are exceedingly varied. But even Stefan George's poem about the "totgesagten Park" (the park they say is dead), which was cited above as an example of an almost muted "poetry," is replete with the correlation of perceived outer reality with inner attitude. For as Coleridge says, in a passage we may take as summarizing the whole truth of this aspect of poetry as "content":

As soon as the human mind is intelligibly addressed by an outward image exclusively of articulate speech, so soon does art commence. . . . art itself might be defined as of a middle quality between a thought and a thing, or . . . the union and reconciliation of that which is nature with that which is exclusively human. It is the figured language of thought.

I have spoken somewhat briefly of a feature of "content" that actually could be shown to ramify into subtle examples, and I have done so in order to be able to devote slightly longer discussion to a more elusive aspect: that for which I adopt the term *essentia*. Poetic *essentia* is not dependent upon a linguistic code; it is not

generated by foregrounded arrangement of language and its reference. It is, rather, an awareness that is "existential" or "metaphysical." It is represented by rather than derived from language.
It expresses the nature of human existence, wherein we find ourselves with "such large discourse, / Looking before and after." For
we live always in a "now" looking to a past and future "then."
Our lives are split. We have a double nature: an existence "now,"
which is palpable and concrete, and an existence in the past and
future, which though spectral is none the less truly our own existence. The paradox is what Jaspers recognizes by his two terms for
existence: *Dasein* and *Existenz*. But the paradox, one stresses, is
not the property of philosophers; it is the most inescapable fact of
human life. It is a fact about which there can be no argument
whatever, however strange it may seem when compared to the way
in which a stone or a cow exists.

Poetic *essentia* is generated by the simultaneous awareness of
our existence in these two forms. When we stand in a "now" and
look at a "then," we generate *essentia* by making the sense of
"now" more vivid (and thereby treasuring its nowness), and
simultaneously becoming more aware of its difference from
"then." Or conversely, we may devalue "now" and treasure
"then." In Lear's speech, the gloom of "now" as defeat is impreg-
nated with the joy of "then": "now" is the prospect of "away to
prison," but the tone implies "away to paradise." *Essentia* is the
feeling of the whole of our existence in its cloven reality.

The truth of split existence, however, is more deeply realized
looking toward vanished actuality than toward future possibility.
"I look into past times," says Wordsworth, "as prophets look /
Into futurity." *Essentia* is most typically the sense of a treasured
"now" lost in "then," or the prospect of such loss. It is a sweet
sadness. The sweetness comes from the intensified sense of being,
and the sadness from the intensified sense of being's loss into the
nonbeing of "then." As Shenstone said, in a scarcely expected
aperçu, "The words 'no more' have a singular pathos, reminding
us at once of past pleasure" and of its loss.

Essentia, in its disposition of awareness between "now" and

"then," is accordingly fleeting and intangible—is in the nature of
an evanescence. Indeed, the most immediate awareness of "now"
is not only that which vanishes into "then," but is in itself fragile.
It is noteworthy that Rilke's prescription, in *The Notebooks of
Malte Laurids Brigge,* for how a poet is formed, insists not only
on saturation in *ens* but also on saturation in the evanescences
that characterize the "nows" of *essentia:*

In order to write a single verse, one must see many cities, and men,
and things. . . . One must be able to return in thought . . . to unexpected encounters, and to partings . . . to days of childhood . . .
and to mornings by the sea. . . . There must be memories of many
nights of love. . . . And still it is not yet enough to have memories.
. . . Only when they have turned to blood within us . . . no longer
to be distinguished from ourselves—only then can it happen that . . .
the first word of a poem arises and goes forth from them.

Poe, in cataloguing "the simple elements which induce in the
Poet himself the true poetical effect," comes to a similar conclusion:

He recognizes the ambrosia which nourishes his soul . . . in the
volutes of the flower . . . in the waving of the grain-fields . . . in the
blue distance of mountains—in the grouping of clouds . . . in the
sighing of the night-wind . . . in the scent of the violet.

And the linkage between intensified nowness and evanescence is
further underscored by Coleridge's statement that "poetry is the
blossom and the fragrancy" of human thoughts and emotions.

Because the intensified sense of being alive involves awareness
of the most fleeting elements in our experience, the "then" that
characterizes *essentia* is sometimes poetically implied in a "now"
even without being summoned. We recognize this in such lines as

> Passions of rain, or moods in falling snow;
> Grievings in loneliness, or unsubdued
> Elations when the forest blooms; gusty
> Emotions on wet roads on autumn nights.

Here *essentia* is present though "then" is not stated. As in these
lines from Wordsworth's *Prelude,* the evanescence of a treasured
"now" is emphasized by "then":

And as I was green and carefree, famous among the barns
About the happy yard and singing as the farm was home,
. . . .
All the sun long it was running, it was lovely, the hay
Fields high as the house, the tunes from the chimneys, it
            was air
      And playing, lovely and watery
        And fire green as grass.

There, as in these following lines, the evanescences of a treasured
"now" are made more fragile by loss into a past "then":

    Oh, many a time have I, a five years' child,
    In a small mill-race severed from his stream,
    Made one long bathing of a summer's day;
    Basked in the sun, and plunged and basked again
    Alternate, all a summer's day, or scoured
    The sandy fields, leaping through flowery groves
    Of yellow ragwort . . .

But perhaps no more revealing example of poetic *essentia* could
be adduced than Keats's lines, uttered from the "now" of a visit to
the Elgin marbles:

    Such dim-conceivèd glories of the brain
      Bring round the heart an indescribable feud;
    So do these wonders a most dizzy pain,
      That mingles Grecian grandeur with the rude
    Wasting of old Time—with a billowy main,
      A sun, a shadow of a magnitude.

The "then" of Grecian antiquity is rendered as glimpses of a
"now"—a "billowy main, / A sun, a shadow of a magnitude"—
but the nature of this "now" as glimpse confirms the countertruth
of "then." The "heart," or full emotional awareness, experiences
the recognition of existence's split into "now" and "then" as an
"indescribable feud" or "dizzy pain." "Now" is intensified by the
image of sun, but the specification "a" sun, rather than "the"
sun, holds the sun in the real "now" and identifies the second
sun as lost in "then." The last phrase, "a shadow of a magnitude,"
attenuates evanescence to the remotest point that can be indicated
by words.

The moment when we most truly feel ourselves alive, and in the same awareness most feel ourselves passing into time—that is the lyric instant. That is the poetic *essentia*. It is hardly an exaggeration to say that lyric awareness is always an awareness, however expressed, of "the rude / Wasting of old Time"; or that the ultimate poetic theme is the elegiac theme. Great poems are monuments to our lost selves. "A Poet," says Shelley, in recognition of this unceasing loss of human experience in time's flow, "is a nightingale, who sits in darkness and sings to cheer its own solitude with sweet sounds." [20]

It is the sense of the "now" passing into the "then" that creates the feeling of "current" in Platonic poetry. It is the existential, as opposed to the linguistic, awareness of this movement that accounts for the sense in such poetry that the essence lies outside the words in which it is caught. And it is the evanescence of *essentia* that accounts for that tradition's insistence that poetry comes from an inspired moment of vision rather than from consciously premeditated design.

Sometimes *essentia* occurs even where life is not treasured. Hardy's "The Darkling Thrush" and Donne's "A Nocturnal Upon St. Lucy's Day" come to mind as examples. But the frosty desolation of the first poem, and the emphasis of the second upon "absence, darkness, death; things which are not," generate the positives by which alone their negatives have poetic force. Both poems are realizations of loss; but loss does not exist by itself. Its "intentional structure" (to borrow a concept from Husserl) assures the presence of those correlatives of life and joy displaced by the overt stratagems in each case. The "lovers" and their "next Spring" in Donne's poem, and the "joy illimited" and "blessed Hope" of the bird's song in Hardy's, thereby become hints for an entire unexpressed treasuring of life.

Sometimes, to take another kind of example, the "now" of the poetic observer is desolate, but that of the poetic subject is treasured, so that the subject's "now" becomes the observer's "then," and vice versa. An illustration might be Gray's "Ode on a Distant Prospect of Eton College."

Essentia must be present in all poetry that merits the name, though it need not mark every line of that poetry. The lyric and the poetically essential are one and the same; but the lyric instant, or awareness of *essentia,* is the evanescent and life-giving breath, not the bricks and mortar, of poetry. As Staiger says, "The lyric is the last attainable ground of everything poetic." [21] An individual poem, as contrasted to poetry, may generate much, little, or no *essentia.* Dryden, strong in *substantia* but weak in *ens,* writes page upon page with hardly a suggestion of *essentia* (although there are occasional exceptions, such as "To the Memory of Mr. Oldham"). As Young said, Dryden "was a stranger to the pathos, and by numbers, expression, sentiment, and every other dramatic cheat, strove to make amends for it; as if a saint could make amends for the want of conscience. . . . The noble nature of tragedy disclaims an equivalent; like virtue, it demands the heart; and *Dryden* had none to give."

The lyric instant, however, though related to tragic awareness, is slightly but significantly different from that awareness. The tragic realization is the vision of the conflicts of human aspiration at the brink of nonbeing; yet the tragic "then" is a future "then," usually symbolized by death. But the lyric instant does not involve a social perspective; it is rather art's most distinctive tribute to our individual selfhood. It looks upon the world from our own inner selves, not from the standpoints of interacting characters. The lyric instant occurs when, gazing directly from our own being into the double awareness of life as "now" and "then," we understand both what we treasure and what we lose.[22] The lyric "then" is less typically a future than a past, less a death than a loss in time (death as such is treated in lyric as the form of loss rather than as the tragic terminus). Keats's "Ode on Melancholy," where sadness is found to live not with darkness but with the sense of life ("She dwells with Beauty—Beauty that must die, / And Joy, whose hand is ever at his lips / Bidding adieu"), represents exactly the defining simultaneity of treasuring and loss suspended in *essentia.*

In "Mr. Flood's Party," which we have rather casually adduced to provide examples of *substantia* and *ens,* poetic *essentia* accordingly reveals itself in such lines as

> Alone, as if enduring to the end
> A valiant armor of scarred hopes outworn

and in general is revealed by the sense of the isolation of the old man and of his separation from his youthful existence:

> There was not much that was ahead of him,
> And there was nothing in the town below—
> Where strangers would have shut the many doors
> That many friends had opened long ago.

In these lines we feel the essence of poetry.

Poetic *essentia* can often be found in the same group of words that embody *ens;* but the two aspects of "content" are not at all the same. The line, "Their hearts have not grown old," quoted from Yeats's "The Wild Swans at Coole" to illustrate *ens,* also illustrates *essentia.* The correlation of human emotion (hearts) with an object of nature (the swans) reveals *ens;* the simultaneous emphasis on the "now" of the observer and the "then" of his former self that is conveyed by the idea of growing old reveals *essentia.* For the line, in saying that "Their hearts have not grown old," actually conveys the meaning "My heart *has* grown old."

"The Wild Swans at Coole," indeed, illustrates very well the way in which poetic *essentia* is generated. The first stanza establishes the almost palpable presence of "now."

> The trees are in their autumn beauty,
> The woodland paths are dry.
> Under the October twilight the water
> Mirrors a still sky;
> Upon the brimming water among the stones
> Are nine-and-fifty swans.

The counting of the swans, which is further foregrounded by the archaic form "nine-and-fifty," provides transition to another form of counting—that in which the "then" is opposed to the "now":

> The nineteenth autumn has come upon me
> Since I first made my count;

And the two succeeding stanzas develop the poignance arising from the gap between "now" and "then":

I have looked upon those brilliant creatures,
And now my heart is sore.
All's changed since I, hearing at twilight,
The first time on this shore,
The bell-beat of their wings above my head,
Trod with a lighter tread.

Unwearied still, lover by lover,
They paddle in the cold
Companionable streams or climb the air;
Their hearts have not grown old;
Passion or conquest, wander where they will,
Attend upon them still.

Essentia arises not only from the movement of poetic argument, but inheres naturally in certain images. Among these we may think of twilight, which fuses the "now" of day with the "then" of night; of autumn, which fuses the "now" of summer's warmth with the "then" of winter's coldness; of flowers, which underscore the beauty of "now" while, by their fragility, they intensify the sense of loss into "then." For instance, the first stanza of "The Wild Swans at Coole" quoted immediately above suggests, by its images of "autumn beauty" and "October twilight," the lyric concatenation of "now" and "then."

Such images are the very stuff of poetic *essentia,* and are used again and again by poets. Consider Hopkins:

Márgarét are you gríeving
Over Goldengrove unleaving?
Leáves, líke the things of man, you
With your fresh thoughts care for, can you?
Áh! ás the heart grows older
It will come to such sights colder
By and by, nor spare a sigh
Though worlds of wanwood leafmeal lie;
And yet you wíll weep and know why.
Now no matter, child, the name;
Sórrows spríngs áre the same.
Nor mouth had, no nor mind, expressed
What heart heard of, ghost guessed:
It ís the blight man was born for,
It is Margaret you mourn for.

The correlation of human sadness with the falling leaves of autumn is a classic example of *ens*. The contrast of the observer's "now" with the child's "now," however, emphasizes an unspoken contrast between his "now" and the "then" of his own childhood, and also emphasizes that Margaret's "now" will become the "then" of the observer's "now": the sense of loss in falling leaves is that of the loss of self in time: "It is Margaret you mourn for." This is poetic *essentia*. In *essentia* "Sórrows spríngs áre the same": the loss of "now" in "then." The concern in this poem with the knowledge that "the heart grows older" is the same *essentia* revealed in Yeats's poem by the line, "Their hearts have not grown old."

Hopkins's use of the *essentia* inherent in autumn might be compared with Rilke's variation, incorporated into a greater poetry:

> Herr: es ist Zeit. Der Sommer war sehr gross.
> Leg deinen Schatten auf die Sonnenuhren,
> Und auf den Fluren lass die Winde los.
>
> Befiehl den letzten Früchten voll zu sein;
> Gib ihnen noch zwei südlichere Tage,
> Dränge sie zu Vollendung hin und jage
> Die letzte Süsse in den schweren Wein.
>
> Wer jetzt kein Haus hat, baut sich keines mehr.
> Wer jetzt allein ist, wird es lange bleiben,
> Wird wachen, lesen, lange Briefe schreiben
> Und wird in den Alleen hin und her
> Unruhig wandern, wenn die Blätter treiben.

> Lord: it is time. Most great the summer was.
> Lay your shadow down upon the sundials now,
> And across the meadows set the winds loose.
>
> Make the last fruits mellow on the vine;
> Spare them but two further southern days,
> Speed them to fullness, and press
> The last sweetness through the heavy wine.
>
> Whoever does not have a house will build one now no more.
> Whoever dwells alone now will long remain alone,
> Will wakefully write long letters, read,
> And restless to and fro
> Will wander in the alleys, when the leaves are blown.

Here, in addition to a Keatsian opulence of *ens,* the lines "reek" (to misappropriate Donald Davie's term) of *essentia.* The "now" of summer is held in autumnal suspension with the "then" of winter by such phrases as "den letzten Früchten," "zu Vollendung," "die letzte Süsse." The restlessness—an inspired combination of sadness and expectation—of the line "Wird wachen, lesen, lange Briefe schreiben" makes the sense of "Unruhig wandern" more poignant; for to write long letters is to attempt to reclaim life from "then" into "now," an attempt the more elegiac in the context of "allein" and blowing leaves.

The images of autumn and twilight coalesce with the metaphor, "In me thou see'st the glowing of such fire, / That on the ashes of his youth doth lie," and together they generate the *essentia* of Shakespeare's sonnet 73:

> That time of year thou mayst in me behold
> When yellow leaves, or none, or few, do hang
> Upon those boughs which shake against the cold,
> Bare ruin'd choirs, where late the sweet birds sang;
> In me thou see'st the twilight of such day
> As after sunset fadeth in the west;
> Which by and by black night doth take away,
> Death's second self, that seals up all in rest:
> In me thou see'st the glowing of such fire,
> That on the ashes of his youth doth lie,
> As the death-bed whereon it must expire
> Consum'd with that which it was nourish'd by.
> > This thou perceiv'st, which makes thy love more strong,
> > To love that well which thou must leave ere long.

The best of Shakespeare's sonnets, indeed, seem almost Platonic paradigmata for *ousia's* interfusing of *substantia, ens,* and *essentia.* Despite Ransom's unseeing attack on these poems, despite animadversions by Winters, despite a recent disparaging remark by Auden, I agree with Keats that Shakespeare here "has left nothing to say about nothing or anything," with Wordsworth that in no other part of Shakespeare's writings is there found "in an equal compass a greater number of exquisite feelings felicitously expressed," and with Coleridge, who stated that no other sonnets were "so rich in metre, so full of thought and *exquisitest* diction."

Of the cycle as a whole, Coleridge judged that "These sonnets
. . . are characterized by boundless fertility and laboured condensation of thought, with perfection of sweetness in rhythm and
metre."

Above all, they reek of poetic *essentia*. "Now" is again and
again embodied and cherished in the motif of love and the beauty
of the beloved, caught in metaphors of light, flowering, and sum-
mertime; "then" is indicated again and again in time's corrosion
of those metaphors:

> When I do count the clock that tells the time,
> And see the brave day sunk in hideous night;
> When I behold the violet past prime,
> And sable curls all silver'd o'er with white;
> When lofty trees I see barren of leaves,
> Which erst from heat did canopy the herd,
> And summer's green all girded up in sheaves
> Borne on the bier with white and bristly beard,
> Then of thy beauty do I question make,
> That thou among the wastes of time must go.

The opposing tensions that generate *essentia* are perhaps nowhere
else so powerfully realized as in the first two quatrains of sonnet 65:

> Since brass, nor stone, nor earth, nor boundless sea,
> But sad mortality o'ersways their power,
> How with this rage shall beauty hold a plea,
> Whose action is no stronger than a flower?
> Oh how shall summer's honey breath hold out
> Against the wrackful siege of batt'ring days,
> When rocks impregnable are not so stout,
> Nor gates of steel so strong, but Time decays?

Here the images of permanence in the first line—which pounds
like the waves of the sea—are juxtaposed against equally powerful
images of destruction by time, all made more memorable by extraordinary richness of *ens* and intricacy of *substantia* (as, for
instance, in the consonantal *s, t* variations that permeate the diction, reaching an apex in the eighth line).

In Shakespeare's sonnets, finally, is achieved the truest relationship between "content" as poetry and "form" as poem. For that relationship is not merely the interpenetration of *substantia* by *ens* and *essentia*. It is also a radically paradoxical melding of disparate resistances to time. Poetic *essentia* is an evanescence—a "honey breath" assaulted by "the wrackful siege of batt'ring days." *Dum loquimur, fugerit invida aetas: carpe diem.* Poetic *substantia,* in absolute contrast, is that which abides. *Exegi monumentum perennius aere.* As Blackmur points out:

Poetry names and arranges, and thus arrests and transfixes its subject in a form which has a life of its own forever separate but springing from the life which confronts it. Poetry is life at the remove of form and meaning; not life lived but life framed and identified.[23]

And Valéry, as noted above, emphasizes that "the poem . . . does not die for having lived: it is expressly designed to be born again from its ashes and to become endlessly what it has just been." So the paradox is this: poetry, the evanescent mingling of the sense of life's value within its loss, is itself free from such loss within the unchanging artifice of poem—"Ah happy, happy boughs! that cannot shed / Your leaves, nor ever bid the Spring adieu." Of the many expressions of this ultimate paradox none is more satisfying than those supplied by Shakespeare's sonnets. The wonderful sonnet 107 concludes:

> And thou in this shalt find thy monument,
> When tyrants' crests and tombs of brass are spent.

Sonnet 60, which begins with the *ens* and *essentia* of "Like as the waves make towards the pebbled shore, / So do our minutes hasten to their end," concludes with the couplet:

> And yet to times in hope my verse shall stand,
> Praising thy worth, despite his cruel hand.

The exquisite sonnet 18 provides an almost flawless example of the ideal balance of *substantia, ens,* and *essentia,* as well as an illustration of the fully realized relationship of poetry to poem:

> Shall I compare thee to a summer's day?
> Thou art more lovely and more temperate:
> Rough winds do shake the darling buds of May,
> And summer's lease hath all too short a date:

> Sometimes too hot the eye of heaven shines,
> And often is his gold complexion dimm'd;
> And every fair from fair sometimes declines,
> By chance, or nature's changing course, untrimm'd;
> But thy eternal summer shall not fade
> Nor lose possession of that fair thou ow'st
> Nor shall Death brag thou wand'rest in his shade
> When in eternal lines to time thou grow'st:
>   So long as men can breathe or eyes can see,
>   So long lives this, and this gives life to thee.

The sonnet does not exhibit quite so much richness of word and sound as does sonnet 30 ("When to the sessions of sweet silent thought"), but it exemplifies as well the complete poetic act—the coming together of evanescent "poetry" and immutable "poem"—as any in the whole inspired cycle.

NOTES

1. *La Deffence et illustration de la langue Francoyse,* ed. Henri Chamard (Paris, 1961), pp. 105–06.

2. Though capable of true poetic achievement on some occasions, Arnold was peculiarly prone to create "bad poems." See, for instance, Leavis's devastating critique of the sonnet to Shakespeare. *Education & The University* (London, 1965), pp. 73–76.

3. "The Formalist Critics," *The Kenyon Review,* 13 (1951), 72.

4. For a survey of modern attitudes toward the idea of form, and incidentally of content, see Wellek's "Concepts of Form and Structure in Twentieth-Century Criticism," *Concepts of Criticism* (New Haven, 1963), pp. 54–68.

5. *In Defense of Reason,* 3d ed., p. 11.

6. But it is interesting to note, in view of our equation of "poetry" with Platonic current of feeling, that Susanne Langer, in her discussion of "feeling" and "form," equates the former with music, which is above all a current, e.g.: "The tonal structures we call 'music' bear a close logical similarity to the forms of human feeling. . . . Music is a tonal analogue of emotive life." *Feeling and Form; A Theory of Art* (New York, 1953), p. 27.

7. (New York, 1949), p. 18.

8. "The Analysis of Compression in Poetry," *Foundations of Language: International Journal of Language and Philosophy,* 7 (1971), 40 n.

9. "Poetry and Abstract Thought," *The Art of Poetry,* trans. Denise Folliott (New York, 1958), pp. 71–72.

10. *A Prague School Reader on Esthetics, Literary Structure, and Style,* trans. Paul L. Garvin (Washington, 1964), pp. 9–10.

11. Ibid., p. 10.

12. "Standard Language and Poetic Language," *Essays on the Language of Literature,* ed. Seymour Chatman and Samuel R. Levin (Boston, 1967), pp. 241–43.

13. *Russian Formalist Criticism: Four Essays,* trans. Lee T. Lemon and Marion J. Reis (Lincoln, Neb., 1965), pp. 12, 21–22.

14. Ibid., p. 127. So too Croce, although from a different standpoint: "The aesthetic fact . . . is form, and nothing but form"; "Poetical material permeates the souls of all: the expression alone, that is to say, the form, makes the poet. . . . when we take 'content' as equal to 'concept' it is most true, not only that art does not consist of content, but also that *it has no content." Aesthetic,* trans. Douglas Ainslie (New York, 1955), pp. 16, 25.

15. "Standard Language and Poetic Language," p. 245.

16. I have in mind Kant's dictum that "to coin new words" is a "desperate expedient," and that we ought rather to "look around in a dead and learned language" to find appropriate terms (*Gesammelte Schriften,* Akademie Ausgabe, III, 245).

17. One of the ways in which *ens* can reveal itself in *substantia* is through onomatopoetic metrical cadence. Cf. Emil Staiger's observation: "Je reiner lyrisch ein Gedicht ist, desto mehr verleugnet es die neutrale Wiederholung des Takts, nicht in Richtung auf die Prosa, sondern zugunsten eines im Einklang mit der Stimmung sich wandelnden Rhythmus. Das ist nur der metrische Ausdruck dafür, daß in lyrischer Dichtung ein Ich und ein Gegenstand einander noch kaum gegenüberstehen" (*Grundbegriffe der Poetik* [Zürich, 1963], p. 28). Examples might be such lines as "And hear the mighty waters rolling evermore," or "The murmurous haunt of flies on summer eves."

18. *Literature and the Irrational* (Englewood Cliffs, N.J., 1960), p. 275.

19. *The Poetry of Experience* (New York, 1963), p. 53.

20. Cf. another realization of the same sadness: " 'Ungeborgen, hier auf dem Bergen des Herzens,' so hat Rilke, selber aus dieser existentiellen Erfahrung heraus, die ganze Ausweglosigkeit des . . . Menschen zu bezeichnen versucht." O. F. Bollnow, *Neue Geborgenheit; Das Problem einer Überwindung des Existentialismus* (Stuttgart, 1955), p. 15.

21. *Grundbegriffe der Poetik,* p. 207.

22. Consider Heidegger's insight that poetry's measure is not solely metric: "Poetry is a measuring. But what is it to measure? . . . To write poetry is measure-taking . . . by which man first receives the measure for the breadth of his being. . . . Only man dies—and indeed continually, so long as he remains on this earth, so long as he dwells. His dwelling, however, rests in the poetic. Hölderlin sees the nature of the 'poetic' in the taking of the measure by which the measure-taking of human beings is accomplished" (". . . . dichterisch wohnet der Mensch. . . ," *Vorträge und Aufsätze* [Tübingen, 1954], p. 196).

23. *Form and Value in Modern Poetry* (New York, 1952), p. 339.

Aggression and Satire:
Art Considered as a Form of Biological Adaptation

ALVIN B. KERNAN

The naive question "If that is what the poet meant, why didn't he say so plainly?" comes very close to the heart of poetic things. It is a question about the value of art and style, about the utility of the images, the rhythms and rhymes, the tropes, and the complex structures with which the poet informs his matter. The most familiar answer to this question is, of course, that the poet is saying what he has to say in as clear and direct a fashion as possible, that what is said cannot be separated from how it is said, and that a complex style carries equally complex meaning. But some uneasiness apparently remains, for in the last two hundred years or so—since we lost the easy belief that the chief functions of literature were to imitate, instruct, and amuse—some strange additional explanations of the images and structure of poetry have been either developed from earlier hints or discovered new. The myth critic explains the elaborate forms of literature by telling us that they preserve primal rites and ancient explanations of the origin of things and the fundamental relationships of man and nature. The aesthetic critic explains the art of poetry as the manifestation of abstract beauty and idealized form, greatly superior to anything to be found on this side of the imagination. The psychoanalytic critic treats the indirections of art as disguises for the mysterious energies of the id, the configurations of the collective unconscious, the illogicality of dream, and the strange images and "grammar" of preconscious thought process.

In recent years a few critics have sought a charter for poetry neither in the deeps of the self and the primal past, nor on the transcendental heights of imagination where pure beauty is seen, but in the area of biological behavior. Susanne Langer in *Feeling and Form* sees art as the formalized expression, the "virtual" enactment, of basic attitudes necessary to man's proper orientation in nature and society. Comedy in her view, for example, is an artistic elaboration of the teleological tendency that enables all living things—the vine crawling up the masonry wall, the mouse nesting in the warmth of the chimney, the man evading some rigid law that forbids pleasure and life—to deal with and survive the chances and changes of a hostile universe. For Morse Peckham in *Man's Rage for Chaos: Biology, Behavior, and the Arts,* art is an "adaptational mechanism" which purposely throws us into unfamiliar situations and disappoints our expectations to make us "aware of the disparity between behavioral pattern and the demands consequent upon the interaction with the environment. Art is rehearsal for those real situations in which it is vital for our survival to endure cognitive tension" (p. 314). Joseph Campbell in *Primitive Mythology,* the first of his four-volume work *The Masks of God,* seems to argue (he never quite commits himself) that our most powerful symbols are comparable to isomorphs, those innate images imprinted in the brains of animals, as the image of hawk is present in the mind of the newly hatched chicken, who runs for shelter whenever the shadow of the hawk moves across the ground. Perhaps the most interesting of Campbell's examples is that of the grayling butterfly, a kind of insect Platonist, who always pursues females of the darkest hue. An artificial female of a darker color than occurs in nature will draw him from the living creature toward the ideal. In *The Seamless Web,* Stanley Burnshaw, somewhat in the manner of I. A. Richards, treats poetry as man's attempt to regain a primal unity of being, balancing the conflicting forces of diencephalon and cerebral cortex, civilization and "creature knowledge," translating everything we perceive into organic processes.

The indebtedness of these biological theories to older critical theories is obvious. Campbell, for example, is really only using a little biological lore to support a familiar theory of myths; and, though Peckham may be an exception, the central effort in these and most similar writing follows Shelley in trying to capture biology and science for poetry, not genuinely in investigating whether the making of poetry might have a physiological basis or whether art might function as a complex form of biological adaptation. The very largeness and vagueness of the concepts used— Langer's "brainy opportunism," Campbell's isomorphs, and Peckham's "seamless web" of an organic All—make testing such concepts impossible. In order to explore whether biology, and particularly "ethology," the study of animal behavior, offers us any help in understanding what poetry is and how it functions we need a more precisely defined and limited situation which can be investigated with some precision and in some detail. Certain striking similarities between that kind of poetry we call satire and the ways aggression is used and handled at a biological level might well constitute the needed conditions.

Satire has been identified in many different ways, but it seems to me that literary tradition has selected and called satire only those works which have as their primary and consistent motive an attack upon someone or something. In short, aggression lies at the heart of satire. In the type of satire known as "Juvenalian" the aggression is so direct, so violent, and so sustained as to make us distinctly uneasy, as in this Eskimo flyting:

> I beat you
> I kill you
> I cut off your head
> I cut off your arm
> And then the other
> I cut off your leg
> And then the other
> The pieces for the dogs
> The dogs eat.

In "Horatian" satire the aggression may be so muted and indirect as to make us doubt who or what is being attacked, or whether there is any attack at all; but the teeth marks are there on Settle's reputation when Pope finishes his couplet:

Now Night descending, the proud scene was o'er,
But liv'd, in Settle's numbers, one day more.

It is not the intensity of the attack which identifies satire and distinguishes it from other literary kinds, which nearly always contain some amount of aggression, but its dominance, its persistent
refusal to be bled off into tragedy's compassionate awareness of the
inevitability of error and suffering, or comedy's joyous sense that
life always finally outwits folly. On the rare occasions when we
are allowed to see the face of the satirist plain—Timon cursing life
at the end of Shakespeare's *Timon of Athens*, Molière's Alceste
with his green ribbons sitting in his dark corner, Gulliver living
in the stable with the horses he prefers to men—his distinguishing
feature is a pronounced, unmistakable hostility toward other men.

But if Juvenal's *saeva indignatio* expresses the primary energy
of satire, Dryden's remark in the *Essay on Satire* about that "vast
difference betwixt the slovenly butchering of a man, and the
fineness of a stroke that separates the head from the body, and
leaves it standing in its place," reminds us that we do not ordinarily allow the term "satire" to be used for such crude forms
of verbal aggression as cursing, denunciation, diatribe, invective,
sarcasm, pasquinade, or what Benjamin DeMott has called the
"language of overkill," that "mindless cycle of super taunts" so
prevalent in our age of "habitual irascibility" ("The Age of
Overkill"). To be true satire, verbal aggression must, we seem to
believe, be artfully managed, witty, indirect. To this requirement
of a high degree of stylization in the attack, we must also add the
further traditional requirements: that satire speak true, not
lie about what it attacks; and that it be morally responsible, not
an expression of mere ill will or personal animus. In practice these
requirements have all worked toward the same end, the creation of
an art of satire which controls and shapes the energy of aggression
in a socially acceptable way. This art functions in a remarkably
analogous way to the controls used to manage aggression at more
basic levels of life.

Disagreement among biologists on whether aggression is an
instinct or a reflex is matched by satirists' disagreement on why

they write. Juvenal (*si natura negat, facit indignatio versum*) and Pope ("Fools rush into my Head, and so I write") would seem to argue that satire is a reflex, while Marston ("I cannot chuse but bite") and Swift ("Drown the world! I am not content with despising it, but I would anger it, if I could with safety") seem to sense satire as instinct. But whatever its origin, in the response to the dangerous situation or in the chemistry of living things, aggression is a basic vital energy, and like all such energies cannot be said to be either a simple good or a simple bad. Its values for biological life are fairly obvious: the prevention of uneconomic concentrations of members of the same species in a limited food-gathering area, the protection of the brood from predators, and making certain that among herd animals the physically strongest males will sire the next generation and thus ensure the survival of the species. Its dangers are equally apparent. Melville describes an island in which "the chief sound of life . . . is a hiss" ("The Encantadas"), and the terrors of a world in which intraspecific aggression is uncontrolled appear nowhere more clearly than in the scene of the rat pack, all members of the same blood clan, gathering around a strange rat and delicately but inexorably nibbling him to pieces; or in that insane setting, the nesting ground of the night heron, where the nests must be placed at least two neck-lengths apart, and any bird happening to walk mistakenly between the nests and come within reach of those snaky necks and constantly probing bills is instantly pecked to death.

Among the strongly aggressive species, evolution has favored those which developed ways of limiting and directing aggression without eliminating it or blunting its useful functions. The great majority of these control devices in the animal world are purely mechanical or chemical. For example: a female smell which prevents attack by males; the "cheeps" of the young turkey which inhibit the aggression of the mother; the smell signs deposited by cats and dogs to signal their presence; or the suppression at appropriate times of bright colors and ostentatious structures, which seem among tropical fish, for example, to elicit aggression. A little more interesting are the "threat gestures" and the "submission gestures." Threat gestures, or bragging, limit aggression by frightening the opponent out of fighting. The poster fish, for example, when angry blow themselves up, get as bright as possible, and turn broadside to display themselves from the most fearsome perspective, meanwhile stirring the water rapidly with ferocious movements of their fins. The submission gesture works, of course, in exactly the opposite way. The puppy turns over on its back and dribbles when approached by an older animal; the weaker wolf offers its unprotected throat to a stronger antagonist; and the defeated crane lowers its neck and offers the vulnerable area of its head to the victor. Related human submission gestures would be, I suppose, bowing, holding up the hands, or the custom of supplication found in Homer in which the defeated warrior drops to his knees and clasps the legs of his opponent.

But the most elegant method of directing and managing aggression is ritualization, a process in which aggression is both expressed and channeled by certain rhythmic, formalized, and habitual actions. The range of these rites of aggression in the animal world is extraordinary, but for our purposes we can limit our discussion to two types. The first might be called the "war-dance type" in which aggression is first ritually aroused and then redirected. As an example of this way of handling aggression we can instance the case of the tropical fish in which the female makes all the signals—bright colors, inflation, hostile movements—which arouse the male fish to such a fury that he charges her. But just before he would ram her, he swerves aside and his charge carries him on into the territory of the neighboring fish of the same species, where he proceeds to take out his anger on the neighbor. In the "war-dance ritual" aggression is allowed to reach the point of actual attack, but in the next type, which we might call "the game ritual," aggression is released but carefully managed and stopped before it comes to the point of serious fighting and injury. An example of this type of ritual aggression would be a fight between stags where the issue is decided by locking horns and struggling without the fight usually coming to wounds or death. Similarly, certain species of fish rush at each other again and again but stop short of impact, until one or the other decides that it has been bested and withdraws from the contest.

Despite certain obvious similarities between the ways men and animals handle aggression, *Homo sapiens* has, according to Konrad Lorenz, from whose book *On Aggression* these details are taken, a uniquely difficult problem with aggression. Among those species which can kill with one slash of the fang or the claw, evolution has favored those with strong inhibitory mechanisms, such as the smell or sound signals described earlier. But man falls among a group of animals who are not inherently dangerous to their con-specifics, and therefore evolution did not operate on him as on the tiger to select varieties with strong controls on intra-specific aggression. But at a very late date in his biological development man invented tools and became at once the most dangerous of all creatures. In respect to aggression, man is then an evolutionary anomaly, extraordinarily aggressive, extraordinarily dangerous, and extraordinarily lacking in automatic controls on his hostility toward other members of his species. His culture has therefore been forced to supply under great pressure the controls he lacks by nature.

The art of satire, I would now like to suggest, might profitably, or at least interestingly, he approached as one instance of the way in which man has learned to control aggression and manage it to useful ends. There are a number of points at which that art is remarkably similar to the aggression-inhibiting and -controlling devices of the animal world. Lorenz notes, for example, that fiery colors and ostentatious physical structures express and elicit aggression, and that certain animals frighten their opponents and thus prevent death struggles by blowing themselves up as big and glowing as brightly as possible. The submission response to this bragging technique also controls aggression but by suppressing the signs of antagonism: a fish who "wishes to appease a superior opponent . . . grows pale, draws in its fins, displays the narrow side of its body, and moves slowly, stealthily, literally stealing away all aggression-eliciting stimuli" (p. 126). These two methods happen to correspond very nicely with the two principal stances assumed by the writers of satire. On the one hand there is the "hard-attacker," the bragging satirist like Juvenal or Aretino who flaunts his violence, threatens his enemies, stresses the power of his dark magic, and in general tries to make anyone afraid to disagree with or cross him. As an example of this stance we might take Pope's pride "to see Men not afraid of God, afraid of me." On the other hand there is the sly retiring satirist, like Chaucer, Erasmus, or Gay, a very humble sort of fellow, so simple that he doesn't know that it is wrong or dangerous to tell the truth in this world, so friendly that he can't imagine that anyone might take offense at being shown to be a bore or fool. Horace in *Sermones* 1.4 creates the archetype of this satiric stance, thanking the gods for making him "slow-witted, gentle, and hesitant to speak."

While a certain amount of ingenuity will produce a number of this kind of close parallel between the art of satire and the way animals manage aggression, such exact comparisons would be in the long run misleading. But since the problem of the management of aggression remains the same for men and other animals, we might reasonably expect to find that while the controls differ, the function remains the same. Biology would then provide a model of how the art of satire functions, not a catalogue of the devices the satirist uses to control aggression sufficiently to make it tolerable. We might test the value of this assumption by looking briefly at what has always been taken as one of the primary requirements of satire, the management of the attack in a witty fashion. Unrelieved and earnest denunciation may have an undeniable power, as in the curse or the sermon, but true satire seems to require a certain amount of cleverness, of indirection, of unexpected and shocking juxtaposition in the single details and in the arrangement of the whole. The history of western satire supports this view of the necessity of wit, and the great works of attack, those which comprise satire proper, are a succession of witty devices and clever techniques for expressing aggression in an oblique and humorous way: the beast fable, mock epic, the false utopia, the journey to strange lands and the factual observation of strange customs, the letters of obscure men, the praise of folly, the adventures of the booby hero, the dialogues of the gods, and the fairy tale cynically retold. The very titles of the most famous satires constitute a catalogue of these witty devices, *The Frogs, Dialogues of the Dead, Animal Farm, Candide, The Dunciad, Gulliver's Travels, Brave New World, Alice in Wonderland.*

The satirist seems always to pretend to praise what he is in fact blaming, or merely to describe in the most objective manner possible the abominations he encounters; and though we all recognize the game for what it is, know in fact that the blame is intensified by the pretended praise, such irony still seems necessary. Dryden, in the *Essay on Satire,* is aware of both its necessity and its effect when he comments on his portrait of Buckingham, "the character of Zimri in my *Absalom* is, in my opinion, worth the whole poem; it is not bloody, but it is ridiculous enough; and he, for whom it was intended, was too witty to resent it as an injury. If I had railed, I might have suffered for it justly; but I managed my own work more happily, perhaps more dexterously." The wit made the attack less painful and injurious to its target and at the same time preserved its author from the counterattack he might have "suffered . . . justly." This is pretty much what Freud also tells us in *Wit and Its Relation to the Unconscious* where he demonstrates that most jokes and sallies of wit are sanctioned releases of severely repressed feelings, particularly hostility. Both Dryden and Freud bring us to the point where we can understand that the use of wit to convey an attack functions similarly to techniques used among the animals to release aggression and yet at the same time control it, making attack less dangerous to both attacker and attacked. Just how wit functions in this way is not, however, entirely clear. Freud theorizes that the witty way of perceiving things is a kind of primitive language requiring less effort than more precise and logical ways of thinking and that therefore its use, and the perception of it by a listener, requires less mental energy. The sudden surplus of energy gained by dropping back into an "easier" language is experienced as pleasure, and this coupled with the additional pleasure gained from the expression of the repressed hostility is sufficient to overcome any negative feelings normally accompanying aggressive acts.

It would not, I think, be unreasonable to doubt a theory such as this which treats the play of wit as a low-energy form of mental activity, creating pleasure by slackness and muddiness of thought. It would seem on the other hand quite reasonable to think of wit in the more traditional manner as a high-level *rational* activity, simultaneously perceiving similarities and differences in an instant, joining with lightning speed those things which are usually separated, playing with many possibilities at the same time without confusing them. If this view of wit were correct, if it were a function of the conscious mind working at its highest speed and greatest power, then our explanation of how it functions in connection with aggression would be quite different from Freud's. We would have to say that the characteristic situation of satire, a witty expression of aggression, is a combination of an irrational emotion, hostility, which is normally repressed, and of a certain flashing, brilliant play of rationality. It would then seem to follow that the release of aggression becomes acceptable because we are reassured through the presence of the wit that the rational and conscious mind is still very much in control of the irrational aggressive energies. The situation would be much like that in a game in which violent and potentially destructive energies are released, but released in the reassuringly controlled circumstances of game—rules, boundaries, referees, time limit—which prevent any disastrous killing outcome.

Such an explanation of how wit functions to make aggression acceptable also seems to fit very well other aspects of the art of satire. Rhyme, carefully controlled metrical patterns, exact placement of words and images, tropes, the structured order of the parts and the whole, and all the many other poetic techniques shared with other art forms, work in satire to reassure us that at every point aggression is not raging free but is being carefully controlled and ordered by art, by the conscious mind and the rational faculties. The aggression, if it can be measured at such levels of intensity, is about equal in the two following passages, but it is far less threatening in the second example because it is so carefully patterned and so ingeniously worked out.

Now, the rotten diseases of the south, the guts-griping ruptures, catarrhs, loads o' gravel in the back, lethargies, cold palsies, raw eyes,

dirt-rotten livers, wheezing lungs, bladders full of imposthume, sci-
aticas, lime-kilns i'the palm, incurable bone-ache, the riveled fee-simple
of the tetter, and the like, take and take again such preposterous discoveries! [Thersites in *Troilus and Cressida*, v.1.17–24]

> Let Courtly Wits to Wits afford supply,
> As Hog to Hog in Huts of *Westphaly;*
> If one, thro' Nature's Bounty or his Lord's,
> Has what the frugal, dirty soil affords,
> From him the next receives it, thick or thin,
> As pure a Mess almost as it came in:
> The blessed Benefit, not there confin'd,
> Drops to the third who nuzzles close behind;
> From tail to mouth, they feed, and they carouse;
> The last, full fairly gives it to the *House*.
>
> [Pope, *Epilogue to the Satires*, II.171–80]

In recent years, however, the art of satire has not been identified
so much with its skillful use of wit and rhetoric as with its exploitation of a particular set of symbols and characteristic configurations. The Myth of Satire presents a decaying metropolis in
which a tyrant rules a polyglot mob, a countryside of ruins and
jungle in which savage animals stalk their prey, and a heaven from
which the gods have long departed. The dying city has many
names, Sodom, Babylon, The City of Man, The City of Dreadful
Night, Rome, London, Hollywood, but within it life and things
always disintegrate into dense, disorganized messes—chaos, the
mob, the junk pile, jungle growth, babble—and the world moves
frantically but meaninglessly, running on a treadmill, turning
giddily on the wheel in Luna Park, spreading over everything like
an oil spill and making it into nothing. This is, in the terms of
Northrop Frye, the world that man fears, that desire rejects; and
the strategy of the satirist has always been to associate these images
of fear with the men and practices he attacks by making the latter
the embodiments and the causes of the feared conditions. There is
a world of difference between Juvenal and Lenny Bruce, as there
is between the Asiatic customs and the bourgeois values they respectively attack, but both satirists show the things and men they
hate creating the same fragmented and senseless world. The causes
of disaster or the targets of aggression differ from satire to satire,

but the effect is always the same, and that effect is the Myth of
Satire. It would, I suppose, be possible to argue that the persistent
appearance of this myth in satire functions in somewhat the same
way as wit, rhetoric, and structure to make aggression acceptable
by showing it under rational control. After all, if satirists tell the
same story again and again, no matter how apparently different
their subject matter, then familiarity, maintenance of tradition,
and repetition reassure us each time that the old dangers are being
controlled in the old ways. This feeling of reassurance is strength-
ened by the fact that the images of the myth give a negative value
to the illogical and the irrational, to the formless, the meaningless,
that which comes from nowhere and goes nowhere. All this may
be so, but the fears which the myth images and the satirist exploits
seem not to originate in our conscious minds so much as in our
bones or, to use a more modern metaphor, in the irrational darkness of our unconscious. To bring these primal fears into play at
the same time that the forbidden aggression is released would
seem to produce such an intense concentration of the irrational as
to evoke all our rational ego defenses. The result would then be a
reaction against aggression rather than its licensed release. Something of this sort does indeed happen, I believe, in the most powerful satires and accounts to some degree for the persistent distaste
for such works, even when they are admired. Aristotle's view
(*Poetics,* VI) that the authors of satire represent "vicious and contemptible" men and are of a meaner sort than the authors of
hymns and encomia may have been modified over the years, but
it has not been changed. Satire, even at its best, is still regarded
with great suspicion.

By the strategy of the satirist is finally much more complex
than merely mixing a sufficient amount of the rational with aggression to smuggle it past the social censor. He plays an elaborate
game in which threat gestures are matched with their opposites,
submission gestures, and the control exercised by the rational is
reinforced by the fear of the irrational. To understand just how
this works we must turn to that other type of control society exercises on all releases of aggression, including satire. In order to
be acceptable, satire must not only be witty and well wrought,

but it must attack only out of moral zeal and only those who have broken some generally accepted value system, and the charges it makes must be true. "Moral doctrine . . . and urbanity, or well-mannered wit," is the way Dryden describes the requirements, and his phrasing would be difficult to improve upon: "There can be no pleasantry where there is no wit; no impression can be made where there is no truth for the foundation." In other words, we do not allow the satirist to "rail without a decent cause" (Byron, *Don Juan*, II.119); the release of aggression is sanctioned only when the thing attacked is shown to be wrong and dangerous. In practice this has seemed to mean that the satirist must show his enemy to be the enemy of society and all good men, and this is usually done by holding him up against some standard of morality or good sense, e.g. Horace's famous "mean" and the quiet life on the Sabine farm, or Aristophanes' appeals to sturdy common sense. But there is, interestingly enough, usually a good deal of doubt about how seriously these moral standards are to be taken in satire; and in a great many famous cases, such as *Gulliver's Travels* or *Don Juan*, just exactly what they are or whether they are even present is in doubt. My own view is that the real standard is more often a negative than a positive one and that it is to be found in the Myth of Satire. If the images and configurations which compose that myth are indeed the things that all men fear, then the satirist has found the most powerful sanction available for his attack when he shows his enemies creating or being responsible for these conditions. If the bourgeois society legitimized by the Congress of Vienna leads to cannibalism in an open boat, as it does indirectly in *Don Juan*, or if in a later form it causes men to turn into a herd of bellowing, thundering, thick-skinned rhinos, as in Ionesco's *Rhinoceros*, then *it*, the object of attack, is discredited by a deeply rooted standard from which there is no appeal. If it brings about what we fear the most, or *is* the thing we fear the most, then no matter how powerful the prohibitions against aggression, the attack, however savage, is justified.

To meet the corresponding requirement that aggression is allowable only if the charges leveled at the target are true, satirists have developed a large number of conventional techniques for establishing a tone of veracity For example, authors of satire consistently make an effort to persuade their readers that their works, no matter how bizarre or grotesque, are plain, straightforward literal descriptions of the world as it really is if men would only see it in their "steel glass." To buttress these claims, satirists regularly disclaim being poets and present themselves as simple truth-tellers; they call attention to the plain, everyday language they use; and they make elaborate, though ludicrous, attempts at specificity and verisimilitude, naming streets, drawing maps, providing graphs. Indeed, though the progress has not been at all constant, the major tendency in western satire has been toward the creation of an illusion of objectivity, and therefore of implied truthfulness. This process is best seen in the author's gradual withdrawal from the satire in order to remove any suspicions that the attack might result from his own bias, personal antagonisms, and misanthropy. Where Juvenal and Horace deliver their attacks in their own name, Swift and Molière are gone from their satires and their places taken by Gulliver and Alceste. By the time we reach Evelyn Waugh and George Orwell even the fictitious satirist is gone, the voice of the narrator is almost obliterated, or at least neutralized, and the fools present themselves in all their folly, without any awareness that they are being watched. "What," the satirist is then in a position to say, "could be more truthful than this?"

In a recent (1971) speech in Vienna, accepting the dedication of Freud's house as a museum, Anna Freud remarked, "My father said that the first man to use abusive words instead of his fists was the founder of civilization." But while the shift from blows to words to express aggression was a great step forward, the movement from hard words to satire was equally necessary, for words too can harm and even kill, and aggression in any form in such a potentially dangerous power that society must always manage it carefully by ringing it with rigorous controls. We have in satire, I believe, a brief schematic history of man's attempts to manage this explosive but useful energy which can tell us a great deal about human efforts throughout history to find a way of successfully handling aggression. We might also speculate further that since the effort has apparently been more successful in the greatest satires than in society—compare, say, *The Dunciad* with the situation in Northern Ireland—satire might well offer at least some practical guidance for understanding and dealing with aggression in society.

I suppose that the easiest charge that can be made against the approach to understanding the art of satire proposed in these pages, and against any attempt to use biological models to explain art, is that it is reductive. In this view, it might be charged, wit, art, morality, and truth become no more meaningful in and of themselves than the automatic cheep of the young turkey which inhibits the hen from pecking him to death, or the smell emitted by the female lizard which chemically depresses the aggression of the male. Wit and the turkey's cheep are then but variant forms of the same function in two different species of animals, and both "signals" have been favored by evolution because they contribute to the survival of the species by controlling and limiting intraspecific aggression.

Even if this were the case, I would still argue that to place satire, or any other form of art, at or near the center of one of the most fundamental, persistent, and critical activities engaged in all life, with the stakes nothing less than survival or extinction of the species, is not to reduce its importance but to increase it enormously. But the charge of reductionism can be met in other ways as well. Men are not after all turkeys or lizards, and while they may have the same problems with aggression and their solutions may function in the same way, the methods they use, though they overlap here and there, differ greatly. And in that difference we can find out something about our uniqueness as men, even as we remember that we share some of our most fundamental energies and powers with the rest of life.

Notes toward a "Class Theory" of Augustan Literature: The Example of Fielding

W. B. COLEY

A very crucial and very little known event in English literary history occurred when a group of critics and authors undertook in the late seventeenth century to alter the literary codes and canons of the day from conformity with a predominantly aristocratic, to conformity with a predominantly middle-class ideal.[1]

A salient feature of the literary man in the Augustan age is a certain amphibiousness—in political, religious, and, more broadly, in social relations. Before the rise of the great reading middle classes (during Pope's lifetime) the man of letters had been dependent on his patrons, and even in Pope's day he found it important to have aristocratic friends. His friendships had much to do with determining whether a poet wrote or did not write, wrote well or badly, starved in a garret or gave suppers in a villa. This fact was not merely a social and economic cause of literature; it entered into the very mind of the writer and gave him a certain kind of matter and a cast of thought. . . . A situation of superiority in talent and inferiority of privilege had produced a special way of talking—and perhaps even of seeing—double.[2]

Satire was thus an upper-class preserve in the main, with the satirists in the free or paid service of their social superiors, if they were not themselves members of a high social group. . . . It may be that it was only in England, and only in the period 1660 to say 1760, that satire was widely practised and also usually had its darts pointed horizontally or downwards in the social scale, but not upward. . . . It would seem an appropriate task for literary critics and social historians to discover why, in ancient times, in the late Middle Ages, in eighteenth-century France, and in nineteenth-century England, but not

in the Augustan Age of English satire, there were writers who resorted
to the satiric lance as a weapon serviceable in promoting concerted
action against the poverty, the misery, the social degradation, of the
depressed masses.[3]

I am afraid that both my title and my introductory quotations
stand in need of explanation, if not justification. The term "class"
in my title will undoubtedly mislead some readers into thinking
this essay is trying to pass for Marxist criticism. While I should
not mind particularly if this were the case, my credentials in
this respect are hardly orthodox. My purpose is to suggest, however, that some sort of socioeconomic, ultimately even "cognitive," [4] distinction manifested by many writers of the Augustan
period provides us with additional clues to the nature of its
literature—clues to its theory, to its rhetorical strategies and
idiom, even to some of its themes and subject matter.

The two classes I have in mind comprise, on the one hand, the
men of letters who actually depended on their writing for most of
their livelihood and, on the other, the patrons upon whom the
writers depended for support of their writing. Fundamentally,
this distinction is economic, if by no means exclusively so. Patrons
either had money to distribute to their writers or else had access
to "places" or positions in which their writers could be employed
gainfully. In Augustan England such places often involved the
writing of political journalism, and not so often the magnum opus
which in an earlier time would have brought a certain glory to its
supporter and a certain security to its creator. It is easy perhaps to
exaggerate the abruptness of such a change in the writer's position.
Fielding did dedicate *Tom Jones* to Lord Lyttelton. However,
the prior relationship between the two men was longstanding
(they were fellow Etonians) and in many respects extraordinarily
political in nature. Dedications there continued to be, and
Dodingtons to feed on them. But the quid pro quo relationship
that always existed between poet and patron increasingly demanded of the former that he supply something a little more
practical than a dedication. Noting this fact to be true of the
age of Addison and Swift, Alexander Beljame proposed that the

involvement of these and other writers in the pamphlet wars and political in-fighting had the effect of draining off their energies from the accomplishment of more *literary* productions.[5] This proposal may tell us why the writers of the Augustan Age did not produce more masterpieces. But it does not tell us much about the nature of what was produced, and that is the purpose of the present essay.

If the distinction between the two classes I have postulated was at bottom economic in nature, it had some noneconomic ramifications as well. The second of my quotations asserts that in some degree his aristocratic friends dictated not only whether the Augustan man of letters published or not, but also the nature and even the quality of what he did write. To put it another way, unless he had independent resources, he controlled neither the means of production nor the entire nature of the thing produced. In *Joseph Andrews* Mr. Wilson derives the custom of printing books by public subscription from the fact that booksellers allowed authors so little profit, even from "the best Works," that the patrons of literature had to devise other means of encouragement.[6] To an author this must have seemed like conjoining one dependency with another. It was the second which had its social side.

If I am using "class" in a special, perhaps heterodox, sense, I am also taking liberties with the idea of "theory." What I aim to do, inspired partly by my three authorities, is to combine their suggestions into something resembling a theory by which to account better for what otherwise seem to be unrelated features of Augustan literature. Clearly I hold that an accommodation between classes, whether it be dignified by the term "struggle" or not, was operating in the period under discussion. I further hold that although such accommodation involved many social nuances, some of them quite striking, at bottom it was an economic matter, involving one class of persons who made things but did not control the marketing of what they made, and another class of persons who did not, as a rule, make the same things or make them as regularly or as well but who did control the marketing of the things made by the first class. This proposition is much too rudimentary and derivative to lay strong claim to be called a "theory." Nevertheless, I am encouraged to persist in using this term by the plurality of meanings assigned to it by the recipient of this volume. In his essay "Rhetoric and Poems: Alexander Pope" Mr. Wimsatt distinguishes "five main types of relation between theory and poems," the fourth of which ("when in a given era a theory helps to determine poems not as subject matter but as an influence or cause why they are written in a certain way") seems fairly close to the definition I have in mind.[7] That I will attempt to lay out and support my theory chiefly in terms of the career and production of one writer is but another indication of the provisional nature of my essay. If the theory has any validity, readers will be able to supply their own examples.

The precedent for some sort of class theory of this period, though not for my particular version perhaps, is found in the essay from which I take my first introductory quotation. That essay holds that in the late seventeenth-century dialectic between men of wit and men of sense the issues seem to have been joined along class lines. "Wit" was essentially an aristocratic standard, a genteel vice. "Sense," with its implications of common sense, met with great appreciation among middle-class dissenters and those with a more sober, mercantile predilection. As practiced by "Dryden and his Crew" wit was charged with denigrating not only literature but virtue itself—in business, the arts, the church, and the law. The solution, in the metaphor of its commonest expression, was to refuse to take in the productions of wit at the Muses' exchequer, thereby debasing wit's currency and presumably driving it out of circulation the way a domestic embargo might drive out French silks and wine.[8] There is no question that wit lost many of its original intellectual and metaphysical qualities at this time. It seems plausible to suppose that the pace of this loss was accelerated by the critics who imputed to wit all the old aristocratic vices of untruthfulness, impiety, anticlericalism, and the like. In short, the metamorphosis of wit was a bourgeois triumph.

My second introductory quotation, though respectful of the

Krapp thesis, offers something of an alternative, one that is in many ways closer to what I am proposing here. In trying to account for the characteristic tone or idiom of poetry written in the manner of Dryden or of Pope, Wimsatt first considers its irony: "not the irony of Greek tragedy, for example, nor the romantic irony of sardonic introspection, nor that of metaphysical paradox, but just the irony . . . of a professional class which pays compliments for reward to men higher but duller." [9] Such a formulation may not quite meet the requirements of a class-struggle hypothesis, but it does point to sociological fact and to the possible relation of that fact to the production of literature.

My final quotation provides some necessary parameters for any serious case on behalf of a class theory of Augustan literature. If the Wimsatt quotation implies that satire may have been the most appropriate mode for the Augustan man of letters, given his situation in the scheme of things, the Viner quotation observes that Augustan satire, whatever its "causes," was not very revolutionary. It attacked not the basic system so much as the hypocrisies and failings of those who ran the institutions which comprised it. Viner goes on to suggest that Augustans may have preferred satire as a vehicle with which to express these attacks because satire allowed them to satisfy "a nostalgia for obscurity, contrivance, impenetrability, while on the surface conforming to new standards of lucidity and clarity." [10] Perhaps this suggestion points, without being fully aware of it, to the same profound ambivalence which critics of many different types have detected in Augustan literature: sniping and carping and flaying, without going the whole route and saying that the "system" itself was radically imperfect; betraying, in fact, lingering predilections for the obliqueness and witty complicatedness associated with a literature and even a social situation by then outmoded and in increasing contradistinction from its own; betraying such predilections, we might possibly argue, not just for nostalgia's sake but out of hostility, expressing itself clandestinely via irony and similar indirections. With Viner's suggestion we are close, it seems, to the position of those rhetorical studies which find surface "statement" combined with almost metaphorical obliqueness in, say, the couplets of

Pope,[11] and also to those studies which trace the element of witty seriousness in the Augustan mode, a "kind of licensed escape or leave of absence from serious rules which it could not wholly afford to repudiate." [12] I am not sure whether the economist and the rhetorical critic would both assent to a thesis connecting rhetorical strategies with class considerations, but there is no inherent contradiction.

In summary, the first of my three quotations advances the view that considerations of class entered into matters of literary theory and, possibly, literary production in the early part of our period. The second quotation makes a similar suggestion with respect to the rhetoric of Augustan literature. The third notes the unusually "safe" subject matter of Augustan satire and attributes it to the class basis of such satire in the aristocracy or in its dependents.

The Augustan Age is generally agreed to have been marked by a considerable interpenetration of literature and politics. There is further agreement that the Augustan man of letters differed from his seventeenth-century counterpart in the degree to which he was required to exploit political connections rather than the more traditional connection between patron and poet. What does not seem agreed, however, is how much and in what ways politics influenced the nature and production of literature, and vice versa. One obstacle to such agreement is the failure to reach another, prior agreement, namely, that concerning the real nature of Augustan politics itself. Before we can satisfactorily assess the effect on the writer of his political dependency, we must be able to say something more precise about its probable form. Was it primarily a matter of ideology? Of diverting his energies into a species of writing which may not have much interested him? Of developing positions in which he may not have believed? Or was it more likely to be a matter of holding onto some sort of sponsorship regardless of its ideological demands? The curse of party or the curse of patron?

It used to be that one could argue straightforwardly about the influence of political conviction upon literary theory, although not so much was said about the influence in reverse. Whiggism, to take one example, was credited with providing some of the theoretical underpinning for the rise of sentimentalism in literature. And at least a plausible case could have been suggested for presumed Tory support of the authoritarian principles of French neoclassicism. Such cases rest, of course, on the presumption that there really were (or continued to be) such entities as Whig and Tory ideologies or even real parties by those names. Since the work of Lewis Namier much has been done to discredit the idea that Georgian England was run on a two-party system or that there was any fixed body of principles to which party labels could be attached with consistency. The Namierian revisionism proposed that English politics was no longer (perhaps never had been) a matter of confrontation over principles; rather it was increasingly a matter of personal, familial, educational, and geographical connections, such connections expressing themselves most clearly in the factionalism which splintered the groupings traditionally labeled Whig and Tory. Connection, not ideology, was held to be what made the political world go round. Ideology in fact was so ubiquitous that the idea of a patriot king, generally credited to the metafactionalism of Bolingbroke and other Tory extremists, was taken over in the late 1740s by nominally Whig pamphleteers arguing for unity behind George II so as to assist Pelham in his efforts to create the right conditions for a broad-bottom coalition.

Lately, however, there has been something of a return to the earlier view, an antirevisionism, let us call it, which argues that Georgian politics did derive its main dynamics from the ideological contest between the two traditional parties. The later Plumb in particular has found considerably less to praise in Namier's depreciation of the two-party system and his depreciation of concepts in general as a political force. Plumb's Ford Lectures, published in 1967 as *The Origins of Political Stability: England 1675–1725*, have been supported in their antirevisionism by Geoffrey Holmes, whose *Politics in the Age of Anne* (1967) goes even further in restoring the value of party policy and principles.

In the face of such fundamental disagreement what does the nonhistorian do? Without presuming to prejudice the more profound historical questions, I am going to draw (without citation)

on a background of readings in the political ephemerae of the
1730s and 1740s to assert that any paradigm of the Augustan man
of letters must emphasize his close dependency on the support of
men in or around the seats of power and that this dependency
presented him with two unavoidable difficulties: ideological inconstancy and the threat of the loss of the dependency itself. Surprising as it may seem, there was no necessary connection between
the two, though in practice they might often be connected. For
one thing, the politicians themselves were frequently inconstant
in their professed convictions, so that it would not have been
logical to expect more of their dependent writers. A contributor
to the Pelhamite journal, *The True Patriot*, is clear about the
political inconstancy at least.

In this Case, who can deny that it is the Duty of a Man of Honour to
change and to prefer the Safety of his Country to that Reputation for
Steadiness which is, in Fact, no better than a fair Name for a very
ill Quality, I mean Obstinacy. . . . By thus fairly stating the Question,
we have an Opportunity of seeing that *Change,* with Respect to
Politicks, is so far from being altogether indefensible, that the contrary
Conduct may be *truely* stiled so.[13]

It is true that this sort of reasoning was more common among
those in power than among those out of power. It is also true
that as the half-century wore on, there was more of it altogether.
Furthermore, there is little evidence that inconstancy on the
patron's side ever prompted his literary dependents to sever a
useful connection. Although writers found themselves writing on
different sides of the same question at different times in their
careers, the relative complacency with which they seem to have
lived with this condition, at least in public, implies that it was
more or less taken for granted as a fact of life. Much more likely
to terminate a dependency was the patron's indifference to what
his writer was doing for him. Perhaps he felt he no longer required such services or that he was not getting value for money.
Fielding's references to Chesterfield, for example, even those in
nonpolitical contexts, diminished sharply in number after the
latter began to disengage himself from active politics.

What happened when a writer's political dependency was terminated obviously depended on what other sources of support were available to him. Fielding, whose dependency on the politicians and other nonliterary sources of support was in some ways more degrading than we realize, puts the case with considerable bitterness.

Why is an Author obliged to be a more disinterested Patriot than any other? And why is he, whose Livelihood is in his Pen, a greater Monster in using it to serve himself, than he who uses his Tongue to the same Purpose?

To confess the Truth, the World is in general too severe on Writers. In a Country where there is no public Provision for Men of Genius, and in an Age when no Literary Productions are encouraged, or indeed read, but such as are season'd with Scandal against the Great . . . the Temptation to Men in desperate Circumstances is too violent to be resisted; and if the Public will feed a hungry Man for a little Calumny, he must be a very honest Person indeed, who will rather starve than write it.[14]

These are familiar, almost reflexive arguments: no double standard, the general distress of literature in the absence of public support, the priority of starvation to ethical scrupulosity. However, the fact that they were familiar and even conventional does not necessarily mean that those who made them did not believe them. It would be difficult to show that the lot of the Grub-Street writers was relatively harder than that of their counterparts at other times. For one thing, their very existence as a distinct class was a fairly recent development. For another, without considerable evidence of other kinds one is reluctant to take literally their statements of distress. Dr. Johnson must have thought he was stripping the issue of its "luxury of sorry Feeling" when he made his statement about no man but a blockhead ever writing except for money. Fielding's point, however, is quite different. Johnson was simply asserting that writers did not write for love, so to speak. Like other people, they expected to get paid for whatever it was they did. Fielding is saying that in the end bad causes are better than starvation. In other words, not the profit motive in literature, but the question of the right to subsist.

Although Fielding's statement sounds extreme, I have already suggested there is no reason to believe that he and others who made essentially the same case did not believe in the truth of what they were saying. Now I would go further and say that neither the problem of sincerity nor the problem of truth to the facts of the matter seems entirely relevant to my point. The increasingly paranoid visions of the Grub-Street writers will not satisfy either the economic or the social historian as a fair account of the way things really were. But the critic must attend to them as clues to the influence or cause why the literature took the shape it did.

At this point we need an example.

Fielding's *Jacobite's Journal* passage, quoted above, is an interpolated extenuation of an attack he was making on his friend and former colleague, James Ralph. In 1748 Ralph, then and earlier a dependent of Dodington's, was editing *The Remembrancer* in support of the Opposition party centered around Leicester House and the Prince of Wales. As a Pelhamite journalist, Fielding was more or less expected to take the measure of Opposition writers like Ralph, and in this essay he comes down hard on him: "the Drummer of Sedition . . . fights in the Cause of Popery and Slavery, under the Standard (as he pretends) of the Constitution." After a good many remarks in a similar vein Fielding asks the question which leads to the passage already quoted: "Why did not the Ministry secure such a Writer to themselves, or at least purchase his Silence, when he offered himself to them?" Not the least interesting thing about this question and the answer it prompted is the general applicability of both to Fielding himself. Although he concludes the essay by saying that Ralph's apostasy, understandable in times of tranquillity, is unforgivable in times of crisis, the lengthy extenuation of the writer in need sounds very much like a satirist's apology—after the fact instead of before. It is hard not to think that Fielding had his own journalistic career in mind when he wrote this digression.

As yet we do not know very much about Fielding's political affiliations during the early part of his career. What we do know suggests that he followed closely the patterns set by his Etonian

friend and patron, George Lyttelton. Fielding's political affiliations, like Lyttelton's, switched around a good deal during his active years, enough in fact to draw the attention of hostile journalists, who affected to find Fielding's career remarkable in this
respect. Curiously, though, such activity does not seem to have
damaged the underlying expectations of friendship or connection.
A recently discovered letter from Fielding to the Duke of Richmond, dating from 1749, implies that the two men had continued
their relationship, whatever it may have been, and that the former
continued to hope for favors from the Duke.[15] To be sure, Fielding had dedicated a play (1733) and a poem (1739, 1743) to Richmond and had praised him several times. But by 1735 their political paths had sharply diverged, as Richmond threw strong support to Walpole, Fielding having given signs a year earlier that he
had followed Lyttelton and Chesterfield into the opposite camp.
For the sometime editor of the scurrilously anti-Walpole *Champion* to expect favors from one of the Great Man's staunchest supporters is further testimony to the "amphibiousness" of the social
and political situation of writers.

Another example of the disjunction between friendship and
politics is provided by Ralph himself. Three years after he had
been roasted in the *Jacobite's Journal* Ralph is invited to dine
with Fielding at Dodington's, no other guests being recorded, and
he accepts. In fact, according to Dodington's journal he had Fielding (twice with Mrs. Fielding) to dinner nearly a dozen times during the period 1750–52,[16] and this despite the fact that the attacks on the supposed seditiousness of *The Remembrancer* were
in effect attacks on the politics of Dodington himself. Unlike the
ideologues of other times, Georgian politicians seem generally to
have maintained something of a distinction between their politics
and their friendships. In the special case of friendships involving
dependency, however, there may have been an awareness by both
parties that the position of one of them verged on servility and
hence was less unexceptionable than that of an equal. Fielding's
enemies sometimes took him to task for not behaving like the
gentleman he had been born. Fielding himself may have betrayed
concern over his own station by insisting on the honorific "Esq;"

after his name, to the delight of enemy journalists, who rebuked him for his snobbery. But it may well have been just this sense of station that made him more sensitive to the abject elements of dependency, and more bitter.

One of the most intriguing examples of the complex relation between patron and writer is furnished by that between Fielding and Sir Robert Walpole. From almost the beginning of his literary career Fielding showed signs of trying to have it both ways with Walpole. Although the political satire of the earliest plays is comparatively muted or else generalized, it is generally agreed that by 1730 (*Tom Thumb*) or at least by 1731 (*The Tragedy of Tragedies, The Grub-Street Opera*) Fielding was beginning to focus more on the figure of Walpole and the useful concept of the Great Man. Only a year later, however, in the dedication (to Walpole) of *The Modern Husband* (1732) he writes what has struck many readers as either an ironic or an out-of-place entreaty for Walpole's patronage. The entreaty may well have been serious—Fielding was in no very secure financial state and he does not seem to have been on more than the fringes of any political circle—but the fact that many have read it ironically testifies to the ubiquitousness of that way of seeing and writing "double" which Wimsatt has found so characteristic of this period.

At apparently the same time, Fielding composed (but did not then publish) two verse epistles to Walpole, poems which their modern editor has called "jesting" but which exhibit at the very least an intriguing ambiguity.[17] The first and more important of these epistles begins encomiastically: Walpole is signalized as the helmsman of the ship of state, "Our Nation's Envy, and its Pride" (l. 2). It then develops the witty paradox that Walpole's poet ("Your Bard"), i.e. the "author" of the epistle, is in fact "a greater Man" than Walpole himself. This may already be ironic. Though he does seem to have gone three times to see *Tom Thumb* in 1730,[18] Walpole was notoriously indifferent to the needs of playwrights and poetasters alike. However much Fielding may have wished for such a connection, there is no hard evidence that he had made it, then or later.

The paradox of the poet's superiority to the Great Man is developed in a series of syllogisms. If there be no necessary connection between greatness and happiness; if indeed to be wretched is to be great; then the poet is great: "Forbid it, Gods, that you should try / What 'tis to be so great as I" (ll. 15–16). Social conventions are such that the greatest families dine at a later hour than the less great. By such a convention the poet, who "ne'er dines at all," is the greatest. Even in architecture the poet is superior, with his castles in the air and his lofty garret, from which he can look down on a whole street of important people: "We're often taught it doth behove us / To think those greater who're above us" (ll. 25–26). If crowds at a levée are a sign of the greatness of the person who holds it, the poet is once again superior: the duns press round him, not two days a week, but every day save Sunday.

For all his greatness, however, the poet will "come down, with wond'rous Ease / Into whatever Place you please" (ll. 45–46). What he is fittest for, in short, is a sinecure. This may indeed be "jesting," but if so, it is jesting of a special sort, in the tradition of witty seriousness that Fielding is elsewhere more explicit about. The situation of superiority in talent and inferiority of privilege has here produced a curious way of seeing double, servility perhaps, but with a sting. The irony of the poet's situation is that he must "come down" in order to survive in a world not noticeably encouraging to poesy. It might be argued that this is nothing more than a conventional Augustan treatment of the "distressed poet" theme, that there is no sign of the influence of class. About a decade after the supposed date of this epistle, literary gossip rumored that Walpole had at one time gone bail for Fielding, who had been arrested in some country town and was facing jail for want of funds. Fielding, so the account ran, rewarded his benefactor by satirizing him and then turning up at one of his levées. When asked why he wrote so, he is said to have replied that "he wrote so that he might eat." [19] We don't really know just how poor Fielding really was. In *The Journal of a Voyage to Lisbon* (1755) he implies he was getting along on about four or five hundred pounds a year. Recently, however, it has been suggested that he was making something on the order of seven hundred, although spending a hundred more than he was taking in.[20]

Whatever the figures, it should be noted that for his own contemporaries Fielding was a "type" of the distressed poet. A majority of the occasional references to him touch at some point on his impecuniousness. For example, *The Seventh Satyre of Juvenal Imitated* (1745):

> Would you have F——— match what Congreve writ?
> Oh, give him Cloaths, e're you deny him Wit.
> When press'd with Duns, and forc'd to write for Bread,
> The craving Belly checks the teeming Head.

The anonymous poet then goes on to handle the dependency question:

> But he has Patrons, and of these not few—
> Patrons! dy'e call them?—an unthinking Crew,
> In Manners grov'ling, as they're high in Birth,
> Who gives to Strumpets, what they keep from Worth;
> On Hounds and Horses fix their whole Regard,
> Nor spare one Guinea to relieve the Bard.
>
> [81–90]

Again the materials are conventional rather than personal. Whatever his financial difficulties—and at times he spoke of them gloomily—there seems to be little question but that Fielding had enough to eat. To the struggling man of letters, whether he be Fielding or the author of the Juvenal imitation, patrons, of course, never give enough. The point to be made here is that to many of his contemporaries Fielding was a symbol, perhaps *the* symbol to some, of what was abject in the writer's dependency on the patron.

But what of the view from the other side? What did the patron think of the poet and his relationship to him? Is there evidence that the poet, in addition to the vicissitudes of dependency, had to put up with indifference and loftiness? To get a sense of this other view it is instructive to look at an unpublished poem by Horace Walpole, entitled "The Praises of a Poet's Life" and written in imitation of the *Beatus ille* epode by Horace.[21] The Horatian original deals ironically with a usurer who is contemplating retirement from city life to the joys of country living. After calling in all his funds and moving to the country, the usurer rapidly becomes disillusioned with the bucolic life and hurries back to the city and redistributes his funds. Like Mr. Spectator, he found that country life was not what the poets said it was. Walpole's poem begins with a rehearsal of the supposed blessings of the poet's life. For one thing, it is blessedly free, free from the sort of thing which plagues the life of a man of politics—no required attendance at Parliament; no need to listen to dull speeches; no servility to the demands of party. Friend only to virtue, the poet's muse is impartial and eulogizes heroes of all parties. Nor does the poet have to exchange the Muse for the Bar: "To quit the happy Mask of specious Lore, / And without *Grecian* Wings attempt to soar" (ll. 17–18).

Parenthetically, we might note the unfavorable comparison between the speciousness of the knowledge conferred by and necessary to poetry, on the one hand, and the implicitly hard and true "Sense" (the word is Walpole's) required by the law, on the other. This looks suspiciously like the same ambivalence toward the value and meaning of poetry that one catches sight of in Pope's preface to the 1717 edition of his poems, where in one breath he utters pleasantries about poetry as the product of leisure hours and of an indifference to matters of great significance, and in another refers to the life of a wit as warfare upon earth. Both Walpole and Pope seem to hint at a kind of schizophrenia in the Augustan poetic, one to which the class situation of the poet must have contributed profoundly.

Walpole's poem then states that the poet's freedom permits him to shun "Those noisy Scenes . . . The factious Seats of Int'rest's venal Sons" and to flee from the "Levees of the Haughty Great," including, specifically, those of Sir Robert Walpole and Samuel Sandys, his successor as chancellor of the Exchequer (ll. 23–26). In the summer of his career, according to the poem, the poet can live apart from the annoyances of the real world. Indeed, he is pictured leading the "ductile Metaphors," working with similes and rhyme, crafting descriptions and digressions, culling the beauties of his predecessors, and fitting "old Histories to modern Days" (ll. 27–36).

But for the poet, as for the rest of the world, the seasons change. With the advent of autumn a certain change comes over the town and the poet, too, who now gathers up sententiae from the classical masters and in the dedication of his play "vows [them] to be Hints taken from his Patron's Family" (ll. 40–42). In winter, a darker season, the "moody Poet" lampoons the vices of the town and "weaves fine Nets of Flatt'ry's viscous Glue / For Popularity's ambitious Crew" (ll. 53–54), in return for which he is given the inevitable "Hares and Partridges," the surplus, as it were, of the Great Man's larder. After an obscurely placed digression on love and the superiority of British beauties, the poem draws near a conclusion with a vision of security, as it were, vouchsafed the imagining poet:

> How gratefull thus to each new Delight to try,
> With Wealth to change one's Pleasures, Taste t'enjoy!
> In one's own Coach how sweet all Day to roam,
> At night to loll, and roll supinely Home!
> The lazy Footmen round the Door to see,
> The plump, sleek Swarm of a Rich Family!
>
> [ll. 81–86]

That this vision is in some sense deeply ironic is clear from the final lines of the poem, which attribute the vision to Fielding, who is said to have that morning received a subscription fee, presumably for the *Miscellanies* to come, and to have thereby redeemed his snuffbox from pawn. In a note glossing the reference to Fielding, Walpole describes him as "a Writer of great Humour, Extravagance, & Poverty," the second attribute presumably contributing to the third.

The poem is unfinished, or at least wanting in some of its transitions. But if it implies, as I think it does, that we take the type of poet to have been modeled on Fielding—he is the only poet mentioned by name—and if it further implies that its occasion was partly Fielding's attempt to realize the vision of security ("With

Wealth to change one's Pleasures") by means of the subscription to the *Miscellanies,* then perhaps we are able to read it better in the light of the class differentiation between poet and patron. The irresponsible freedom of the ideal poetic life, the theme of the speciousness of poetry in comparison to the law, the picture of the poet crafting away while the real work of the world goes on elsewhere, the shift in his mood and position as he begins to "come down," however unpleasantly, into the society around him, the visions of love and riches generated (or so the poem seems to say) from a context of flattery and obsequiousness—all these go to make up the case, the patron's case, be it said, against the poet. Their weight comes down hardest on the poet's wanting to exercise his unproductive craft—unproductive in the materialist sense —as if free from the demands of practical experience while at the same time wanting also to participate in the pleasures which are created only when those demands are in some way satisfied. The poet is charged, in short, with wanting to have his cake and eat it too.

So much for dependency as seen from the other side. The doubling of perspective may have helped us see better the perilous balance required of the Augustan man of letters. To judge merely from the literary expressions of it, his self-esteem appears to have been a precarious thing, maintained chiefly by indirect means: irony, obliqueness, apology, self-deprecation, parody. These means have been isolated and studied carefully in recent years, for the most part against a background of intellectual history or theories of sensibility: for example, as the working out of the tradition of wit, or as a last-ditch effort to live with the obsolescent Rules by which literature was still theoretically supposed to be produced. According to the latter account, Augustan writers had to find a way of living with the Rules because they were not yet able to repudiate them.

I wish to suggest that a similar situation existed with respect to the class of writers. As a class, it was still subservient to a class we have called patrons. But the relationship was becoming uneasy, not merely (with Beljame) distracting. Lacking the convictions necessary to repudiate the system which produced such class differentiae, Augustan writers of satire did not take "concerted action against the poverty, the misery, and the social degradation, of the depressed masses." [22] Instead they played games, serious games perhaps, with the system, with its aristocratic representatives, and with its Rules. For an example one may look, say, at a late Fielding farce (*Pasquin*), where a variation of the "sessions piece" formula shows a mini-system headed by a Queen called Common-Sense, who is overthrown, in what Shaftesbury would have called a "triumph in reverse," by the forces of Ignorance, the whole a parody of what Fielding and his friends affected to believe was happening under Walpole's administration. Or one might catalogue some of the other variations on the theme of dependency: authority, the Great Man, justice, patronage, paternity, law, Scripture, master-servant, high-low.

In asserting the link between wit and seriousness Augustan writers may indeed have been repudiating the so-called dissociation of sensibility.[23] My contention here is that they were doing more than that. Restlessly and wittily, they were playing with—not frontally attacking—the dependency between classes, with an aspect of the great chain of being, if you like, which they could no more repudiate than they could the Rules. They may be faulted for insufficient conviction or for lack of revolutionary ardor, but they cannot be faulted for taking refuge in a sorry sentimentality or a cynical withdrawal.

NOTES

1. Robert Martin Krapp, "Class Analysis of a Literary Controversy: Wit and Sense in Seventeenth-Century English Literature," *Science and Society,* 10 (1946), 81.

2. William K. Wimsatt, Jr., *Alexander Pope: Selected Poetry and Prose,* Rinehart Editions no. 46 (New York, 1951), "Introduction," pp. xvi–xvii.

3. Jacob Viner, "Satire and Economics in the Augustan Age of Satire," in *The Augustan Milieu: Essays Presented to Louis A. Landa,* ed. Henry Knight Miller et al. (Oxford, 1970), pp. 86, 87, 100–01.

4. I use "cognitive" here to mean known in the sense of felt or sensed or unconsciously apprehended.

5. *Men of Letters and the English Public in the Eighteenth Century: 1660–1744,* trans. E. O. Lorimer (London, 1948). The original French editions date from 1881 and 1897.

6. Henry Fielding, *Joseph Andrews,* ed. Martin C. Battestin (Oxford, 1967), pp. 215–16. The passage is from bk. 3, chap. 3.

7. Reprinted in *The Verbal Icon* (Lexington, Ky., 1954), pp. 169–85. The quotation is from p. 171.

8. Krapp, "Class Analysis," pp. 84–85, with additional examples from William K. Wimsatt, Jr., and Cleanth Brooks, *Literary Criticism: A Short History* (New York, 1967), p. 241.

9. "Introduction," *Alexander Pope,* pp. xviii–xix.

10. "Satire and Economics," p. 81.

11. For example, Maynard Mack, " 'Wit and Poetry and Pope': Some Observations on His Imagery," in *Pope and His Contemporaries: Essays Presented to George Sherburn,* ed. James L. Clifford and Louis A. Landa (Oxford, 1949), pp. 20–40.

12. William K. Wimsatt, Jr., "The Augustan Mode in English Poetry," *ELH,* 20 (1953), 1–14; and William B. Coley, "The Background of Fielding's Laughter," *ELH,* 26 (1959), 229–52. The quoted matter is from Wimsatt, "The Augustan Mode," p. 14.

13. "The Present History of Great Britain," in the issue (no. 25) of Tuesday, April 15, to Tuesday, April 22, 1746. Although Fielding was the editor, he does not seem to have written this particular installment. Its views, however, are compatible with his views on the matter.

14. *Jacobite's Journal,* no. 17 (March 26, 1748), p. 1.

15. Mary Margaret Stewart, "Henry Fielding's Letter to the Duke of Richmond," *Philological Quarterly,* 50 (1971), 135–40.

16. Lewis M. Knapp, "Fielding's Dinners with Dodington," *Notes and Queries,* 197 (1952), 565–66.

17. See Henry Knight Miller, *Essays on Fielding's "Miscellanies"* (Princeton, N.J., 1961), p. 127. The titles of the epistles give their dates of composition as 1730 and 1731, respectively, a dating which Miller, "General Introduction" to the Wesleyan edition of the *Miscellanies* (Oxford, 1972), p. xliv, accepts. For a different dating, see Hugh Amory, "Henry Fielding's *Epistles to Walpole*: A Reexamination," *Philological Quarterly,* 46 (1967), 236–47.

18. Charles B. Woods, "Fielding's Epilogue for Theobald," *Philological Quarterly,* 28 (1949), 423.

19. *An Historical View . . . of the Political Writers in Great Britain* (London, 1740), pp. 48–51, first cited in this connection by Howard P. Vincent, "Henry Fielding in Prison," *Modern Language Review,* 36 (1941), 499–500. The shilling pamphlet was listed in the "Books in September and October, 1740" in *Gentleman's*

Magazine, 10 (1740), 528, which suggests that this particular anecdote may have been derived from slightly earlier accounts in the newspapers, for example, in the *Gazetteer* of July 30 and August 1 and 2, 1740, which also allude to Fielding's supposed overtures to Walpole.

20. Hugh Amory, "Fielding's Lisbon Letters," *Huntington Library Quarterly,* 35 (1971), 81.

21. "HW's Poems and Other Pieces," fols. 52–54, in the collection of Wilmarth S. Lewis, to whom I am indebted for permission to quote. See also W. B. Coley, "Henry Fielding and the Two Walpoles," *Philological Quarterly,* 45 (1966), 168–69, where the poem is cited in a different connection.

22. Viner, "Satire and Economics," pp. 100–01.

23. Wimsatt, "The Augustan Mode," p. 14.

The Fictional Contract

MARTIN PRICE

We have been offered countless definitions of the novel. They range from the novel as a picture of life to the novel as dramatic poem, from an autonomous formal structure to a uniquely compelling moral force. These definitions may be frank efforts at persuasion, deliberate raids upon the prestigious name of the novel conducted in the hope of directing its future. Or they may be efforts to get beneath the accidental differences to the essential form of the novel, to determine what it really is. In either case, the effect is to promote a particular kind of novel and to claim our attention for it. Other forms of the novel may be shown respect so long as we acknowledge that they can no longer be pursued. Often we lavish praise on the dead because they no longer threaten us; the tribute we pay is a measure of our relief, as if the majesty of the tomb served in part to make the burial more secure.

These persuasive definitions have their uses, and they are the very stuff of literary manifestoes. The difficulty arises when the meaning of a term is restricted under the guise of being analyzed and the experience it denotes suffers a corresponding contraction. Such a definition obstructs our response to experience and limits our perceptions. What I propose to do is simply to survey some of the principal functions the novel has in fact served. I shall try for adequate range, but with no hope of completeness. Once I have discussed these functions separately, I want to consider briefly the extent to which they limit or reinforce each other. How fully can the same novel satisfy a range of functions at once? If this suggests a definition in turn, I shall leave it for the reader to draw.

There are three principal families or groups of functions I wish to discuss: the novel as game or pure form; the novel as expressive act; and the novel as a source of knowledge, as record or model.

It is the nature of games that they are self-enclosed, creating a world that obeys fixed rules but also presents one with much that is accidental or unpredictable. The resistance may come of chance (the fall of the cards) or of competition (the strategy of an opponent). To win the game one must follow the rules in order to shape the unpredictable into a form that is prescribed; one cooperates with chance or outmaneuvers an opponent, but one can win only by observing the procedures agreed upon. A game is, moreover, an end in itself. We may play it for distraction or use it as a means of aggression; we may rage in frustration or crow with self-satisfaction at the close; but the game has a definable end, whatever else we may make of the process. We know, of course, that games like novels may provide valuable exercise in skill and even moral training; but these are uses to which it may be put rather than essential to the game itself.

We may regard the process of reading a novel as a game between two players, one the reader and the other the author; or we may see it as a game like solitaire, where the reader is required to impose some kind of order on the materials that are given to him. The latter view stresses the novel as artifact, self-contained and without reference to an author. But it presents problems. To read a novel is to discover the order latent in its materials rather than simply to impose one by a set of rules. In some sense each novel discloses to the reader the order he may expect to find, in its use of convention and by its opening movement: we could not speak of suspense unless there were a limited range of expectations, within which there remains crucial unpredictability. In that sense, the novel both sets the rules and provides the challenge, whether or not we become fully aware of the author's presence behind the work he has created. When we become fully aware of that presence, we may wish to speak of the rhetoric of the novel.

So long as we engage in the game, it bounds our awareness and holds our attention; if we turn away from it, we know we are leaving the area it circumscribes. This is largely because the rules of the game create a world of "institutional facts," to which our responses are regulated and even defined by a system of "constitutive rules." [1] We do not confuse the words of fiction with statements of fact or references to fictional characters with allusions to real people. In fact, one may speak of artistic representation as itself an institution. As Richard Wollheim observes of a similar case, "it is hard to see how the resemblance that holds between a painting or a drawing and that which it is of would be apparent, or could even be pointed out, to someone who was totally ignorant of the institution . . . of representation." [2]

There are novels which insistently call attention to the rules they impose and even mock us with the strenuous efforts they demand of us. We are not allowed to lose ourselves in the game, and yet the reminder that we are playing, however strenuously, has a liberating effect as well: we are made aware of our own contribution to the game, of the skills we are required to employ and of the pleasure we find in exercising them. The self-conscious game is a special case of the gamelike aspect of most novels, but it helps us see what is present all the time.

In a different way we can see the gamelike aspect of the novel more clearly by considering a relatively pure case: the detective story. We read it for the exercise of the puzzle, and we hardly recall it more than we do any other puzzle we have completed unless its impurities give it other kinds of interest. When we read a detective story, we do not really regard murders as murders, for we are interested in the problems that the convention of a murder creates. The problems, moreover, are presented in a distinctive way. We take for granted that much of the information we are given will be ambiguous; clues may be misleading or false in emphasis. It is our task to play against the author, remaining vigilant where he most wishes to lull our suspicions, refusing what strike us as false leads, inventing surmises that go beyond his proffered evidence. Some detective stories present a series of solutions, each new one overturning and correcting the last, until by the close we reach the one adequate solution that takes into account every possibility that has been raised. Anyone who reads detective stories knows that there are certain moves the author should not make: he should not allow the solution to depend upon evidence that is withheld from the reader, and he should not make the criminal a character who is introduced late in the story. Such moves are regarded as cheating, as is the reader's turning to the back of the book before he earns his way to it.

The detective story is more game than novel. Its characters may be rudimentary (unless the puzzle involves complex motives rather than the mechanics of opportunity), and its plot tends to be more ingenious than plausible. We should hardly tolerate this mode of narration if its function were not precisely to tease and test us, although we accept something close to it in Henry James or Joseph Conrad in return for a different kind of reward. The detective novel reduces the problems of following a story to those of making appropriate inferences and avoiding false suggestions. But upon such procedures (with less need for eluding the author's tricks) all the more complex experience of the novel is based.

To treat the novel as a game is to concentrate our attention upon the puzzle-solving aspect and perhaps to recognize it as more fundamental than we usually do. The puzzle shows, in a trivial and therefore all the more obsessive way, a concern with form—with imposing, discovering, at any rate achieving it. Passive participation in games of mere chance involves little more than hopeful waiting; but most games involve some skill, and therefore an active effort to bring form into being. The success of a game depends, in large measure, on its providing sufficient resistance to call forth exertions and yet not so much as to make the effort futile. There are times when the game is already won but must still be played out, the outcome no longer seriously unpredictable and the resolution almost mechanically worked out, according to set laws. One may see this as the counterpart of what has often been criticized as the schematic in the novel: a pattern is so firmly established that, once it is mastered, its application presents no new problem and becomes only passive execution. Things do not simply fall into place; they jostle one, as it were, in their readiness to get there, and one feels oneself more the instrument of a design than the discoverer, much less the creator, of one.

The impulse to achieve form and order need not detain us. It is so general and so fundamental as to need little explanation: we may see it as the impulse to control, to humanize, to shape the casualty of events to the order of our minds, to abolish waste and obscurity by converting disorder to design. The goal of the impulse is to convert all content to form, that is, to trace in every element of the work some purposiveness that makes it necessary rather than accidental, to find relevance in every detail and meaning in every event. This is a grand ambition and not one to be achieved; the goal simply shapes the direction of the impulse. To state it in terms of meaning is already to look beyond the merely gamelike or formalistic aspect of the novel, and, if one were cautious enough, one would use a term like pattern rather than meaning. For while the novel is composed of words with meanings that designate events which in turn have meanings, the question at stake is whether the novel as a whole is controlled by meaning. One can readily think of novels which "come out" merely as games or as rituals come out; they achieve a rounding or closing of form, a binding of loose ends, a resolution that satisfies all the expectations that the form has aroused.

In practice, whatever the goal, the full achievement of form is scarcely to be attained. For the movement to the goal begins in the arbitrary and accidental, and these remain in some degree unpurged, untransformed. They become an embarrassment for any tyrannical ideal of form, and they impugn the value of the ideal. The forming process rather than the achieved form tends to be the primary interest of game-player or novel-reader. The completion of the form is an acceptable resting point, a sufficient resolution, not a total extinction of accident. What makes a resolution sufficient? In a game we know when we have won. We have attained the degree of order that the rules require, and this will vary with the nature of the materials. Loose ends remain. A checkmate does not require a swept board, and a slam will require a certain number of tricks. In the arts we do not know when we have won, and we tend to be haunted by an ideal conception of form—for example, that of organic unity—that induces despair or, worse, encourages desperate ingenuity in exacting a design. If unity were the sole end of structure, we should be able to attain it at the sacrifice of all that makes unity interesting; but, in fact, only such a degree of unity is desirable as will accommodate other functions.

Here the analogy with the game breaks down: without clear rules, the novel cannot be won or lost, it can only be more or less satisfactorily resolved. What such resolutions can mean becomes most clear where critics have discussed the question of how a given novel might have been completed (Dickens's *Mystery of Edwin Drood* or Mann's *Confessions of Felix Krull*) or whether an open novel like *Tristram Shandy* has in fact been completed. But in a sense every critical dispute about the interpretation of a novel is a dispute about how it is resolved, that is, to what end it moves. What is striking is that there is general agreement that such novels are in fact resolved even where there is strong disagreement about which of the possible resolutions one should accept. The situation is reminiscent of the multiplied endings of detective stories, each containing the previous ones.

The forming process varies with the kind and degree of form that is sought, but it underlies all kinds and degrees as something more constant than any of them, and it becomes an occasion for attention in its own right. Michaelangelesque, Mozartian, and Wordsworthian are terms that have as much weight as the titles of particular works, and they are terms invoked as readily by passages as by completed works. Yet none of these terms would have its full weight if the formative power it names did not include the formation of a complete work. The game provides a simple analogy again; once a game is won or lost, we may—if there is record or notation, even sharp enough memory to permit it—wish to replay it, to trace a sequence of moves in order to enjoy once more the mastery they exhibited. There is a fine instance of the power such a passage may have in Kenneth Clark's discussion of Rembrandt's self-portraits:

More than any of the series, the Kenwood portrait grows outward from the nose, from a splatter of red paint so shameless that it can

make one laugh without lessening one's feeling of awe at the magical
transformation of experience into art. By that red nose I am rebuked.
I suddenly recognise the shallowness of my morality, the narrowness
of my sympathies and the trivial nature of my occupations. The
humility of Rembrandt's colossal genius warns the art historian to
shut up.[3]

Clark is referring to more than formal mastery, but all else is
grounded in that and follows from it.

Something of the sort may be seen in the criticism of the novel.
The large and loose works permit one to talk with great precision
only about passages. The passages presuppose the larger, resolved
form and gain their full import only from their reference to what
precedes or follows, quite literally from their status as passages.
Yet it is here, in the local situation, where ends and means are
concentrated in a complex moment, where all the difficulties of
playing are raised by the crux of possibilities engendered by the
past and governed by the future, that the full value of the game is
felt. One can, in the novel, speak of such moments as instances of
"truthfulness," of full respect for the casualty and complexity of
the actual; but they are constituted by the form and by what the
form itself is constituted to admit. To put it in bizarre but emphatic terms, they are moments of institutional life. If they recall
comparable moments of actual experience and seem true to them,
it is in large part because we conceive actual experience in their
terms.

I have so far discussed games of skill and chance. One might, as
an approach to other functions of the novel, glance at the kind
of play that might be called mimicry, or impersonation. Whether
or not it is based on actual models or on invented selves, it becomes a release from constraint, a freeing of the power to choose
one's identity or roles, a holiday from the life one has inherited or
earned. This is that "power of improvisation and joy" that Roger
Caillois calls *paidia,* and it can be related to those cases of self-
induced vertigo or intoxication he also treats (as *ilinx*). So it can
unless it acquires discipline and exemplifies as well something of
the "taste for gratuitous difficulty" Caillois calls *ludus.*[4] One thinks
of those imagined worlds that novelists not only create but rather

compulsively map, codify, and particularize—down to street names, income figures, and shopping lists that will never enter into the novel itself. These have been explained by the need to imagine fully that some novelists feel; one can accept that but still ask further questions. These model worlds are not designed to reveal some aspect of the actual world but to create an alternative world whose rules are tighter than the actual world's and are gratuitously imposed. In effect, their very "realism" turns the actual into game. Caillois cites the theater as a form of activity that disciplines mimicry; the novel can serve more obliquely but perhaps even more elaborately—since it does not require powers of performance—to achieve the same end. Related to this, and perhaps more clearly tied to psychic needs, is the novel as ritual: constantly reenacting patterns of conflict and resolution—as in the traditional genres of light fiction, the western or romance—and providing (whatever else) the reassurance of the reconstituted form.

As the second group of functions the novel serves I have in mind the ways in which it engages and shapes the feelings of both author and reader. This raises questions of projection and identification, of fantasy and, in a special sense, of therapy. The game as such is self-contained, but as it is turned to expressive uses it becomes not simply an arena marked off by institutional rules but a playground for feelings that cannot otherwise be exercised. The institutional rules are essential to this exercise, for the fear of these feelings—the resistance to acknowledging and expressing them—is alleviated by the formal pattern into which they can be admitted. We can start from either side of the transaction, as it were, with the feelings that require a formal structure, or with the structures that admit a kind of feeling (in some sense regressive) that we usually suppress. The first approach is closer to Freud's treatment of dreams, the second to his treatment of jokes. Both require the elaborate and highly poetic devices of condensation and displacement, but both exhibit them in a process of local or small-scale ordering. The fluidity of dreams permits rapid transitions from which one need not look back; the structure need not achieve a sustained consistency. The brevity of jokes permits a compact, if intricate, structure, often generated by a single act of verbal play. Neither can account in itself for the sustained form of the novel or provide more than a partial and suggestive analogy.

To speak of fear of our feelings need not conjure up specters of repressed sexual impulses, although they clearly have a central place. Let me cite instead two passages from Raymond Williams on the Victorian social novel:

Like Alton Locke, Felix Holt becomes involved in a riot: like him, he is mistaken for a ringleader; like him, he is sentenced to imprisonment. This recurring pattern is not copying, in the vulgar sense. It is rather the common working of an identical fear, which was present also in Mrs. Gaskell's revision of John Barton. It is at root the fear of a sympathetic, reformist-minded member of the middle classes at being drawn into any kind of mob violence. John Barton is involved in earnest, and his creator's sympathies are at once withdrawn, to the obvious detriment of the work as a whole. Sympathy is transferred to Jem Wilson, mistakenly accused, and to Margaret's efforts on his behalf, which have a parallel in Esther's impulse to speak at the trial of Felix Holt. But the basic pattern is a dramatization of the fear of being involved in violence: a dramatization made possible by the saving clause of innocence and mistaken motive, and so capable of redemption. What is really interesting is that the conclusion of this kind of dramatization is then taken as proof of the rightness of the author's original reservations. The people are indeed dangerous, in their constant tendency to blind disorder. Anyone sympathizing with them is likely to become involved. Therefore (a most ratifying word) it can be sincerely held that the popular movements actually under way are foolish and inadequate, and that the only wise course is dissociation from them. . . .

These novels, when read together, seem to illustrate clearly enough not only the common criticism of industrialism, which the tradition was establishing, but also the general structure of feeling which was equally determining. Recognition of evil was balanced by fear of becoming involved. Sympathy was transformed, not into action, but into withdrawal. We can all observe the extent to which this structure of feeling has persisted, into both the literature and the social thinking of our own time.[5]

While Williams's analysis seems just, I find troubling the fact that he scants the problem of game or form. These are novels written according to certain rules, or at least certain conventional expectations, of which the resolved and "happy" ending is one of the most conspicuous. We have to acknowledge that these novelists worked within such forms and brought to them the awareness, however disabled by fear, that Williams discusses. The form of these works did not provide the vehicle for meeting the problems he cites. It provided instead the vehicle for expressing feelings that can only yield somewhat strained resolutions. But this use of the novel has a counterpart in work of the preceding century like Fielding's *Tom Jones*. Fielding constructed a novel in which an artlessly imprudent hero could not hope to acquit himself with success in a world of self-interest. Fielding insists upon the need for prudence, but he presents many portraits of men whose self-regard is both prudent and contemptible. In contrast, Jones's generosity of spirit makes him all but incapable of prudence and at most a somewhat theoretical convert to it at the close. In order to extricate his hero from the consequences of imprudence, Fielding must perform the work of a wise providence; the contrivance of the plot is the perfect vehicle of the author's ambivalence, and the reconciliation is imposed by means as "magical" as in the novels Williams treats. Yet without the contrivance we could not have had the celebration of generosity.

What I have done is to reverse Williams's direction, to insist that the vehicle releases feelings rather than that it exhibits a fear of them; that it does both is my real argument. For it admits only those feelings that can be acknowledged, and only to the degree that they can be; if it expresses no more, it has at least given these a form. The process of shaping that makes feelings admissible recalls the structure of games; one can see the structure both as a self-imposed gratuitous difficulty and as a release. Dryden wrote in this vein about rhyme; the difficulty it imposed often produced the happy discovery of the inevitable word. For most of us, the self-imposed difficulty of the form is the author's concern; what he offers us (as the punster offers his audience) is the release from the conventional limits of logic into a realm where words seem to perform magical acts. What W. K. Wimsatt has called the counter-logical use of language is at once obedience to conventional forms, metrical and rhetorical, and a restoration of that childhood power of manipulating words with all the authority of Humpty Dumpty.

So with the form of the novel: it may give experience the coherence of romance, the moral clarity of melodrama, the causal inevitability of tragedy. These forms are gratifyingly schematic and, as it were, lucidly rule-bound; but they admit the complexities that would otherwise be chaotic or overwhelming. As Ernst Kris puts it, the "maintenance of the aesthetic illusion . . . stimulates the rise of feelings which we might otherwise be hesitant to permit ourselves, since they lead to our own personal conflicts. It allows in addition for intensities of reaction which, without this protection, many individuals are unwilling to admit to themselves." The pleasure of such an aesthetic experience as what Aristotle calls catharsis is "a double one, both discharge and control." We destroy reality in order to construct its more tolerable and comprehensible image: "Every line or every stroke of the chisel is a simplification, a reduction of reality. The unconscious meaning of the process is control at the price of destruction. But destruction of the real is fused with construction of its image." Most of all, the process is a tribute to the power of the ego in ordering its world: "The control of the ego over the discharge of energy is pleasurable in itself." [6]

This last point brings us to the problem of identification. We may feel involvement in a game: our pride and interest—a quite deep-lying sense of self—may ride on our success or failure. But there is another kind of involvement we feel in a novel. The experience of which we read gains immediacy; we entertain it as if it were our own. We feel with some of the characters, and we accept their situation as one in which we imagine ourselves as actors.

How completely do we enter into the experience of the characters? As in a dream our own capacities for feeling are exercised by the characters in which we invest them. ("A dream," as Freud remarked, "does not simply give expression to a thought, but represents the wish fulfilled as a hallucinatory experience.") When we speak of identification, the feelings are so fully exercised as to preclude even marginal self-awareness. Such a state is perhaps pathological if it is more than transitory, and it may be more easily sustained in adolescence than later. The common process is far more complex and interesting. We may enter into a character to a considerable degree and "perform" his feelings somewhat as a musician performs a sonata. But we tend to retain some power of disengagement: we may be able to move back from or out of the character, to see him with detachment as well as sympathy. This will, in fact, be encouraged by the novelist's own presence: at the very least, the composing power of the novelist will serve to detach us from simple identification. Beyond that, we have the explicit voice of the novelist, as he recounts the story, or even as he presents the character's thoughts through indirect discourse. The difference between the words in which the character might himself think and the words in which the novelist presents his thoughts produces at least a trace of dissonance or a shadow of irony. And in the larger structure of the novel we are as readers constantly aware of patterns, of relevances, that the characters may exhibit without recognizing. In a novel of multiple plot, for example, like George Eliot's *Middlemarch,* any one story is embedded in a structure of relationships with other stories that have as much prominence for us but may be at the margin of a given character's awareness or totally beyond his ken. At its most pointed, this will be dramatic irony; but in a more tenuous form it is present everywhere and affects our sense of any character or event.

Again, the words in which the novelist writes are words he will have applied to other characters in the same story; each novel is a verbal matrix, and, while the degree or ordering will vary from case to case, there is at least the likelihood that the words will bind and relate elements as the elements themselves can scarcely imagine. All of these devices serve, then, to keep us aware of the fictionality of the work and of the characters. Yet they do not rule out a large degree of sympathy; we are flexible enough to move in and out, back and forth, without totally sacrificing one aspect for the sake of others. The game modifies the possibilities of identification but does not annihilate them.

As the form of the novel emerges, our identification shifts more and more from character to author. "We started out as part of the world which the artist created; we end as co-creators: we identify ourselves with the artist." As Kris observes, "however slight, some degree of identification with the artist, unconscious or pre-conscious, is part of any aesthetic reaction," [7] and it may be awakened early in our reading by the overt play in the language or narration as well as by the narrative voice. As the novel approaches resolution, however, the process is intensified. The central character, with whom we have identified, may himself undergo precisely this kind of shift, a broadening of awareness that takes in the whole pattern of which he is a part, a release from the peculiar blindness or limitation that has beset him and produced the complications of the plot. If so, the shift of identification is a twofold one: both character and, with him, reader move toward and effectively reach the author's awareness. The central character who signally fails to do so, who remains essentially blind or obtuse, seems often to have too little consciousness to permit sufficient identification: it is the complaint made about Emma Bovary by readers as different as Henry James and D. H. Lawrence.

This opening out of awareness becomes, often, an exemplary therapeutic moment. The central character may enact it, or the reader may come to it alone. At some point the constrictions of selfhood give way to an openness and objectivity of vision, as in Dorothea Brooke's looking through the window near the close of *Middlemarch* or Emma's recognition of her love for Knightley and her fear for the fate of that love in Jane Austen's novel. Iris Murdoch has frequently written about this therapeutic power of art and made it the subject of some of her novels. Her view of our normal condition stresses the blindness of our egoism. "We are anxiety-ridden animals. Our minds are continually active, fabricating an anxious, usually self-preoccupied, often falsifying *veil* which partially conceals the world." We are cured in part as we can "take a self-forgetful pleasure in the sheer alien pointless independent existence of animals, birds, stones and trees." So art, while it can easily fall into "self-consoling fantasy," is at its best "a thing totally opposed to selfish obsession."

Good art reveals what we are usually too selfish and too timid to recognize, the minute and absolutely random detail of the world, and reveals it together with a sense of unity and form. This form often seems to us mysterious because it resists the easy patterns of the fantasy, whereas there is nothing mysterious about the forms of bad art since they are the recognizable and familiar rat-runs of selfish daydream. Good art shows us how difficult it is to be objective by showing us how differently the world looks to an objective vision. We are presented with a truthful image of the human condition in a form which can be steadily contemplated; and indeed this is the only context in which many of us are capable of contemplating it at all. Art transcends selfish and obsessive limitations of personality and can enlarge the sensibility of its consumer. It is a kind of goodness by proxy. Most of all it exhibits to us the connection, in *human* beings, of clear realistic vision with compassion. The realism of a great artist is not a photographic realism, it is essentially both pity and justice. . . .

The great deaths of literature are few, but they show us with an exemplary clarity the way in which art invigorates us by a juxtaposition, almost an identification, of pointlessness and value. The death of Patroclus, the death of Cordelia, the death of Petya Rostov. All is vanity. The only thing which is of real importance is the ability to see it all clearly and respond to it justly, which is inseparable from virtue. Perhaps one of the greatest achievements of all is to join this sense of absolute mortality not to the tragic but to the comic. Shallow and Silence. Stefan Trofimovich Verhovensky.[8]

I am not so much interested in Miss Murdoch's view of the therapeutic power of all art as in the therapeutic process as it emerges within the novel. It emerges as form emerges and our identification shifts from character to creator. And it involves as well, to recall Kris's point, the assertion of the powers of the ego. This need not be, as in Miss Murdoch's analysis, a triumph over self-consoling fantasy; it may even be a triumph for such fantasy if our culture has imposed a distrust of self and a submissiveness to institutions that defrauds us. Stendhal's world of post-Napoleonic France and Italy is such a culture, and, while Stendhal is no uncritical proponent of instinct, his heroes gain their dignity in part from the jealous protection of their ego from culture. Philip Rieff has stated the problem very well:

To maintain the analytic attitude, in the everyday conduct of life, becomes the most subtle of all the efforts of the ego; it is tantamount to limiting the power of the super-ego and, therewith, of culture. The analytic attitude expresses a trained capacity for entertaining tentative opinions about the inner dictates of conscience, reserving the right even to disobey the law insofar as it originates outside the individual, in the name of a gospel of a freer impulse. Not that impulse alone is to be trusted. It is merely to be respected, and a limit recognized of the ability of any culture to transform the aggressiveness of impulse, by an alchemy of commitment, into the authority of law. Freud maintained a sober vision of man in the middle, a go-between, aware of the fact that he had little strength of his own, forever mediating between culture and instinct in an effort to gain some room for maneuver between those hostile powers. Maturity, according to Freud, lay in the trained capacity to keep the negotiations from breaking down.[9]

The point I would draw from Rieff to supplement or balance Miss Murdoch's is that the novel may favor either culture or instinct in its expressive function, or it may reach for that balance that Rieff and many literary critics as well have called maturity.

Finally, we must consider the expressive function of the novel that is evoked by the term myth. It is difficult to separate the descriptive from the evaluative force of that term, but in its modern use, drawn from the comparative study of religions and popular beliefs, it seems to mean a narrative (or set of narratives) that offers a large-scale interpretation of shared experience. It has, therefore, generalizing force as well as concreteness, and it builds community by creating the patterns by which men shape their lives. Whether myth wins full credence or not need hardly arise; its effect is like that of a common sacrament, whatever dogma may underlie it. The hero is each of us, or rather all of us; and the episodes of his history become a scripture in which we can read our nature.

So at least the "myth critic" might assert, and he may, like Northrop Frye, see all literature as the vestiges of primitive myths, displaced from their original form by secularization, fragmented as one aspect or another of the hero, or of the cycle of his myths, is given prominence. Behind each literary work, for Frye, looms the original, integral cycle of myths or at least a systematic vision of all literature as its reassembled fragments. Not all myth critics share Frye's love of system, but most see some allusive element in the reenactment of a mythical pattern in a novel. The reenactment is, as a rule, unconscious and imperfect. The myth is relived through necessity rather than deliberately performed. It is imperfectly embodied in modern circumstances and in limited actors (who may be heroic but scarcely heroes); and the author, if he is fully conscious of the myth he evokes, will probably be as much moved by an ironic sense of its somewhat frustrate survival as by a trust in its power to invest events with profound suggestions.

Implicit in all of this is the belief that both author and reader reach some deeper level of reality, or at least more spacious awareness, through the recognition of a mythical dimension in the novel. There is, for one thing, often an allusion to titanic figures and to those large bare spaces in which their drama was once played out. There is also a vast recession to the prehistorical time of myth and, along the way, through the various reenactments—the numerous Prometheus figures or earth goddesses, let us say—we can discern in history and literature. (If we stress the way in which myth exists in a time other than historical, we can imagine a sheer transcendence of time as we know it.) Corresponding to the long recession in time there may be a sense of deep descent into the most elementary feelings of man, as recorded in those narratives which retain a recognizable archaic identity through all their later adaptations.

If this view of myth has any validity, it could explain the revelatory power the novel sometimes seems to achieve—revelatory of the mysterious forces within man through myths in which they were first and most forcefully projected. Such revelation is tied to what I have called therapy. The myths seem to awaken and even to endorse primitive impulses, that is, to invite regression and to celebrate instinct. Much of the recent celebration of myth sees it a necessary corrective to the costly repressions and featureless attenuation of feeling and of identity that civilization has exacted. The feelings, critics would claim, need to recover their elemental grandeur; it is their reality that we have neglected. To restore our awareness of them may lead once more to a reality principle but on better terms.

I have presented the case for myth criticism in as neutral a way as I could, but some problems must be raised. Critics often imply that the recognition of myth in a novel confers power and complexity. This is doubtful. In contrast, the appeal to myth often makes for distention and rhetorical coercion, a vehement insistence upon more than the author's imagination can realize. One must recognize that it is an ironic and self-conscious use that is made of myth by novelists of great stature—Mann, Joyce, and Gide come at once to mind. Further problems arise when the work makes no direct allusion to myth but is credited with mythical power by enthusiastic critics. And where it does make direct allusion, is that allusion an evocation of a full myth or is it similar to many other allusions, historical or literary, that call up exemplary figures in particular aspects? Is George Eliot's evocation of Saint Theresa in the Prelude to *Middlemarch* a reference to myth or history? Does not the novelist need, in some measure, to re-create the myth if he is to make full use of it?

One can recognize in certain novelists a tendency to surround their heroes with mystery and to make them loom larger in the mists of surmise. If this is accompanied by the use of a somewhat primitive setting, as in Conrad's use of Patusan in *Lord Jim,* it may have the effect of mythicizing the central character. In the case of the "Jim-myth," the process of generalizing, of making Jim a representative man and his case a universal predicament, is conducted by Marlow; one might even say that Marlow mythicizes Jim more than Conrad does. One might, but in fact Conrad shows similar tendencies elsewhere and even in the opening chapters that precede Marlow's narration in this novel. Still, to be a myth-maker is to adopt a technique which is in itself allusive, and to see a myth in the process of creation is hardly to respond to myth in the full sense that many critics propose.

The third group of functions may be called cognitive; they include all the ways in which the novel provides knowledge, informs us or gives us new insight into the world about us. In the simplest sense, the novel often provides a record of how people live. We read novels to learn about the career of a scientist, the customs of a fishing village, the manners of a bygone age. The novel may set out to be documentary, or it may become a document. The kind of record it provides will vary in degree and kind of ordering. Novels may be profuse in details of the surfaces of life, acute in fixing social attitudes, sometimes quite theoretical in analyzing what they represent. In the last case the narrative moves toward illustration and example, offering an instance of general principles that may be explicitly stated or at least strongly implied. One thinks of those novels which fuse socialist realism with Marxist analysis; but more often such novels are transparently allegorical.

How committed the author himself may be to a hypothesis, or how conscious of one, does not matter. Any novel can provide the reader with a sense of experiment, of regarding his experience under a certain aspect, of trying out a set of values or a new archetype. I have not tried to distinguish between a new way of seeing and a new way of judging. Each tends to imply the other. The testing of values may encourage a more metaphorical or symbolic technique. One thinks of the satiric works that strip away all those elements that make conduct plausible, or that magnify latent motives by making them deliberate. One gets a mechanized world, without the confusions and pretexts of actual society, where certain motives can be seen in bold clarity. Is there really anything more, the satirist may ask. Isn't this what it really amounts to? And can you bear to face it without disguise?

Whether the governing spirit is satirical or sympathetic, whether the novel's form is documentary or symbolic, the shaping of experience will move toward what might be called a model. The value of the model is that it finds a manageable scale or form. It encloses a section or isolates a dimension of reality upon which we wish to concentrate our attention, and it frees it of distracting irrelevance. In the scale model of a street, for example, we may include a typical number of cars and pedestrians moving in normal patterns, but we are primarily interested in the pattern of traffic flow rather than the dress of the people or the make of their cars. Like the game, the model is highly conventional and operates according to a scale and to laws of its own. But its end is to study the reality it represents and perhaps to manipulate it experimentally.

Satiric models tend to exhibit the neglect of a significant value. They are dystopias, presenting as intention and as system the obliviousness or muddle of conventional societies. Utopias, or the green worlds of pastoral romance and comedy, are societies which release in turn natural powers that man rarely allows himself to enjoy in conventional society. But all novels serve in some measure as a testing of values, an exploration of what their realization costs or confers. Any novel tends to reduce the pluralism of values that the world offers and to concentrate upon a few. In the simplest fiction, the values at stake are two, and they stand in simple opposition. It creates characters who are significantly related to each other by simple contrast or likeness. In complex fictions, we deal with what Ludwig Wittgenstein calls family resemblances. Characters bear asymmetrical relationships to each other. If Emma Woodhouse resembles Mrs. Elton in certain respects, she resembles Frank Churchill in others, and all three of these characters are tied together by resemblances like members of a family. It may be the nose that constitutes the resemblance in one case and the eyes in another. Characters do not form simple uniform classes, for what they have in common is more elusive, and less easily extricated from their individuality. They embody common values, but they embody them in different ways and to different degrees. The difficulty of discovering the values of the novel is like the difficulty of following the story. In both cases, the difficulties are created by elements that are seemingly opaque or irrelevant.

To discern those principles which govern the novelist's creation of a set of asymmetrical characters requires delicacy and tact, almost as much as governed the creation in the first place. For the complexity of relationships corresponds precisely to the complexity of the principles that the novelist, however consciously, has embodied in them. One finds oneself saying, "not this, but somewhat more like that," "not quite, but almost," "in this respect but not in that." If one asks whether such models can be said truly to simplify what they present, the answer must lie in the very process of deliberation they impose. We have been given the weights and quantities, as it were, by which to calculate. That we can never reach a precise sum or balance is to be expected. That we can become aware of where such a balance might lie, that all of the structure may be imagined in relation to this balance, is itself a striking simplification. We have simplified certain elements in order to get with precision at the peculiar complexity that, in a given novel, most matters.

Models may exist on different scales within the novel that is itself a model for the outward reality. In Dickens's *Little Dorrit* the Marshalsea prison is a self-contained world with its own social structure. It proves to be the counterpart of the larger social world, the "superior sort of Marshalsea" that William Dorrit's family enters upon his release. Within the novel are other small models of self-imprisonment: the Circumlocution Office, with its wholehearted dedication to the program of How Not To Do It; the tutelage in respectability under Mrs. General; Mr. Merdle's captivity by the Chief Butler. If each reinforces the next, it does so in a different key, or scale, or context; the common relationships that each of these models embodies are extended in scope but also in meaning as they are fused into the one large model that is the novel itself.

Can we call such models metaphors? The models of science, as Max Black observes, have much in common with metaphors. "They, too, bring about a wedding of disparate subjects, by a distinctive operation of transfer of the *implications* of relatively well-organized cognitive fields. And as with other weddings, their outcomes are unpredictable." The use of a model may "help us to notice what otherwise would be overlooked, to shift the relative emphasis attached to details—in short, to *see new connections.*" We may wish to distinguish theoretical models that are purged of their "negative analogy" and can become fully accurate accounts of real operations rather than mere analogues. But, in fact, as Black points out, there "is no such thing as a perfectly faithful model; only by being unfaithful in *some* respect can a model represent its original." And as with all representations, "there are underlying conventions of interpretation—correct ways for 'reading' the model."

Yet the operational model—whether it is a scale or a relational model—exists for the sake of studying what it represents. It is "designed to serve a purpose, to be a means to some end. It is to show how the ship looks, or how the machine will work, or what law governs the interplay of parts in the original; the model is intended to be enjoyed for its own sake only in the limiting case where the hobbyist indulges a harmless fetishism." [10] In the case of the literary model it is precisely that kind of play which may be indulged, just as we find the metaphorical action of poetry generating images that are intrinsically interesting. In novels the model may achieve the roundness of a fictional "world," with its own coherence, and with a rich enough surface to allow one to enter into it imaginatively without needing to be aware of its application or its metaphorical status. We may enjoy it as vicarious experience, we may try to come to terms with it as we might play a game. To the extent that it is like reality but tellingly different from it (as a model must be), it may offer just that playlike release of dislocation into a simplified order. And we enjoy the pleasure of being for a while someone of supremely demanding impulse who is securely locked into a structure, like Alice's Red Queen. While the novel may serve many of the functions Black attributes to the model, it serves others as well; and each delimits the adequacy with which others can be met.

To discuss the novel as model calls attention to its representation of the actual and to its formalization of it, but neglects the movement of narrative. To recover this we must turn, as critics have increasingly done, to the analogy with historical narrative. Perhaps the boldest analogy has been drawn by the philosopher W. B. Gallie, who analyzes the structure of histories by considering what it means to follow a story. Gallie opposes that view of history which sees its proper function as formulating laws by which actual events can be predicted and therefore explained. Such a view of history would transform it into a social science whose distinctive property would be the pastness of its subject matter; it would free history of its concern with the temporal, for the laws to be formulated would make at most incidental reference to time (as in Boyle's law of gases). Gallie, like other historical narrativists, sees history as having a radically different structure: it is a "species of the genus Story," and its narrative form is essential to its mode of explanation. The conclusion of a story is "not something that can be deduced or predicted," and the sense of following a story "is of an altogether different kind from the sense of following an argument so that we see that its conclusion *follows.*"

Gallie's account of followability stresses the presence of contingencies—"through or across" which we follow the story—and the acceptability of its events rather than their necessity or causal chain. The acceptability of events will depend upon their providing "some indication of the kind of event or context which occasioned or evoked," or at least made possible, succeeding events. This "main bond of logical continuity" leads toward the conclusion, which we cannot predict but which ("often without being even vaguely foreseen") "guides our interest almost from the start." Gallie compares following a story with following a game; in both "we accept contingency after contingency as so many openings up of yet other possible routes towards the required although as yet undisclosed conclusion. In the case of a story, where there are no definite rules to help us decide what contingencies can be accepted into it, it is up to the writer to vindicate his acceptance of a given contingency in terms of the subsequent, sufficiently continuous, development of his story." [11]

Gallie's strong emphasis on the following of a story has been criticized by Louis Mink, who distinguishes sharply between following and *having followed* a story. While "experiences come to us *seriatim* in a stream of transience" they "must be capable of being held together in a single image . . . in order for us to be aware of transience at all." This "thinking together in a single act" Mink calls comprehension. "To comprehend temporal succession means to think of it in both directions at once, and then time is no longer the river which bears us along but a river in aerial view, upstream and downstream seen in a single survey." What Mink does is to transform the process of temporal succession into one of spatial comprehension; "in the understanding of a narrative the thought of temporal succession as such vanishes—or perhaps, one might say, remains like the smile of the Cheshire Cat." [12] Mink seems to me to be surrendering the narrativist position altogether in such a case. True, he reduces narrative to configuration rather than to the deductive application of general laws, but history becomes for him like the elaborate "spatial" pattern of images we may extract from a novel at the sacrifice of its process of unfolding. We are back to the model, but we have lost the narrative.

Mink overemphasizes the fact that Gallie's open conclusion is not available to the historian who knows how things come out or to the reader who has been through a novel before. It is true that we may know the actual conclusion of a series of events and will not be drawn on by suspense; yet it is clear that if we cannot suppress such knowledge we can depress its force. It is too simplistic a view of the reading process to say that we must either know the end or be moved by curiosity to discover it, for we can recover the sense of surprise with which we meet each new contingency and, even more, see how it is absorbed into a more complex pattern of continuity. Relieved of the urgency of sheer curiosity, we may attend all the more to the emergence of pattern. As Gallie observes, we may at moments feel we *are* the hero, through full identification, and at other moments become the "detached inactive observer." It is not, as he puts it, "any subordination of the observer's standpoint to that of the agent, but rather an unusually rapid movement and interplay between the two standpoints that characterises our appreciation of the story's development." [13]

The last phrase is telling: we are not simply following the story but appreciating its development. We have moved to some degree from identification with characters to what Kris calls identification with the author, and it is this movement I have discussed as a therapeutic function of the novel. Mink makes a similar point about the relation of narrative to life. "Life has no beginnings, middles, or ends; there are meetings, but the start of an affair belongs to the story we tell ourselves later, and there are partings, but final partings only in the story." [14] Or, in other terms, the shaping of experience frees it of immediacy as it gives it form; we move from immersion to reflection, from temporal anxiety to spatial comprehension, from the attitude of an agent to the attitude of an understanding observer or creator. This process has begun within the narrative itself. As the story progresses, the options a character may take become fewer, the patterns of continuity become clearer, the conclusion seems ready to emerge. The interplay between standpoints begins to favor the detached one, unless in fact the hero we follow reaches that standpoint, too, and we share it with him.

But this does not exhaust the problematic relation of the novel to historical narrative. One can say of the latter that for the most part the author must designate his subject initially. Its limits may not be clear, and the themes that govern the account will emerge only gradually; but there is, in a work that is avowedly expository and tied to the factual, an explicit initial commitment, and the historian must show or argue, as he progresses, the relevance of what he includes. It is this subject that becomes the figure in his design, emerging from a ground of contingencies that do not trouble us so long as they provide the figure with definition and extension. It is only when such contingencies disturb the figure itself and create a new figure–ground relationship that they become significant contingencies, and earn our full attention.

In the novel the subject remains far more open. The reader starts with the assumption that a pattern of significance will emerge; this is, so to speak, one of the terms upon which the institution of the novel rests. The material adduced is chosen by the author with this end in view; it seldom, therefore, provides the resistance of historical materials. The consequent ordering should, as a result, be fuller and more intense. As in historical narrative, there are figure-ground relationships, and the inevitable contingencies and irrelevancies that form the ground will be accepted so long as they provide occasions for the figure to maintain itself or develop. The comparatively high degree of coherence the novel promises may lend more expectation that each element—even those that normally constitute ground—will emerge as significant, and as a rule a greater proportion will, many having been created with just such a function in mind. The elements of the novel are, one might say, saturated with purposiveness as true historical materials cannot be. Accordingly, the reader is ready to accept a greater measure of apparent irrelevancy and of discontinuity and is prepared to wait for implicit connectedness to be revealed in the process of unfolding. Because of the greater openness of subject and form and the greater coherence that emerges in the narrative, the narrative process may become more crucial than in history, less guided by expository suggestion and explicit assertion of pattern. The presentiment of the conclusion becomes, as Gallie indicates, more magnetic for being held off and for only gradually emerging.

The more the novelist tries to create the surface density and complexity of actual experience, the more he will create detail that has the resistance of historical fact. Some of the detail may be actual historical event or literal and identifiable setting; that may extend to the customs and manners of a given segment of society. These become limits within which the novelist must work, and they are all the more readily accepted as ground by the reader, for, as Gallie observes, it is "in contrast to the generally recognised realm of predictable uniformities that the unpredictable developments of a story stand out, as worth making a story of, and as worth following." [15] I should prefer to alter terms somewhat, for the very contingency of everyday life is predictably unpredictable and readily accepted as the ground of those significant contingencies that fully engage the figures and alter their nature. The full significance of the predictably unpredictable may be established in retrospect, as when Fielding makes clear, once we know the identity of Mrs. Waters, how adroitly he managed the casual comings and goings at Upton so as to prevent her being seen (and thus identified) by Partridge.

The novel often admits contingencies that make sense in symbolic terms. When Jacky Bast turns out, in Forster's *Howards End,* to have been Mr. Wilcox's mistress, this has a moral aptness that makes it persuasive, and the self-concious artifice of Forster's narrative provides us with a key of expectation that makes acceptance complete. In a novel whose central phrase is "Only connect," such a connection is precisely the sort that needs to be made; and it is only Mr. Wilcox who finds it difficult to face. There are, of course, novels much more fully controlled by such symbolic relationships or "magic" causality than Forster's, and such novels encourage the comparison that Frank Kermode has chosen to draw with a theological rather than secular history—with a history that, through such correspondences as typology and through a strong teleological vision of first and last things, can overcome the resistance of historical fact and make its materials as malleable as the novelist's. The chief resistance Kermode treats is the necessary postponement of promised apocalypse, when historical fact fails the teleological pattern imposed upon it and requires that the teleological narrative be revised so as to accommodate a new ending. In other ways the divine historical narrative resembles the fictions of the novelist, saturated as they are with purposiveness, ready to trace surprising connectedness, and eventuating in a completed pattern such as only story (rather than history) can provide.

What I have been charting might be called the "overdetermination" of the form of the novel. Freud uses the term in his analysis of dreams to show how one manifest or surface meaning can express several separate wishes or latent meanings. This is achieved by condensation, by that formation of composite images, like verbal puns, that accommodate several meanings. But overdetermination works no less in jokes and, in fact, in all our behavior. Whatever choices we make will represent the convergence or resultant of several forces: our rational estimate of the future, our sense of what we owe to ourselves in the way of consistency of purpose, our latent and unacknowledged impulses. Some of these forces may be overwhelmed by the urgency of others, for the forces will inevitably vary in power for each act.

When we try to explain our choice we may resort to a principle of complementarity, seeing the action as the result of one force or another; for each will serve to account for it. But this kind of explanation often proves inadequate, for each force more or less subtly dislocates or subdues the others, and the full explanation requires an awareness of all. One of the dangers of enthusiastic psychoanalytic explanation of literary works is that the action of latent impulses may be traced without sufficient regard for the structure which shapes their expression and without whose protection they might remain suppressed. On the other hand, to trace the cognitive structure of a work—its pattern of meanings—will explain the occasion for the psychological expression but may not be able to estimate its force; and it is this difficulty that, with whatever success, myth criticism often tries to meet. Nor do most of our critical approaches do justice to the element of play in fiction except in those works that insist upon it—Nabokov and Borges come to mind among recent authors of such works, as Sterne does among earlier—or perhaps in the rather isolated treatment of the comic.

I have no illusions that calling attention to the multiple functions of the novel will solve any problems of interpretation. If anything, it will create new ones. If it achieves any end, that may be to make us more fully aware of the structure of novels. We tend, for good reason, to concentrate upon the cognitive functions of the work, to extract from it a structure of meanings. We tend at times to be foolishly rigorous in our search for meaning, and the result is the kind of bathetic rhetoric of overinterpretation, of forced profundities and of evangelical platitudes (each church, including those that favor the inner light, having its own). In part, I think, this is trying to make our statement of the meaning suggest what we cannot or do not directly treat: the other functions that are served in the structure. It is true that any of these functions, if it is explored deeply enough, leads us to the others; but we had better know what we are doing. Clearly, a discussion of a Henry James novel as game could be as tedious and joyless as any other, but there is value in recognizing to the full the contrivances and artifice, the manipulation of evidence and the control of disclosure, in order to recognize not merely the meaning that is ultimately disclosed but (what is really part of that meaning) the processes by which meaning is reached and the resistances to it that must be overcome.

What I am most eager to make clear is the artifice of narration, the fictional contract that binds reader and author. No general statement can specify the terms of the contract that is drawn, as it were, for each novel. All one can provide is one of those forms, such as we can buy at a stationer's, that observes the general legal procedures in its letterpress and leaves large blanks to be filled in by the participants. For to recognize the artifice of narration is not to divorce it from experience but to restore a fuller sense of the omnipresence of art and convention in all our experience. The

novel is about life. I would be ready to deny its ultimate autonomy, if I could even imagine what that would mean; but I should
be equally ready to insist upon the institutions that govern our
experience of life, that give it form and make for our comprehension.

NOTES

1. John R. Searle, *Speech Acts: An Essay in the Philosophy of Language* (Cambridge, 1969), pp. 50 ff.

2. Richard Wollheim, *Art and Its Objects* (New York, 1968), sec. 13.

3. Kenneth Clark, *Looking at Pictures* (London, 1960), p. 197.

4. Roger Caillois, *Man, Play, and Games* (1958), trans. Meyer Barash (London,
1962), pp. 27–29.

5. Raymond Williams, *Culture and Society 1780–1950* (Penguin Ed., 1963), pp.
114–15.

6. Ernst Kris, *Psychoanalytic Explorations in Art* (New York, 1952), pp. 45–46,
52, 63.

7. Kris, pp. 56, 58–59.

8. Iris Murdoch, *The Sovereignty of the Good* (London, 1970), pp. 84–87.

9. Philip Rieff, *The Triumph of the Therapeutic* (New York, 1965), p. 31.

10. Max Black, *Models and Metaphors: Studies in Language and Philosophy*
(Ithaca, N.Y., 1962), pp. 237, 220.

11. W. B. Gallie, *Philosophy and the Historical Understanding* (London, 1964),
pp. 24, 28, 40.

12. Louis O. Mink, "History and Fiction as Modes of Comprehension," *New
Literary History*, 1 (1969–70), 547, 554–55.

13. Gallie, pp. 47–48.

14. Mink, p. 557.

15. Gallie, p. 26.

John Crowe Ransom's Theory of Poetry

RENÉ WELLEK

In "Philosophy and Postwar American Criticism" (1962, reprinted in *Concepts of Criticism,* New Haven, 1963), I tried to relate the main contemporary American critics to their explicit or implicit philosophical backgrounds. I classed Ransom confidently with Bergsonism, stressing his isolation among the New Critics who could be called rather Coleridgeans. Today, on second thought, after reexamining Ransom's books and reading many of his scattered uncollected writings for the first time, I have come to the conclusion that this alignment must be modified and his position defined differently.[1]

It is true that Ransom sympathizes with Bergson's attack on scientific abstraction (*GT,* 219),[2] with his defense of qualities (*GT,* 259), with his rejection of psychophysics (*GT,* 229), and that in a review of Wyndham Lewis's *Time and Western Man* (*SR,* 37 [1929], esp. 358–59) Ransom defends Bergson's idea of flux and of nature's invincible contingency. But Ransom wanted to have Bergson go much further: "I am sorry to say that Bergson has not been interested in defending the particularity of physical objects. He has devoted himself to defending the particularity of living organisms and of states of mind." He might, continues Ransom out-Bergsoning Bergson, "just as well have saved the inorganic objects, too." For "a thing is of inexhaustible variety and its concrete energy will never submit to determination. . . . The things too are whole and free" (*GT,* 218–19).

This is Ransom's primary insight, his point of departure both as a philosopher and aesthetician. The world is a loose assembly of objects, particular, individual, concrete, dense, but also contingent, heterogeneous, and diffuse. With obsessive frequency Ransom varies this one motif: "A real thing is a bundle of complementary qualities and an inexhaustible particularity" (*SR*, 37, [1929], 361). "The object appears to us as a dense area of contingency, that is concretion" (*KR*, 7 [1945], 284). The world has body, is made of objects which have "a qualitative density, or value-density" (*NC*, 293).

At a crucial point of *The World's Body* Ransom uses the German word, *Dinglichkeit*, which he translates as "thinginess" (*WB*, 121, 124), for this primary insight. It is a most unusual term, which points to a German source. It does not figure in any German dictionary with the single exception of Grimm's *Wörterbuch*. A word list dating from 1482 translates it *entitas, Wesentlichkeit,* a sense which would be about the opposite from Ransom's. The term does not occur in Kant, Schelling, or Schopenhauer. Hegel uses *Dingheit* in *Die Phänomenologie des Geistes* (ed. Georg Lasson [Leipzig, 1928], pp. 91–92, 145, 257, 264, 407) and so does Heidegger in his famous lecture on "Das Ding" (1950, in *Vorträge und Aufsätze* [Pfullingen, 1954], II, 42–43). As far as I have been able to ascertain, Nietzsche first uses *Dinglichkeit* in *Götzendämmerung* (1889) in the context of a discussion of Heraclitus who, Nietzsche tells us, recognized "die Lüge der Einheit, die Lüge der Dinglichkeit, der Substanz, der Dauer" (*Werke* [Leipzig, 1919], VIII, 77). It occurs again in an aphorism included in the posthumous miscellany *Der Wille zur Macht* (1901). Nietzsche asserts there: "Wir haben nur nach dem Vorbilde des Subjekts die Dinglichkeit erfunden und in den Sensationen-Wirrwarr hineininterpretiert" (*Werke,* XVI, 55). Thomas Mann, an avid reader of Nietzsche, uses it again in *Der Zauberberg* (1924). Mynheer Peeperkorn is said to be averse to theoretical discussion: "Peeperkorns Verlangen nach Dinglichkeit entsprang aus anderen Gründen" ([Stockholm, 1966], p. 820). Here the pejorative use in Nietzsche takes on a more favorable turn, remote, however, from a clearly philosophical use. The passage in Johannes Volkelt's *System der Aesthetik* ([Munich, 1925], III, 421) in which he contrasts poetry and painting with architecture and music according to "Dinglichkeit und Undinglichkeit des Gehaltes" is also different. Husserl's term is closest to Ransom when in 1907 he gave a whole lecture course on the "thing" and called his theme in a notebook "Versuch einer Phänomenologie der Dinglichkeit und insbesondere der Räumlichkeit," but this entry was not printed until 1950 (see Walter Bienel, "Einleitung," in *Die Idee der Phänomenologie* [The Hague, 1950], p. xi). Recently, presumably under the influence of phenomenology, *Dinglichkeit* has become common in German philosophical and critical writing, e.g. Käte Hamburger, in her *Philosophie der Dichter* (Stuttgart, 1966), discussing Rilke uses the word as much as four times on a page (p. 202). Thus it seems possible that Ransom invented the term himself, forming it on the analogy of such words as *Zärtlichkeit, Männlichkeit,* and so on, to judge from a letter (dated October 29, 1971) which he wrote me in answer to an inquiry about the word's source.

But why did Ransom make up or pick up a German term? He seems not to have been aware of the great role which "thing" played in the works of two contemporary poets: in Rilke, who celebrated things in his speech on Rodin (1907) and wrote a whole series of famous *Dinggedichte;* and, more recently, in Francis Ponge, who since *Parti pris des choses* (1942) writes his poems about things including pebbles and soap. Sartre, in an essay on Ponge, "L'Homme et les choses" (1944, in *Situations* I [Paris, 1947], 245–93), developed the theme in terms of Husserlian phenomenology.

Ransom's *Dinglichkeit* must have been inspired by his study of German philosophy: of Kant, Hegel, and Schopenhauer. Kant particularly is invoked as "his mentor" (*PE*, 159), and he includes himself among "Kantians" (*PE*, 185). This seems puzzling, as he had realized very early that Kant is a "rationalist of the sternest order" (*GT*, 274). Ransom could not approve either his view of religion (*GT*, 78) or his view of "sentiment as moral weakness" (*WB*, 219), though recently Ransom agreed with Kant "not daring to make images of the Unknown God" (*So R*, NS 4 [1968], 596). Kant, quite differently from Ransom, had changed the dogmatic concept of thing to a purely logical system of relations and conditions of knowledge. The explanation of Ransom's "Kantianism" must be sought not in any philosophical allegiance but in Kant's aesthetics.

In spite of his complaint against Bergson's failure to defend the freedom of inanimate objects, the world of things is for Ransom not only a world of sticks and stones but of "precious objects," objects beyond price, anything to which our affective life is attached: father and mother, husband or wife, child, friend; one's own house, but also the sun and moon, sky, and sea; and even such objects as one's nation, church, God, business, "causes," and institutions (*KR*, 9 [1947], 643). The love of a shabby old place, an old horse, or an old wife, of anything which is cherished irrationally, "exempted from the fair or market valuation" (*WB*, 213), constitutes this world of precious objects.

Ransom calls a knowledge of this world of things "ontology," in a sense very different from the historical meaning of the term which was invented by the Calvinist theologian Rudolf Goclenius (1547–1628) and adopted by Christian Wolff. Wolff, the dominant German philosopher before Kant, understood ontology to mean the study of the nature of the real in abstraction from its specific embodiments, in contrast to cosmology and psychology. Ontology is concerned with the general formal characteristics or categories— a conception which is almost the opposite of Ransom's concern with the qualitative particularity of the world. Kant substituted "the modest name of Analytic of pure understanding for the proud name of ontology" (*Kritik der reinen Vernunft*, B 303) and demolished the so-called ontological argument for the existence of God.

In Ransom "ontology" is often used as a synonym for any concern with actual reality. The term is grossly misunderstood if it is equated with "aesthetic" or "formalist." Ontology, on the contrary, is knowledge of Being, which is not to be understood as the highest abstraction and not at all in the sense of existentialist thought, but as the assembly of real things, as "nature." One must admit that in the *New Criticism* Ransom uses the term in almost any combination, often very loosely. There is "ontological speculation" (327), "consideration" (318), "interest" (302), "principles" (293), "argument" (290), "question" (288), "law" (327), "efficacy" (336), "intimations" (330), "brief" (331), "sense" (331, 335), "triumph" (333), "competence" (333), "density" (335), and possibly more. Still, in many cases "ontological" means Ransom's conceptions of particular being, as when he tells us that science has no "realistic ontology" (*NC,* 80).

All this amounts to a conception of a pluralistic universe, realistic rather than Platonic and idealistic (*IC,* 124). Ransom speaks of his "Platonic and metaphysical days" as a thing of the past (*KR,* 5 [1943], 280) and shows considerable sympathy with naturalistic points of view: "naturalism" in a biological sense, as shown by his interest in Freud, dating back as far as 1924 (a review of *Beyond the Pleasure Principle,* in *Sat R,* October 4, 1924, 161–62), in Dewey and Santayana. A review of Maritain's *Dream of Descartes* says expressly, "Of religion one is obliged to think that we need a better anthropology, a better psychology, to define this kind of experience and accord to it its rights—not a more ingenious metaphysics." He even concludes, "It does not seem immoderate to say that there is no hope of understanding religion unless it can receive a modern and therefore a secular description" (*SR,* 54 [1946], 154, 156).

Thus Ransom's surprising declaration of being a Kantian is by no means an endorsement of idealism. Ransom expressly disapproves of "the hole of subjectivism" (*So R,* 7 [1942], 534). He characterizes Coleridge as "a not always intelligible adapter of German idealism, cloudy and rhetorical and insistently metaphysical" (*WB,* 163). He considers Hegel "Plato's pious and dutiful successor" (*LC,* 33), upholder of "an extravagant monism" (*KR,* 6 [1944], 119), and dismisses the dialectics as mere "wordplay" (*KR,* 6 [1944], 117). The admiration for Kant seems largely limited to the aesthetics "which I took, and take, to be of the highest human authority" (*So R,* NS 4 [1968], 587), and thus to the *Critique of Judgment,* "the foundation of systematic aesthetics" (*LC,* 31), which is interpreted mainly as an exposition and defense of two ideas Ransom embraces as his own. Kant is seen in contrast to Hegel as a defender of "natural beauty" (*PE,* 171) whose view of nature as "free and purposive" supports Ransom's feeling that the natural world is our home. Kant also teaches that "the meaning of beauty is an effect that external nature accomplishes, not man" (*KR,* 26 [1964], 254). He also answers the question of what is poetry? "Kant's view is simple, and for all except the new 'symbolist' critics (who covet for poetry a 'creativity' upon which there are to be no limits) it will be adequate: Poetry is the representation of natural beauty" (PE, 171). Thus Ransom can praise Wallace Stevens as "a nature poet according to Kant," "a very good Kantian" (KR, 26 [1964], 239, 231). One other idea struck Ransom in the *Critique of Judgment*, the view that "it did not matter to poetry whether the world it set up has real existence or was only imaginary" (SR, 74 [1966], 399) or that "the aesthetic judgment is not concerned with the existence or non-existence of the object" (WB, 131). Kant thus appears as "the most radical and ultimate spokesman for poetry that we have had" (PE, 169).

Kant is thus called upon to authorize a very old theory of poetry: a version of mimesis. The poet presents or represents the world of objects and thus makes us know it. The poet makes this knowledge explicit in a work of art (WB, 231), articulates what may have remained inarticulate. He makes us realize the world, brings home to us what we may have known either dimly or abstractly. The poet does not impose an alien, superior mind on an inert world, but he discovers and liberates what had been hidden in the objects. This knowledge of the poet obviously implies a claim for the truth of poetry. Ransom speaks of the "cognitive integrity—the truthfulness of poetry" and asserts that poetry has "more truth than science cares to tell" (NC, 93) and that poetry at least "seeks truth" (WB, 155).

This truth of poetry is insistently set off against the truth of science. As early as 1923 Ransom told us that art "fishes out of the stream what would become the dead abstraction of science, but catches it still alive" (*Literary Review* of the *New York Evening Post*, July 14, 1923) and in 1929 he spoke of works of art as "psychic exercises which are just so many rebellions against science" (*Sat R*, September 14, 1929, p. 125). Most strikingly, in a footnote tucked away in *The World's Body*, the conflict of art and science is put into a historical perspective. "In all human history the dualism between science and art widens continually by reason of the aggressions of science. As science more and more completely reduces the world to its types and forms, art, replying, must invest it again with body" (*WB*, 198*n*). Art, in a paradoxical reversal of ordinarily assumed chronology, is "considered late, post-scientific, rebellious against science. . . . Back of art, there is the embittered artist, whose vision of the real has been systematically impaired under the intimidations of scientific instruction" (*SR*, 37 [1929], 362). Art "comes after science." It "attempts to restore the body which science has emptied." Quoting a simple observation: "the trees stood up against the sky" Ransom argues that "the line, and the poem have improvised a successful immunity which preserves the object, a 'total situation,' from suffering siege and reduction" by science (*KR*, 1 [1939], 198–99).

Ransom conceives of science almost always as utilitarian, practical, applied, identical with technology. The speculative scientist is never considered. "Science," he says, "belongs to the economic impulse and does not free the spirit" (*WB*, 49). Art differs in being disinterested, an idea known mainly in the Kantian formula of *interesseloses Wohlgefallen,* which Ransom, however, quotes several times in Schopenhauer's version: "Art is knowledge without desire" (*GT*, 315; *WB*, 45, 325; *IC*, 103), while he alludes to Kant's teaching only once (*WB*, 307). Obviously he preferred Schopenhauer's "knowledge" to Kant's "satisfaction." The odd reversal of the succession of art to science can be defended by extending the concept of science to include any and all practical activities.

How does Ransom concretely envisage this special knowledge conveyed by poetry? How, in practice, is this investing of the world with body to be accomplished by poetry? Sometimes he draws distinctions between the assertions poets make. They either observe the world as particularity when they say something as simple as "the trees stood up against the sky." Or they animate the inanimate; they commit what Ruskin called "the pathetic fallacy"—no fallacy to Ransom—or they even animate "abstract qualities" (*WB*, 158–59). At other times Ransom describes the process of knowing as a series of identifications: "Images are perceptions, and perceptions are assertions; perceptions are as true and as false as propositions." He appeals to the "Neo-Hegelians" from whom "he received his fullest understanding of what is implied in a perception" (*WB*, 156–57). As far as I could discover, there is no

authority for the statement that "perception *is* assertion" in either
Green or Bosanquet, while Bradley does teach that simple assertions about our feelings (e.g. "this hurts, I am hot") imply an
analytic judgment of sense. But whatever Ransom's exact source
may be, the progression—images, perceptions, assertions, propositions—allows him to argue for the truth of poetry, for poetry as a
true knowledge of the world. Knowledge, we could object, must
mean here something like "realization," "awareness," as when we
say, "You don't really know what it is like before you have lived
through it." It is the function assigned to poetry by the Russian
formalists or by Max Eastman who, differently from Ransom, uses
realization or awareness to relegate poetry to a lowly place below
science. While one can hardly refuse the use of the term "knowledge" in Ransom's sense, it will not satisfy those who have a more
systematic, rational, and coherent ideal of truth in mind.

But what is meant by "investing with body," "restoring the concrete world," or in an alternate phrase "recovering the denser and
more refractory original world which we know loosely through
our perceptions and memories" (*NC,* 281)? These transactions
seem to reduce poetry to the humble function of somehow tighten-
ing or sharpening our everyday perceptions, of reminding us of
the actual world of manifold qualities. They seem to make poetry
a dispensable luxury for the man of vivid perceptions and acute
awareness.

Greater claims for poetry are made intermittently. Whimsically,
Ransom can draw on the old microcosm-macrocosm parallel. "Is it
not splendid if it is true that a small book of small poems contains
just so many miniature or local editions of the cosmos itself, the
whole bookful being of a size to go into a coat pocket, and any one
of them of a size to go into a pocket of the brain?" (*Texas Quarterly,* 9 [1966], 191). Elsewhere an appeal is made to Wordsworth's
"spots of time" and the "timeless moment" of Eliot's *Four Quar-
tets,* to an epiphany which establishes a communion with God. It
is an aesthetic moment which "seemed to bring us into the presence of the unknown God who gave us the sense of beauty and
caused beauty to appear in his creation, establishing at least a

moment of communion." "Beauty," says Ransom referring to his earlier views," ranked even above morality, and was our highest natural faculty" (*So R*, N.S. 4 [1968], 587–88).

In an unargued transition Ransom shifts the function of poetry from the display, knowledge, and restoration of the real world or from a sudden contact with the supernatural to an adoration and glorification of this world. Art celebrates the concrete, the highly sensible (*GT*, 22). The poet's piety is "natural piety." "In romantic art"—and Ransom prefers it to classical art, differing from his fellow-critics—"we revel in the particularity of things, and feel joy of restoration after an estrangement from nature. The experience is vain and aimless for practical purposes. But it answers to a deep need within us. It exercises that impulse of natural piety which requires of us that our life should be in loving *rapport* with the environment" (*Sat R*, September 14, [1929], p. 127). "The poet's faith, I should say, is that this is 'the best of all possible worlds' " (*PE*, 183). Poetry is not only festal, not merely a celebration of the beauty of nature but also, in a slight contradiction, nostalgic, commemorative, "in the past tense," even the pluperfect (*WB*, 250). Once it is conceived as yearning for the Lost Paradise. "The little world [poetry] sets up is a little version of our natural world in its original dignity, not the laborious world of affairs. Indeed, the little world is the imitation of our ancient Paradise, when we inhabited it in innocence" (*PE*, 100).

The religious implications and motives are obvious in the late passages as they are in the early book *God without Thunder*. I would not want to decide how they can be reconciled with the strong naturalistic statements quoted before, with the view that poets are "prodigious materialists" (*WB*, 326) or that "to the theologian the poet might want to say, One world at a time" (*PE*, 184). Transcendence seems expressly denied in these pronouncements.

Some corollaries for a theory of poetry follow from Ransom's concept of poetry. Ransom plays down the personality of the poet, a motif well worn in modern theories since Flaubert and Mallarmé. "Anonymity is a condition of poetry. . . . A good poem, even if it is signed with a full and well-known name, intends as a work of art to lose the identity of the author" (*WB*, 2). "By the doctrine of expressiveness art is disreputable" (*WB*, 308), presumably because it would be self-indulgence.

It follows also that Ransom has little use for affective theories of poetry. Ransom argues that there is "no emotion at all until an object has furnished the occasion for one," as "emotions are correlatives of the cognitive objects" (*NC*, 201). Feelings are "calls to action, and always want to realize their destiny, which is to turn into actions and vanish" (*WB*, 290) and thus presumably are not aesthetic. But elsewhere Ransom can say that "the human importance of the art-work is that it 'touches the heart' " (*KR*, 12 [1950], 202), and sentiment (obscurely different from emotion and feeling) is sometimes equated with the aesthetic experience. The sentence "Sentiment is aesthetic, aesthetic is cognitive, and the cognition is of the object as an individual" (*WB*, 216) sounds almost like Croce, though elsewhere Croce is chided—wrongly, I think—for assuming that art is "simple child's play" (*SR*, 37 [1929], 362). His "aesthetics denied him a criticism" (*SR*, 52 [1944], 558), says Ransom, in defiance of Croce and almost all of Italy.

Precious objects are prized by our affections, but there is, for Ransom, a difference between the genuine artist who distances and thus overcomes sentiment and the sentimental artist who has "the right sentiment for the object, but articulates the object no better than a man who has merely the sentiment" (*WB*, 231). Art feels cold, not hot.

Consistently, Ransom has little use for Aristotelian catharsis. In the traditional interpretation as "a gross physiological metaphor," it seems to him "inept" and in the refined version of S. H. Butcher merely "an agent of moral improvement" (*WB*, 179). "Its object is to intensify the aesthetic moment in order to minimize and localize it, and clear the way for the scientific moment" (*WB*, 211), "scientific" meaning here something like practical or even civic. Aristotle wanted to purge the Greeks of their sense of cosmic evil. He wanted them to be good citizens (*WB*, 187).

"Art gratifies a perceptual impulse and exhibits the minimum of reason" (*WB*, 130). But criticism, in contrast, is conceived as rational and scientific, if we mean by science not any imitation or claim for the method of the exact sciences but a systematic approach toward a general theory of poetry and the arts. "Criticism is a science, and a science must know what it is doing" (*Sat R*, March 24, 1934, p. 574). "Criticism must become more scientific, or precise and systematic" (*WB*, 329). It must be based on theory and ultimately on aesthetics. "Theory, which is expectation, always determines criticism and never more than when it is unconscious" (*WB*, 173). "The authority of criticism depends on its coming to terms with esthetics" (*IC*, 92). Criticism must concentrate on the "objective literature itself" (*NC*, 75) and must be distinguished from interest in biography, literary history, and sociology. Ransom can be caustic at the expense of the pedants in the English departments, on the "indefensible extravagance in the gigantic collective establishment of the English faculties" who fail to teach criticism (*KR*, 2 [1940], 349–50). He is quite explicit in rejecting the Marxist approach of Bernard Smith's *Forces in American Criticism* (in *Free America*, 4 [January 1940], 19–20), though much later Ransom says casually that "at any rate, the social conscience [of the Marxist critics] influenced him very deeply" (*KR*, 12 [1950], 208). I am not aware of any public evidence for this influence, at least on Ransom's literary criticism.

The advocacy of systematic criticism induced Ransom to support criticism in American universities and colleges as an academic subject. Particularly the essay "Criticism, Inc." (1937) and the book *The New Criticism* (1941) gave Ransom a commanding, elder statesman's position in the movement he had named. The term is an old one. The Schlegels called themselves "neue Kritiker," and Croce, when referring to his own views, speaks of "la nuova critica." From there J. E. Spingarn took the term for a little book, *The New Criticism* (1911), which expounded Croce in a diluted version. Ransom's book is highly critical of the critics there considered. It is far from a celebration of the New Criticism, as Ransom sharply criticizes Richards for his psychologism, for "very nearly severing the dependence of poetic effect upon any standard of objective knowledge or belief" (*IC*, 95). He makes many objections to Eliot's criticism, its emotionalism, and its concept of tradition. A review of Eliot's *Use of Poetry and the Use of*

Criticism (*Sat R*, March 24, 1934, p. 574) criticizes him for disdaining theory, just as he was later to charge him with "theoretical innocence" (*NC*, 145). Quite as sharply Ransom rejects Yvor Winters's moralism (which earned him a virulent reply in *The Anatomy of Nonsense*).

The other critics to whom the label has stuck are by no means immune from Ransom's criticism, even though he may have seen them as allies in the general cause. Empson is praised as "the closest and most resourceful reader that poetry has had" (*NC*, 102), but even the Richards chapter in *The New Criticism*, which endorses some of Empson's gross misreadings, recognizes the "overreading" of the "bare ruined choirs" passage in Shakespeare's sonnet. An earlier essay, "Mr. Empson's Muddles" (*So R*, 4 [1938–39], 322), more stringently criticizes his "almost fanatical devotion to puns" (326). Empson's interpretation of Marvell's "The Garden" seems to Ransom "the most extreme example of what I regard as Mr. Empson's almost inveterate habit of overreading poetry" (331). Empson is "a solipsistic critic, because he has much to say about anything, and not the strictest conscience about making what he says 'correspond' with what the poet says" (333). His ambiguity is rather multiplicity. The meanings may be irrelevant to each other, inconsistent, or at the worst contradictory (336). He and Richards admire "all possible complications, all muddles, indiscriminately" (337).

Similarly Cleanth Brooks is praised as "the most forceful and influential critic of poetry that we have" (*PE*, 148), as "the most expert living reader or interpreter of difficult verse" (*KR*, 2 [1940], 247), but Ransom disagrees with Brooks's preoccupation with paradox, wit, and irony. Paradoxes must be resolved (*KR*, 9 [1947], 437). "Opposites can never be said to be resolved or reconciled merely because they have been got into the same poem" (*NC*, 95). Irony in poetry should occur only occasionally. Paraphrase, condemned by Brooks, is "a critical function" (*KR*, 9 [1947], 442). The defense of poetry "must be of its human substance and on the naturalistic level" and not by some "fairly impenetrable esoteric quality" postulated by Brooks (*KR*, 9 [1947], 438).

Of the two prominent critics more loosely associated with the

New Criticism, R. P. Blackmur and Kenneth Burke, Ransom admires Blackmur more. Quoting him on Shelley and Emily Dickinson, he praises these passages as "in depth and precision at once beyond all earlier criticism in our language" (NC, x). *Language and Gesture* is called "the official classic in exegesis of the poetry of an age" (PE, 102). But neither does Blackmur live up to Ransom's ideal of a critic. He remains a formalist. He forgets "that there are substantive as well as formal values in the poem" (PE, 108). "Substantive" must here mean something like Ransom's "ontological."

Ransom admires Kenneth Burke as "of all our critics philosophically the subtlest, temperamentally the most ironic" (*New Republic*, February 18, 1946, p. 257), as "a master of innovations even upon the most modern forms of Dialectic" (*Texas Quarterly*, 9 [1966], 191). But Burke is said "to play too near the rational surface of the poem and the reason it does not go deeper is that he is no lover of nature" (KR, 14 [1952], 231). Poetic metaphor is not to be identified with scientific analogy (So R, 7 [1942], 530n) as Burke tries to do. Burke, "the most bristling with modern technicalities," drawn from psychology, anthropology, sociology, and linguistics, is on the side of modern rationalism (KR, 10 [1948], 684, 687) and thus fails to understand poetry.

Of all English and American critics of the recent period only Allen Tate seems to have commanded Ransom's complete assent. Tate's essays "Three Types of Poetry" and "Poetry as Knowledge" move on the lines of Ransom's thought. It might be difficult to establish priorities between teacher and pupil.

Thus Ransom differs sharply from the other New Critics (with the exception of Tate) in his concern for the world of nature, for what he calls "ontology." *The New Criticism* concludes with a chapter "Wanted: An Ontological Critic" (279 ff.), i.e. a critic who would be concerned with the relation between the words of the poet and "the world beyond words," "that dense, particular, individual world of objects." The final desideratum is an "ontological insight" (IC, 112), an insight into nature, an aim shared by criticism and poetry. Criticism is then "pure speculation" (IC, 91), not distinguishable from aesthetics and ultimately from philosophy.

I have deliberately postponed the discussion of Ransom's most widely known and criticized idea, the dichotomy of structure and texture. "A poem is a logical structure having a local texture" (*IC*, 110) is the main formula, in which "structure" is used not in the sense of linguistic structuralism as totality or system but as rational argument (which Ransom somewhat confusingly calls "logical"), while "texture" is the presentation of the qualitative density of the world. "The texture is ubiquitous; and to put it simply it consists in interpolated material which does not relate to the argument" (*KR*, 5 [1943], 286). This dichotomy has been called a revival of the ancient form-content duality and has been seen even as a relapse into the view of poetry as decoration: images, metaphors, and so on embellishing the rational or moral content. Ransom later saw a parallel to his structure-texture dualism in Freud's ego-id contrast. "The thought-work in the poem" is the ego's, while "the play upon substance" is the id's (*KR*, 9 [1947], 655). This contrast would assume that the texture of a poem is somehow arrived at unconsciously, hardly a view which can be defended, as Ransom's other reflections assume a conscious working-out of the metaphorical and metrical texture of the poem. Nor can one be convinced by his attempt to relate structure to Eliot's emotions and texture to feelings (*NC*, 156), as structure is always defined as a logical or rational argument (*NC*, 156).

Mostly Ransom makes the structure-texture dualism so sharply distinct that texture appears as "redundant," "irrelevant," "adventitious" in relation to structure. But on the other hand, there is the prose argument which is equally indispensable. We are told, "No prose argument no poem" (*KR*, 5 [1943], 286) and that "a poet who argues badly is a reproach to poetry" (*Hika*, 5 [1939], 10), a standard which is used to disparage poems Ransom considers poorly argued, such as Joyce Kilmer's "Trees," or poems which are only strings of images or scenes, such as *The Waste Land*, severely criticized as incoherent in 1923 (*Literary Review*, 3 [July 1923], 825–26).

Metaphor is the main element of texture. The abandonment of metaphor would mean the abandonment of poetry (*PE*, 181). Metaphor serves to "remove the object from classification and dis-

position, as a particular always qualitatively exceeds the universal"
(*LC*, 23). Metaphor "serves to obscure the pointer relation of prose
language or serves to densify the imagery and to increase 'naturalism' " (*SR*, 52 [1944], 568). "Naturalism" here must mean "ontology," mimesis and not naturalism as it is understood in Zola's
sense, which Ransom always condemned when he discussed the
modern American novelists (see *American Review*, 7 [1936], 301–
18). Metaphor is "one militant way of defending nature" (*PE*,
181), as it is "a going to the Concrete of nature for its analogy"
(*PE*, 180).

Ransom rejects the version of metaphor, expounded by I. A.
Richards, as an "interanimation of tenor and vehicle." "The prof-
its of the transaction do not amount to much in themselves" (*NC*,
77). He doubts Richards's account of Coleridge's example of
imagination from *Venus and Adonis* as a case of modification or
interanimation between Adonis and the shooting star. He shows
that Richards can mistake the vehicle for the tenor in a well-
known passage comparing the Thames with the flow of the mind
in Denham's *Cooper's Hill* (*NC*, 68–72). Metaphor for Ransom is
simply "a sort of second poem attached to the given poem" (*NC*,
77). "The vehicle must realize itself independently and go beyond
its occasion" (*NC*, 85). Antony (in a scene with Eros in *Antony
and Cleopatra*), comparing the change in himself with the changing
shapes of clouds, is an example that proves to Ransom that "few of
the images have anything to do with Antony's own situation" (*NC*,
85). They live their own life. They are importations, or "im-
porters" (*KR*, 12 [1950], 505).

The independent life of the metaphor is one of the reasons for
Ransom's preference for the poetry of the metaphysicals. "The
conceit," he argues, "has no explicit tenor, but only a 'vehicle'
covering it. . . . The tenor of a metaphysical poem is," at most,
"conventional and generalized, while the texture is thick and odd"
(*NC*, 188–89). Ransom even states that a metaphysical poet makes
"the whole poem, or some whole passage of it, out of the single
unit metaphor" (*NC*, 185). He can, however, produce only "The
Exequy" of Henry King and the compasses passage from Donne's
"Valediction: Forbidding Mourning" as examples. But there are

many genuinely metaphysical poems such as "Twicknam Garden" which do not fulfill this supposed requirement. It is simply not true that "a single extended image bears the whole weight of the conceptual structure" (*So R*, 1 [1936], 10) in a metaphysical poem.

Beyond the metaphor there is myth." "Myths are conceits, born of metaphor" (*WB*, 140). Poets are "constantly creating little local myths" (*GT*, 66) with their metaphors. The great myth, religion, has decayed and has made myth unavailable to the modern poet. Yeats, however, "disproved" this (*KR*, 1 [1939], 311). He alone among modern poets created a new myth, though, in other contexts, Ransom dismisses "the phases of the moon" as "a private system: the work of a prose thinker" (*So R*, 7 [1941–42], 526). Also, "the Ossianic and Irish mythology produced nothing that is worthy of his ultimate stature as a poet" (*KR*, 1 [1939], 314).

Ransom argues mostly for the structure-texture dichotomy. "Texture is the thing that peculiarly qualifies a discourse as being poetic; it is its differentia" (*NC*, 220). Sometimes, he considers meter either to be a third equal element making a triad of the poetic transaction—comparing the head with structure, the heart with texture, and the feet with the meter (*KR*, 16 [1954], 560), or he makes meter and "the phonetic effect" serve as "a sort of texture to the meaning" (*NC*, 318). He defends meter as "bringing about the abdication of prose" (*WB*, 258) and providing the poet with a mask (*WB*, 257), thus supporting the anonymity and impersonality of poetry. Ransom, however, does not believe in the expressiveness of meter. He frequently ridicules the usual assumptions about sound symbolism (*WB*, 95–97). He "cannot discover a fixed scheme" in free verse (*NC*, 262). He opts thus for a bold, rhythmical reading of poetry in preference to a reading emphasizing the spoken prose rhythm. The chanting Yeats, we might add, was a better reader of poetry than the subdued, prosy Eliot.

It all comes to a rejection of organicism, of what for Ransom is the superstition of totality, coherence, unity, *Gestalt*. A poem, he says memorably, is "much more like a Christmas tree than an organism" (*KR*, 7 [1945], 294–95), or with different metaphors, a poem is like a democratic state and not a totalitarian government (*IC*, 108), or a poem is like a house with the paint, paper, and tapestry comparable to the texture, and the roof and beams to the structure (*IC*, 110–11). Once, he seems to admit that a work of art is an organism with parts functionally attached to each other, producing a whole. However, he immediately withdraws this apparent concession, insisting that this view of totality would apply also to a machine or to a scientific operation (*KR*, 7 [1945], 289–91). Ransom finds it odd that literary critics, "so many of them," should claim "that this same rigorous organization obtains within a poem; that the Universal or logical plan of the poem is borne out perfectly in the sensuous detail which puts it into action" (*PE*, 164). Still, after arguing as usual for the concrete and particular, Ransom concludes that "it would be wrong to give the impression that in a poem, necessarily, the intellectual Universal has always disappeared from sight and now exists only in the Concrete." Rather, "it is my impression that as often as not a poem will recite its two versions, side by side" (*PE*, 174). We are back to the unresolved dichotomy. The idea of a reconciliation or synthesis presented by the Hegelian Concrete Universal (revived by Bosanquet in the second lecture of *The Principle of Individuality and Value* [London, 1912]) is finally rejected as "a gaudy paradox" (*KR*, 6 [1944], 121). There is no "resolution," no "fusion" in poetry (*IC*, 109). In unusually strong terms Ransom asserts that "it is a lie to say that contradictories may not coexist, for they do it in poetry" (*So R*, 4 [1938–39], 338). "We must not become fools of the shining but impractical ideal of 'unity' or of 'fusion'" (*NC*, 183). The reconciliation of opposites formulated in a famous passage by Coleridge, endorsed by Cleanth Brooks, is rejected. "I cannot but think that the recent revival of Coleridge's involved critical language has been obfuscating" (*KR*, 9 [1947], 439). There is also no identification of subject and object, no such integral experience as propounded by Dewey (*KR*, 7 [1945], 286). The work of art as Dewey describes it becomes "too fluid for human identification" (*KR*, 7 [1945], 288). In short, "poetry is an inorganic activity" (*KR*, 5 [1953], 290).

There are a few occasions where Ransom tries to escape the difficulties of his dualism. He picked up the term "icon" from Charles Morris (who in turn derived it from Charles Saunders

Pierce) as an alternative to image. The term avoids the association, in English, of image with visibility, which Ransom uses even later when he says that "the artistic vision . . . makes the vast depth of natural contingency visible" (*KR,* 7 [1945], 291). "Icon" certainly emphasizes that the aesthetic sign must be a whole object, and in the note on the term explaining the title of *The Verbal Icon,* W. K. Wimsatt defines "icon" as "an interpretation of reality in its metaphoric and symbolic dimensions." But Ransom objects to Morris for considering the icon "only a medium denoting, by embodying, a value," while for Ransom "the icon is a body imitating some actual embodiment of the value" (*NC,* 289). Ransom drops the talk of value quickly, as value interests the consumer and he is concerned with "body" though he somewhat whimsically confesses that "he does not know what the body is for" (*NC,* 291). Morris's theory, Ransom concludes, remains "another version of affective or psychologistic theory" (*NC,* 289). Immediately following the account of Morris, Ransom tries, even with a diagram, to illustrate the relation between meter and meaning by a clash or struggle which seems to correct the usual irrelevance theory. "The composition of a poem is an operation in which the argument fights to displace the meter, and the meter fights to displace the argument" (*NC,* 295). The poet makes adaptations both of meter to meaning (introducing Indeterminate Sound) and of meaning to meter (introducing Indeterminate Meaning) (*NC,* 302). Some interplay, some mutual modifications are suggested. As Ransom said later, "I had the idea of a poem as a great 'paradox,' a construct looking two ways, with logic trying to dominate the metaphors, and metaphors trying to dominate the logic" to which he added meter to give the poem "the form of a trinitarian existence" (*PE,* 157). The image of head, heart, and feet also suggests such an ultimate reconciliation with organicism. In a recent paper the metaphor Ransom uses of the "skeleton of summary and syntactic language" contrasted with the "flesh" of connotative poetic meaning points also to a unity of the two (*Texas Quarterly,* 9 [1966], 192).

But we must not try to assimilate Ransom to this central tradition, even when he makes concessions to it. His original insight remains the experience of the natural world as an assembly of qualities, as heterogeneity which it is the task of poetry to present to us who have forgotten this world of precious objects, of private experiences. Poetry thus shields us against the abstractions and exploits of science and technology which Ransom saw as destructive of the saner and happier ways of life in the South of his youth and the agrarian past of his region. As any poet-critic, Ransom writes also in defense of his own poetic craft: he obviously, like Valéry, practiced it as a balancing of sound and meaning, as a continued compromise between meter and sense, metaphor and argument. Whatever defense can be put up for organicism, for the ultimate indissolubility of content and form, of the what and the how, of style as meaning, we should grant to Ransom that there is a dichotomy, or as Roman Jakobson would say, a "binary" relation in all language utterances which, in a theory of poetry, we may rechristen theme and style, sound and meaning, and even, with Ransom's peculiar vocabulary, structure and texture. We should also grant him the merit of having revived the ancient doctrine of the imitation of nature and to have given it a new twist with his insistence on nature's particularity and heterogeneity reflected in poetry.

NOTES

1. *John Crowe Ransom: Critical Essays and a Bibliography,* ed. Thomas Daniel Young (Baton Rouge, 1968), is indispensable for its list both of Ransom's articles and reviews and of comment on Ransom's criticism. Since then James E. Manger, Jr., *John Crowe Ransom: Critical Principles and Preoccupations* (The Hague, 1971) deserves attention.

2. The following abbreviations for writings by John Crowe Ransom are used in this paper:

GT   *God without Thunder* (New York, 1930).

IC   "Criticism as Pure Speculation," in *The Intent of the Critic,* ed. Donald A. Stauffer (Princeton, 1941).

LC   "The Literary Criticism of Aristotle," in *Lectures in Criticism: The Johns Hopkins University,* ed. Huntington Cairns (New York, 1949).

NC   *The New Criticism* (Norfolk, Conn., 1941).

> **PE**   *Poems and Essays* (New York, 1955).
> **WB**   *The World's Body* (New York, 1938).

Periodicals are quoted with the abbreviations used in *PMLA:*

> **KR**   *Kenyon Review*
> **Sat R** *Saturday Review of Literature*
> **SR**   *Sewanee Review*
> **So R**   *Southern Review*

Structure

"Sense Variously Drawn Out": Some Observations on English Enjambment

JOHN HOLLANDER

"The music of the English heroic line," said Dr. Johnson, "strikes the ear so faintly, that it is easily lost, unless all the syllables of every line cooperate together; this cooperation can only be obtained by the preservation of every verse unmingled with another as a distant system of sounds; and this distinctness is obtained and preserved by the artifice of rhyme. The variety of pauses, so much boasted by the lovers of blank verse, changes the measures of an English poet to the periods of a declaimer; and there are only a few happy readers of Milton who enable their audience to perceive where the lines end or begin. *Blank verse,* said an ingenious critic, *seems to be verse only to the eye.*" [1] To an age like our own which is so accustomed to purely graphic meters and visual formats for poetry, such a comment seems hard-of-hearing; we would more properly want to say this of pure syllabics, for example. Of more central concern, however, is the short shrift given to "the variety of pauses," a variety not only basic to the metrical system of *Paradise Lost,* but one which has become more and more important in the recent history of prosody.

Johnson's concern here was with the integrity of the poetic line. There is a long tradition for his anxiety about line terminus as a guardian of that integrity. The Virgilian hexameter, overflowing with syntax, nevertheless marked its rim with an almost inevitable accentual close, a stress pattern of $['\cdots'\cdot]$ [2] accompanying the unvarying quantitative schema $[-\smile\smile-\smile]$ no matter how little alignment of stressed syllable with long one had occurred in the first four feet. [3] Dryden, in an amusing anticipation of Dr. Johnson's

201

disparagement of blank verse as opposed to more powerful rhymed couplets, hankered after just this kind of marked terminus which he knew the classical, heroic hexameter to possess: "For imagination in a poet is a faculty so wild and lawless that, like an high-ranging spaniel, it must have clogs tied to it, lest it outrun the judgment. The great easiness of blank verse renders the poet too luxuriant." [4] The unbridled forward surge of language, Dryden argues, is specifically to be curbed by linear closure. This same marking function, whether considered in its melodious, chiming role or as a more prosaic ticking, is invoked by other arguments for rhyme, down to a very different sort of neoclassicism from Dryden's, in Paul Valéry's remark about how "Rhyme establishes a law independent of the poem's theme and might be compared to a clock outside it." [5]

If rhymes are clogs, dampers, or restraints, it is an exuberantly generative linguistic faculty upon which they operate. Milton himself, in defending his own "variety of pauses," denounced rhyme, "the Invention of a barbarous Age," as a "troublesome and modern bondage." [6] It is, however, poetry itself, lines handcuffed together, rather than the poet's creative faculty, which he specifically wished to liberate ("'ancient liberty recover' to Heroic poem"). In this he was preceded by Ben Jonson, whose image of the fetters of rhyme applies wittily and profoundly to its internal constraints—

> Joynting Syllabes, drowning Letters,
> Fastning Vowells, as with fetters
> They were bound! [7]

—as he was followed, strangely, by Blake: "Poetry Fetter'd, Fetters the Human Race." [8] Even though Blake was talking here of the chains of Miltonic blank verse (now having outgrown the antithetical role it played, as against rhymed couplets, in *Paradise Lost,* and become the primary mode itself), he could quote Milton in claiming it to be "derived from the modern bondage of Rhyming." It might be observed in passing that the tying down of line-endings comes to stand for such a restraint—on the generative wit that races across them—primarily in a neoclassical reaction against Miltonic verse.

Milton's own reference to his "variety of pauses" appears in the prose preface on "The Verse," added after the first 1667 printing of *Paradise Lost,* rejecting rhyme as being of "no true musical delight; which consists only in apt Numbers, fit quantity of Syllables, and the sense variously drawn out from one verse into another." Allowing for a terminological confusion between stress and quantity common in Renaissance English poetic theory (where, actually, stress is thought of as English quantity), Milton is asserting that the music of his verse will lie in its being in fact accentual-syllabic blank verse, and in its instrumentalized enjambments. *"Sense variously drawn out"*—this is clearly the heart of the matter. He is arguing specifically against the notion that only rhyme is musical, the notion that "stumbled" many readers, and for this reason it is the figuratively "musical" variation in the character of his line termini which he underlines. Recent sophisticated discussions of Milton's style during the last decade have begun to analyze the amazing repertory of effects, at once both subtle and profound, of which Milton's language in *Paradise Lost* was capable. Within the context of such discussions, it should now be clear that, as with all "musical" devices in *Paradise Lost,* the intricately related demands of local meaning and larger vision are being served by the many ways in which Milton's line-endings variously fetter and spur the exuberance of syntactic production.

One need only look at a celebrated example, the opening line of *Paradise Lost:*

> Of Man's first Disobedience, and the Fruit
> Of that Forbidden Tree, whose mortal taste . . .
>
> [1.1–2]

Here we have a paradigm of the poem's unique mode of linearity: a line characterized by an architectonic structure in its unfolding array of syllabic distribution (three monosyllabic words, then, central in every sense, a word of five syllables, then three monosyllables again) exhibits a closed unit of what Alistair Fowler has discussed as "triumphal form." [9] But its stasis is immediately disturbed by the brilliant line-ending. "Fruit" might well have led to something like "Thereof" in the following line, thus being taken in the figurative sense of "results"; actually, the line which follows thrusts us into the primary, literal sense of *that* fruit of *that* tree. "Disobedience" has the importance of staged centrality, "Fruit" the urgency of a terminal place which reveals both its own positional ambiguity and that of the word occupying it. These two impulses—the one toward systematic, static pattern, the other toward periodic flux and articulated paragraphing—are the warp and weft of the verse fabric of *Paradise Lost*. Whenever brilliantly framed and patterned lines occur, they are opened out at their closing to allow their apparent syntactic closure to flow forward. Thus, for example, when the inner state of Satan on Mount Niphates is being described:

> horror and doubt distract
> His troubl'd thoughts, and from the bottom stir
> The Hell within him, for within him Hell
> He brings, and round about him . . .
>
> [IV.18–21]

The perfect schematic chiasmus of line 20 swirls up as a momentary picture in an agitated phantasmagoria, until our attention moves on, dragged by the force of continuing syntax and its tugging toward completion (we must have the verb, however inverted, for which "Hell" is an object, as well as a symmetrical tessera in a mosaic pattern). But consider the "stir" in line 19: it produces nothing that we would ordinarily call a prominent enjambment. The pattern [verb / Object] (where the slant-dash stands, as usual, for line-break) represents no more than a moderate flow of sense. But what hangs on at the end of the line is the likelihood of the verb's intransitivity, i.e. it might have gone on: "stir / From their dark slumbers Thoughts more troubl'd yet." The *contre-rejet,* or continuation of the enjambed unit, shows it to be surprisingly transitive, and it is this surprise which lights up the following line. Even more shocking is the dissolution of the linear façade a few lines further on, where conscience

> wakes the bitter memory
> Of what he was, what is, and what must be
> Worse; of worse deeds worse sufferings must ensue.
>
> [IV.24–26]

Here the static pattern of line 25, framing the formula from the prayerbook ("As it was in the beginning, is now and ever shall be"), is jolted by the revelation that "be" was merely predicative (and of "worse," at that), rather than existential. As if to confirm the intention of that jolt, "worse" is repeated twice in the line.[10]

In short, Milton's "variety of pauses" is a powerful and delicate device, "musical" if one must, for choreographing the reader's attention, for directing, focusing, and moving the highest and finest perceptions both of the text he reads and of his own act of reading. Closure and flow, the opposed features of Milton's verse form, oppose themselves in ways parallel to the opposition of visual and acoustic modes, respectively, of poetic language. More interestingly, the "pauses" are employed to point up other conceptual dimensions in the meanings of the text—not merely the local sense of the lines which they connect, but of the mind of the whole poem. The opening line of Book I moves us from the general to the concrete and local, and from the figurative sense of a word to the literal one. These are both crucial categorical pairs in the poem, confusions in which will entangle both Satan's thought and its echoes in human dialectic. Throughout the poem, the dynamics of line terminus will point up such dimensions as can be revealed by grammatical shift—a verbal-nominal ambiguity points up another kind of lexical one, such as that of original (Latinate or Greek or Hebrew) meaning versus a derived one (itself a metaphorical dimension of the poem, emphasizing the distinction between the Original and the Fallen). Thus

> this *Assyrian* Garden, where the Fiend
> Saw undelighting all delight, all kind
> Of living creatures . . .

> [IV.285–87]

where a shade of the *O.E.D.* adj. 5 sense of "kind" ("benevolent"), reinforced by an off-rhyme and by internal assonance, hangs over the line-end, as if to continue "all kind / And loving creatures," for example. Or, again, the line break can affect the lexical quality of a word lying beyond that break, playing an unfallen against what Christopher Ricks has designated an "uninfected" meaning.[11] So as in Satan's cry of delight

> O fair foundation laid whereon to build
> Thir ruin!

[IV.521–22]

Donald Davie has called attention to the "oxymoron revealed" in the line transition,[12] but he neglects the dimensions of "ruin." Owen Barfield has commented on the shift in meaning of the word from that of a process ("ruining") to the residues of that process ("rubble"); [13] here there is indeed an oxymoron only when "build" is literal and "ruin" equals "ruins." But we are led also to consider the other case, where "build" is figurative, and "ruin" means undoing, and where there is no oxymoron at all.

Often, the Miltonic line-juncture will startle in a complex mimetic way, operating on words and their designata at once. Thus, of the two contiguous trees in Paradise—"And next to Life / Our Death, the Tree of Knowledge" (IV.220–21)—it is "Our Death," not just "Death," which is imminent even in the garden, Free Will being what it is. Or again, Satan (at IV.197–98) "sat devising Death / To them who lived" and the ambiguity of "devising" first suggests the creation and institution of death itself, until, with the *contre-rejet* of the new line, the mere sense of "plotting" is revealed. And here, too, the axis of general versus particular is underlined.

These examples show us that it is always a grammatical operation which the "sense variously drawn out" effects, and only thereby a semantic and, ultimately, an imaginative one. In the lines given below, it is actually a matter of a shift in antecedent—from the "expected" to the "discovered"—which forces an ironic point:

> Satan, now first inflam'd with rage, came down,
> The Tempter ere th'Accuser of man-kind,
> To wreck on innocent frail man his loss
> Of that first Battle, and his flight to Hell:

[IV.9–12]

Linearity itself shapes our expectations in blank verse, and our first impulse is to take a line like 11, far from being an architectonic one as it is, as completing a period. "His" would then, given lexical richness of "wreck," refer to "man"; the enjambment revealed itself reveals the true antecedent, but the ambiguity of the pronoun reflects the fact that, in the poem, Satan's loss is not only a type of Adam's, but a cause of it.

Paradise Lost bristles with such instances, and one is tempted to quote dozens of them. From Book IV again, Eve's account of her displacement of Narcissistic admiration onto a recognition of Adam's as an objectified beauty, concludes "and from that time I see / How beauty is excell'd by manly grace" (ll. 489–90), where the literal sense of "see" dissolves into a figurative one ("see how" as "understand that"), with a lingering hedging of her commitment. Or

> hideous ruin and combustion down
> To bottomless perdition there to dwell
> In Adamantine Chains and penal Fire
>
> [1.46–48]

where, again without a conserving pattern, "down" has a fleeting, illusory (because, ultimately, grammatically impossible) adjectival quality, "dwell" seems first to be followed by a stop, and the following *contre-rejet* maintains the effect of bottoms dissolving into mirages as dropping continues.

The taxonomy of the "variety of pauses" would yield some interesting results for students of Milton's imagination,[14] perhaps with respect to a way he seems to have of making metaphoric use of a phenomenology of language: grammar, syntax, and diachronic morphology, as the reader is aware of them, become elements of experience which are, in subtle ways, moralized in the poem. But at this point I should like to abandon the gathering of instances, and turn from the "variety" to the "pauses," to some of the procedural problems for prosodic analysis which the notion of "pause" sets up.

What we have in fact been considering is a variety of enjambments, even though we usually reserve that term only for what appear to be the more abrupt or sharp of these. In discussions of caesura in various languages, the word "pause" is misleadingly used to describe a situation whose necessary and sufficient condition is a word boundary; [15] such a boundary will coincide with a wide array of junctures, some of which would indeed be projected into speech as "pauses," or be represented by punctuation in writing. In enjambment, however, linear terminus exercises an even more marked cutting effect; ironically enough, our convention of separating lines of verse with a slant-dash in prose format suggests a more useful model for treating enjambment than the usual pair of opposed terms "enjambed" versus "end-stopped" evokes.

Let us choose instead a kind of spectrum, along which we would arrange all the possible ways of terminating lines, considered not as boundaries or termini, but as the kinds of cutting into syntax which the slant-dash notation illustrates. At either end of this spectrum, we would put a trivial case, one of extreme "softness" of cut, where the slant-dash really divides nothing, and the other of "hardness," where an unusually strong linkage is severed. In order to accommodate a diachronic view of the English poetic line since Chaucer, the spectrum must be sufficiently wide to include such normally trivial cases. Thus, on the right, the terminus of

Through *Eden* took their solitary way. /

makes a total closure—of phrase, clause, period, book, and *Paradise Lost*. At the other end of the spectrum, let us place a cut so sharp as to be analogously senseless, so sharp that it has no phonetic, let alone grammatical, consequences whatsoever, a cut not even between graphemes (as in b / Etween), but between two subcomponents, as in the disyllabic couplet

And al-
Though Paul [16]

In between these, we might arrange the possible cuts in a kind of ordered array.[17] Certainly [xxxxx; / Xxxxx] would be far over toward the right, while [a / (any noun)] would be toward the left or "hard" side. The best way to show such an array might be to consider the effects of alternative cuts, of pathological versification, in a familiar passage. Consider the famous "self-descriptive" couplet from Pope's *Essay on Criticism:*

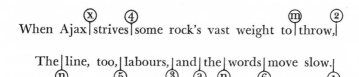

I have numbered from 1 to 6 in this diagram some possible points at which a contemporary poem in free verse might, in quoting Pope's lines, break them. I have also shown the possible ordered array [n < m < a] (where [<] means a harder cut), and I have raised a question whether the consonantal clusters at [x] enforce a different order of cut from the one its merely grammatical status of [subject / Verb] would make.

The effect of such a spectrum is to allow a treatment of line-breaks as marking or indicating syntactic groups, and sometimes as performing a trick not unlike covering up one end of a line of English inscription, inviting the reader to guess at the nature of the hidden text, and then revealing it. Milton, and Blake when he follows him, is in effect employing the half-covered line, the guess, the correct "answer" and even the moment of *anagnorisis*, of discovery of the truth with its slight rebuke, as part of the marking process. Certainly the marking or annotating is done within the metrical resources of the verse. But just as certainly is it being effected by a kind of metalanguage—not one as sharply differentiated from its object language as are prosodic signs, brackets, the symbols of sentence-diagram, and so forth, but clearly as separated. This operation is an concrete an instance of the abstractness of meter, in the sense argued for it by W. K. Wimsatt and Monroe Beardsley,[18] as one could hope to find.

The Miltonic tradition of enjambed blank verse deploys its variety of line-endings to annotate syntax, primarily; when a lexical ambiguity is being developed, it is a control exercised over the act of sequential reading which points it up. But even within the line, accentual-syllabic meter can do its work of notating and annotating the syntax of a text. Contrastive, or other sorts of emphatic stress, provide the most obvious surface upon which the effects of iambic positioning can operate, even when the results are not specifically those of contrast. Let us consider an ambiguous sentence cited by Chomsky as requiring two syntactic descriptions,[19] but whose ambiguity is easily resolved by the informal notation of italics:

1. They don't know how good meat tastes

can be immediately associated with one of its two possible syntactic descriptions (the one involving the relation, as Chomsky gives it, "meat tastes good") by means of italicization in ordinary prose:

2. They don't know how good *meat* tastes

Here there is an implicit contrastive treatment of "meat" ("They don't know how good meat can taste, having fed only on rice and fish"). Note, however, that an alternative treatment

3. They don't know how *good* meat tastes

while assigning a different syntactic description still retains some ambiguity because of the emphatically contrastive "good." That is, 3a, "how *good* meat tastes (not just slightly *salty*)" versus 3b, "how *good* meat tastes (*Prime* meat, not that stringy U.S. Good you've been eating").

Now, because of its conventionality, accentual-syllabic verse can do its own sort of italicizing. We could just as easily use versification to resolve the syntactic ambiguities in our example. When recast into iambic pentameter, the ambiguity of 1 can still be preserved, although shaded toward the readings of 3:

4. "But they don't know how good meat tastes," he said

This line retains another possibility as well, one to which Chomsky might have assigned a third syntactic description, and which emerges in the italicized version:

5. They don't know how good meat *tastes*

and where the emphatic stress could yield 5a, "how good meat *tastes,* rather than *looks*" versus 5b, a noncontrastive terminal emphatic stress that we might style the girlish petulant, a version, in meaning of either 2 or 3b, but not, I think, of 3a.

As a line of verse, 4 could certainly yield readings 2, 5a, or 5b, and, less likely, 3a. This uncommitted quality is characteristic of self-consciously iambic modern metrical styles (in this case, for example, Robert Frost's in his blank-verse eclogues). But consider another iambic treatment of our example, from another hypothetical Frost poem:

6. "They don't know how good meat tastes."

"Silas does."

Here 3a and 3b are ruled out, by the implicit italicization of "meat." It is obvious, too, that other accentual-syllabic rhythmic settings could reinforce the effects of 4 or 5 even more obviously. Thus, we could render the sense of 3 more clearly as

7. They don't know how good meat tastes!
   The missing joys! the needless wastes!

Alternatively, an elided anapestic movement could do the work of 6, as in

8. They don't know how good meat tastes
   In the misty mid region of Weir!

But all of these effects are much more powerful when deployed around the line terminus than among iambic positions alone. In the case of this example, let us consider

9.   they don't know how
   Good meat tastes

and

10.   they don't know how good
   Meat tastes

and

11.   they don't know how good meat
   Tastes

and

12.   they don't know
      How good meat tastes

Here we must decide not only which of the meanings charted in
2, 3, and 5 are assigned by the positioning of the line-break, but
how the discovery of the *contre-reject* may revise that decision. As
we actually read 1, Chomsky's unannotated string in its un-
avowedly literary context (that is, as an *example* in a linguistic
treatise), the various possibilities of 2, 3, 5, etc., flicker on and off,
within the transparency of the line of text, like the alternating
readings of the duck-rabbit cited by Wittgenstein.[20] With the discovered *contre-rejets* in these lines, we are prodded into one decision or another; thus, in 9, the primary revelation is that "how"
will *not* be followed by "to" and its infinitive, while the secondary one is that we are left with a case of 2 because of the stressed
position of "meat."

In 10, the possibilities of 2, 3, and 5 do not waver so much as
jam up against each other, and we are required to consider the
possibility of simultaneous readings. 11 tends to rule out 3, combining 2 and 5—except for the hint of 3b in 5b. Finally, 12, of all
the possibilities, retains the slow ambiguity of 4, and, through it,
of 1.

Now to return to the enjambment spectrum discussed earlier:
while it is clear that 12 represents the softest of these cuts in syntax,
dividing verb and complement, 9 and 10 both present interesting
problems. In order to assign them places along the scale, we should
not only need an extremely sophisticated system of gradation, but
we should have to resolve ambiguities about where the cut, in
fact, occurs. In 10, for example, the reader arrives at the line-
ending believing that the cut is being made as in

10a.   they don't know how good
      He is

—where, because of the inversion, the cut is being made between
predicate adjective and its verb. But the discovered *contre-rejet*
reveals the possibility of an adjective-noun (and thus, initial foot-
reversal as well). If previously introduced material has prepared
a reading of 3a or 3b—for example,

10b. Their beef is rotten; they don't know how good
  Meat tastes

—then the enjambment will have been harder than in

10c. They love its hue, but they don't know how good
  Meat tastes

Some of these distinctions may seem overly delicate, but they are very powerful in determining the pace and texture of metrical style, and not for the music, but the doctrine there—not merely for their abstract rhythm of percussiveness, however clothed in the melody of rhyme or assonance, however modulated by alliteration the attack. Operating within the line, through the action of stress-maximum positioning on monosyllables, they hum out a melody which can be hauntingly characteristic. Thus the lines about the hen

> Who cackles every morning from her perch
> To tell the servant girl new eggs are laid

and, later on in the same poem, about the boy who

> takes his hat and hopes to find it full,
> She's laid so long so many might have been
> [John Clare, "Hen's Nest"]

sound particularly like Robert Frost in his mode of wielding the controlling tool of positioning. Similarly with Dante Gabriel Rossetti's

> Our speed is such the sparks our engine leaves
> Are burning after the whole train has passed
> ["Antwerp to Ghent"]

which sounds equally like Frost, and where the colloquial syntax allows a clause, with an ellipsis of the relative pronoun, to glide into terminal position before the main verb of the *contre-rejet*.

Neither of these metrical gestures brandishes its implements as do those of Browning. I am thinking of an instance like

> Sétèbòs, Sétèbós, and Sétèbós!
> ["Caliban upon Setebos"]

where the two possible ways of handling an initially-stressed tri-syllabic word in an iambic context are flourished with a kind of measured panache: ['··] or ['·'] will both do (but never [·'·, ·'', or ''·]), and so *do* they both. There are so few problems in the accen-tual-syllabic accommodation of polysyllabic words that many areas of metrical controversy of the past two decades might have been bypassed if there were no monosyllables in English. In these re-marks I am only indirectly concerned with the theoretical back-ground of the iambic pentameter line, and shall merely suggest that in the present discussion, I have been thinking of phrases as polysyllabic words,[21] and clauses as phrases built from these. "Nat-urally dactyllic" words like "Setebos" or "Trumpington," and compounds like "scatter-brained" and "whistle-stop" are stressed in the same ways as phrases like "scatter it," and their stress-positioning in a line would be isomorphic to Browning's (i.e. "Scatter it, scatter it, and scatter it").[22]

Much of what happens in strong or hard enjambments, then, forces a reinterpretation of the position of the syntactic cut at the line break, based upon the discovered *contre-rejet*. As we have seen from Milton, other revisions can depend upon the syntactic re-reading: the discovered transitivity or intransitivity of a verb, the verbal status of a participle, can also force an accompanying ac-ceptance of an etymologized or earlier historical usage. Particu-larly in contemporary English, a level of diction might be implied by a *contre-rejet*. Consider the following possibilities:

> . . . and I go.

> . . . and I go
> Homeward

> . . . and I go
> Home on Wednesdays

> . . . and I go
> Without my lunch

where the difference of aspect between the second and third cases reinforces the difference between the archaic and the colloquial levels upon which the cases are arranged.

There are other metrical considerations which can affect the hardness or softness of enjambments. English adaptations of classical meters, whether stressed analogues of quantitative meter, or visual codings of the meters themselves (by which I would include all the Elizabethan experiments from "Master Drant's rules" to Campion's experiments), can modulate enjambed effects:

> Glory too God, the father, and his onlye
> Son, the protectoure of us earthlee sinners,
> Thee sacred spirit, labourers refreshing,
>   Stil be renownèd
> [Richard Stanyhurst, "A Prayer to the Blessed Trinity"]

These lines compose a stressed Sapphic strophe (perhaps Stanyhurst had given it a quantitative coding as well—he did this elsewhere). "Onlye / Son" is rather hard; "refreshing / Still" is rather soft, and yet the boundary between lines 3 and 4 is frequently violated by hyphenation (and hence, one of the hardest of cuts) in classical authors (Sappho, Catullus), as if the stanza really were a three-lined one, with two Lesser Sapphics and a longer terminal. Thus Campion: "Author of number that hath all the world in / harmony framèd" forms the conclusion of a Sapphic strophe. In both these cases, normal accentual-syllabic line-end expectations are suspended as a result of the reader's recognizing the Sapphic pattern, which will allow none of the variation, in the accentual version of it, generated by the English iambic line (if a purely quantitative version, the line will have no audible integrity in any case).

Rhyme is, of course, another factor in modulating the effects of terminal cuts. Robert Herrick ("Upon Himself"), echoing in his small way Ben Jonson's powerful and famous enjambment across not only a line, but a labelled strophe-break "And there he lives with memorie: and *Ben / Jonson*, who sung this of him," immediately rhymes internally upon his discovered monosyllable, as if to reassure the reader of his intention:

> And learn'd Musicians shall, to honour *Herricks*
> Fame, and his Name, both set, and sing his Lyricks.

Or take Marvell's celebrated four lines from "To His Coy Mistress":

> Thy beauty shall no more be found,
> Nor in thy marble Vault shall sound
> My ecchoing Song: then worms shall try
> That long preserved Virginity.

The movement of these lines is extremely characteristic of Marvell, showing the balanced swing from a somewhat hard, open line-ending of one couplet back to closure which, in four stresses, anticipates Pope in five. But the force of "sound / My ecchoing Song" is in the discovered subject of "sound." If the first couplet were closed, "sound" would be uninverted, with "beauty" as its subject, and figurative (beauty being silent); but although it is not, our false surmise lingers on for a bit after the continuation.

In other cases, the rhyme merely gives a final stamp to a closure made in other ways. The famous "imitative effect" of the refrain of Marvell's "The Mower's Song," supposedly so suggestive of the motion of scything—

> For Juliana comes, and she
> What I do to the grass, does to my thoughts and me.

—comes from the inverted clausal pattern, and its postponed predicate. Aided by the tendency of the English Alexandrine to break into trimeter fragments, the completion of the main clause, as if in a reciprocal return: "do to the grass"—"does to my thoughts" (the architectonic chiasmus of ["I do to . . . does to me"] also helps) makes us fancy we "hear" the swaying, reciprocating motion of the scythe. In a taxonomic classification of enjambment, this might represent a species in which the *contre-rejet* reveals an almost pathological syntactic inversion or deferment.

In other instances, a rhyme occurring after the discovery may work to reinforce, in a strange, brief kind of restrospect, the discarded initial syntactic reading of the first line. Thus, in Frost's couplet from "After Apple Picking":

> But I was well
> Upon my way to sleep before it fell

there is the effect of the discarded semantic unit's being confirmed by the very revised one to which it gives way as "well" is reread adverbially, not so much in Milton's manner, but by a kind of general implication—if p stands for "But I was well," and q for "But I was well upon my way to sleep," then p *implies* q is true. But notice, for example, how much less total poetic force accompanies the syntactically harder cut in the otherwise similar dummy (from a hypothetical "After Cucumber Picking"?)—"But it was ill / Fitted for pickling without thyme or dill." It is not only because the covert associations of sleep and death in Frost's poem are absent from the ludicrous dummy that it has little power, and it should be hardly necessary to invoke such instances to show that the prominence of verse patterning and its effectiveness do not necessarily generate poetic or even rhetorical power. But whether or not a strong effect of alliteration or enjambment will startle, reassure, tire, or redirect the reading attention is surely a function of the role of that device in the total poetic style.[23] When enjambment is systematic, as in *Paradise Lost* or some of William Carlos Williams's free verse, a wide range of effects ensures that even strong, pointed cuts at line-breaks will never startle by their mere occurrence but, if at all, for what they reveal—about language, about the world, or because of when and where, in the course of the poem, they show it. But when the style avoids strong enjambment, the effect may be to shock per se: T. S. Eliot's "Entertains Sir Ferdinand / Klein" occurs in a context of archly rhymed and stopped Gautier-like quatrains.[24]

But where, in twentieth-century verse, an enjambment can occur without interest in shock or abruptness as a mimetic effect by itself, the Miltonic operations on the lexical level can occur. A paradigmatic case is from William Carlos Williams in a well-known poem which uses the device almost as if in a manifesto:

so much depends
upon

a red wheel
barrow

glazed with rain
water

> beside the white
> chickens [25]

The rigorous metrical convention of the poem demands simply three words in the first line of each couplet and a disyllable in the second. But the line termini cut the words "wheelbarrow" and "rainwater" into their constituents, without the use of hyphenation to warn that the first noun is to be part of a compound, *with the implication that they are phenomenological constituents as well.* The wheel plus the barrow equals the wheelbarrow, and in the freshness of light after the rain (it is this kind of light which the poem is *about,* although never mentioned directly), things seem to lose their compounded properties. Instead of Milton's shifting back and forth from original to derived meanings of words, Williams "etymologizes" his compounds into their prior phenomena, and his verbal act represents, and makes the reader carry out, a meditative one. The formal device is no surface trick. But in an even more famous poem from the same group, Williams employs an enjambment which is directly in the line of Milton's type of revisionary disclosure:

> By the road to the contagious hospital
> under the surge of the blue
> mottled clouds driven from the
>
> northeast—a cold wind. Beyond, the
> waste of broad, muddy fields
> brown with dried weeds, standing and fallen [26]

"Blue" in the second line might be nominal, and the surge of azure sky might be a too-easily gained sign of spring; the enjambment pulls it back into adjectival status, paired with, and half-modifying, "mottled." The fairly hard but merely systematic enjambments of "the" in the next two lines tend to soften, in retrospect, the modulation of "blue," as if to suggest, perhaps, that closure is no norm, that linearity has no marked integrity other than the rough typographical width of somewhere around thirty ems.

In all the variations of verse system which twentieth-century poetry has produced, the role of enjambment has expanded considerably: in many kinds of free verse, the mere modulation of degrees of hardness or softness along the spectrum is a more fundamental means of maintaining pace and dramatic build, of controlling the motion of attention along the flow of language, than modulation of line length itself. But this legacy from Milton descended in no closed line of succession. Indeed, Milton's functional, rather than merely rhythmic "music" in his "variety of pauses" seems to have gone largely unheard in the eighteenth century. Even in bald stylistic parody, where perceptions of structure are mechanically heightened and gears creak where, in the original, energy flowed, there is no sense of it. In "The Splendid Shilling," John Philips can only broadly mock an inverted syntax which an Augustan ear could take but as delayed, even tardy complement. Invariably a sinking or mock-heroic descent occurs when the reader is dropped into, rather than discovers, the object of the verb in such cases as

> if he his ample Palm
> Should haply on ill-fated Shoulder lay
> Of Debtor
>
> [ll. 60–62]

In Philips's parody, the wit moves in a direction opposite to that of usual mock-heroic, in that the honest substance of Grub Street life ridicules the high style. At its best, the repeated effect is very funny, as at the first appearance of the dun:

> What should I do? or wither turn? amaz'd,
> Confounded, to the dark recess I fly
> Of woodhole
>
> [ll. 42–44]

The "dark recess" is made of no embrowning shades, as only the hypallage underlined by the line-break reveals. This is one of the few instances in the poem of that form of discovered incompleteness of the previous line. When Philips continues with "strait my bristling hairs erect / Through sudden fear" he cannot take advantage, as Milton would, of the hypothetical adjectival status of "erect" simply because his periods are un-Miltonically short, and because he has not prepared for the effect in the texture of the insufficiently Latinate lines.

Throughout the eighteenth century, Miltonic blank verse tended to neglect the poetic effects of syntactic modulation which degrees of enjambment might achieve. Young and the Wartons wrote what was the next thing to unrhymed couplets, in this respect. Cowper's line-endings in *The Task* show a "variety of pauses," but they are ineffective for anything more than control of pace. Thomson occasionally generates an expressive effect, but they are only of the type which either call attention to the terminal word, or act mimetically through pacing. Thus, in the latter instance, the sounds of the hunt in *Autumn* are recapitulated:

> O'er a wild, harmless, flying Creature, all
> Mix'd in sad Tumult, and discordant Joy.[27]

[ll. 428–29]

The young William Blake, in the flagrantly experimental blank-verse poems of *Poetical Sketches,* would show himself to be as attentive a reader of the verse of *Paradise Lost* as he was responsive to its dialectic. The systematic variation of iambic pentameter lines in the poems to the seasons, and "To the Evening Star," for example, distort accentual-syllabic patternings both in the direction of pure syllabism ("Thy soft kisses on her bosom; and put") and the strange accentualism that occasionally operates in the adapted fourteeners of the long poems later on (as in this Alexandrine from "To Winter" functioning as a pentameter: "Is driv'n yelling to his caves beneath mount Hecla"). This kind of systematic variation may have been part of the young poet's war with eighteenth-century pseudo-Miltonic blank verse. But the "variety of pauses" in these five poems is even more considerable.[28]

In "To Spring" the line-endings suggest those of Cowper or Thomson, the cuts being made frequently between monosyllabic verb and object: "turn / Thine angel eyes"; "taste / Thy morn"; "put / Thy golden crown," etc. But "To Summer" starts out with a more forceful breaking:

> O Thou, who passest thro' our vallies in
> Thy strength, curb thy fierce steeds, allay the heat

[ll. 1–2]

The *contre-rejet* reveals an unexpected power of word and designation—the "fierce steeds" come hard upon the shock of discovery that summer will assault, rather than caress, and that the second line terminus is iambic, "the heat" being reinforced by its assonance with "fierce steeds." Several such cuts accumulate in the second stanza, where terminal words, normally unstressed in their phrases, receive syllabic attention at the line break:

> Sit down; and in our mossy vallies, on
> Some bank beside a river clear, throw thy
> Silk draperies off, and rush into the stream
>
> [ll. 10–12]

—whereas in the final strophe, the line endings are cut at clausal or parallel phrasal breaks, giving a strong, resolved, declamatory cast to the individual lines.

It is in "To the Evening Star," however, that Blake makes his most sophisticated and truly Miltonic use of "sense variously drawn out":

> Smile on our loves, and, while thou drawest the
> Blue curtains of the sky, scatter thy silver dew
> On every flower that shuts its sweet eyes
> In timely sleep. Let thy west wind sleep on
> The lake; speak silence with thy glimmering eyes
>
> [ll. 5–9]

The cut at "the / Blue curtains" initiates an accentual Alexandrine, bracketed by the *contre-rejet* "Blue" and its rhyming "dew"; its architectonic plan is not allowed to remain frozen, however, as "scatter" is modified and made more specific. But it is the "sleep on / The lake" which represents a response to Milton's most complex enjambments. It is of the type we have been examining, which forces a reinterpretation of the syntax when the opening words of the run-over line are indeed discovered to be a true *contre-rejet*— "sleep on" could be closed, and mean "continue sleeping undisturbed," a reading enforced by the terminal stress position of "on." But this reading (the complete verb phrase, call it *A*) gives way to *B*, a truncated prepositional phrase, whose stress pattern would be "sleep on" (as in "sleep on the floor," for example). As we read, we expect *A*, discover that *B* is meant, and are left with the blurred superposition of the two syntactic alternatives, "keep on sleeping (because?) on the lake" being the resulting phantom image.

Blake's sensitivity to Milton's device is understandable, as is his eventual lack of interest in developing its use in the long poems,[29] where it might have seemed to function more as Blake's hated color or harmony, than as his beloved line or melody. Perhaps, too, he saw Milton's use of it as an attempted substitute for the ultimate intransigence of English word-order syntax. Latin verse can produce phantom images by nonsyntactic adjacency alone, as in

sed nox atra caput tristi circumvolat umbra

[Aeneid, vi.866]

where "head" is surrounded by "black" and "sad," neither of which actually modifies it, but *seems to,* or modifies metaphorically. Milton was to see that the *simultaneous* variousness of the drawing-out of sense from one verse to another could produce such hovering effects, which would vanish in the paraphrase of prose as totally as those of their Latin counterparts would do in translation. Milton's English iambic pentameter was better able to produce such effects, utilizing the underlinings and emphases given by iambic stress-maxima, by cutting into its own syntax—producing scholia of and on itself—than even his Latin predecessors could. What Donald Davie has called "syntax as music" certainly claimed the youthful Milton's ear when he encountered the enjambments of the sonnets of della Casa.[30] But he was able, by plying that most remarkable instrument of English meter, seeming to work midway in the mind between eye and ear, to invent a new mode of image-making in English poetry. Even as lexical diachrony could function in *Paradise Lost* as an emblem of fall or rise, so, at a higher (or deeper, as recent linguistic theory would suggest) level, he could work with syntax (or at least, the experience of scanning it) as image. His invention proved so subtle as well as so powerful that with few exceptions (some instances in Keats and G. M. Hopkins, for example) it would go unused until the syllabic and accentual integrity of the poetic line broke down in twentieth-century improvised metrical styles.

NOTES

1. Samuel Johnson, "Milton," *Lives of the English Poets.*

2. I shall use [˘, ´] to mean unstressed and stressed syllables in accentual-syllabic verse; our commonly used, casual [∪ ´] notation borrows its two markers from quantitative and accentual notational systems, and is rather like a mixed metaphor or a Graeco-Latin compound.

3. Whether or not this effect is merely statistical, given the consequences of the penultimate stress rule in Latin, is problematic. See Charles Gordon Cooper, *An Introduction to the Latin Hexameter* (Melbourne and New York, 1952), for an excellent treatment of these matters, as well as the discussion of applications to English in G. L. Hendrickson, "Elizabethan Quantitative Hexameters," *Philological Quarterly,* 28 (1949), 237–60. The reader of modern English, too, can perceive the effects of a terminus marked by features *outside* the metrical system: consider three lines of pure syllabic verse, à la Marianne Moore or W. H. Auden, with ten syllables and no assigned stress patterns. In the following example they will all terminate in an accentual iambic close; or, if one prefers the terminology of Halle and Keyser, stress maxima in even positions:

> Open windows in the morning are bright;
> Closed transoms give on the hallway and spill
> No intriguing pale yellow squares of sun. . . .

4. John Dryden, *Epistle Dedicatory to "The Rival Ladies"* (1694), in *Essays* (Everyman Ed.), pp. 187–88.

5. Paul Valéry, *Analects,* trans. Stuart Gilbert (Princeton, 1970), p. 102.

6. John Milton, *Paradise Lost,* prefatory note on "The Verse." The text, as in all quotations from Milton throughout, is that of M. Y. Hughes (New York, 1957).

7. Ben Jonson, "A Fit of Rime Against Rime," ll. 10–12.

8. William Blake, "To the Public," preface to *Jerusalem;* the text is that of David V. Erdman and Harold Bloom (New York, 1970), p. 144.

9. Alistair Fowler, *Triumphal Form* (Cambridge, 1970).

10. Further study may show this to be a widespread convention for assuring the attentive reading that the shock it felt was deliberately intended. Thus, in "The Tunnel" section of Hart Crane's *The Bridge,* in an almost exclusively closed iambic pentameter environment, we get: "That last night on the ballot rounds did you / Shaking, did you deny the ticket, Poe?"

11. Christopher Ricks, *Milton's Grand Style* (Oxford, 1963).

12. Donald Davie, "Syntax and Music in *Paradise Lost*" (in *The Living Milton,* ed. Frank Kermode [London, 1960]), pp. 70–84, opened up many of the problems

of line-ending in *Paradise Lost* and was able to argue, before many other critics of Milton's verse, from the phenomenology of the act of reading.

13. In *Poetic Diction* (2d ed., New York, 1957), 120–22.

14. Seymour Chatman set up the category "alternative" lines (midway between "run-on" and "end-stopped") in which, loosely defined as it is, these Miltonic examples might fall. See "Comparing Metrical Styles," in *Essays on the Language of Literature,* ed. Seymour Chatman and Samuel R. Levin (Boston, 1967), pp. 148–49; but the insensitively performatory approach to the nature of the poetic line (as in "Caesura, end-stoppage, and enjambment only exist in actual performance, since they are phonological, not orthographic phenomena," p. 148) tended to confirm the suspicions of W. K. Wimsatt and others that Chatman's methods could contribute little to the understanding of English meter and its role in the poetic process.

15. See for example, "Caesura," in the *Encyclopedia of Poetry and Poetics,* ed. Alex Preminger and Frank Warnke (Princeton, 1965). In classical verse, the rule that the caesura must fall within a foot serves to give it a *linking* role, and diaeresis, the coincidence of foot and word-boundary, falling at the end of the third foot of the heroic line, would have a cutting function.

16. A line should be drawn at this point between a linguistic, and a purely graphic, effect. This extreme left-hand end of the spectrum is only engaged by twentieth-century verse in any case, but certainly an accentually-syllabic strict couplet like "O, now / A Cow," done as

O, NOV / V A COW

is "concrete poetry," and hence a branch of graphic art; cutting a grapheme as it does, it is not annotating language, but abstracting forms.

17. My colleague Samuel R. Levin recognized, in "The Conventions of Poetry" (in *Literary Style: A Symposium,* ed. Seymour Chatman [London and New York, 1971], pp. 172–74) the need for some kind of hierarchy of junctural features. In another context, Roger Fowler observed that the shorter the lexical unit, the less likely it is to be enjambed.

18. In "The Concept of Meter: An Exercise in Abstraction" (1959, reprinted in *Essays in the Language of Literature,* pp. 91–114), some problems raised by Chatman's approach led to a formulation tacitly assumed throughout the present essay, and affirmed in different form in the author's own "The Metrical Emblem" (1960), reprinted in the same volume, pp. 115–26. "The Rule and the Norm," in which Wimsatt and Beardsley refined their argument with respect, this time, to the schematic treatment of English iambic meter by Halle and Keyser, appeared in *Literary Style: A Symposium,* pp. 197–215.

19. "Topics in the Theory of Generative Grammar," in Noam Chomsky, *Selected Readings,* ed. Allen and Van Buren (London, 1971), p. 11.

20. Ludwig Wittgenstein, *Philosophical Investigations,* II.11; I think this is more appropriate an analogy than the alternating readings of, say, the Necker cube, as the graphic conventions being punned upon in the first instance are more like linguistic ones of the kind at work in our example.

21. As Hopkins seems to do in the hard cut at the end of the first line of "The Windhover": "morning's minion, king- / Dom of daylight's dauphin."

22. But note that in "A halfpenny will help you scrape a knee," the allowable stressings for "hálfpènny" and "scrápe à knée," permit one to give way, and the iambic context to dissolve (when sung, for example, to the tune of Richard Rodgers's "To Keep My Love Alive"). The [′ · ′] metrical treatment mediates between two other extremes:

$$[\; ′ \; \cdot \; \cdot \;] \; \text{halfpenny} \rightarrow \; ′ \; \cdot \; ′ \; \leftarrow \text{scrape a knee} \; [\; \cdot \; \cdot \; ′ \;]$$

One of the reasons that trisyllabic rhyming played such an important part in the history of light verse from Browning through Old Possum is that it allows for the momentary comic fiction that syllables or morphemes are punning words in another syntactic context—as in Lorenz Hart's sequence "Like a wreck to me—appendectomy" from the song mentioned above.

23. Allen Mandelbaum has pointed out to me that whereas Dante presents a brilliant and subtle range of enjambments across particles like *quando*, it is not until Canto 17 of the *Purgatory* that a strong cut appears, where it is quickly tempered by the eventual rhyme. Thus

> Questi è divino spirito, che ne la
> Via d'andar su ne drizza senza prego
> E col suo lume sè medesmo cela

[II.17, 55–57]

24. Or, even more abrupt a case, from *The Wasteland* (ll. 253–54), "When lovely woman stoops to folly and / Paces about her room again, alone," where the surprise is reversed when we discover that the famous Goldsmith quotation will not end the line, and the "and" is promoted metrically and syntactically both. Such a joke of promotion may stem from Lewis Carroll's "And when I found the door was shut, / I tried to turn the handle but."

25. "Spring and All," 22 (1923).

26. "Spring and All," 1.

27. Or, in the former mode, "Immortal Peter! First of Monarchs! He / His stubborn country tam'd" (*Winter*, ll. 965–66).

28. Alicia M. Ostriker discusses the meter of the *Poetical Sketches* and the enjambments in particular (*Vision and Verse in William Blake* [Madison, 1965], pp. 36–40); her definition of enjambment as "run-on or absence of pause at the end of the line" prevents her from realizing the syntactic possibilities of the Miltonic type, and she has nothing of interest to say about specific cases.

29. Ostriker comments usefully on this, pp. 134–36.

30. The discussion of this in F. T. Prince, *The Italian Element in Milton's Verse* (Oxford, 1954), pp. 14–33, remains the most authoritative one.

Swift and the Poetry of Allusion: "The Journal"

AUBREY WILLIAMS

Jonathan Swift spent most of the summer of 1721 at Gaulstown House, country seat of Lord Chief Baron Robert Rochfort, and one consequence of this sojourn was a small and charming poem called "The Journal," which Sir Walter Scott described as a "humorous poetical record of the occupations of the family and visitors." [1] Seemingly a most slight piece, the poem nevertheless prompted a considerable amount of invidious comment in Swift's own day. For one thing, he was severely criticized because one short passage, in which the household is described assembling for dinner, seemed to some a blasphemous allusion to the Last Judgment. As Scott noted:

> The Dean has been censured, on an idle supposition of this passage [ll. 25–34] being an allusion to the day of judgment. So says Mr. Faulkner, in corroboration of which I observe, that, in "Gulliveriana," the passage is printed in Italics, with an index placed opposite, to call the attention. In the Whitehall Journal, the editor refuses to believe that the piece is Swift's, "because so pious a person as the Dean could not possibly forget all respect and reverence for things sacred, as to turn the day of judgment so openly into ridicule, as the author of this lampoon most manifestly does in this burlesque piece." [2]

There is no evidence that Swift was in any way perturbed by such comment as this, but there is testimony that he was exasperated by charges that his poem represented an act of rude ingratitude toward his hosts at Gaulstown. Because he had scorned certain pomposities of William Percival, Dean of Emly, and had also therein disdained some paltry chatter of the Dean's wife, Percival was incensed enough to publish a poetical reply, called "A Description, In Answer to the Journal." Designed primarily as an indictment of Swift for avarice and inhospitality in the management of the deanery of Saint Patrick's, Percival's poem also charges Swift with a gross lack of gratitude to the Rochforts:

> Sometimes to Gallstown he will go,
> To spend a month or two, or so,
> Admires the baron, George and's spouse,
> Lives well, and then lampoons the house.[3]

It was not from Percival alone, however, that such charges were directed at Swift. When "The Journal" was reprinted, in 1723,[4] in the *Whitehall Journal*, a prefatory letter from Dublin contained these paragraphs:

The malevolents amongst us cast invidious reflections on the Dean for writing this poem; and say that it was odd in him, after the kindest entertainment for some months together at Mr. Rochfort's house, who was Lord Chief Baron in this kingdom, in the last reign, to vanish away one morning *sans ceremonie;* and that it was ungrateful, after having sucked all the sweets of Gaulstown, to leave the following sting behind him.

If you give this packet a place in your Journal, you will oblige a vast number of your admirers in this kingdom, who are impatient to see the Dean's satire upon the hospitable Baron, and the rest of his friends and messmates, for almost a whole summer.[5]

Some ten years later, after publication of "The Grand Question Debated, Whether Hamilton's Bawn should be turned into a Barrack or a Malt-House," Swift felt obliged to refute charges of ingratitude against that poem as well as revived charges against "The Journal." Writing to the Reverend Henry Jenny on June 8, 1732, he opens with a reference to a set of verses passed about Dublin:

The subject was my great ingratitude and breach of hospitality in publishing a copy of verses called Hamilton's Bawn. The writer hath likewise taken severe notice of some other verses published many years ago by the indiscretion of a friend, to whom they were sent in a letter. It was called a Journal, and writ at Mr. Rochfort's; and the consequences drawn from both by this late writer is, that the better

I am used in any family the more I abuse them; with other reflections that must follow from such a principle.[6]

In his correspondence during the summer of 1721 Swift refers several times to the actual mode and circumstances of life at Gaulstown, with no hint of dissension or even annoyance—until a letter written shortly after his departure thence. In early July he tells Esther Vanhomrigh that at Gaulstown he is "as deep employd in othr Folks Plantations and Ditchings as if they were my own Concern." In early September he tells Knightley Chetwode the weather has been so bad for ten weeks that he has been "hindered from several rambles," but on the same day he writes to the Reverend John Worrall that, though he plans to return to Dublin by October 1, "a fit of good weather would tempt me a week longer," and he continues, "but I row or ride every day, in spite of the rain, in spite of a broken shin, or falling into the lakes, and several other trifling accidents." Toward the end of September, in a letter to Archbishop William King, he again mentions the daily activities that will eventually appear as events in the poetical record:

My Lord, I row after Health like a Waterman, and ride after it like a Post boy, and find some little Success; but *subeunt morbi tristisque senectus*. I have a Receipt to which you are a Stranger; my Lord *Oxford* and Mr. *Prior* used to join with me in taking it, to whom I often said, when we were two Hours diverting ourselves with Trifles, *vive la bagatelle*. I am so deep among the Workmen at Mr. Rochfort's Canals and Lakes, so dextrous at the Oar, such an Alderman after the Hare. . . . [7]

Yet on October 6, from Dublin, he writes to the Reverend Daniel Jackson, one of his fellow guests at Gaulstown, a letter that suggests he did indeed terminate his summer visit *sans ceremonie,* and also suggests that both he and his hosts had found his stay growing tense and tedious. Here is the start of his letter to Jackson, still at Gaulstown: "I had no mind to load you with the secret of my going, because you should bear none of the blame. I talk upon a supposition, that Mr. Rochfort had a mind to keep me longer, which I will allow in him and you, but not one of the family besides, who I confess had reason enough to be weary of a man, who entered into none of their tastes, nor pleasures, nor fancies, nor opinions, nor talk." [8]

However much he outstayed his welcome at Gaulstown, and whatever vexations he endured there, Swift nevertheless attempted in his letter to Jenny ten years afterward, to make it clear that he considered such poems as "The Journal" and "The Grand Question Debated" as being among those trifles in verse which fell from him, not as abuses of hospitality, but as "amusements in hours of sickness or leisure, or in private families, to divert ourselves and some neighbours, but were never intended for publick view, which is plain from the subjects and the careless ways of handling them." [9] Yet trifles were important to Swift, as his "Receipt" of *vive la bagatelle* indicates, and often his triflings become something more than mere beguiling divertissements, a fact shrewdly noted by Bolingbroke in a comment addressed to Swift during the very middle of his stay at Gaulstown: "you see I amuse myself *de la bagatelle* as much as you, but here lyes the difference, yr *bagatelle* leads to some thing better, as fiddlers flourish carelessly before they play a fine air, but mine begins, proceeds, and ends in bagatelle." [10] Far from being a graceless lampoon on his hosts and messmates at Gaulstown, "The Journal" may rather be seen as something better—a humorous yet telling illustration of the way in which the quite humdrum, and quite autobiographical, events of a manorial day may be turned into an artful and canny comment on the inherent dissatisfactions of mortal life, no matter how tranquil and secure that life may seem to be, at first, amid the patterns of life in rural retreat.

When "The Journal" was reprinted in the Pope-Swift *Miscellanies* of 1732, its title became "The Country Life." Either title seems especially appropriate, though "journal," with its meaning of a record of diurnal activities, may seem more relevant to the actual structure of Swift's poem. This structure is essentially horological, a narration of events in a typical day on a country estate in an hour-by-hour fashion. At the same time, the poem is divided into two distinct parts, the second of which constitutes a gloss on the first—a gloss that is fundamentally ironic and comic, but also crosshatched with darker lines of human discontent.

The very opening line hints at the ultimate conflation of the idyllic, the comic, and the serious in the poem, for in it Swift invokes Thalia, the muse not only of comedy but also of pastoral or bucolic poetry, and yet asks that she inspire him with "sober" verse:

> THALIA, tell in sober Lays,
> How George, Nim, Dan, Dean pass their Days.

George is the eldest son of the Lord Chief Baron, and Nim is the Baron's second son, John, an ardent hunter. Dan is the Reverend Daniel Jackson to whom Swift was later to write the explanation of his sudden departure from Gaulstown, while Dean is of course Swift himself. These persons, along with Lady Betty, George's wife, and the Baron, are the chief characters of the poem.

The first sixty lines of the poem tell the hours of a country day from the moment when Swift, a bustling and rather officious personage in his own poetical record, rises at seven and, in his

> Night-gown drest,
> Goes round the House to wake the rest,

until the close of the day when the "weary Dean goes to his Chamber." The course of the day seems marked by pursuits of an essentially cheerful and tranquil nature, and it scarcely seems a merely casual fact, furthermore, that in the first assemblage of the day, even before the family and guests collect at breakfast,

> grave Nim and George Facetious,
> Go to the Dean to read Lucretius.

Now it is true that Swift and his friends could just as well have spent an hour every morning reading Horace or Virgil or even Shakespeare. But it is also most appropriate that a record of the felicities of rural retirement should show each day beginning with a small domestic reading or discussion of the De rerum natura, the great poem which celebrated the doctrines of Epicurus. As Sir William Temple had noted, Epicurus passed "his Life wholly in his Garden" and considered that no life other than one of rural retirement contributed so much to the true happiness of man, for there the

Sweetness of Air, the Pleasantness of Smells, the Verdure of Plants, the Cleanness and Lightness of Food, the Exercises of Working or Walking; but above all, the Exemption from Cares and Solicitude, seem equally to favour and improve Contemplation and Health, the Enjoyment of Sense and Imagination, and thereby the Quiet and Ease both of the Body and Mind.[11]

A principal aim of Lucretius in *De rerum natura* had been the freeing of man from fear, particularly fear of death and fear of punishment by the gods after death. But he had also wanted to free man from the other vanities of life which could only bring cares and vexations of all kinds in their train. And so the opening lines of Book II of his poem (lines alluded to in scores of late seventeenth-century English poems on the blessings of country life) treat with scorn those "mistaken Mortals" who

> with Cares and Dangers vex each Hour
> To reach the Top of Wealth, and Sov'reign Pow'r.

In contrast to such, Lucretius extolls those who understand that "frugal Nature seeks for only Ease," and also extolls those who strive to achieve

> A Body free from Pains, free from Disease;
> A Mind from Cares and Jealousies at Peace.[12]

Whatever stress one may wish to place upon the daily readings of Lucretius at Gaulstown, it is nevertheless true that the first half of "The Journal" proceeds to describe a country day which seems to exemplify, though in humorous terms to be sure, a life of mild bucolic labors along with conviviality of conversation and tranquillity of mind. When the reading of Lucretius is interrupted by Lady Betty at ten, even her small tyrannies seem the affectionate exercise of wifely authority:

> At Ten, my Lady comes and Hectors,
> And kisses *George,* and ends our Lectures:

> And when she has him by the Neck fast,
> Hawls him, and scolds us down to Breakfast.

Squandering an hour or so at this meal, the four men disperse during midday to follow their "peculiar Whimseys": some to rowing, others to reading or darning hose or gardening, another to peeping "in the Ponds to look for Spawn." Their various diversions, moreover, seem to be given a special orientation when each is associated with one of the four elements:

> At Two or after we return all,
> From the four Elements assembling,
> Warn'd by the Bell, all Folks [13] come trembling,
> From Airy Garrets some descend,
> Some from the Lakes remotest end.
> My Lord and *Dean,* the Fire forsake;
> *Dan* leaves the Earthly Spade and Rake,
> The Loyt'res quake, no Corner hides them,
> And Lady *Betty* soundly chides them.

It was this passage which provoked some of Swift's contemporaries to charge him with a blasphemous allusion to the Last Judgment, though any irreverence in the lines would seem to derive mainly from a beam in the eye of a malicious beholder. At the same time, if we keep in mind the daily sessions spent in reading Lucretius, the lines may seem especially ironic, for as noted earlier one of the specific aims of *De rerum natura* was to free man from any fear of judgment and punishment after death. But however one may interpret such a bit of covert fancy on Swift's part, the introduction of the four elements into the poem does seem to suggest a microcosmic world in which the concordant activities of labor and recreation have become so harmonized as to be almost indistinguishable. An allusion to the four elements in a poem on country life seems, in fact, to have had a special propriety; as Abraham Cowley noted in his essay "Of Agriculture," the "Principles" of a "Country life" are "the same which *Ennius* made to be the Principles of all Nature: Earth, Water, Air, and the Sun." It seems no accident, therefore, that Jonson's "To Penshurst" should celebrate an estate which "joy'st in better marks, of soil, of air, /

Of wood, of water," or that Pope's "Windsor-Forest" should celebrate a landscape whose features are

> as the World, harmoniously confus'd:
> Where Order in Variety we see,
> And where, tho' all things differ, all agree.

In summoning the inhabitants of Gaulstown from the four corners
and elements of their own little world, Swift may simply be claiming for his own poem a place in the poetry of country life, and
perhaps also claiming that in certain ways his poem may be a comparison of small things with large.

After dinner, with its observations of the traditional pieties
("Now Water's brought, and Dinner done, / With Church and
King"), and after an interlude of napping or reading or card-
playing, the mild exertions of the day are resumed, though still in
keeping with the cadences already established, and in keeping,
indeed, with the diurnal pace of the sun itself:

> *George, Nim* and *Dean* set out at Four,
> And then again, Boys, to the Oar.
> But when the Sun goes to the Deep,
> Not to disturb him in his Sleep;
> Or make a rumbling o'er his Head,
> His Candle out, and he a Bed.
> We watch his Motions to a Minute,
> And Leave the Flood when he goes in it.

With the departure of the sun so respectfully observed, the household goes to prayers, to cards, to supper, to a final hour of drink or
chat. And then Swift brings the first half of his poem, and the benign cycle of its day, to an emphatic close:

> So when this Circle we have run,
> The Curtain falls, and we have done.

In the first half of "The Journal" life at Gaulstown seemed to
parallel that felicitous Epicurean state "in which there are very
many necessary Goods, very few Ills, and in which it is permitted
to lead a Life so sweetly, so quietly, and constantly, as the Com-

pany, Course of Life, Constitution of Body, Age, and other Circumstances will allow." [14] But the real theme of Swift's poem is announced at ll. 115–17, where he tells Patrick Delany (to whom the poem is addressed):

> But you, who are a Scholar, know
> How transient all things are below:
> How prone to change is human life,

And so, picking up the stage metaphor with which he had closed the first half ("The Curtain falls"), he begins the second half by explicit recognition that, to this point, there had been certain omissions in the poetical record:

> I might have mention'd several facts,
> Like *Episodes* between the Acts;
> And tell who loses, and who wins,
> Who gets a Cold, who break their Shins.

From this point on the poem proceeds by a systematic shattering of the atmosphere of bucolic tranquillity and conviviality established in the first half. Dan, who so far has appeared the assured and expert fisherman, is now seen to have "caught nothing in his Net," and we are further told, indeed, "how his Boat was over set." Certain actual events related in the correspondence of the summer also begin to appear: "For brevity," says Swift, "I have retrench'd, / How in the Lake the *Dean* was drench'd." And he goes on:

> It would be an Exploit to brag on,
> How valiant *George* rode o'er the *Dragon;* [15]
> How steady in the Storm [16] he sat,
> And sav'd his Oar, but lost his Hat.
> How *Nim,* no Hunter 'ere could match him,
> Still brings us Hares when he can catch them:
> How skilfully *Dan* mends his Nets,
> How Fortune fails him when he sets:
> Or how the *Dean* delights to vex
> The Ladys, or Lampoon the Sex.

The household which had seemed so amiable is now discomposed, furthermore, by interlopers who ruffle its society and disturb its peace. The tranquillity is initially shattered by the Dean Percival who was later to malign Swift for a supposed lampoon of his hosts, and by his wife, "that Female Pedant." Swift says that he

> might have told how oft *Dean Per——l*
> Displays his Pedantry unmerciful,
> How haughtily he lifts his Nose,
> To tell what ev'ry School Boy knows.

His wife, in utter tediousness of detail, "Shews all her Secrets of House keeping," and so prates on and on about how she

> Was forc'd to send three Miles for Yest,
> To brew her Ale, and raise her Paste:
> Tells ev'ry thing that you can think of,
> How she cur'd *Charley* of the Chincough;
> What gave her Brats and Pigs the Meazles,
> And how her Doves were kill'd by Weezles:
> How Jowler howl'd, and what a fright
> She had with Dreams the other Night.

Twaddling as her speech may be, Mrs. Percival's topics neverthe-less swell the catalogue of petty cares, mischiefs, and mischances so common to the human lot—and so noticeably absent from the first part of the poem.

The disruption of Gaulstown by the Percivals seems slight, however, when compared to the possibility of a much more foreign invasion next seen as engrossing the brain of the lord of the manor. Having "gone so far on" as to admit such blots on domestic peace as the Percivals, Swift decides to give a "word or two of Lord Chief *Baron*," hitherto a scarcely noticed personage on his own estate. More particularly Swift will tell

> how little weight he sets,
> On all Whig Papers, and Gazets:
> But for the Politicks of Pue,
> Thinks ev'ry Syllable is true.

Lord Rochfort had been Attorney-General of Ireland and Speaker of the Irish House of Commons. From 1707 to 1714 he was Chief Baron of the Exchequer, but on the accession of George I he was deprived of this office because of his strong Tory prejudices, and his stubborn adherence to these is indicated by his blind faith in the "Politicks" of *Pue's Occurrences,* a Dublin daily paper of a strong Tory cast. With these facts in mind, Swift's next few lines seem to implicate him in (or at least show him sympathetic to) the various attempts, in the second decade of the eighteenth century, to engage Charles XII of Sweden in an invasion of England for the purpose of restoring a Stuart monarch to the throne.[17]

Charles XII was killed in December 1718, and "The Journal" was not written until 1721. Yet the Lord Chief Baron for some time apparently has not wished to concede his death or give up hopes of the plotted invasions, for Swift writes that

> since he owns the King of *Sweden*
> Is dead at last without evading; [18]
> Now all his hopes are in the *Czar,*
> Why *Muscovy* is not so far.

Relations among England, Sweden, and Russia during this period were strained and complicated. The English king and his Whig supporters were understandably anxious: both at home, because of threatened Jacobite invasions, and abroad, because disputes in the Baltic area were a threat to the territorial interests of George's electorate of Hanover. And with Charles XII and Peter the Great united in hatred and resentment against George, the danger to him as well as to England is clear from the bare outlines of Charles's grand scheme "to wrest from Denmark and Hanover the conquests they had made, to ruin the Hanoverian power, to replace Augustus by Stanislaus on the throne of Poland, to invade England or Scotland in person with a Swedish army transported in Russian ships, and to change the whole tenour of English policy by a restoration of the Stuarts." [19]

Whether or not the Lord Chief Baron actually desired a direct military invasion of England by Muscovite forces (now that Charles was dead) is not clear from the poem. What is clear is that he has not been able or willing to disengage himself from politics and thereby achieve, amid his life of rural retirement, any real detachment or tranquillity of mind. And if the daily readings of

Lucretius are to be seen as having any special import for the way events in the poem are to be viewed, then it is worth remembering that the Latin poet had particularly argued "for avoiding the Miseries of intestine divisions and Civil Wars, the Calamities that in his Days affected the Republick of Rome." [20] It may be worth noting too that only a couple of years before he wrote "The Journal" Swift himself had written a letter to Charles Ford in which he not only expressed a deep personal longing for detachment from political factions, but also used a phrase which associated his thoughts quite specifically with the memorable opening of Book II of *De rerum natura:*

It would be an admirable Scituation to be neither Whig nor Tory. For a Man without Passion might find very strong Amusements. But I find the turn of Blood at 50 disposes me strongly to Fears, and therefore I think as little of Publick Affairs as I can, because they concern me as one of the Multitude; and for the same Reason I dare not venture to play at threepeny Bassett, because it is a Game where Conduct is of no use, and I dare not trust to Fortune as the younger Folks do, and therefore I divert my self with looking upon others at Play mea sine parte pericli [*De rerum natura,* II, 6], which if a Man could do in what concerns the Publick, it would be no ill Entertainment.[21]

In Creech's translation the opening of Book II goes thus:

> 'Tis Pleasant, when the Seas are rough, to stand
> And view another's Danger, safe at Land:
> Not 'cause he's troubled, but 'tis sweet to see
> Those Cares and Fears, from which our selves are free.
> 'Tis also pleasant to behold from far
> How Troops engage, secure our selves from War.
> But above all, 'tis pleasantest to get
> The Top of high Philosophy, and sit
> On the calm, peaceful, flourishing Head of it.
> Whence we may view deep, wondrous deep below,
> How poor mistaken Mortals wand'ring go,
> Seeking the Path to Happiness:

Far from seeking the detachment of mind recommended by such a passage, the master of Gaulstown agitates himself with useless conjectures and most vain hopes. Viewed from the vantage point of Swift's poem (if not exactly from the "Top of high Philosophy"), the perturbations of the Baron's spirit make him seem a good and comic emblem of man's capacity for folly and self-delusion:

> Now all his hopes are in the *Czar,*
> Why *Muscovy* is not so far,
> Down the black Sea, and up the Streights,
> And in a Month he's at your Gates:
> Perhaps from what the Packet brings,
> By *Christmas* we shall see strange things.

Comic as the Baron's fretful speculations may seem, even more absurd appear the anxieties aroused in the other inhabitants of the manor by a petty invasion of Gaulstown that now actually occurs. This last event of his poem Swift introduces with those sententious lines that now seem fully justified in view of the ways, whether lamentable or vexatious or ludicrous, the tranquil country day has been altered for the worse: "How transient all things are below: / How prone to change is human life." And then he goes on:

> Last Night arriv'd *Clem* [22] and his Wife.
> This Grand Event hath broke our Measures,
> Their Reign began with cruel Seizures;
> The *Dean* must with his Quilt supply,
> The Bed in which these Tyrants lie:
> *Nim* lost his Wig-block, *Dan* his Jordan,
> My Lady says she can't afford one;
> *George* is half scar'd out of his Wits,
> For *Clem* gets all the dainty bits.
> Henceforth expect a different survey,
> This House will soon turn topsy turvey;
> They talk of further Alterations,
> Which causes many Speculations.

Now all those who started a day of bucolic retirement with the study of Lucretius are shown as having failed miserably in achieving any kind of ideal of tranquillity, whether Epicurean or otherwise. Utterly disordered and resentful at the arrival of additional guests, the expropriation of a quilt or wig-block or chamber-pot for the newcomers' use can only be regarded, in the exaggerations of their disquiet, as acts of cruel and tyrannical seizure, while the award of a few "dainty bits" to Clem is enough to make George "half scar'd out of his Wits." The seemingly tranquil patterns of country life displayed in the first part of the poem have now been fully shattered.

The fact that Swift apparently chose in 1732 to change the title of his poem to "The Country Life," should alert us to its alliance with the scores of other poems celebratory of rural retirement written during the seventeenth and eighteenth centuries. And as Maren-Sofie Røstvig has shown in her superb treatment of such poems,[23] the vast majority of those written during the latter part of the seventeenth century were saturated with Epicurean and Lucretian attitudes and values. Whether translations or paraphrases of Horace or Virgil and other classical authors, or more original celebrations of the virtues of country life, such poems were almost always influenced by the Epicurean stress on tranquillity of mind and indolency of body [24] or by the Lucretian image of the "Detached Spectator" (Professor Røstvig's phrase) in the opening lines of Book II of *De rerum natura*. And since Lucretius was the avowed espouser of Epicurean ethical thought as well as of Epicurean metaphysics, it is not exactly improbable that in his own poem on the subject of rural retirement Swift should use the name of Lucretius alone to stand for the thought of both.

But while the daily readings of Lucretius may seem to suggest "The Journal's" kinship with earlier English poems of country life, and also may remind us of their Lucretian/Epicurean tenor, we yet can see that the second half of Swift's poem directly challenges any notion that man can achieve perfect tranquillity of mind or indolence of body in this life, no matter how idyllic the circumstances of his rural retreat may seem. Far from being a discourteous lampoon of his hosts at Gaulstown, Swift's poem seems rather a seriocomic controversion given to a poetic genre that had come to be associated with a whole set of soft-headed Epicurean notions about human nature and the human condition. And of course Swift's overturn of the illusions about human nature fostered in earlier poems of country life is exactly what we should expect from such a Christian realist.

Swift's dispute with Lucretius (if the poem can indeed be regarded as such) was scarcely an eccentric one and had many parallels in other seventeenth-century writings. A good illustration of this can be found in a sermon by the Reverend Isaac Barrow, where it is argued, against the Epicureans specifically, that "all present enjoyments are transient and evanid; and of any future thing, in this kingdom of change and contingency, there can be no assurance." (This statement, given the two contexts, is remarkably similar to the one moral sentence of Swift's poem: "How transient all things are below: / How prone to change is human life.") Barrow then describes the Epicurean vision thus:

The Epicureans did conceit and boast, that having by their atheistical explications of natural effects, and common events here, discarded the belief and dread of religion, they had laid a strong foundation for tranquillity of mind, had driven away all the causes of grief and fear, so that nothing then remained troublesome or terrible unto us; and consequently, what, said they, could forbid, but that we should be entirely contented, glad and happy?

Against such a "conceit" Barrow argues that unless the Epicurean can "trample down reason, new mould human nature, subjugate all natural appetites and passions, alter the state of things here, and transform the world, he will yet in the greatest part fail of his conceited advantages; very short he will fall of triumphing in a contented and quiet mind." Contrary to all Epicurean expectations, there can be nothing on this earth that is not liable to disappointments and crosses, for, no matter what, man's reason, "reflecting on present evils, and boding others future, will afflict him," and at the same time "his own unsatiable desires, unavoidable fears, and untameable passions, will disquiet him." [25]

Swift seems to agree fully with Barrow, for the strophe and antistrophe of his poem show how lamentably fallacious an image of rural tranquillity may be. His manorial residents (including himself) are ludicrously unable to escape not only such mishaps as

drenchings and seizures; they are also ludicrously unable to escape
the cares, resentments, fears, petty jealousies, and griefs that, from
any realistic point of view, are a perennial and intrinsic portion of
fallen human nature. Seemingly so slight and familial, constructed
out of a visit during which the Dean really did break his shin and
catch a cold, "The Journal" may finally seem to be, in Bolingbroke's words, "some thing better" than a mere bagatelle, or an
ungracious lampoon. So charming a little poem may also help us
to realize that, next to Pope, Swift was the best and most subtly
allusive poet of his time.

NOTES

1. *The Works of Jonathan Swift,* ed. Sir Walter Scott, 19 vols. (Boston, 1883),
I, 252.

2. Ibid., XIV, 165–66.

3. The entire poem is printed in ibid., I, 253–56. See also *The Poems of Jonathan
Swift,* ed. Harold Williams, 3 vols. (Oxford, 1958), I, 277.

4. Apparently it was first published in 1721.

5. *Works,* XIV, 164.

6. *The Correspondence of Jonathan Swift,* ed. Harold Williams, 5 vols. (Oxford,
1963, 1965), IV, 26.

7. Ibid., II, 393, 401, 402–403, 406.

8. Ibid., II, 407–08.

9. Ibid., IV, 27.

10. Ibid., II, 400.

11. "Upon the Gardens of Epicurus," in *The Works of Sir William Temple,* 2 vols.
(London, 1720), I, 175.

12. *T. Lucretius Carus, Of the Nature of Things,* tr. Thomas Creech, 2 vols.
(London, 1714), II, 11, 12–13, 19–20.

13. Some versions read "Flocks."

14. Thomas Stanley, *The History of Philosophy,* 3rd ed. (London, 1701), p. 547.

15. The Dragon was "My Lord Chief Baron's smaller Boat."

16. Some versions read "Sterne."

17. A sense of the contemporary response to the threat of a Swedish invasion can be gathered from a pamphlet, attributed to Daniel Defoe, called *What If the Swedes Should Come?* (London, 1717).

18. Some versions read "Invading."

19. W. E. H. Lecky, *A History of England in the Eighteenth Century*, 8 vols. (New York, 1891), I, 256.

In view of all these facts, Swift's own admiration for Charles XII during this period is intriguing, particularly when it is recalled that he intended to dedicate his *Abstract of the History of England* to the Swedish king (see *Correspondence*, II, 311*n*) and had hoped to visit the Swedish court (*Correspondence*, I, 153). Even more interesting is Swift's decision, the year after Charles's death, to dedicate his *Abstract* to the Count de Gyllenborg, the Swedish ambassador to England who was arrested in January 1717 and expelled from the kingdom a few months later for complicity in Charles's plot to support a Jacobite uprising with 12,000 Swedish troops (see *Correspondence*, III, 63*n*).

20. Lucretius, *Of the Nature of Things*, I, d4ᵛ.

21. *Correspondence*, II, 312.

22. Clement Barry, a "chief Favourite and Governour of Gallstown."

23. Maren-Sofie Røstvig, *The Happy Man: Studies in the Metamorphoses of a Classical Ideal*, 2 vols. (Oslo, 1954, 1958).

24. I.e. freedom from bodily pain or suffering.

25. "The Profitableness of Godliness," in *Theological Works of Isaac Barrow*, ed. Alexander Napier, 9 vols. (Cambridge, 1859), I, 211, 213–14, 215–16.

The Strategies of Biography and Some Eighteenth-Century Examples

FRANK BRADY

The rudimentary state of biographical theory can be blamed on biography's anomalous status among literary forms. It is based on fact, and modern criticism hardly knows what to do with the factual. Our critical position presents a curious inversion of eighteenth-century literalism: "The value of every story depends on its being true. A story is a picture either of an individual or of human nature in general: if it be false, it is a picture of nothing." [1] So Dr. Johnson, whose writings and conversation demonstrate how narrowly he interpreted "truth." But for the modern critic the only meaningful truth, in a *literary sense,* is the truth of the imagination. If the truthful is also "factual," if it claims to portray directly the world of present or past, it is cast into the literary limbo known as "descriptive or assertive writing." Imaginative literature must not be contaminated by anything more than incidental reference to historical experience, or it becomes suspected of such pernicious aims as trying to change our opinions or influence our behavior.

This argument from the necessity for "disinterest" provides one basis for the modern attitude toward the factual. Another assumption behind this attitude is that primarily factual material, like biography, is artistically unworkable, though an occasional life may inherently display that shapeliness, drama, or coherence characteristic of the best fiction. [2] When fact and fiction are inescapably mixed, as in Shakespeare's history plays, critics ordinarily reduce the historical material to fictional status, which conveniently eliminates any possible theoretical problems posed by this combination. Yet problems remain. Hugh Kenner remarks about *Robinson Crusoe:* "For to be told, poker-faced, that it is not the fabrication we would gladly accept, but the very thing that is normally fabricated—a memoir, a testimony—this somehow changes a book, even when we do not believe what we are being told about it." [3] Yes, but how does it change a book? Consider, for example, the peculiarly unsettling effect of certain short stories by Borges, where fiction masquerades as fact.[4]

Just a narrative device, the critic may comment, and in any case biography is safely factual. If it takes the form of a fictional reconstruction of the thoughts and actions of real persons, it is usually dismissed as a hybrid hardly worth despising. Biography indeed could be comfortably subsumed under history if it did not reveal some suspicious resemblances to the novel in plot, character, and setting. Also at its inception in the eighteenth century, the English novel was so intertwined with biography that the resemblances between these forms will not go away.[5] In terms of plot, the full-scale (birth to death) biography belongs in the same class with its fictional counterpart, the "Life and Adventures of" or "History of" novel. The biographer still faces the same problems that confronted Defoe in *Moll Flanders* and Fielding in *Tom Jones*—and, incidentally, should be as ruthless as they are in skipping over uneventful periods in his hero's life. This birth-to-death plot structure may seem primitive, unless shaped with the sophistication of a Fielding or a Flaubert, but what the biography loses in smoothness and coherence may well be compensated for by its sense of actuality. For while fiction (poetry, drama) is superior to biography (history) in its intensive and generalizing properties, biography carries a greater feeling of authenticity than fiction. We grant to truth what we would refuse to imagination.

Novelists have exploited the fundamental plot resemblances between biography and fiction from the novel's beginning, but biographers with disastrous innocence have too often conceived of themselves as chroniclers. Chronicle is merely the basis of biography, the gathering of its material, not biography itself.[6] Depending on his material, the biographer can assume some of the novelist's structural freedoms: he can emphasize the fictional or the thematic (as Northrop Frye defines these terms); or allegorically, portray the life as journey or battle; or experiment with the handling of time.[7] Also he can shift point of view with less sense of strain than the novelist. Given the feeble lead of Mason's *Memoirs of Gray,* Boswell in the *Life of Johnson* achieves complex variations in perspective by mingling the first-person forms of the diarist (the subject seen by himself in the present) and the autobiographer (the subject seen by himself in retrospect) with third-person forms: the limited (the subject seen by contemporaries) and the quasi-omniscient (the subject seen by the biographer).

The handling of plot and point of view, two formal aspects of biography, make up part of the grander strategy every good biographer must settle upon in shaping his material. (In loose analogy, the novelist is to the biographer as the painter is to the sculptor: the painter can choose his materials freely, while the sculptor must be more conscious of the "resistance" of his material.) Since the biographer himself seems so often unaware that his work has either formal aspects or a general strategy, it is not surprising that the critic usually appears ignorant of any formal aspects in biography comparable to those he could at once specify in a novel or poem. As for larger questions of biographical strategy, they so seldom enter a critic's head that he can hardly believe that they exist. To account, then, for the merit of a biography the critic tends to generalize about historical accuracy, vividness, authenticity, and so forth. But good biographers have defined their subjects strategically for a long time.

In *Tom Jones,* Fielding insists on our participation in the artistic problems he faces. What do we call this thing he is writing? What materials can he properly use? How shall he handle questions of time and tone? What standards should be employed to judge it? In the *Lives of the Poets,* Johnson was also experimenting with new forms, but he leaves the reader to work out their rationales for himself. He had for precedent those various models so faithfully rehearsed by historians of biography: Plutarch's fusion of narrative, portrait, and commentary; Cavendish's extension of the *de casibus* tradition; Walton's secularized version of the saint's life; the Theophrastian sketch as revived in the seventeenth century; collections of ana and memorabilia from Xenophon to Ménage. None of these patterns suited his purpose.[8] He had told Boswell on their Hebridean tour that "he did not know any literary man's life in England well-written. It should tell us his studies, his manner of life, the means by which he attained to excellence, his opinion of his own works, and such particulars."[9] All these points he covered in his *Life of Pope*, the acknowledged paradigmatic example among the *Lives of the Poets*, but no single point directs our attention to the basic organizing principle of its long biographical section. Taken as a group, they do.[10]

Modern study of the *Life of Pope* has stressed the extent to which Johnson is relying on and responding to previous biographers and critics of Pope,[11] or remarked on such thematic concerns as "the vanity of human wishes."[12] In his examination of the *Lives of the Poets*, Lawrence Lipking goes futher to discuss perceptively various general ways of looking at the *Life of Pope*, but he seems puzzled by what may be called its "local structure": "Too much of it concerns local quarrels, and depends on references or on sequences of thought that are not specified, for it to possess the self-contained harmony of art."[13]

Before discussing this local structure, one general comment: part of our difficulty with the *Life of Pope* as a whole lies in the critical expectations we bring to a study of Pope. For example, Johnson discusses the "Ode on St. Cecilia's Day" and the translation of the *Iliad* at length, while he brushes aside the Imitations of Horace. In an age which prized sublimity, which regarded the ode and the epic as the great poetic forms, this emphasis is natural. Likewise, Johnson's familiarity with Horace leads him to react to Pope's imitations with about the degree of attention we give to Pope's versions of Donne.

The larger problem posed by the *Life of Pope* derives from our sense that it is a great biography combined with a failure to see what holds together by far its longest part, the biographical section. As suggested earlier, the critic then takes refuge in such general attributes as the "air of authority, the energy of the expression, the seeming fairness, the clarity and arresting directness of its thought."[14] Unquestionably these are important motives for our reaction to it, but they fail to consider any of the work's formal aspects, and in particular Johnson's basic organizing principle which also defines his strategy in dealing with Pope's life.

That organizing principle is a simple one which Mr. Lipking's reservations, just quoted, about the *Life of Pope* point straight toward. Why at the beginning, for instance, does Johnson make so much of Dennis's attack on the *Essay on Criticism?* Dennis's critique is a mixture of shrewdness, irritability, and dogmatism apparently of little interest to later readers. But this critique was the opening gun in the lifelong battle between Pope and many of his lesser contemporaries that was to culminate in the *Dunciad.* Johnson's organizing principle is that he is writing the life of a man whose "primary and principal purpose was to be a poet." Pope, he says, "considered poetry as the business of his life, and, however he might seem to lament his occupation, he followed it with constancy: to make verses was his first labour, and to mend them was his last." [15] But Johnson's conception of the poet involves neither the Romantic interest in poetry as the outpouring of a noble soul nor the modern concentration on the poet's psychological makeup. In a typically eighteenth-century way, Johnson sees Pope as a poet in relation to other men, in his social context, in his *public* character.

If the opening section of the *Life of Pope* is read as a study of the poet in society, almost every detail falls into place. The various stories on which it centers—the cockfight for preeminence with Addison, the possible patronage of Halifax, even the "open war" with Hervey and attacks on the Ministry when Pope "forgot the prudence" (pp. 178, 179) with which he had earlier avoided politics—make the *Life of Pope* a judicial commentary on the public image of himself that Pope displays in the *Epistle to Arbuthnot* and elsewhere. For from the opening paragraphs in which Johnson contrasts his information about Pope's ancestry to Pope's assertions about it, Johnson plays his views of Pope as poet, thinker, and man against those of Pope's contemporaries and Pope's own. Johnson finds proper subjects for attack in the implied justification for suicide in the *Elegy to an Unfortunate Lady* and the simple-minded or misleading doctrines of the *Essay on Man* because the aim of poetry is to instruct by pleasing: the poet has an important role in society. (In this respect Johnson takes Pope more seriously than modern critics take Pound or Eliot or Yeats when they minimize or disregard the poet's political and social views.) Elsewhere Johnson concentrates on such "social" matters as literary collaboration, the poet's financial arrangements, and the letters which show Pope as he wished to appear to posterity.

Pope's character necessarily emerges in this biographical section as a product of Johnson's strategy in presenting him as a public figure. Sometimes using Dennis or Addison as a stalking horse, Johnson implies that Pope was affected, hypocritical, devious, snobbish, and vengeful.[16] But he also gives due weight to Pope's filial piety, loyalty to his friends, and public charity. Pope as a man turns out to be a compound of virtues and vices, like the rest of us. Yet all these details reflect the poet's character in relation to other people, to his reputation, rather than in relation to himself. (Since almost every incident has literary significance, the account of Pope's narrow escape from an overturned coach stands out as an awkward exception.) Pope's sex life, sparse as it was by his own admission, would demand considerable scrutiny in any modern biography; apart from an indirect allusion to "an idle story" of Cibber's (p. 185), Johnson never mentions it. Even Pope's long attachment to Martha Blount becomes linked to literary history, to Pope's relations with Allen and Warburton. Johnson's sense of the poet's role in society is so strong that he cannot bring himself to believe that Pope's expressed desire for solitude was sincere, though Johnson's own dependence on society obviously affects his judgment on this point.[17] Interesting personal details Johnson reserves for the following character sketch, and even of those Johnson provides just enough to mark the "peculiarities" of Pope's private character and life.[18]

On 20 April 1781, "somebody" remarked to Johnson that "the life of a mere literary man could not be very entertaining." Having just finished his *Life of Pope,* it is obvious why Johnson replied, "But it certainly may. . . . Why should the life of a literary man be less entertaining than the life of any other man? Are there not as interesting varieties in such a life? As *a literary life* it may be very entertaining." [19] As well as the *Life of Pope,* the *Life of Dryden* and to a lesser extent several of the remaining *Lives of the Poets* are literary lives.[20] In striking contrast to the simple but sufficient organizing principle used in these lives is the complex interweaving of patterns exhibited by the *Life of Savage.*

The basic problem to be resolved about the *Life of Savage* is its genre. Taken intentionalistically it is of course a biography, but factually it must be considered a very poor biography. Boswell's conclusion still holds about its *donnée,* that Savage was the illegitimate son of the Countess of Macclesfield: "The world must vibrate in a state of uncertainty as to what was the truth" (*Life,* I, 174). Further, Johnson transposes two of the major events in Savage's life, his killing of Sinclair and consequent trial, and Tyrconnel's patronage of him; while many other of Johnson's "facts" are incorrect. Here we are on the borderline between fact and fiction with a vengeance, and the proper approach may well be to consider the *Life of Savage* a work of the imagination, taking it as a great short novel as Cyril Connolly did. But as a great short novel it is a most peculiar one, since its author was under the impression he was creating a factual work. In turn the reader vibrates in a state of uncertainty as to what is "factual" and what is not, an uncertainty compounded by Johnson's bewilderment in the face of the monstrous "facts" supplied him, and his attempt to reconcile them by the test of probability with the usual principles governing human motivation and conduct.[21] In his discussion of Savage's life before they became acquainted and even later, Johnson seems at times to be going through the equivalent of a Rorschach test. Johnson's view of Pope is sharply differentiated from Pope's view of himself in the *Life of Pope;* in the *Life of Savage,* Savage is constantly refracted through Johnson's effort first to understand him and then to explain him to the reader. Yet, like the grin of the Cheshire Cat, Savage's own voice—in indirect conversation, in his speech at the trial, in poems, and in letters—erupts and fades throughout the story. The *Life of Savage* brings out with unusual clarity the three patterns inherent in any biography: the subject's view of himself, the biographer's view of the subject, and the reader's view of both subject and biographer.

It is apparent that the *Life of Savage* offers a glorious tangle of theoretical problems, which mainly will be avoided here. From the point of view of Johnson's central strategy as embodied in its basic structural patterns, the *Life of Savage* can be classified as a fictional work masquerading as fact, with an unreliable narrator who thinks he is reliable; in short, I will treat it as if it belonged to the same genre as *Moll Flanders*. (I am well aware that Johnson did not think of it in these terms, nor will the reader respond with the same "mental set" to both works.) When the two works are taken together, it becomes evident that the biography is more intricately ordered than the novel.

If, as Benjamin Boyce suggests, the *Life of Savage* finds some of its antecedents in "secret histories" or rogue stories—the underbrush of fiction—as well as in novels like *Roxana*,[22] Johnson surely transcends them as he did the putative models for the *Life of Pope*. To make sense at all of Savage's life, Johnson had to organize it very tightly, and the initial organizing pattern, established in the opening sentence, centers on the terms *nature* and *fortune:* "It has been observed in all Ages, that the Advantages of Nature or of Fortune have contributed very little to the Promotion of Happiness." [23]

"Nature" and "fortune" are the two assumed axes of the chart on which a man's life was commonly plotted in the eighteenth century. Nature resembles our term, heredity, with the distinction that nature emphasizes inherent disposition and abilities rather than what is given by genetic transmission. But fortune and our corresponding term, environment, are quite different. Environment suggests interaction, and often struggle, between the individual and his society. Fortune suggests, first, chance or vicissitude, a man's shifting place in this world as determined by Fortune's wheel. In this sense it evolves into one of Johnson's *Dictionary* definitions: "the good or evil that befalls man." By the eighteenth century, however, two further and overlapping definitions of fortune have become significant: "one's condition or standing in life," and "position as determined by wealth" (*OED*, 5, 6).[24] Johnson blends the earlier and later meanings of fortune in the *Life of Savage*. As one of its overall patterns it shows "a turning of the

Boethian wheel of Fortune," [25] but this pattern when specified in the repeated use of "fortune," "misfortunes," "miseries," and so forth, usually takes on the later meanings of fortune.

Fortune and nature mesh in complicated ways, the complications arising because Johnson maintains two views of Savage in equilibrium. The first view is that Savage is a hero characterized by "intellectual Greatness" (p. 3), though heroic mainly in his suffering. Johnson establishes this view early: "The Heroes of literary as well as civil History have been very often no less remarkable for what they have suffered, than for what they have atchieved . . ." (p. 4). In his heroic aspect, Savage's encounters with Fortune construct a *de casibus* pattern, of which the great early example in English biography is Cavendish's *Life of Wolsey*. But deluded and self-destructive as Savage is in Johnson's portrait, he is not the Micawberesque antihero that he has recently been taken for.[26] There is nothing ironic in Johnson's description of Savage at the time he was writing his tragedy about Sir Thomas Overbury: "Out of this Story he formed a Tragedy, which, if the Circumstances in which he wrote it be considered, will afford at once an uncommon Proof of Strength of Genius, and Evenness of Mind, of a Serenity not to be ruffled, and an Imagination not to be suppressed" (p. 21).

Rising fortune enhances Savage's literary reputation and Johnson comments, "So powerful is Genius, when it is invested with the Glitter of Affluence; Men willingly pay to Fortune that Regard which they owe to Merit" (p. 44). When Savage loses Tyrconnel's favor, a different relationship between nature and fortune emerges: "As many more can discover, that a Man is richer than that he is wiser than themselves, Superiority of Understanding is not so readily acknowledged as that of Condition; nor is that Haughtiness, which the Consciousness of great Abilities incites, borne with the same Submission as the Tyranny of Wealth" (p. 100).

As the fortunes of Savage decline, Johnson's portrayal of him becomes increasingly somber. Yet with enough flaws to supply a half-dozen tragic heroes, Savage maintains "the same invincible Temper" (p. 99): "In his lowest State he wanted not Spirit to assert the natural Dignity of Wit, and was always ready to repress that

Insolence which Superiority of Fortune incited, and to trample the Reputation which rose on any other Basis than that of Merit" (p. 99). More and more isolated from his society, even exiled into Wales, Savage still retains "the insurmountable Obstinacy of his Spirit" (p. 109); he was, Johnson says, "a Lion in the Toils" (p. 118). In his independence, resentment, insolence, and self-delusion, there are some touches of Satan:

> that fixt mind
> And high disdain, from sence of injur'd merit . . .
> And study of revenge, immortal hate,
> And courage never to submit or yield.
>   [*Paradise Lost,* 1.97–98, 107–08]

But only touches. Johnson's central reaction to Savage as intellectual hero is to deplore the enormous waste of genius: "On a Bulk, in a Cellar, or in a Glass-house, among Thieves and Beggars, was to be found the author of the *Wanderer,* the Man of exalted Sentiments, extensive Views and curious Observations, the Man whose Remarks on Life might have assisted the Statesman, whose Ideas of Virtue might have enlightened the Moralist, whose Eloquence might have influenced Senates, and whose Delicacy might have polished Courts" (p. 97). This reflects Savage's view of himself, of course, as he expresses it in a letter from prison shortly before his death: "As to the World, I hope that I shall be endued by Heaven with that Presence of Mind, that serene Dignity in Misfortune, that constitutes the character of a true Nobleman" (p. 123).

The second view Johnson presents of Savage is the prudential one, taking "prudential" in Aristotle's sense as conducting oneself wisely in the world. This view has been too often discussed to need development here. In terms of prudence, the *Life of Savage* reads like a tragic version of *Tom Jones,* with intellectual greatness taking the place of instinctive benevolence as the hero's main attribute. Fortune waits on prudence in this world, or supposedly so: actually Tom never shows much prudence. Even so, Tom's cheerful benevolence leads naturally to his rescue by friends at the end of the novel, just as the deep solipsism lying under Savage's surface companionability inevitably provokes his friends' abandonment of him. What is remarkable about Johnson's two views of Savage's character is that they never fuse; they proceed side by side until they conclude in the double ending that has puzzled critics. The last paragraph comes down heavily on the necessity for prudence, while the three preceding ones eloquently reiterate that Savage had "a Genius truly poetical" and "a great Mind, irritated by perpetual Hardships." Of Savage as hero Johnson reminds us, "they are no proper Judges of his Conduct who have slumber'd away their Time on the Down of Plenty."

The unresolved tension between these two main structural patterns accounts, I think, for much of the interest generated by the *Life of Savage*. They are supplemented by a number of crisscrossing character, thematic, and verbal patterns: Savage as child in relation to his supposed mother and parental surrogates; the contrast between his theory and practice, between that "Knowledge of Life [which] was indeed his chief Attainment" (p. 136) and his inability to apply it in any proportion to his talent; the close connections between his life and his writings; even Johnson's use of maxims and legal metaphors.[27] Underlying these patterns is Johnson's attempt to make psychological sense of the melodrama that marked Savage's life, complicated by his double attitude toward Savage's character: a recognition, often amounting to admiration, of Savage's independence of the world, and the realization that such independence can only be maintained at excessive cost.[28] And, finally, there is the mystery of Savage himself, who emerges for the reader with the complex opacity that characterizes someone we have known well and long but really have never understood. Whatever he makes of Savage, each reader almost surely seems a different Savage than the one seen by subject or biographer.

The two main structural patterns of the *Life of Savage* lead in two different biographical directions. In the *Life of Johnson*, Boswell domesticates the heroic, one clue to his purpose being stated in the advertisement to the second edition: "It seems to me, in my moments of self-complacency, that this extensive biographical work, however inferior in its nature, may in one respect be assimilated to the ODYSSEY. Amidst a thousand entertaining and instructive episodes the HERO is never long out of sight; for they are all in some degree connected with him; and HE, in the whole course of the History, is exhibited by the Authour for the best advantage of his readers." Boswell then quotes two lines from Horace, given here in Francis's translation:

> To show what wisdom and what sense can do,
> The poet sets Ulysses in our view.

Boswell's central thematic purpose is to construct an epic, a moral epic of heroic proportions, in which a man with greater strengths and weaknesses than ordinary, struggles with the problems of daily life and overcomes them. The remote model for that epic is the *Odyssey* with its archetypal journey pattern, the *Life* substituting a journey in time for one in space. Boswell presents a definite ethical pattern in Johnson which is for "the best advantage of his readers," because Johnson deals on a large scale with the common problems of ordinary people. Of all the versions of epic produced in the eighteenth century—*The Rape of the Lock, The Dunciad, Tom Jones, The Decline and Fall of the Roman Empire,* even Blake's major prophecies—Boswell's remains the most immediate to our everyday concerns.

The other biographical direction suggested by the *Life of Savage* leads to Goldsmith's *Life of Nash,* that "inimitable mock heroic, conferring immortality on a marionette of supreme quality." [29] Where Savage totally rejected the prudential, Beau Nash followed the path of "prudence" to excess. Our final impression of Savage is of someone profoundly different from those around him; in Nash, Goldsmith says, "I attempt the character of one, who was just such a man as probably you or I may be, but with this difference, that he never performed an action which the world did not know, or ever formed a wish which he did not take pains to divulge." [30] The mock-heroic form, however, indicates that Goldsmith's strategy is to take Nash at his face value. He was King of Bath; he gave his little province rules; "neither rank nor fortune shielded the refractory from his resentment" (p. 304). "Birth and fortune" (p. 294) replace nature and fortune as measuring sticks, because Nash was completely concerned with those surfaces of society called rank and fashion. Goldsmith treats Nash with the same blend of amusement and seriousness with which he surrounds the Reverend Charles Primrose. For though surfaces are the natural matter of comedy—think of *The School for Scandal* with its Surfaces, screen scene, disguises, portraits and character paintings—they are also where much of life goes on. Goldsmith seems close to a pun when he says, "The relations of great events may surprize indeed; they may be calculated to instruct those very few, who govern the million beneath, but the generality of mankind find the most real improvement from relations which are levelled to *the general surface of life;* which tell, not how men learned to conquer, but how they endeavoured to live . . . " (p. 290, italics added). When Johnson defined politeness as "fictitious benevolence," he was recommending it as "of great consequence in society" (*Life,* v, 82, 21 August 1773). Nash's mistake, of course, lay not in regulating the superficial manners and customs of society but in equating these manners with "manners" in the deeper sense, the whole span of social behavior. Surface becomes everything and Nash swells with importance: his full-length statue is placed between the busts of Newton and Pope; his funeral is pompously royal. But his life is increasingly empty, and all he leaves behind him are a small collection of books, some family pictures, and a few trifles that Goldsmith is careful to enumerate: "an etui mounted in gold . . . a silver terene . . . and some other things of no great value" (p. 367). Amiability mistook itself for greatness.[31]

Against the prudential example—in a double sense—supplied in Nash, Goldsmith counterpoints an instance of "heroic" excess: the story of Miss Sylvia S——, whose romantic imprudence led to suicide. The same kind of counterpointing, but in a thorough and integrated fashion, characterizes Boswell's "Memoirs of Pascal Paoli." Boswell's main purpose was to compose a portrait, modeled on those of Sallust and Plutarch, of a classical hero.[32] But essentially Boswell discovered a new biographical strategy: the biographer becomes the most important other character in his subject's biography. The "Memoirs of Pascal Paoli" revolves around a giant and a dwarf star, the mature Paoli and the naive

Boswell, who exists to ask the innocent, revealing question, to evoke the grand response, to highlight the hero. In the process, Boswell exaggerates his own limitations: "Never was I so thoroughly sensible of my own defects as while I was in Corsica. I felt how small were my abilities and how little I knew" (p. 189). At most Boswell can playact the ruler, riding out on Paoli's own horse with his party of guards; real state and distinction, real power, rest in Paoli. Yet he is a human hero, kind to his young and ingenuous friend, and he displays both "great and amiable" virtues (p. 189).

In the Benbridge portrait of Paoli, commissioned by Boswell (opp. p. 190), the background consists in some rather stylized rocks, trees, and hills, and Boswell treats his background, Corsica and the Corsicans, in much the same generalizing fashion: a rugged country inhabited by a brave, unspoiled, and rather primitive people, who throw Paoli's stern and active virtues into sharp relief. Boswell's tour with Johnson to the Hebrides offered the possibility of a more complex and exciting arrangement. Scotland becomes an active entity, initially set in ambivalent opposition to Johnson, their hostility well publicized. In this ready-made scenario, Boswell casts Johnson as John Bull, the "true-born Englishman." Boswell, as mediator, defends Scotland when necessary, but prefers the neutral, detached role of "a citizen of the world" (*Life*, v, 19–20).

Even before the two leave Edinburgh, Boswell has set up this triangular plot, of which I shall cite one example. In the Records Room of Parliament House, the sight of the Treaty of Union between Scotland and England aroused Boswell's *"old Scottish sentiments"* about the loss of independence. Johnson, taking the bait, responded with one of the traditional sneers at the Scots, their failure to rescue Mary, Queen of Scots, from her English prison. Boswell then expands the scene dramatically:

[JOHNSON.] ". . . and such a Queen too! as every man of any gallantry of spirit would have sacrificed his life for." Worthy *Mr. James Kerr, Keeper of the Records.* "Half our nation was bribed by English money."—JOHNSON. "Sir, that is no defence: that makes you worse." Good *Mr. Brown, Keeper of the Advocates Library.* "We had better say nothing about it."—BOSWELL. "You would have been glad, however, to have had us last war, sir, to fight your battles!"—JOHNSON. "We should have had you for the same price, though there had been no Union, as we might have had Swiss, or other troops. No, no, I shall agree to a separation. You have only to *go home.*" [*Life,* v, 40–41, 16 August 1773]

Within this triangulation the narrative proceeds day by day, offering in its minute factuality the most resistant material imaginable to formal structuring. Johnson described its basis to Mrs. Thrale: "Boswel writes a regular journal of our travels, which, I think, contains as much of what I say and do, as of all other occurrences together—'For such a faithful Chronicler as Griffith.' " [33] And later readers of Boswell's journal may be pardoned for thinking, like Johnson, of Boswell as essentially a faithful chronicler. In contrast, Johnson, in his *Journey to the Western Islands,* is constantly concerned with philosophical generalization about the flow of history. Even in acknowledging the "local effect" of Iona, Johnson characteristically rises beyond "sensation" in defining it: "Whatever withdraws us from the power of our senses; whatever makes the past, the distant, or the future predominate over the present, advances us in the dignity of thinking beings." [34] But the *Tour to the Hebrides* is immersed in sensation, in the here and now. Reading the two works side by side can suggest that some eighteenth-century equivalents of Don Quixote and Sancho Panza are describing the same journey, and indeed the contrast between Johnson and Boswell within the *Tour* alone recalls some of the differences between Cervantes's great figures. (Also the *Tour,* like *Don Quixote* and many of its successors, includes an interpolated tale: the wanderings of Prince Charles Edward among the Hebrides, a grandly romantic counterpoint to Boswell's own main story.)

Based on the recurrent rhythm of daily experience, the journal is the only literary form that is truly open-ended, and any formal patterns it discloses must be "accidental." Yet in the *Tour* this rhythm is not particularly insistent; our interest in what the travelers are saying and doing often overrides our sense of time and place. And, at the level of daily existence, the journal builds up a loose unity through the repetition of subjects (emigration, subordination, and so forth) and the links or comparisons among people, settings, and events. These might be considered as equivalent to thematic or symbolic patterns in a novel. But the *Tour* is given a more general shape by the contrast between expectation and experience, testifying to Johnson's dictum that "the use of travelling is to regulate imagination by reality, and instead of thinking how things may be, to see them as they are." [35]

Generically the *Tour* is antiromance, and specifically it is an inversion of the usual Grand Tour account. The ordinary tourist on that expedition traveled back in time to the sources and monuments of Western culture, especially to the Rome of the first centuries, the golden age of civilization. To visit the semi-barbarous Scottish outlands tested an opposed vision of the past, which maintained that the primitive was superior to the civilized, that the groves of Eden might be approximated in the islands of the South Pacific or some other unspoiled region. (The primitive in this instance, of course, would take the form of a feudal or pastoral society.) Johnson, as might be expected, was skeptical that Nature's plan was anywhere near this simple or, if it was, that art did not improve upon it considerably. But it would be exciting to observe society in an earlier stage of culture. Boswell states their expectations, simply and naturally, as being to explore "a system of life almost totally different from what we had been accustomed to see" (*Life*, v, 13).

The contrast between expectation and experience runs throughout the *Tour* as a strong, complicated patterning force. It may be helpful to recall a few landmarks: the debate between Johnson and Lord Monboddo over the relative happiness of the London shopkeeper and the savage; the inspection of the old woman's hut near Loch Ness, which provides the first encounter with pastoral actuality; Johnson's vigorous lecture to Sir Alexander Macdonald on the behavior proper to a feudal chief; the travelers' enjoyment of the simple but civilized pleasures of Raasay and Dunvegan; the pursuit and destruction of Ossian; finally, the climactic visit to Iona, where Johnson and Boswell felt, if momentarily, in firm and exalted touch with the past. And the gradual realization that they had come too late to find the pure patriarchal society they anticipated. Perhaps it was just as well; by the time they returned to civilization they were prepared to laugh heartily "at the ravings of those absurd visionaries who have attempted to persuade us of the superior advantages of a *state of nature*" (*Life*, v, 365, 27 October 1773).

All the while using himself as a mediating figure, in his journal as on their jaunt, Boswell keeps the *Tour* skillfully centered on Johnson. Boswell may be the only important biographer who has composed both a portrait (in the *Life*) and a narrative account (in the *Tour*) of the same subject. When he draws far back from his material, Boswell can speak of their jaunt as "the transit of Johnson over the Caledonian hemisphere" (*Life*, v, 382, 6 November 1773): instead of the Johnson at rest that the *Life* mainly provides, here is Johnson in constant motion, resilient, patient, formidable, always himself. We tend to recall the *Tour* as a series of sharply defined episodes in which Johnson, "led" by Boswell, moves across a barren landscape densely populated with figures.

Two episodes deserve particular mention. Reduced to entertaining themselves one night, says Boswell, "I took the liberty to put a large blue bonnet on his head. His age, his size, and his bushy grey wig, with this covering on it, presented the image of a venerable *Sennachi* [Gaelic oral historian]; and, however unfavourable to the Lowland Scots, he seemed much pleased to assume the appearance of an ancient Caledonian" (*Life*, v, 324–25, 17 October 1773). It was Johnson's most unexpected role, this transformation in which Boswell suggests the momentary reconciliation of opposites.

The other episode is the great unwritten scene in Boswell's journal, the quarrel between Johnson and Lord Auchinleck. Boswell must have reduced his account of this scene to safe generalities with the greatest of reluctance, for not only did it set his intellectual against his physical father but it provided a natural climax to the confrontation between Johnson and Scotland, here stoutly represented in its most Whiggish and Presbyterian aspects. What life gave to art with one hand, it took away with the other: custom and reverence prohibited Boswell from giving his narrative its proper denouement.

This interference of life with art also enters into the last and

oddest of Boswell's biographical strategies—perhaps tactic, here—
in the *Tour:* the use of the journal itself. At the heart of Boswell's
journal lies a paradox. He presents each day's events and impressions in a totally unselfconscious way, a record of the normal flow
of experience. At the same time, the journal is highly self-conscious, an account intended for Johnson, who read and occasionally corrected it. It was clearly preparation for the biography of
Johnson Boswell meant to write. Johnson himself called it "a very
exact picture of a portion of his life" (*Life,* v, 279, 3 October
1773), and wished it twice as long as it was. And it raised his
opinion of Boswell.

As the tour proceeded, the journal took on a shadow existence
of its own that affected the relationship between the two men, as
when Boswell continued an argument in it that Johnson then
answered. Boswell even had the boldness to record some of Johnson's peculiarities, such as his not wearing a nightcap, or talking to
himself and "uttering pious ejaculations," hoping that Johnson
would explain them (*Life,* v, 307 and n. 2, 12 October 1773). Johnson passed over these remarks without comment. Also the journal
could get in the way. When Johnson complained at one point
that they saw little of each other, Boswell blamed it on the need
to post his journal. And once he confesses, "I did not exert myself
to get Dr. Johnson to talk, that I might not have the labour of
writing down his conversation" (*Life,* v, 159, 7 September 1773).
As well as *realizing* the present, the journal is shaping life itself.
This blurring of life and art is a peculiarly Boswellian trait, but
it suggests once again that the range and variety of strategies
available to the biographer remain largely unexplored.

NOTES

1. James Boswell, *Life of Samuel Johnson,* ed. G. B. Hill, rev. L. F. Powell, 6 vols.
(Oxford, 1934–64), II, 433 (16 March 1776). Hereafter cited as *Life,* with volume and
page numbers.

2. As Aristotle conceded that in certain instances dramatists could derive plots
from historical events (*Poetics,* chap. 9). In his *Enquiry Concerning Human Understanding,* Hume asserts that "the unity of action . . . which is to be found in
biography or history, differs from that of epic poetry, not in kind, but in degree"

(quoted in Leo Braudy, *Narrative Form in History and Fiction* [Princeton, 1970], p. 32).

3. *The Counterfeiters* (Bloomington, 1968), p. 84.

4. N. N. Holland gives an interesting explanation for the reader's uneasiness when confronted with such works (*Dynamics of Literary Response* [New York, 1968], pp. 98–99). I have tried to deal with some of the problems involved in the relationships between fact and fiction in an essay called "Fact and Factuality in Literature," to be published in a *festschrift* in honor of Henry W. Sams.

5. D. A. Stauffer provides an historical account of the early indistinctness of biography and fiction in *The Art of Biography in Eighteenth-Century England* (Princeton, 1941), vol. 1, chap. 2.

6. As recently as 1965 an historian of biography in English, R. D. Altick, thought it necessary to insist that "strong plots" appear in the lives of real people (*Lives and Letters* [New York, 1965], pp. 355–60). An excellent example of a proper and useful chronicle is L. J. Courtois, *Chronologie critique de la vie et des oeuvres de Jean-Jacques Rousseau* (Geneva, 1924).

7. As Leon Edel has argued persuasively in *Literary Biography* (Garden City, Anchor ed., 1959), chap. 5.

8. Following a remark of Sir John Hawkins, George Watson asserts that Johnson's model was the Countess d'Aulnoy's (or Fontenelle's) *Recueils des plus belles pièces de Poètes François* (*The Literary Critics*, New York, 1964, pp. 86–88). If Johnson used this work or Elizabeth Cooper's *The Muses' Library* or Theophilus Cibber's *Lives of the Poets* as models for his *Life of Pope*, he is about as little indebted to them as Boswell is to Mason's *Life of Gray* (see Lawrence Lipking, *The Ordering of the Arts in Eighteenth-Century England* [Princeton, 1970], pp. 415–28).

9. *Boswell's Journal of a Tour to the Hebrides,* ed. F. A. Pottle and C. H. Bennett (New York, rev. ed., 1961), p. 204 (22 September 1773).

10. I assume agreement that the *Life of Pope* is divided into a long biographical section, a character sketch, and a short critical section with appendixes; also that the *Lives* of Cowley and Savage are organized quite differently; and finally that Johnson lacked either the materials or the interest to organize many of the little *Lives* with much care.

11. Benjamin Boyce, "Samuel Johnson's Criticism of Pope in the *Life of Pope*," *Review of English Studies*, n.s. 5 (1944), 37–46; F. W. Hilles, "The Making of *The Life of Pope*," in *New Light on Dr. Johnson*, ed. F. W. Hilles (New Haven, 1959), pp. 257–84.

12. Paul Fussell, *Samuel Johnson and the Life of Writing* (New York, 1971), chap. 9.

13. Lipking, p. 452. Mr. Lipking finds a thematic center for the *Life of Pope* in the concept of *poetical prudence* (ibid., p. 450).

14. Boyce, p. 46.

15. *Lives of the Poets*, ed. G. B. Hill, 3 vols. (Oxford, 1905), III, 86, 217–18.

16. And at least once Johnson turns Pope verbally upon himself: describing Pope's shuffling response to Hill's expostulation about being included in the *Dunciad*, Johnson remarks, "he first endeavours to wound, and is then afraid to own that he meant a blow" (p. 151).

17. In contrast, Johnson's *Life of Gray* shows the poet of solitude.

18. I am assuming that Johnson omitted many of the details that Marchmont must have supplied to him. Also, Boswell gave Johnson a copy of his notes of his own conversation with Marchmont (*Boswell in Extremes*, ed. C. McC. Weis and F. A. Pottle [New York, 1970], pp. 332–39). On the subject of marking "peculiarities" in character, see the conversation between Johnson and Boswell of 17 September 1777 (*Life of Johnson*, III, 154–55).

19. *Life of Johnson*, IV, 98, 20 April 1781 (italics in original). For the date of composition of the *Life of Pope*, see Hilles, pp. 258–60.

20. The pattern is perhaps more clearly marked in the *Life of Dryden* in which, as Mr. Lipking points out, "Johnson's eye keeps steady watch not so much upon Dryden as upon Dryden's transactions and relations with his public" (Lipking, p. 444).

21. See William Vesterman's discussion of this point, in "Johnson and *The Life of Savage*," *ELH*, 36 (1969), 666–70.

22. "Johnson's *Life of Savage* and Its Literary Background," *Studies in Philology*, 53 (1956), 578, 590–93.

23. *Life of Savage*, ed. Clarence Tracy (Oxford, 1971), p. 3.

24. I had intended to demonstrate, rather than merely to assert, the pervasiveness of the nature-fortune pattern as a basic eighteenth-century assumption, but the matter grew under my hands and will have to be reserved for separate notice.

25. J. A. Dussinger, "Style and Intention in Johnson's *Life of Savage*," *ELH*, 37 (1970), 565. See also pp. 577–80.

26. Fussell, pp. 259–61.

27. Mr. Vesterman elaborates this last point as well as the "unnaturalness" which characterized Savage's relationships with others (Vesterman, pp. 671–74). Mr. Dussinger's ingenious discussion of Savage as "child" is not always convincing. He calls the *Life of Savage* "a fiction with an essay superstructure, a sympathetic but resolute account of tragic alienation from the recognized norms of the envisioned world" (Dussinger, p. 580).

28. This can be contrasted to Johnson's attitude toward Pope's affected indifference and real anxiety about his reputation and his relations with "the Great."

29. The anonymous article, "Biography," in the *Harmsworth Encyclopedia*, quoted in W. H. Dunn, *English Biography* (New York, 1916), p. 92.

30. *Life of Richard Nash* in *Collected Works of Oliver Goldsmith*, ed. Arthur Friedman (Oxford, 1966), III, 291.

31. As Goldsmith says gently, "his virtues were not of the great, but the amiable kind" (p. 364).

32. F. A. Pottle and I have discussed Boswell's guiding principles at greater length in *Boswell on the Grand Tour: Italy, Corsica, and France* (New York, 1955), pp. 143–48. All references to the "Memoirs" are to this edition.

33. *Letters of Samuel Johnson,* ed. R. W. Chapman (Oxford, 1952), I, 370–71.

34. *Journey to the Western Islands of Scotland,* ed. Mary Lascelles (New Haven, 1971), p. 148.

35. *Letters,* I, 359.

Reynolds among the Romantics

FREDERICK W. HILLES

Together with some of Johnson's writings, the *Discourses* of Sir Joshua Reynolds are quoted in the fifteenth chapter of Wimsatt and Brooks's *Literary Criticism: A Short History* as a convenient way to sum up certain critical opinions of "the last classical generation." In a footnote rebutting these opinions are some of the "pungent comments" that Blake wrote in the margin of a copy of Sir Joshua's *Works,* now in the British Museum. Blake's marginalia are thoroughly Blakean. As a control it should be worth while to compare with them the marginalia in another copy of Sir Joshua's *Works,* one that I acquired when it turned up at Sotheby's in 1936. These volumes (the third edition, published in 1801) were "purchased & presented" to Benjamin Robert Haydon by his father, presumably in 1804 soon after young Haydon had convinced his reluctant family that he was to become a painter.[1] Earlier, even before attending the Plympton Grammar School where Reynolds had also studied, Haydon had done a good deal of drawing and had dreamt of becoming an artist. Then one day, while browsing among the books of his father's apprentice, "Accidentally tumbling his collection over I hit upon Reynolds's *Discourses*. I read one. It placed so much reliance on honest industry, it expressed so strong a conviction that all men were equal and that application made the difference, that I fired up at once. I took them all home and read them through before breakfast the next morning. The thing was done. I felt my destiny fixed. The spark which had for years lain struggling to blaze, now burst out for ever." [2]

Obviously young Haydon was not a critical reader. His knowledge of painting at that time was limited; his hero worship of Sir Joshua, extreme and quite understandable. As he grew older he found much in the *Discourses* to criticize, but when in 1823 he picked up a new edition of them, he wrote: "The pleasure I felt at regaining a copy of a work with which so many, many dearest associations of early study are connected cannot be conceived." [3] Twelve years later, in the lectures that he published shortly before his death, references to the *Discourses* are plentiful. The mature Haydon took exception to a number of pronouncements, but his admiration for Reynolds he never lost.

The annotations he made in the first copy he owned can be dated roughly between 1808 and 1820. To distinguish between those marginalia written early and those late could perhaps be done by any expert in handwriting, but no specialized training is needed to prove that the comments are spread over a number of years, and it is reasonable to assume that the majority of them were written in the middle of the second decade of the century, when he was writing various essays and articles for *Annals of the Fine Arts*. Several early notes are dated. When in the third discourse Reynolds speaks of the hours of study demanded of the painter, a study that he calls "painful," Haydon comments: "Why talk of its being painful? Why give this handle to indolence? Any great work is painful (i.e., an effort). It was painful for Buonaparte to fight the battle of Austerlitz, but what great man thinks about the pain or exertion when he has an object in view? Dec. 1808." Later in the same discourse, when Reynolds wrote, "A man is not weak, though he may not be able to wield the club of Hercules," young Haydon's characteristic remark is: "But every man should be determined to lift it if it crushed him the next minute. Dec. 1808." Unhappily, Haydon's handwriting is often difficult to decipher, and in these two notes the last digits are questionable. We do know from his diary that he spent several evenings in December 1808 writing notes on painting for his friend Prince Hoare. He might well have turned to Reynolds for suggestions at this time.[4] There is another relatively early note. In Malone's memoir at the beginning of the first volume is mention of young Joshua's early drawings, under one of which his father wrote, "Done out of pure idleness." At this point Haydon adds: "There is also one at Plympton in the room where he slept, executed with his finger (it appears) in ink against the partition. Dr. Johnston with Sir Joshua called to see it when in Devonshire."[5] This drawing we know Haydon saw in 1809;[6] perhaps the note was written at that time. Later he added, "it has been, since I wrote this, painted over by a stupid fellow who painted the house 1812."

In London Haydon had formed the habit of calling upon Sir Joshua's ablest student, James Northcote, another Devonian. Here in 1812 he first met William Hazlitt, "that interesting man, that singular mixture of friend and fiend, radical and critic, metaphysician, poet and painter. . . ."[7] Unsuccessful as a painter, Hazlitt was at this time about to embark on his career as journalist, and he often dropped in on Haydon, once he got to know him. Glimpses of what went on when the two men were together are supplied by reminiscences of Haydon's pupil, William Bewick. Haydon, according to Bewick, was "energetic, explanatory, voluble, and eager to convince." Hazlitt is quoted as saying: "I find him well read up in the literature of the day; never at a loss for subjects of conversation, whether of books, politics, or men and things. The only subject he seems to desire to eschew, with me at least, is the fine arts." Bewick's comment is, "Hazlitt was ever urging the painter into questions about art, and when it did not seem agreeable (as it seldom was) for Haydon to acquiesce in this, he would start off upon his own views and opinions, and Haydon listened with great attention to his fresh and vigorous observations on the practice of the art, and his just and discriminating conclusions on the Italian schools of painting."[8]

By the middle of 1814 Hazlitt was, among other things, in charge of the department of fine arts for the young periodical *The Champion*. Toward the end of that year he wrote a series of essays on Sir Joshua and the *Discourses,* essays which were reprinted a few years later in *Annals of the Fine Arts*[9] and were partly incorporated in his article on "Fine Arts" written in 1817 for the *Encyclopaedia Britannica*. It was apparently when he was planning these essays that he first borrowed Haydon's copy of the

Discourses, entering numerous comments in the margins of the book.[10] He must have again borrowed the volumes in 1820 or thereabouts, for certain marginalia of his tie in, not with the earlier essays but with those included in *Table Talk* (1821). Haydon's comments on Hazlitt's comments could have been entered at various times.

On the last day of 1821 Haydon wrote in his diary, "Bewick, my pupil, has realized my hopes." It may have been at about that time that he gave the profusely annotated copy of Reynolds to his successful former pupil. Then, possibly in the following spring,[11] he asked that the volumes be returned to him. Long after this (1864) Bewick wrote: "When I was in Edinburgh in 1824 a friend called upon me with a book that he said I ought to possess. It had been bought [in June 1823] at the sale of Mr. Haydon's things, and brought to Edinburgh. This was 'Reynolds' Lectures,' in three volumes, with notes and sketches by the well-known hand. The work had been given to me by Haydon as a keepsake, and after I had had it some time he said to me, 'Bewick, I think you must give me back the Reynolds that I gave you.' So I took it back to him, and it was curious enough that I should be fated to get it by purchase after all, and in the round-about fashion I did. I still have the work, and treasure it as containing remarks and sketches by Haydon in his younger days." In a postscript to this letter Bewick added that his copy also contained "notes by my late friend W. Hazlitt, who had borrowed it to write his essay on Reynolds in the *Edinburgh Review*." [12] Bewick himself annotated the copy modestly in pencil in his small neat hand, but his comments lack the fire that underlies those of his predecessors.

What follows is a sampling of the marginalia, in which obvious slips of the pen are silently corrected and such matters as capitalization and punctuation are normalized. The same liberty has been taken with the quotations from Blake.[13] Sir Joshua's text is here printed in italics, preceded by a roman numeral for the number of the discourse, an arabic for the number of the page. The handwriting of Hazlitt and Haydon, normally very different, can at times be surprisingly similar. Haydon occasionally inked over, in order to preserve them, some of Hazlitt's penciled comments that he wished to refute, and in doing so tended to make Hazlitt's handwriting resemble his own. He also at times added Hazlitt's initials to such comments. Where marginalia are not initialed, the author can usually be identified with a good deal of confidence, but there are some about which an editor is forced to guess. I have indicated my doubts.

II.36 — *enter into a kind of competition* [*with the Old Masters*], *by painting a similar subject,* . . . *place it near the model, and compare them carefully* . . .

Intense feeling for perfection needs no such helps. [B.R.H.]

Cf. Blake's "What but a Puppy will dare to do this?"

III.52f. — *instead of endeavouring to amuse mankind with the minute neatness of his imitations, he must endeavour to improve them by the grandeur of his ideas.*

Pshaw: is there nothing in nature but minute neatness? Is there no medium between the superficial & the insipid? W.H.

He does not say there is not, but that you must *rather* do the one than the other. B.R.H.

Cf. Blake's "Without minute neatness of execution the sublime cannot exist!"

III.55 — *enthusiastick admiration seldom promotes knowledge.*

i.e., in things not calculated to excite enthusiastic admiration. Dr. Johnson's though[t] of poetry applied to painting.[14] [W.H.]

Cf. Blake's "Enthusiastic admiration is the first principle of knowledge & its last."

— *He examines his own mind, and perceives there nothing of that divine inspiration, with which, he is told, so many others have been favoured.*

Then he need not look for it any where else. W.H.

If he does, he won't find it. B.R.H.

Cf. Blake's "The man who on examining his own mind finds nothing of inspiration ought not to dare to be an artist. He is a fool & cunning knave suited to the purposes of evil demons."

III.55f. — *He never travelled to heaven to gather new ideas* . . .

There [is] nothing so likely to meet with cordial welcome as sneers at any pretensions to inspiration or inherent superiority of capacity. B.R.H.

Yet the intellectual dignity lays the line betw[een] the mere mechanic & the inspired painter. W.H.

Cf. Blake's "The man who never in his mind & thoughts traveld to heaven is no artist."

III.56 — *he finds himself possessed of no other qualifications than what mere common observation and a plain understanding can confer.*

If he does not, he is not the man. [W.H.]

Milton, Shakespeare, Homer, Buonaparte, Raphael, Mich. Angelo, Phidias, we suppose, found themselves possessed with no other qualifications? Weakness! B.R.H.

Cf. Blake's "Artists who are above a plain understanding are mockd & destroyd by this President of Fools."

III.57 — *Could we teach taste or genius by rules, they would be no longer taste and genius.*

Extraordinary inference. What becomes of the "solidity & truth of principle on which alone we can practise," &c. [W.H.? The reference is to what Reynolds had said on the preceding page.]

Cf. Blake's "This must be how liars reason."

III.57f. — *the whole . . . grandeur of the art consists . . . in being able to get above all singular forms, local customs, particularities, and *details of every kind.*

* no. [B.R.H.]

A sweeping charge. W.H.

This has been the ruin of the English School. [B.R.H.] [15]

Cf. Blake's "A folly. Singular & particular detail is the foundation of the sublime."

III.59 — *This idea of the perfect state of nature, which the Artist calls the Ideal Beauty, is* the great leading principle by which works of genius are conducted.*

* is a farce. W.H.

Cf. Blake's "Knowledge of the ideal beauty is not to be acquired; it is born with us."

III.60 — *an artist becomes possessed of the idea of that central form . . . from which every deviation is deformity.*

Central is wrong certainly it should be *leading*. [B.R.H.]

Cf. Blake's "One central form composed of all other forms being granted, it does not therefore follow that all other forms are deformity."

III.61 — *[Bacon's] meaning is sometimes doubtful.*

Yours is always. [W.H.]

Cf. Blake's "The Great Bacon he is calld (I call him the Little Bacon) . . . is like Sir Joshu[a] full of self-contradiction & knavery."

—If he means that beauty has nothing to do with rule, he is mistaken.

Why, damn it, you said but now that if genius could be subject to rules it would no longer be genius. W.H.

He said if you teach. [B.R.H. He refers to top of p. 57.]

III.62 *— Every object which pleases must give us pleasure* upon some certain principles: but as the objects of pleasure are almost infinite, so their principles vary without end, and every man finds them out, not by felicity or successful hazard, but by care and sagacity.*

* It may give pleasure on certain principles, but that is no reason it was produced by the artist knowing those principles. How is it you often get expressions of moment, & characters which you can never repeat, or tell how you did it? [B.R.H.]

This is as flat, shallow, abortive stuff as ever was penned. Do you know why every object pleases before it can please you? W.H.

No, but that is no reason it should not please you on principle though you may be ignorant of it. B.R.H.

III.63 *— And as there is one general form, which . . . belongs to the human kind at large, so in each of these classes there is one common idea and central form, which is the abstract of the various individual forms belonging to that class.*

i.e., something between a Greek head & an African. W.H.

Cf. Blake's "There is no end to the follies of this man."

III.63f. *— the highest perfection of the human figure is . . . not in the Hercules, nor in the Gladiator, nor in the Apollo; but in that form which is taken from all, and which partakes equally of the activity of the Gladiator, of the delicacy of the Apollo, and of the muscular strength of the Hercules.*

Why not extend this to animal nature & form, also to male & female forms? Grotesques? W.H.

Cf. Blake's "Here he comes again to his Central Form."

III.64 *— perfect beauty in any species must combine all the characters which are beautiful in that species.*

These discourses seem written by an Hermaphrodite. W.H.

III.65 *— when he has reduced the variety of nature to the abstract idea; his next task will be to become acquainted with the genuine habits of nature, as distinguished from those of fashion.*

If perfection consists in abstraction, where stop? But perfection or excellence consists in some qualities or example[s] of pleasure or power, & a greater degree of perfection or excellence must consist in more of that quality, not in less; i.e., in neutralising it by others incompatible with it. Exchange is not progress. The principle of all works of imagination [is] to give the strongest impression on [i.e. of ?] any thing in one individual image. To attempt to give [   ] is nonsense. W.H.

Cf. Blake's "What folly. Is fashion the concern of artists? The knave calls anything found in nature fit for art."

III.75 — *A firm and determined outline is one of the characteristics of the great style; . . . he who possesses the knowledge of the exact form which every part of nature ought to have, will be fond* of expressing that knowledge with correctness . . .*

But this an error; all your science should be concealed as in Elgin marbles.

* He may be fond, but this is no proof he may be right. [B.R.H.]

Cf. Blake's "A noble sentence! Here is a sentence which overthrows all his book."

III.75 — *To conclude; I have endeavoured to reduce the idea of beauty to general principles: . . . bringing [contradictory observations] under one general head, can alone give rest and satisfaction to an inquisitive mind.*

That you have not done. W.H.

Not completely. . . . The leading error of this whole discourse is not having a clear idea of the abstract leading form, or an abstract idea of the true art. Reynolds takes the art as he found it, & lays it down as an axiom that the great style as it exists in the present great works of art, are the infallible landmarks, whereas art is in an imperfect state, and its perfection is yet unrealized. B.R.H.

Cf. Blake's "Sir Joshua proves that Bacon's philosophy makes both statesmen & artists fools & knaves."

IV.83 — *Even in portraits, the grace, and, we may add, the likeness, consists more in taking the general air, than in observing the exact similitude of every feature.*

More, why not both? [W.H. ?]

Cf. Blake's "How ignorant!"

IV.90 — *[The historical painter does not] debase his conceptions with minute attention to the discriminations of Drapery. . . . the cloathing is neither woollen, nor linen, nor silk, sattin, or velvet: it is drapery; it is nothing more.*

All this depends on the character represented: a King must not be drest like an apostle! and Michel Angelo even in the Capella Sistina has given variety of stuffs. Reynolds was too fond of reducing every thing to one principle, which narrows instead of enlarging the basis of art. [B.R.H.]

Cf. Blake's ironical "Excellent remarks!"

IV.95 — *Such as suppose that the great style might happily be blended with the ornamental, that the simple, grave and majestick dignity of Raffaelle could unite with the glow and bustle of a Paolo, or Tintoret, are totally mistaken.*

Certainly, but there is no reason to assert that the simple grandeur of Raphael would not be still more grand, & more impressive, if his tones were more harmonious, & his colour purer. His gravity is required by his brickdust tints &, not encreased, the expression & passion keep up the feeling of grandeur by their power, subdue the ill effects of his worst deep colour, but it does not follow that what he neglected ought to be neglected or that because he did [not] adopt colour, colour ought not to be adopted. [B.R.H.]

Cf. Blake's "What can be better said on this subject? But Reynolds contradicts what he says continually. He makes little concessions, that he may take great advantages."

IV.98 — *Michael Angelo . . . after having seen a picture by Titian, told Vasari . . . "that he liked much his colouring and manner;" but then he added, "that it was a pity the Venetian painters did not learn to draw correctly in their early youth, and adopt a better manner of study."*

Now what does this prove? Not that colour is incompatible with the grand style, but that it was a pity Titian had not adopted a better style of fundamental study. From what follows in Vasari which Reynolds has left out [16] it is evident Michl Angelo approved rather [than] disapproved the union [of colour and design]. "Se quest'huomo fusse punto aiutato *dall'arte, e dal disegno,* come e dalla natura e massimamente nel contrafare il vivo, non si potrebbe far piu ne meglio, havendo egli bellissimo spirito, & una molto vaga el vivace maniera. If this great man was as well assisted by art & design as he [was] by nature, no man could *have done better."* Is this anything but saying Titian began at the wrong end? And because the Venetian Painters neglected what they ought to have attended to, it does not follow that what they did not do, ought not to be done: the Romans neglected colour, *therefore* colour is incompatible with the grand style; the Venetians neglected design, therefore design is incompatible with colour. Was there ever such logic! All parts of the art ought to be united, to show those expressions, and inasmuch as they contribute to this devellopement, they are essentially requisite to the perfect idea of Art founded on Nature. When any of the means attract attention to the exclusion of the end expression they assert & prove not their incompatibility with the end expression but the incompetence of the man who weilds them in making them the end & not the means only. [B.R.H.]

Cf. Blake's "Venetian attention is to a contempt & neglect of form itself & to the destruction of all form or outline, purposely & intentionally. . . . Mich. Ang. knew & despised all that Titian could do."

v.116 — *If you compass [the higher excellencies] and compass nothing more, you are still in the first class. . . . you may be very imperfect; but still, you are an imperfect artist of the highest order.*

Affectation from first to last. [W.H.]

Cf. Blake's "Caesar said he'd rather be the [first in] a village [than] second in Rome. Was not Caesar [a] Dutch painter?"

v.119 — *[Where Raphael] may have attempted this expression of passions above the powers of the art [he may have] by an indistinct and imperfect marking, left room for every imagination, with equal probability, to find a passion of his own.*

Nonsense: in aiming at a middle form, not indistinct, making excellencies from defects raises the Genius to this highest perfection. [W.H. Questionable reading. Cf. end of essay xiv in *Table Talk*.]

Cf. Blake's "If Reynolds could not see variety of character in Rafael, others can."

v.125 — *[Raphael] never acquired that nicety of taste in colours, that breadth of light and shadow, that art and management of uniting light to light, and shadow to shadow, so as to make the object rise out of the ground . . .*

All true. [B.R.H. ?]

Cf. Blake's "Rafael did as he pleased. He who does not admire Rafael's execution does not even see Rafael."

v.127 — *It is to Michael Angelo, that we owe even the existence of Raffaelle.*

How excessively unjust! Raphael had painted the Sacrament & School of Athens before Michel Angelo had painted any thing in Rome. Raphael has never been fairly criticised. No life was written of him, while Michel Angelo's pupils Vasari & Condivi both wrote his life & took care to give every claim to Michel Angelo. [B.R.H.

Cf. his article on this subject in *Annals of the Fine Arts*, 3 (1818), 531–41.]

Cf. Blake's "I do not believe that Rafael taught Mich. Angelo, or that Mich. Angelo taught Rafael, any more than I believe that the rose teaches the lilly how to grow, or the apple tree teaches the pear tree how to bear fruit."

v.128 — *Raffaelle had more Taste and Fancy, Michael Angelo more Genius and Imagination. The one excelled in beauty, the other in energy.*

Quere. Origin of Coleridge's distinction? [W.H. Cf. chap. 18 of Wimsatt and Brooks's *Literary Criticism: A Short History.*

Cf. Blake's "What nonsense!"

v.131 — *another style . . . though inferior to the former, has still great merit, because it shows that those who cultivated it were men of lively and vigorous imagination. This . . . may be called the original or characteristical style . . .*

Afterbirths; variety of nature & art cannot be reduced to your standard. [W.H.]

Cf. Blake's "Original & characteristical are the two grand merits of the Great Style. Why should these words be applied to such a wretch as Salvator Rosa?"

v.135 — *Opposed to this florid, careless, loose, and inaccurate style, that of the simple, careful, pure, and correct style of Poussin seems . . .*

Incorrect. [W.H. ?]

Cf. Blake's "Opposed to Rubens's colouring Sr Joshua has placd Poussin, but he ought to put all men of genius who ever painted. Rubens & the Venetians are opposite in every thing to true art," etc., etc.

v.139 — *if the Figures which people [Poussin's] pictures had a modern air or countenance, if they appeared like our countrymen . . . how ridiculous would Apollo appear instead of the Sun; an old Man, or a Nymph with an urn, to represent a River or a Lake?*

On this principle Thompson is to be censured in the Seasons. [W.H. ?]

Cf. Blake's "These remarks on Poussin are excellent."

vi.153 — *the name of Genius . . . was given . . . to him who had invention, expression, grace, or dignity . . . those qualities . . . the power of producing which, could not then be taught by any known and promulgated rules.*

Against yourself—when it is done by rules, no longer genius. [On opposite page:] Michael Angelo, a copy of.[17] [W.H.]

But when a man has, ignorant of all rules, expressed the passions, composed finely, and given a general air of grandeur to his work, does not this man come under the idea the world has of genius more than one who produces and can produce nothing until acquainted with the rules drawn from works of great men who were ignorant of them? [B.R.H.]

Cf. Blake's "Damned fool!"

VI.154 — *as that art shall advance, its powers will be still more and more fixed by rules.*

It will not go a great way farther. [W.H. ?]

Cf. Blake's "If art was progressive we should have had Mich Angelo's & Rafaels to succeed & to improve upon each other, but it is not so. Genius dies with its possessor & comes not again till another is born with it."

VI.157. — *The mind is but a barren soil; a soil which is soon exhausted, and will produce no crop . . . unless it be continually fertilized and enriched with foreign matter.*

Good. [W.H.]

Cf. Blake's "Reynolds thinks that man learns all that he knows. I say on the contrary that man brings all that he has or can have into the world with him. Man is born like a garden ready planted & sown. This world is too poor to produce one seed"; and "The mind that could have produced this sentence must have been a pitiful, a pitiable imbecillity. I always thought that the human mind was the most prolific of all things, & inexhaustible. I certainly do thank God that I am not like Reynolds."

VI.161 — *We may oppose to Pliny the greater authority of Cicero, who is continually enforcing the necessity of this method of study. In his dialogue on Oratory . . .*

Burke. [W.H.]

Why Burke? Reynolds could read Cicero as well as Burke. Hazlitt always attributes every passage that looks literary or philosophical to Burke. [B.R.H.]

VI.162 — *Nor whilst I recommend studying the art from artists, can I be supposed to mean, that nature is to be neglected: I take this study in aid, and not in exclusion, of the other. Nature is, and must be the fountain which alone is inexhaustible; and from which all excellencies must originally flow.*

Burke again. [W.H., who has underlined from "aid" to "other".]

Stuff. [B.R.H., who has marked the last sentence.]

VI.169 — *it is from his having taken so many models, that [Raphael] became himself a model for all succeeding painters; always imitating, and always original.*

Carlo Maratti. [W.H. Cf. his *Champion* article in *The Complete Works of William Hazlitt*, ed. P. P. Howe, xviii, 64.]

What Raphael was truly excellent for, expression, he acquired from no one; it was only his defects, or his wants, he supplied by ["observation and industry" *crossed out*] by selecting and methodizing the thoughts of others. [B.R.H.]

VI.172 — *a want which cannot be completely supplied; that is, want of strength of parts. In this certainly men are not equal. . . .* Carlo, by diligence, made the most of what he had; but . . .*

*Then how can industry supply the place of talent? 2nd dis- [course. B.R.H.]

Poor Carlo then did not, it seems, by Sir Jos. own acknowledgment, supply *his* deficiencies by industry. [B.R.H. Cf. his "poor Carlo" near the beginning of his first lecture.]

Cf. Blake's "A confession."

VI.180f. — *Whoever has acquired the power of making this use of the Flemish, Venetian, and French schools . . . has sources of knowledge open to him which were wanting to the great artists who lived in the great age of painting.*

Stuff. [W.H.]

What stuff is there in this? [B.R.H.]

VI.186 — *Study therefore the great works of the great masters, for ever. . . . Study nature attentively, but always with those masters in your company; consider them as models . . . to imitate, and . . . as rivals with whom you are to contend.*

Eloquent but false. W.H.

Eloquent & *true*. B.R.H.

VII.200f. — *Colouring is true, when it is naturally adapted to the eye, from brightness, from softness, from harmony, from resemblance; because these agree with . . .* NATURE, *and therefore are true; as true as mathematical demonstration . . .*

A different thing entirely. [B.R.H. ?]

Cf. Blake's "God forbid that truth should be confined to mathematical demonstration."

VII.219 — *that of thinking taste and genius to have nothing to do with*

reason, and that of taking particular living objects for nature.
Nonsense. [W.H. ?]

True. [B.R.H. ?]

Cf. Blake's note on an earlier passage: "It is not in terms that Reynolds & I disagree. Two contrary opinions can never by any language be made alike. I say taste & genius are not teachable or aquirable but are born with us. Reynolds says the contrary."

x.26 — *The folly of attempting to make stone sport and flutter in the air, is . . .*

Happiness of expression. Quere Burke. W.H.

I like thy impertinence, W.H., in always attributing the best expressions to Burke. B.R.H.

xiv.160 — *If Gainsborough did not look at nature with a poet's eye, it must be acknowledged that he saw her with the eye of a painter; and gave a faithful . . .*

Quere. [W.H. ?]

No quere, for it is not true. [B.R.H. ?]

xv.206f. — *It is an absurdity . . . to suppose that we are born with this taste, though we are with the seeds of it, which, by the heat and kindly influence of his genius, may be ripened in us.*

But where did Michel Angelo get it? Has not Sir Joshua [said] that there was no example of this grandeur of line, [p.] 198, and it could only proceed from his own imagination? If it proceeded only from his own imagination, it was born in it, and born in it it was, for his first works, the works of his childhood, equal in principle the works of his manhood. [B.R.H.]

Cf. Blake's note quoted above, VII.219.

These, it should be emphasized, are only samples, selected because they illustrate more readily than others to what extent three different readers agreed or disagreed with Sir Joshua's remarks. All three readers were painters and writers, but the kind of painting or writing each did proves that they were not products of the same school. Blake (1757–1827), though we may often forget it, spent the greater part of his life in eighteenth-century London; Hazlitt (1778–1830), a little younger than his sometime friends Wordsworth, Coleridge, and Lamb, was old enough to share with enthusiasm the hopes raised by the fall of the Bastille; Haydon (1786–1846) was still vigorous after Victoria became queen and after she had married her Albert. We might well expect that there would be great differences of opinion between the three. Certainly they differed in temperament.

Blake is inclined to overstate his objections. He will at times go to the extreme in expressing his opposition, writing silly jingles against "Sir Joshua and his gang of cunning hired knaves," or outrageously exaggerating his opinions and making statements inadmissible as evidence: Reynolds "never was abashed in his life & never felt his ignorance"!

Hazlitt's trademark is amused sophistication. When a portrait-painter writes, as Reynolds does in the tenth discourse, "The face bears so very inconsiderable a proportion to the effect of the whole figure, that the ancient Sculptors neglected to animate the features," Hazlitt becomes Falstaffian: "Call you this backing of your friends?" At other times he will content himself with a brief "My eye" or "Oh ho," and when, in good eighteenth-century fashion, Reynolds paraphrases de Piles (III.69)—"This can only be acquired by him that enlarges the sphere of his understanding by a variety of knowledge, and warms his imagination with the best productions of ancient and modern poetry"—Hazlitt's comment is a mere "Oh Lord"!

In comparison, Haydon's expressions are completely straightforward. When Sir Joshua paraphrases Junius, who was paraphrasing Longinus (II.35: "Consider with yourself how a Michael Angelo or a Raffaelle would have treated this subject: and work yourself into a belief that your picture is to be seen and criticised by them when completed"), Haydon writes: "Sir Joshua is perpetually urging the necessity of artificial stimulants to revive the painter. Cantharides may fire impotence for a moment, but vigorous health is in no want of cantharides." A good example of his controlled criticism comes at the end of the fifth discourse: "Really Sir Joshua Reynolds's advice is so truly excellent as to the moral conduct of the Artist as it refers to Art, so totally opposite to his own habits, his own pursuits, his own line, every atom of which he condemns by such advice, that there is scarcely term sufficiently strong to apply to him for such true comprehensiveness—no paltry excuses for pursuing portrait, no timid sophistry about drawing.

He tells the truth, urges all to pursue the sound, the great road even tho' he must have known that his own intentions and views would be obscured by any one who should successfully pursue his instructions."

The comments of the three men may differ in tone, but the differences are not, it seems to me, significant; basically the three are in agreement. Haydon may at times correct Hazlitt's misreadings of the text, Blake may occasionally be led by his emotions to write nonsense, but in general the three read with the same spectacles. Certainly, as these samplings testify, the three agree in opposing the Johnsonian concept of the Concrete Universal. To them it was right and proper to number the streaks of the tulip; to them great thoughts were specific. Blake's marginalia may be thoroughly Blakean, but it would seem that they are a reasonably accurate reflection of what the romantic generation thought of its immediate predecessors.

NOTES

1. *The Diary of Benjamin Robert Haydon,* ed. Willard Bissell Pope (Cambridge, Mass., 1960), II, 427.

2. *Autobiography of B. R. Haydon,* ed. Tom Taylor (London, 1926), I, 13–14.

3. See note 1 above.

4. Professor Willard Pope agrees that "1808" is probably a correct reading for these two notes. I acknowledge with pleasure the help he has given me.

5. This episode seems to be otherwise unrecorded. See J. L. Clifford's "Johnson's Trip to Devon in 1762" in *Eighteenth-Century Studies in Honor of Donald F. Hyde,* ed. W. H. Bond (New York, 1970), p. 27.

6. *Autobiography,* I, 94.

7. Ibid., I, 160.

8. Thomas Landseer, *Life and Letters of William Bewick* (London, 1871), I, 112, 125, 128.

9. These reprints escaped the eagle-eye of Hazlitt's able editor and biographer, P. P. Howe.

10. Stanley P. Chase, in "Hazlitt as a Critic of Art," *PMLA,* 39 (1924), 187 n., suggests that Hazlitt when writing the *Champion* essays had read the earlier discourses only. Nothing in the marginalia invalidates this suggestion. Perhaps Hazlitt bor-

rowed the first volume only in 1814. Worth noting here is the fact that Blake's marginalia appear only in the first volume.

11. Haydon, *Diary*, II, 364, recording Bewick's serving as Haydon's model. Dates of Bewick's receiving and returning the volumes are highly conjectural.

12. Landseer, *Bewick*, II, 219–20. Bewick's confusion as to the periodical is understandable.

13. Here quoted from *Poetry and Prose of William Blake*, ed. David V. Erdman (New York, 1965), pp. 625–51. I have disregarded Blake's underlinings, deletions, etc.

14. Johnson's comment to Boswell (16 April 1775), "Sir, as a man advances in life, he gets what is better than admiration—judgement, to estimate things at their true value," may have been in Hazlitt's mind, but it did not refer to poetry. Professor Hagstrum suggests that Hazlitt was thinking of Johnson's definitions of wonder, e.g. the opening paragraph of Rambler 137, beginning "That wonder is the effect of ignorance, has been often observed . . . " and the comment on Yalden, "All wonder is the effect of novelty upon ignorance." *Lives of the Poets*, ed. G. B. Hill (Oxford, 1905), II, 302–03.

15. In his fourth lecture Haydon quoted this, adding, "This passage has been literally the ruin of English art, or rather was."

16. In a footnote near the end of his sixth lecture Haydon points out that Reynolds "did not quote all; for, in continuance, Michael Angelo certainly infers colour and design can be united."

17. Cf. Hazlitt's *Table Talk*, essay XIII: "Because . . . a man without much genius can copy a picture of Michael Angelo's, does it follow that there was no genius in the original design?" *The Complete Works of William Hazlitt*, ed. P. P. Howe, (London, 1930–34), vol. viii.

The Native Strain: American Orphism

HAROLD BLOOM

> I do not fear that the poetry of democratic nations will prove insipid or that it will fly too near the ground; I rather apprehend that it will range at last to purely imaginary regions. I fear that the productions of democratic poets may often be surcharged with immense and incoherent imagery, with exaggerated descriptions and strange creations; and that the fantastic beings of their brain may sometimes make us regret the world of reality.
>
> Tocqueville, ca. 1835–40

In September 1866, Emerson, aged sixty-three, set down in his journal an ultimately American insight: "There may be two or three or four steps, according to the genius of each, but for every seeing soul there are two absorbing facts,—*I and the Abyss.*" "Seeing soul" means "poet," and Emerson in his late phase is the poet of the goddess Ananke, the American Necessity he calls "Fate":

> Her planted eye today controls,
> Is in the morrow most at home,
> And sternly calls to being souls
> That curse her when they come.

This grim Muse is hardly the presiding Deity of *Nature* and most of the *Essays,* of *Walden,* of the first three *Leaves of Grass* (1855, 1856, 1860), of Dickinson, or in our time of *Harmonium, The Bridge, Paterson,* and all the other grand monuments of our Optative Mood down to one of the most recent, Mark Strand's conclusion to his lyric "White":

> And out of my waking
> the circle of light widens,
> and the day begins.

Trees turn in the luminous
reaches of sight,
and birds, and the bright
pockets of cloud.
The rim of light
is crowded with hills,
stars, and the pale echoes of night.
It reaches out.
It rings the eye with white.
All things are one.
All things are joined even beyond
the edge of sight.
All things are white.

All things are white, to Strand, when the axis of vision becomes coincident with the axis of things. When all things cease to be one, for him, their opacity appears as a darkness. But for Strand's precursor, Stevens, the whiteness was terrible, and marked an opaqueness rather than a transparency. In the culminating crisis of his vision, Stevens also echoed Emerson, confirming the dialectic of what must be the most central passage in our literature, the extraordinary and much maligned transformation of the Sage of Concord into a Transparent Eyeball. "The ruin or the blank that we see when we look at nature, is in our own eye," Emerson said later in his *Nature,* and the same blankness descends upon Stevens at his nadir of vision:

Here, being visible is being white,
Is being of the solid of white, the accomplishment
Of an extremist in an exercise . . .

The season changes. A cold wind chills the beach.
The long lines of it grow longer, emptier,
A darkness gathers though it does not fall

And the whiteness grows less vivid on the wall.
The man who is walking turns blankly on the sand.

Whether the whiteness is transparent or opaque, what matters is the diminishment of its vividness. When Wordsworth saw the glory fade away, he confronted a fearful life-crisis, which soon enough ended him effectually as a poet. But a British High Romantic, even of Wordsworth's preternatural strength, had the horror only of the loss of a poethood, when vision came to its crisis. Even the Orphic Shelley did not see himself as a liberating god; that was left for his later followers, who apprehended him as a divinity, from Beddoes on through Browning and then to the generation of Lionel Johnson and the young Yeats. The native strain of American poetry, at least from Emerson to my own contemporaries, is a curious variant or version of Orphism, and the crisis of vision in this tradition threatens always a loss of divinity far transcending even the splendor of poetic vocation.

The sources of Emerson's kind of Orphism have been traced in Plato, various Neoplatonists, Cambridge Platonists, and even in the curious New England mode of Swedenborgianism, as represented by Sampson Reed and other exotic contemporaries. But Emerson's Orphism is very much his own, and little is to be apprehended of Emerson by tracking him to any of his precursors, for no other Post-Enlightenment intellect, not even Nietzsche's, has set itself quite so strongly against the idea of influence, and done this so successfully, and without anxiety. Even Emily Dickinson owes more to Emerson than Emerson did to Coleridge, Wordsworth, or any other spiritual father. All that Emerson took from Orphic traditions can be gleaned by any reader with even a slight knowledge of ancient Greek religion. When Emerson, in his essay "The Poet," brings together the "highest minds of the world," those who never cease to explore the manifold meanings of every sensuous fact, he lists an extraordinary seven: "Orpheus, Empedocles, Heraclitus, Plato, Plutarch, Dante, Swedenborg." Presumably, all these excel as figurative interpreters of mere nature, and Orpheus heads the list as though he were an actual poet, with priority over all others. Whether, as Empedocles, Plato, Emerson, and so distinguished a recent scholar as Jane Harrison thought, Orpheus was an actual man, or whether he was only a myth, does not matter for anyone's understanding of Orphism, since what affects followers of so esoteric a faith at any time will be its unique aspects, and not its genetic elements. Orphism differs from every other Greek religion, including the worship of

Dionysus to which it is so strangely both allied and opposed. Orpheus is a kind of shaman, as is Empedocles after him, a master of divination whose quest leads to godhood, if finally also to failure and to a terrible death. The hypothetical lost poems of the Orphics, which Emerson knew in their later, Neoplatonic elaborations, were evidently purgatorial and apocalyptic, offering pathways to release from metamorphic existence. Where Greek thought emphasized always the great reality of human mortality, Orphism was not only a doctrine of immortality, but of the actual if latent divinity of the soul. Such doctrine was Thracian and Bacchic; the Orphics combined it with Apollonian notions of ritual purification to produce a purgatorial faith. There are only two gods who matter deeply to the Orphics, and these are Eros or Phanes, and Dionysus or Bacchus, rather than Zeus and Apollo. I think, to leap ahead, that these are also the only gods who matter to Emerson and to all his descendants in American poetic tradition, though I would add one goddess who is also important in the Orphic pantheon, Ananke or dread Necessity. The divinities of American Romantic poetry are Eros, Bacchus, and Ananke, and the troublesome relations between these giant forms account for much of the peculiar individuality of post-Emersonian American poetry, when we compare it to the British poetry of the same period, continuing on into our own days.

In his essay "History," Emerson tells us that: "The power of music, the power of poetry, to unfix and as it were clap wings to solid nature, interprets the riddle of Orpheus." In a journal entry for November 28, 1836, Emerson illuminates the Orphic riddle:

In what I call the cyclus of Orphic words, which I find in Bacon, in Cudworth, in Plutarch, in Plato, in that which the New Church would indicate when it speaks of the truths possessed by the primeval church broken up into fragments and floating hither and thither in the corrupt Church, I perceive [an adaptation] myself addressed thoroughly. They do touch the Intellect & cause a gush of emotion; [to] which we call the moral sublime; they pervade also the moral nature. Now the Universal Man when he comes, must so speak. He must not be one-toned. He must recognize by addressing the whole nature.

Emerson's Universal Man, he that shall come, is Orphic Man. But what is Orphic Man? Vico traced the lyre of Orpheus to the original possession of Hermes, and though Emerson never mentions Vico he seems to have arrived at just this Viconian connection (possibly by reading French Viconians like Cousin, Ballanche, and Michelet). Orphic Man is Hermetic in having priority, and so in being free of the anxiety of influence. Even as Orpheus dissolved the forms of barbarism so as to nurture Greek civilization (according to Vico), and again in the same way that Emerson's Orpheus brings forth a new flux out of solid nature, so Orphic Man performs rather than suffers a rending. But Orphic Man, who will tear nature apart, is still to come; the Orphic Poet is his prophet.

Emerson's Orphic Poet makes three major appearances, two in *Nature,* and the other in the essay "The Poet." All his appearances are dazzling, and consciously extravagant. In each, Emerson achieves an *ekstasis,* a stepping-out that is truly a wandering beyond limits. If there is a source for these passages, the frequently cited sentence from Proclus will do: "He who desires to signify divine concerns through symbols is orphic, and, in short, accords with those who write myths concerning the gods." In *Nature,* Emerson remarks that what the Orphic poet sings to him may be both history and prophecy. When the Orphic poet teaches Emerson in the essay "The Poet," his song is called "freer speech," and we need to remember that for Emerson "freedom" and "wildness" are synonymous. Yet these central utterances of Emerson's Orphic Poet, though not incompatible with one another, are very different in tone and in direction, the difference being only in part the consequence of the seven years that divided the more experienced Emerson, aged forty, from the apocalyptic and more Orphic Emerson who had reached his own first large utterance at the christological age of thirty-three. Where the first prose-chants of the Orphic poet are in the Optative Mood carried beyond all limits, the later one makes a careful (perhaps an overly careful) distinction between Orphic poet and Orphic poem, admitting a kind of Shelleyan skepticism into the whole category of the Orphic.

Let me attempt to give the center of each crucial Orphic chant, without quoting either fully, as each is so ordered as to make such a center available. In *Nature,* the Orphic poet begins by comparing fallen man, "a god in ruins," to Nebuchadnezzar, the hideous emblem whose degradation is also the climax of Blake's parallel manifesto, *The Marriage of Heaven and Hell*. Nebuchadnezzar— "dethroned, bereft of reason, and eating grass like an ox"—is every man who tries to live by the understanding alone. Yet spirit or "reason" can afflict even Nebuchadnezzar with a terrible cure, or as Emerson more grandly and grimly phrases it: "But who can set limits to the remedial force of spirit?" This is a Jobean rhetorical question, and Emerson answers it with a majestic paragraph that begins: "Man is the dwarf of himself." Once unfallen spirit, Emerson tells us, man was a center from which nature emanated. But the creation is now too large for the self-ruined creator. The Orphic poet concludes, with simple but awesome power, by celebrating in fallen man the faculty of *instinct,* as superior to the will as reason is to the understanding:

He sees that the structure still fits him, but fits him colossally. Say, rather, once it fitted him, now it corresponds to him from far and on high. He adores timidly his own work. . . . Yet sometimes he starts in his slumber, and wonders at himself and his house, and muses strangely at the resemblance betwixt him and it. He perceives that if his law is still paramount, if still he have elemental power, if his word is sterling yet in nature, it is not conscious power, it is not inferior but superior to his will. It is instinct.

By so exalting instinct as our only link to unfallen human potential, Emerson opened himself and his poetic descendants to daemonic influx, for whatever he meant by "instinct," he could not reconcile it with the Transcendentalist faith in Coleridgean "reason." Orphic instinct, in Emerson and in his descendants, manifests itself as Dionysiac possession, and also as a rival possession that begins as Eros and ends as Ananke, love yielding to necessity. Emerson's *Nature* knows only Dionysus and Eros as divinities, but Emerson was not yet at the turning. In the essay "The Poet," which is best viewed as a prelude to Emerson's greatest essay, "Experience," the shadows of instinctual necessity begin to darken instinctual love. Though Emerson calls the poet "the man without impediment" and nature nothing but "motion or change," his later Orphic poet sees Nature as dominant, indeed as Necessity ("Nature through all her kingdoms, insures herself"), while the poet is only a dying creature whose songs are detached from him, by Nature herself, that they may outlive him. Nothing could contrast more with the closing passage of *Nature,* where the Orphic poet returned to prophesy "the kingdom of man over nature, which cometh not with observation," and so counseled every man: "Build therefore your own world." Emerson's first Orphic poet could have written *Song of Myself* or *The Bridge*'s more ecstatic passages; his second Orphic poet could write only lyrics like "As I Ebb'd With The Ocean of Life" or "The Broken Tower." Yet he was right to call both poets Orphics, or at least American Orphics.

Orphism attracted Emerson for reasons akin to the cause of its mingled attraction and repulsion for Plato, and yet more closely akin to its wholly attractive power for Empedocles and much later for the Neoplatonists of all ages, down to certain Late Romantics. For Orphism, uniquely among ancient faiths in the West, came near shamanism without actually quite being a thoroughgoing shamanism. Mircea Eliade lists as shamanistic characteristics in Orpheus his descent to the dead to bring back his wife's soul, his healing art, love for music and animals, his "charms," and—most crucially for us—his power of divination and the posthumous performance of his skull as an oracle. But Eliade also shows that Bacchic (and Orphic) enthusiasm does not equal shamanistic ecstasy, which is rather more extreme. There are moments in Emerson when he almost suggests shamanistic ecstasy, in a few earlier notebook verse fragments, even fewer later prose passages in the Journal, and most memorably in the great poem "Bacchus." Orphic enthusiasm is more generally the expansive or Transcendental atmosphere in Emerson, who is wary almost always as to finding a way back from the influx of power to the stabler ways of prudence.

Yet the shamanistic ecstasy, like the Orphic enthusiasm, is what Nietzsche called "the antithetical"; it is a movement against the merely natural in man. Emerson's poet, like the Orphic adept and like the quasi-Orphic Empedocles, wants us to think of him as a liberating god, and not just as a man. We come back again to the strangeness of Orphism among the classical faiths. It holds that man is wicked, because descended from the Titans who devoured the child Dionysos-Zagreus, and yet also divine, because descended also necessarily from the grotesquely cannibalized Bacchic babe. We have in us what Plato calls "the Titan Nature," our original sin, and we have what was never nature's. Plato mocked the Orphic notion that redeemed life would be "an eternal intoxication," but Emerson welcomed and echoed it. By making his own version of Orphism the revealed religion of American poetry, Emerson did something both frightening and splendid to most of our good poets after him. He committed them to an enterprise that British High Romanticism was either too commonsensical or two repressed to attempt, an enterprise that can be summed up in the single word "divination." If we interpret divination in every possible sense, including the proleptic knowledge of actual experience, and the fearsome project of godmaking, then we have a vision of the outrageous ambition of the native strain in our poetry, or what I have chosen to call American Orphism.

There are a myriad of figures to illustrate American Orphism, but I want to confine myself here first to our very best poets (or those who seem best to me)—Whitman, Dickinson, a certain aspect of Stevens, and Hart Crane—and then to my own contemporaries I admire most, A. R. Ammons and John Ashbery. Frost is a cunningly concealed Orphic, and Pound, in the *Cantos,* a very central one, but a discussion of all our Emersonian poets soon would become very nearly a discussion of all our poets. There are six or seven Emersons in Emerson's prose, and three or four more in his verse, and he would have been delighted at our total inability to reconcile all of them, for more than Whitman he was large; he did contain multitudes of his descendants. He was indeed the American Orpheus, though, as he said, he sang rather huskily in verse, yet so magnificently, I think, in prose. Orpheus turned orator, we could say, or turned sophist as I suppose the late Yvor Winters or Robert Penn Warren might say, in one of their kinder moods toward our greatest ancestor (sometimes they talk of him as though he were Orpheus turned Satan).

Emerson understood that poets, or seeing souls, could not as poets accept mortality. As a man he had to accept rather too much of it: his first wife, his little son, two beloved brothers. As an Orphic orator he began by accepting nothing but Dionysus and Eros, but ended by accepting Ananke, and with her something dread that transcended mortality, the Orphic doom of wandering in repetition, in a netherworld, carrying poetry rather than water in a sieve. Let us call the sieve our American pragmatic temperament, and the spilled poetry the religion of money, since Emerson's disciples included the dreamers who divined a business expansion that would make us liberating gods, the least ambiguous consequence of our Optative Mood. To call the Emersonian Henry Ford a master of divination, and so a major American Orphic, does not discredit the native strain, for Orphism, though esoteric, is a democratic religion.

After Emerson inevitably comes Whitman, since *Song of My-self* is the natural son of Emerson's *Nature* and of the crucial essays, particularly "Self-Reliance" and "The Poet." Whitman, in his three great editions of *Leaves of Grass,* in a religious poet, and his faith is American Orphism. But American Orphism is not a doctrine but a fury, and the rage is for priority. No American poet wants to be an Orphic; they all insist upon being Orpheus. Emerson denounced all influence as pernicious, and his involuntary disciples have fought so bitterly against influence that they have all become one version or another of their brilliantly scattered, ever metamorphic father, whose oracular Yankee skull goes on chanting in their repudiations of Transcendental influx.

Whitman prided himself on telling truths about death that Emerson had not told, as well as truths about the body, sex, and time that went beyond his precursor's knowledge. Perhaps he did, but they are all the same truth and approximate one American Orphic formula: Eros is at once life, love, sleep, and death, or as Jane Harrison said of the ancient Orphic Eros: "a life-impulse, a thing fateful to all that lives, a man because of his moralized complexity, terrible and sometimes intolerable." This Orphic Eros, Jane Harrison also observed, was inseparable from the mother, conceived not as Aphrodite but as the old figure of the Earth-goddess, or if Aphrodite, then the ocean-goddess, or else the

underworld mother, goddess of death. The mysteries of the
Orphic Eros are the mysteries of the mother, and in turning from
his spiritual father Emerson, as from his own phallic father, Whitman turned only toward an even more Orphic vision of death.

Whitman's invocations of the Orphic mother emphasize faith
in a mystery, as here at the close of *The Sleepers* (1855 version):

I too pass from the night;
I stay awhile away O night, but I return to you again and love you;

Why should I be afraid to trust myself to you?
I am not afraid . . . . I have been well brought forward by you;
I love the rich running day, but I do not desert her in whom I lay
    so long:
I know not how I came of you, and I know not where I go with you
    . . . . but I know I came well and shall go well.

I will stop only a time with the night . . . . and rise betimes.

I will duly pass the day O my mother and duly return to you;
Not you will yield forth the dawn again more surely than you will
    yield forth me again,
Not the womb yields the babe in its time more surely than I shall be
    yielded from you in my time.

The riddle of the Sphinx, of human origins, and the greater
riddle of death, are mysteries beyond Whitman's knowledge, but
his moving faith is that the going will be as well for him as the
coming, and that the going is only a return to a further gestation
and to a proper rebirth "in my time," not the time prescribed for
another. "Pure I come from the Pure, O Queen," reads a fragment from one of the Orphic tablets, where the queen addressed
is at once the Earth-mother and the goddess of Hades. "Thou art
become God from Man. A kid thou art fallen into milk," reads
a fragment from another tablet, which could find a number
of contexts in Whitman that would fit. In the Dionysiac afflatus,
Whitman knew his own divinity, as Emerson's writings had
promised he would know. But this is the knowledge of enthusiasm, born from the Orphic flux and doomed to ebb away as
all Orphic intensities ebb. Shamanism, with its archaic and highly
effective techniques of ecstasy, has known always how to avoid

this ebb and flow. Though certain current American Orphics have returned to some of these archaic techniques, they sacrifice their more authentic if more sorrowful heritage by doing so. Emerson definitively prophesied them in "The Poet," when he declared for the Orphic asceticism against the shamanistic immersion in what he called *"quasi*-mechanical substitutes for the true nectar, which is the ravishment of the intellect by coming nearer to the fact." We are to remember that Emerson existed to remind us that a fact was an epiphany of God, and that always we were to ask the fact for the form. Hence the great declaration in "The Poet," that Whitman, Dickinson, Stevens in their lives were to exemplify, and that Hart Crane broke himself by being so tragically unable to heed; this great wisdom, as to substitutes for the true nectar:

These are auxiliaries to the centrifugal tendency of a man, to his passage out into free space, and they help him to escape the custody of that body in which he is pent up, and of that jailyard of individual relations in which he is enclosed. Hence a great number of such as were professionally expressers of Beauty, as painters, poets, musicians and actors, have been more than others wont to lead a life of pleasure and indulgence; all but the few who received the true nectar; and, as it was a spurious mode of attaining freedom, as it was an emancipation not into the heavens but into the freedom of baser places, they were punished for that advantage they won, by a dissipation and deterioration. But never can any advantage be taken of nature by a trick. The spirit of the world, the great calm presence of the Creator, comes not forth to the sorceries of opium or of wine. The sublime vision comes to the pure and simple soul in a clean and chaste body. That is not an inspiration, which we owe to narcotics, but some counterfeit excitement and fury.

This may sound merely conventional, or even tiresomely sensible, but like Whitman's almost pathological emphases on purity and cleanliness and Dickinson's obsession with her White Election, it is a sublime passage of Orphic enthusiasm and about as ordinary as Whitman on death and the mother or Dickinson on what and how she merely sees. For Orphic asceticism, whether ancient or American, is a peculiar kind of purgation, not at all resembling the various asceticisms practiced in Christian traditions. The *askesis* of Empedocles, who was at once a sort of Orphic, a sort of Pythagorean, and something of a Thracian shaman, is much closer to what Emerson urged and Whitman and Dickinson so differently followed. The Purifications of Empedocles are meant to reconcile one goddess to us, and she is Ananke or Necessity. We are daemons, exiled from our true home, and our sin is that we trusted in the principle of strife. The four elements scarcely can bear us, and toss us back and forth, so that we have been all things, even plants and fish. Purifications must redeem us and return us to godhood, and do this by persuading Necessity to remit her oracle that prescribes our wanderings.

Purification, in the shrewd and saintly Emerson, is mostly the process of unlocking our gates, of opening ourselves to vision. How strangely American it is that purification should be release rather than repression, though this is release in the sense best exemplified by Thoreau, a lesser Emerson we have so overvalued in this century, and so oddly and wrongly at Emerson's expense. Purification in Whitman is self-integration and consequent release of imagination, very much in the Emersonian pattern. In Dickinson, purification becomes the most intensely Orphic phenomenon in the history of the American poetic consciousness, and remains more difficult to understand than any parallel process in a major modern creator.

Dickinson's religion, despite the pieties of her biographers-to-date and most of her critics, was no more Christian than the faiths of Emerson, Thoreau, Whitman. Christian imagery she employed always to her own curious ends as she saw fit, free-style, picking it up or dropping it at will. But even as her mind is stronger and more individual, more profoundly original, than Emerson's, Thoreau's, Whitman's, so her American Orphism is more complete and more astringent than theirs. Jane Harrison observed that: "The religion of Orpheus *is* religious in the sense that it is the worship of the real mysteries of life, of potencies (daemons) rather than personal gods *(theoi)*; it is the worship of life itself in its supreme mysteries of ecstasy and love." Bacchus and Eros are

Dickinson's daemons also, but she addressed the third Orphic potency, Ananke, not as Emerson's Fate but as death. Death, which imaginatively failed to interest Emerson, was identified by Whitman with Eros but by Dickinson with Necessity, two startlingly irreconcilable Orphic choices. To understand this contrast, we can return again to the Orphism of Emerson.

What did Emerson ask of life? Ecstasy and love, but also alas a reconcilement with the way things are, not in society or even in our fallen nature, but in the daemonic world. Like Swedenborg, whom he both admired and distrusted, he believed in influx and consequently in contact. It is here that he locates Plato's one defect in power, and "power," for Emerson as for Nietzsche, is the true value-term. He says of Plato "that his writings have not . . . the vital authority which the screams of prophets and the sermons of unlettered Arabs and Jews possess. There is an interval; and to cohesion, contact is necessary." Contact is Dionysian, and returns us to the primal child in ourselves. An Orphic saying of Heraclitus tells us that "Time is a child who plays and moves the pieces, the lordship is to the child." But if our lord Time is a child, then he has all the aggressive and destructive fantasies of a child, and he acts them out. And, unlike a human child, Time can make no reparation.

Orphism, even in the antihistorical Emerson, worships origins, and ultimately therefore worships Time. Time's firstborn, in the Orphic vision, is Eros, who brings us our souls by literal inspiration, by prevailing winds. Our souls then are latent divinities, but if we are to reach this Eros in ourselves we need to get there by Dionysiac enthusiasm. When this influx fails us, when we are left with only the sinful Titanic elements in ourselves, then truly we fall into Time, and finally into Hades. Our souls cease to be airy and become of earth. In the intervals left to us, our religious sense grants us visions of only one deity: Ananke. She abides, and as failed Orphics we must abide with her.

Emerson, when he failed as an Orphic, failed only dialectically, for his temperament was too fortunate for absolute failure. The despair of Melville is both profound and profoundly appealing to us, but Emerson on principle as well as by temperament would not despair, not even if the despair were to be of Whitman's Orphic kind, as in the *Sea-Drift* poems. Here is Emerson in August 1859, lamenting his inability to write consecutively of the beatitudes of intellect:

It is too great for feeble souls, and they are over-excited. The wine-glass shakes, and the wine is spilled. What then? The joy which will not let me sit in my chair, which brings me bolt upright to my feet, and sends me striding around my room, like a tiger in his cage, and I cannot have composure and concentration enough even to set down in English words the thought which thrills me—is not that joy a certificate of the elevation? What if I never write a book or a line? for a moment, the eyes of my eyes were opened, the affirmative experience remains, and consoles through all suffering.

I think a passage like this explains why the later Emerson, of "Fate," "Illusions," "Power," and the other vastations that make up *The Conduct of Life,* is still among the eternally undefeated. Though he yields to Fate and gives to Ananke the worship he once gave to Eros, he can continue to insist that: "We are as lawgivers; we speak for Nature; we prophesy and divine." He had created an Orphism that survives its own ruin; we are not saved, and yet the Dionysian enthusiasm goes on flickering in us. Those who came after him had neither his extraordinary temperament nor his intensely faithless faith. Whitman would not surrender except to Eros, but the Dionysian died in him after his crisis of 1859–60, and like Wordsworth he long outlived his own poethood. Whitman's Orphism is as incomplete as Emerson's is overcomplete.

Dickinson, always too difficult for brief summation, defies all terms not her own. Her religion though, if we try to call it religion or a binding, is a heresy of which the orthodoxy is Emersonian Orphism. Sometimes, but not often, she can be as grim as the older Emerson is about Fate, as in this late fragment:

> We never know we go when we are going—
> We jest and shut the Door—
> Fate—following—behind us bolts it—
> And we accost no more—

But generally she is far subtler in her relations to the goddess Ananke, treating Necessity as a sister not too much more formidable than the poet herself. In the later poems there is rather less transport than in those of the great years, 1859 through 1864, but the Dionysiac enthusiasm, the influx of power, never leaves her, nor does Eros wane to make room for Ananke. Almost from the start, all three deities are in her poetry, and again nearly at her origins Ananke is made one with death. Where Whitman found Eros and death one in the Orphic mother, and Emerson hardly found death at all (in his vision, not his life), Dickinson recognized death's place as rightfully being in the Orphic pantheon. "Why Orphic?" readers of Dickinson may well ask, seeing that she allows Orpheus only one appearance in all of her poetry, though then in a late poem where he is preferred to the Bible because he captivated and did not condemn. Because, like the Orphic poet in Emerson's *Nature,* she tells us powerfully but largely by her example, that reality is consciousness, and this is consciousness of three things: poetic ecstasy, love, and the necessity of dying. The rest, as her pride, power, and exclusiveness of vision imply, do not matter. Life is solipsistic transport, extended to the Bacchic commonal through her poems. Life again is the rapture and cruelty of Eros, in her case always without an object adequate to herself as extraordinary subject. And life, finally yet without paradox, is the confrontation with dying, not as a consequence of Orphic failure in divination, but as the final exercise in divination, the triumphant test that will achieve a decisive priority. For does any other poet whatsoever so persuade us that she will die her own death and not another poet's or person's? Rilke hoped to meet and marry his own death, as Shelley had hoped before him. Both these poets were conscious Orphics, both are persuasive, but both seem dubious or even a little confused about the high individuality of their own deaths when we compare them closely to the more formidable Dickinson. What are we to call her peculiarly self-reliant faith if not a version of Emerson's Orphism, the validly solipsistic, and so ultimately realist doctrine native to American poetry?

As a heretic from Emersonianism, Dickinson declined to entertain inconsistencies, as her precursor could with his outrageous charm. We can name Emerson accurately as a dozen things, and describe all of them with ease and an exuberance he happily supplies us. Unfortunately, we then cannot reconcile that dozen to produce a coherent Emerson. We can name Dickinson accurately as only one thing, but we have failed so far to describe that massive unity, despite all her exuberance, which is not so contagious a quality. The critics of Emerson do not agree, and they are all of them somewhat correct. The critics of Dickinson are all honorable failures.

Yet they have shown us, however tentatively, everything she was not, at times even everything she would not condescend to be. Her hands, as she says, are narrow, yet she says also she can spread them wide: "To gather Paradise—." Elsewhere she tells us Paradise is "an uncertain certainty," and we know she means the Paradise of Poets, which is Orphic. Emerson, who fought against the past as inhibition, was chosen by Orphism because he was susceptible to what he called the Newness, and so asserted his own priority. Dickinson knew every Orphic priority except one, freedom from death's necessity, and so she labored to win a freedom Emerson more happily assumed, the wildness of an absolute priority, an Orphic death that she could die as if no one else had died so inventively before her. More than Emerson or Whitman, she seems now a perfect sphere of a consciousness, a divinity not wholly latent.

Of the Orphic inheritors in modern American poetry, Wallace Stevens is the largest. His most mysterious and difficult poem is the great elegy, "The Owl in the Sarcophagus," where the Orphic trinity appears as sleep, peace, and death: a Dionysiac sleep, erotic peace, and transformed Ananke of a death, all of these oxymorons blending into a Whitmanian consolation for, as an American Orphic, Stevens is closer to Whitman than to Emerson or Dickinson. In *Notes Toward a Supreme Fiction,* Stevens reservedly mentions that: "A dead shepherd brought tremendous chords from hell / And bade the sheep carouse. Or so they said." But this already modified Orphism is darker in the "Owl" elegy, where sleep is "the accomplished, the fulfilling air" that redeems the Orphic soul, yet is also "a diamond jubilance beyond the fire," a reduction of Dionysian enthusiasm to "the unique composure" Stevens will accept as compromise. Eros, always elusive in Stevens, is in his vision of the last things the inhuman figure of peace, of passion spent, "a thousand begettings of the broken bold." Whitman's Orphic mother, divested of her erotic intensities, stands separately in Stevens as a last knowledge that death has, "there on the edges of oblivion." Time as the Orphic child of Heraclitus returns in the poem's moving final image:

> It is a child that sings itself to sleep,
> The mind, among the creatures that it makes,
> The people, those by which it lives and dies.

If this is still Orphic faith, admittedly it is faint, but we may remember the wisdom of Stevens in the even later poem, "The Sail of Ulysses":

> Need makes
> The right to use. Need names on its breath
> Categories of bleak necessity,
> Which, just to name, is to create
> A help, a right to help, a right
> To know what helps and to attain,
> By right of knowing, another plane.

Here Stevens comes full circle around to late Emerson again, for this is the doctrine of *The Conduct of Life,* and Stevens too, for all his ironic wariness, concludes by building altars to the Beautiful Necessity. Emerson and Stevens are allied finally as failed Orphics who refuse to accept defeat.

I conclude though with the most magnificent of failed Orphics, Hart Crane, who was too pure to deny his defeat, and also with a closing glance at the best of our contemporary American Orphics, who understand their tradition perhaps too well. Crane's acts of worship directed to Bacchus and to Eros are clearer than his as intense worship of Ananke, which is simply his love of everything that is irreconcilable, his Shelleyan sense that even love and the means of love are not to be charmed into reconcilement. Crane is profoundly moving when he asks for "That patience that is armour and that shields / Love from despair—when love foresees the end—." The most Orphic poem Crane wrote is "Atlantis," the first section of *The Bridge* to be composed, and the prophecy of this Orphic poet's high spiritual failure (but aesthetic triumph, since it makes no sense to go on calling *The Bridge* a failure, even as the poem becomes more vital with each passing year). "Atlantis" is Orphic rather as its Platonic source is Orphic, that is, on the whole unwillingly. Plato resorts to Orphic mythology, as in his fable of Er, because he needs a purifying vision of judgment, and because he shares the Orphic conviction that our Titan nature requires to be cleansed; but Plato seems uneasy about Orphism, with its necessary emphasis on the irrational soul attaining an airy redemption. Crane too would have liked to have been more rational and less enthusiastic in his glimpses of salvation, but here his poetic tradition may have served him badly. His religious sensibility was too pure and acute to accept the failure of his Dionysiac and erotic quests to attain some reconcilement with the way things were, and it is at least a partial truth to say that Crane's Transcendentalism helped destroy him, which was the violent but insightful judgment of Yvor Winters.

The most convinced American Orphics since Crane were probably the late Theodore Roethke and the formidably active James Dickey, but I choose two poems by my own contemporaries as epilogue for this discussion. One is "Evening in the Country" from the book *The Double Dream of Spring* by John Ashbery; the other is "Prodigal" from the volume *Corsons Inlet* by A. R. Ammons. Both poems are beautifully chastened meditations that combine a kind of convalescence from Dionysiac enthusiasm, a continued erotic hope, and a recognition that necessity is stronger than either poetic influx or love's potential. Though both poets are battered Orphics, they are Orphics nevertheless, Ashbery as Stevens's continuator and Ammons as Emerson's. Ashbery's "Evening in the Country" begins with a declaration of happiness that is also a disavowal of ambition:

> My resolve to win further I have
> Thrown out, and am charged by the thrill
> Of the sun coming up.

From this acceptance of diminishment there rises a poignant declaration of faith in what is essentially an American Orphic act of purification:

> Light falls on your shoulders, as is its way,
> And the process of purification continues happily,
> Unimpeded, but has the motion started
> That is to quiver your head, send anxious beams
> Into the dusty corners of the rooms
> Eventually shoot out over the landscape
> In stars and bursts? For other than this we know nothing
> And space is a coffin, and the sky will put out the light.
> I see you eager in your wishing it the way
> We may join it, if it passes close enough:
> This sets the seal of distinction on the success or failure of your
>   attempt.

The light here is the Stevensian one of the imagination that falls upon reality, adding nothing but itself. One purification is rewarded only by the impulse that may lead to another, and so "the seal of distinction" here will be set without regard to success or failure of a Transcendental attempt. For these are the humane exhaustions of an American Orphism that has burned nearly to the socket.

Ammons's "Prodigal" also addresses itself to a moment of visionary convalescence:

> after the mental
> blaze and gleam,
> the mind in both motions building and tearing down.

But Ammons, though as spent a Dionysiac seer as Ashbery and as much a yielder to the goddess Ananke, moves again toward an Orphic Eros with something of the old Emersonian acceptance and of the great Whitmanian force:

> the mind whirls, short of the unifying
> reach, short of the heat
>   to carry that forging:
>   after the visions of these losses, the spent
> seer, delivered to wastage, risen

into ribs, consigns knowledge to
approximation, order to the vehicle
of change, and fumbles blind in blunt innocence
toward divine, terrible love.

Poem and Ideology: A Study of Keats's "To Autumn"

GEOFFREY H. HARTMAN

"Most English great poems have little or nothing to say." [1] Few
do that nothing so perfectly, one is tempted to add, as Keats's "To
Autumn." Our difficulty as interpreters is related to the way
consciousness almost disappears into the poem: the mind, for
once, is not what is left (a kind of sublime litter) after the show
is over. "To Autumn" seems to absorb rather than extrovert that
questing imagination whose breeding fancies, feverish overidenti-
fications, and ambitious projects motivate the other odes.

It is not that we lack terms to describe the poem. On the contrary, as W. J. Bate has said, "for no other poem of the last two
centuries does the classical critical vocabulary prove so satisfying." We can talk of its decorum, "the parts . . . contributing
directly to the whole, with nothing left dangling or independent,"
of its lack of egotism, "the poet himself . . . completely absent;
there is no 'I', no suggestion of the discursive language that we
find in the other odes," and finally of a perfect concreteness or
adequacy of symbol, the union in the poem of ideal and real, of
the "greeting of the Spirit" and its object.[2]

Yet terms like these point to an abstract perfection, to something as pure of content as a certain kind of music. They bespeak
a triumph of form that exists but not—or not sufficiently—the
nature of that form: its power to illumine experience, to cast a
new light, a new shadow maybe, on things. In what follows I suggest, daringly, that "To Autumn" has something to say: that it
is an ideological poem whose very form expresses a national idea
and a new stage in consciousness, or what Keats himself once

called the "gregarious advance" and "grand march of intellect."

There are problems with *ideological,* a word whose meaning is more charged in Marxist than in general usage. Marxism thinks of ideology as a set of ideas that claim universality while serving a materialistic or class interest. "Ideology is untruth, false consciousness, lie. It shows up in failed works of art . . . and is vulnerable to criticism. . . . Art's greatness consists in allowing that to be uttered which ideology covers up." [3] The attack on ideology in Marxism resembles that on "unearned abstractions" in Anglo-American formalistic theory, except that it engages in "depth politics" to uncover these abstractions. Formalistic criticism can worry overt ideas or idealisms, Keats's "Beauty is Truth, Truth Beauty," for example, yet it accepts gladly the disappearance of ideas, or disinterestedness of form in "To Autumn." There is no attempt to demystify this form by discovering behind its decorum a hidden interest. In a low-risk theory of this kind the presence of ideas can be disturbing but not, obviously, their absence.

The great interpretive systems we know of have all been interest-centered, however; they have dug deep, mined, undermined, removed the veils. The Synagogue is blind to what it utters, the Church understands. The patient dreams, the doctor translates the dream. The distant city is really our city; the *unheimlich* the *heim-lich;* strange, uncanny, and exotic are brought home. Like those etymologies older scholars were so fond of, which showed us the fossilized stem of abstract words, so everything is slain, in interest-theories, on the stem of generational or class conflict.

Yet like nature itself, which has so far survived man's use of it, art is not polluted by such appropriations. Some works may be discredited, others deepened—the scandal of form remains. From Kant through Schopenhauer and Nietzsche, the aesthetic element proper is associated with disinterestedness, impersonality, and resistance to utilitarian concepts. Beauty of this undetermined kind becomes an itch: the mind, says Empson, wants to scratch it, to see what is really there, and this scratching we call interpretation. Most men, says Schopenhauer, seek in objects "only some relation to their will, and with everything that has not such a relation there sounds within them, like a ground-bass, the constant, inconsolable lament, 'It is of no use to me.' " Though the link between art and impersonality is often acknowledged—in New Criticism as well as Neoclassic theory—no very successful *interpretive* use of the principle exists. The notion of impersonality is vulnerable because so easily retranslated into unconscious interest or the masked presence of some *force majeure.*

I try to face this problem of the ideology of form by choosing a poem without explicit social context and exploring its involvement in social and historical vision. This would be harder, needless to say, if Keats had not elsewhere explicitly worried the opposition of dreamer and poet or poet and thinker. Even if "To Autumn" were a holiday of the spirit, some workday concerns of the poet would show through. My use of the concept of ideology, at the same time, will seem half-way or uncritical to the Marxist thinker. In uncovering Keats's ideology I remain as far as possible within terms provided by Keats himself, or furnished by the ongoing history of poetry. This is not, I hope, antiquarianism, but also not transvaluation. It should be possible to consider a poem's *geschichtlicher Stundenschlag* (Adorno)—how it tells the time of history—without accepting a historical determinism. Keats's poetry is indeed an event in history: not in world-history, however, but simply in the history of fiction, in our awareness of the power and poverty of fictions.

My argument runs that "To Autumn," an ode that is hardly an ode, is best defined as an English or Hesperian model which overcomes not only the traditional type of sublime poem but the "Eastern" or epiphanic consciousness essential to it. The traditional type was transmitted by both Greek and Hebrew religious poetry, and throughout the late Renaissance and eighteenth century, by debased versions of the Pindaric or cult hymn.[4] Only one thing about epiphanic structure need be said now: it evokes the presence of a god, or vacillates sharply between imagined presence and absence. Its rhetoric is therefore a crisis-rhetoric, with priest or votary, vastation or rapture, precarious nearness or hieratic distance ("Ah Fear! Ah frantic Fear! I see, I see thee near!"). As these verses by William Collins suggest, epiphanic structure proceeds by dramatic turns of mood and its language is ejaculative (Lo, Behold, O come, O see). Keats's "Hesperianism" triumphs, in "To Autumn," over this archaic style with its ingrained, superstitious attitude toward power—power seen as external and epochal. The new sublimity domesticates with the heart; the poet's imagination is neither imp nor incubus. Though recognizably sublime, "To Autumn" is a poem of *our* climate.

Climate is important. It ripens wits as well as fruits, as Milton said in another context.[5] The higher temperature and higher style of the other odes are purged away: we have entered a temperate zone. What is grown here, this "produce of the air," is like its ambience: Hesperian art rather than oriental ecstasy or unnatural flight of the imagination. Autumn is clearly a mood as well as a season, and Stevens would have talked about a weather of the mind. Yet "mood" and "weather" have an aura of changeableness, even of volatility, while the Autumn ode expresses something firmer: not, as so often in Stevens or in the "Beulah" moments of other poets, a note among notes but, as in Spenser, a vast cloud-region or capability. The very shape of the poem—firm and regular without fading edges but also no overdefined contours—suggests a slowly expanding constellation that moves as a whole, if it moves at all.

Its motion is, in fact, part of the magic. Time lapses so gently here; we pass from the fullness of the maturing harvest to the stubble plains without experiencing a cutting edge. If time comes to a point in "To Autumn" it is only at the end of the poem, which verges (more poignant than pointed) on a last "gathering." The scythe of time, the sense of mortality, the cutting of life into distinct, epochal phases is not felt. We do not even stumble into revelation, however softly—there is no moment which divides before and after as in the "Ode to Psyche" with its supersoft epiphany, its Spenserian and bowery moment which makes the poet Psyche's devotee despite her "shadowy thought" nature. The Autumn ode is nevertheless a *poesis,* a shaped segment of life coterminous with that templar "region of the mind" which the other poems seek, though they may honor more insistently the dichotomy of inside and out, fane and profane. Poetry, to change "the whole habit of the mind," [6] changes also our view of the mind's habitat. To say that "To Autumn" is ideological and that its pressure of form is "English" has to do with that also.

I begin with what is directly observable, rather than with curious knowledge of archaic ode or hymn. In the odes of Keats there is a strong, clearly marked moment of disenchantment, or of illusion followed by disillusion. Fancy, that "Queen of shadows" (Charlotte Smith), becomes a "deceiving elf"—and although the deception remains stylized, and its shock releases pathos rather than starker sentiments, it is as pointed as the traditional turn of the Great Ode. (Cf. the turn, for example, from one mode of music to another in Dryden's *Alexander's Feast* or the anastrophe "He is not dead, he lives" in pastoral elegy.) The transition leading from stanzas 7 to 8 in the Nightingale ode is such a turn, which results in calling imagination a "deceiving elf." An imaginative fancy that has sustained itself despite colder thoughts is farewelled.

There is, exceptionally, no such turn in "To Autumn." The poem starts on enchanted ground and never leaves it. This special quality becomes even clearer when we recall that "La Belle Dame sans Merci," with its harvest background and soft ritual progression, ends in desolation of spirit on the cold hillside. But because the final turn of the Nightingale ode, though clear as a bell, is not gross in its effect, not productive of coital sadness, a comparison with Autumn's finale is still possible. In "To Autumn" birds are preparing to fly to a warmer clime, a "visionary south," though we do not see them leave or the cold interrupt. In "To a Nightingale" the poet is allowed a call—adieu, adieu—which is birdlike still and colors the darker "forlorn," while his complete awakening is delayed ("Do I wake or sleep?") and verbal prolongations are felt. There is no complete disenchantment even here.

"To Autumn," moreover, can be said to have something approaching a strophic turn as we enter the last stanza. With "Where are the songs of Spring? Aye, where are they?" a plaintive anthem sounds. It is a case, nevertheless, where a premise is anticipated and absorbed.[7] The premise is that of transience, or the feel of winter, and the rest of the stanza approaches that cold threshold. The premise is absorbed because its reference is back to Spring instead of forward to Winter; by shifting from eye to ear, to the music-theme, Keats enriches Autumn with Spring. We remain within a magical circle where things repeat each other in a finer tone, as Autumn turns into a second Spring: "While barred clouds *bloom* the soft-dying day." [8] The music now heard is no dirge of the year but a mingling of lullaby and aubade. For the swallows a second summer is at hand (aubade). For us—if we cannot follow them any more than the elusive nightingale—what comes next is not winter but night (lullaby). We go gently off, in either case, on extended wings.

Thus "To Autumn," like Stevens's "Sunday Morning," becomes oddly an Ode to Evening. The full meaning of this will appear. But in terms of formal analysis we can say that the poem has no epiphany or decisive turn or any absence / presence dialectic. It has, instead, a *westerly drift* like the sun. Each stanza, at the same time, is so equal in its poetical weight, so loaded with its own harvest, that westering is less a natural than a poetic state—it is a mood matured by the poem itself. "To Autumn," in fact, does not explicitly evolve from sunrise to sunset but rather from a rich to a clarified dark. Closely read it starts and ends in twilight. "Season of mists and mellow fruitfulness"—though the mists are of the morning, the line links fertility and semidarkness in a way that might be a syntactical accident were it not for the more highly developed instance of "I cannot see what flowers are at my feet . . . ," that famous stanza from the Nightingale ode where darkened senses also produce a surmise of fruitfulness. The Autumn ode's twilight is something inherent, a condition not simply of growth but of imaginative growth. Westering here is a spiritual movement, one that tempers visionariness into surmise and the lust for epiphany into finer-toned repetitions. We do not find ourselves in a temple but rather in Tempe "twixt sleepe and wake." [9] We can observe the ode unfolding as a self-renewing surmise of fruitfulness: as waking dream or "widening speculation" rather than nature-poem and secularized hymn.

Concerning *surmise:* I have suggested elsewhere its importance
for Romantic poetry, how it hovers between factual and fantastic.[10] Its presence is often marked by a "magic casement"
effect: as in Wordsworth's "Solitary Reaper," a window opens
unexpectedly on a secret or faraway scene:

> No nightingale did ever chaunt
> More welcome notes to weary bands
> Of travellers in some shady haunt,
> Among Arabian sands:

Keats has the interesting habit of interpreting pictures (usually
imaginary) as scenes beheld from a magic window of this kind.
Yet since the frame of the window is also the frame of the picture,
he finds himself on an ambiguous threshold, intimately near yet
infinitely removed from the desired place. Most of the odes are a
feverish quest to enter the life of a pictured scene, to be totally
where the imagination is. In the Autumn ode, however, there is no
effort to cross a magic threshold: though its three stanzas are
like a composite picture from some Book of Hours, we are placed
so exactly at the bourn of the invisible picture window that the
frame is not felt, nor the desperate haunting of imagination to
get in. There is no precipitous "Already with thee" and no stylized
dejection.

Something, perhaps, is lost by this: the sense of dangerous
transition, of consciousness opening up, of a frozen power un-
sealing. But the ode remains resolutely meditative. When important images of transition occur they are fully *composed* and no
more vibrant than metrical enjambments: "And sometimes like a
gleaner thou dost keep / Steady thy laden head." Or, "Sometimes
whoever seeks may find / Thee sitting careless." Strictly construed
the "sometimes" goes here both with the seeking and with the
finding: it is factored out and made prepositional. This is a
framing device which further augments the feeling of surmise,
of lighthearted questing. What reverberates throughout, and
especially in this image of the gleaner, the most pictorial of the
poem, is a light but steady pondering. It is not a pondering, of

course, devoid of all tension: "keep / Steady," understood as a performative or "cozening imperative," [11] suggests that the poet is not so much describing as urging the image on, in-feeling it. Let us follow this picture-pondering from verse to verse.

The opening stanza is so strongly descriptive, so loaded with told riches, that there seems to be no space for surmise. A desire to fill every rift with Autumn's gold produces as rich a banquet as Porphyro's heap of delicates in "The Eve of St. Agnes." Thesaurus stanzas of this kind are self-delighting in Keats; but they also have a deeper reason. Porphyro knows that Madeline will find reality poorer than her dream and enhances his value by serving himself up this way. The sumptuous ploy is to help him melt into his lady's waking thought. So Autumn's banquet, perhaps, intends to hold the awakening consciousness and allow the dream to linger. Not only the bees are deceived; the dream "Warm days will never cease" is not in them alone; it is already in Autumn, in her "conspiring." On this phrase all the rich, descriptive details depend; they are infinitives not indicatives, so that we remain in the field of mind. "Conspiring how to load and bless . . . To bend with apples . . . fill all fruit . . . To swell the gourd." As we move through Autumn's thought to the ripening of that thought, we cease to feel her as an external agent.

Thus, the descriptive fullness of the first stanza turns out to be thought-full as well: its pastoral furniture is a golden surmise, imagination in her most deliberate mood. By moving the point of view inward, Keats makes these riches mental riches, imaginative projects. He does not, at the same time, push the mental horizon to infinity: the mood remains infinitive, looking onto "something evermore about to be."

Once we see that what is being satisfied is empathy or in-feeling,[12] and that to satisfy it Keats (like Autumn) fills outsides with more and more inside, the structure of the poem as a progressive surmise becomes clear. In-feeling, in Keats, is always on the point of overidentifying; and even here it demands more than the first stanza's dream of truth. However glowing a prospect Autumn paints, it must still, as it were, come alive. This happens in the second stanza where the drowsy ponderer meets us in person. Now we are in the landscape itself; the harvest is now. The figure of Autumn amid her store is a moving picture, or the dream personified. Yet the two stanzas are perfectly continuous; in-feeling is still being expressed as the filling-up of a space—a figure like Autumn's was needed to plump the poem. Though we approach epiphanic personification in the figure of Autumn, the casualness of "sometimes" "sometimes," together with the easy mood of the opening question, gives us a sense of "widening speculation" and prevents a more than cornucopial view of the goddess.

But the dream is almost shattered at the end of the stanza. The word "oozings" extends itself phonically into "hours by hours," a chime that leads to the idea of transience in "Where are the songs of Spring?" Though immediately reabsorbed, this muted ubi sunt introduces the theme of mutability. Oozings—hours—ubi sunt . . . A single word, or its echoes, might have disenchanted Keats like the turn on "forlorn" in the Nightingale ode. Disenchantment, however, does not occur: there is no reverse epiphany as in "La Belle Dame sans Merci," no waking into emptiness.

We have reached, nevertheless, the airiest of the stanzas. Does a chill wind not brush us, an airiness close to emptiness? Do we not anticipate the "cold hill's side"? Even if the mood of surmise is sustained, it might well be a surmise of death rather than fruitfulness.

Here, at the consummate point of Keats's art, in-feeling achieves its subtlest act. Keats conspires with autumn to fill even the air. Air becomes a granary of sounds, a continuation of the harvest, or *spätlese*. In this last and softest stanza, the ear of the ear is ripened.

More than a tour de force or finely sustained idea is involved. For at the end of other odes we find an explicit *cry*, which is part of their elegiac envoi. Here that cry is uttered, as it were, by the air itself, and can only be heard by an ear that knows how to glean such sounds. What is heard, to quote the modern poet closest to Keats,

> is not a cry of divine attention,
> Nor the smoke-drift of puffed-out heroes, nor human cry.
> It is the cry of leaves that do not transcend themselves.[13]

In lyric poetry the cry is a sign of subjective feelings breaking through and in the cult-hymn of being possessed by divine power. It signifies in both a transcendence absent from this "final finding of the air." Lyricism, in "To Autumn," frees itself for once of elegy and ecstasy: it is neither a frozen moment of passion nor the inscription that prolongs it.

The Grecian urn's "Beauty is Truth, Truth Beauty" remains an extroverted, lapidary cry. However appropriate its philosophy, its form is barely snatched from a defeat of the imagination. "To Autumn" has no defeat in it. It is the most negative capable of all of Keats's great poems. Even its so-called death-stanza [14] expresses no rush toward death, no clasping of darkness as a bride, or quasi-oriental ecstasy. Its word-consciousness, its mind's weather —all remains Hesperian. As its verses move toward an image of southerly flight (the poem's nearest analogue to transcendence), patterns emerge that delay the poet's "transport to summer." Perception dwells on the border and refuses to overdefine. So "full-grown lambs" rather than "sheep." Add such verbal ponderings or reversing repetitions as "borne aloft . . . hilly bourn," a casual chiastic construction, playing on a mix of semantic and phonetic properties. Or the noun-adjective phrase "treble soft" which becomes an adjective-noun phrase when "treble" is resolved into the northern "triple." And consider the northernisms. The proportion of northern words increases perceptibly as if to pull the poem back from its southerly orientation. There is hardly a romance language phrase: sound-shapes like sallows, swallows, borne, bourn, crickets, croft, predominate.[15] And, finally, the poise of the stanza's ending, on the verge of flight like joy always bidding adieu. How easily, in comparison, Hölderlin turns eastward, and converts wish into visionary transport on the wings of an older rhetoric:

> These my words, when, rapt
> faster than I could have known,

and far, to where I never
thought to come, a Genius
took me from my own house. They glimmered
in the twilight, as I went,
the shadowy wood
and the yearning brooks
of my country; I knew the fields no more;
Yet soon, brighter and fresher,
mysterious
under the golden smoke
flowering, rising fast before me
in the sun's steps
with a thousand fragrant hills
Asia dawned

["Patmos"]

Less magnificent, equally magnanimous, "To Autumn" remains a poem "in the northwind sung." Its progress is merely that of repetitions "in a finer tone," of "widening speculation," of "treble soft" surmise. Yet in its Hesperian reach it does not give up but joins a south to itself.

Keats's respect for the sublime poem does not have to be argued. There is his irritation with the "egotistical sublime" of Wordsworth, his admiration for Milton who broke through "the clouds which envelope so deliciously the Elysian field of verse, and committed himself to the Extreme," his anguished attempt to write the *Hyperion,* and the testimony of lesser but affecting verses like those to the "God of the Meridian" in which he foresees madness:

                    when the soul is fled
            To high above our head,
            Afrighted do we gaze
            After its airy maze,
            As doth a mother wild,
            When her young infant child
            Is in an eagle's claws—
            And is not this the cause
            Of madness?—God of Song,

> Thou bearest me along
> Through sights I scarce can bear

The "bear . . . bear" pun shows well enough the tension of epic flight. I must now make clear what kind of problem, formal and spiritual, the sublime poem was.

A first difficulty centers on the relation of romance to sublime or epic. The romance mode, for Keats, is now presublime (and so to be "broken through") and now postsublime. Where, as in the first *Hyperion,* Keats wishes to sublimate the sublime he turns with relief to the "golden theme" of Apollo after the Saturnine theme of the first two books. In the *Fall of Hyperion,* however, romance is an Elysium or Pleasure-garden to be transcended. While in "La Belle Dame sans Merci" romance becomes sheer oxymoron, a "golden tongued" nightmare.

It is best to find a view beyond this special dialectic of romance and epic in Keats, all the more so as that is complicated by the dream-truth, or vision-reality split. No formal analysis will disentangle these rich contraries. It can only reduce them to the difference suggested in the *Fall of Hyperion* between "an immortal's sphered words" and the mother-tongue. This is the dichotomy on which Keats's epic voyage foundered: the opposition between Miltonic art-diction and the vernacular. "Life to him [Milton] would be death to me." "English must be kept up." Yet such a distinction is no more satisfying than one in terms of genre. Vernacular romance is perhaps more feasible than vernacular epic —but we get as mixed up as Keats himself when we define each genre in family terms and put romance under mother, epic under father. In the *Fall of Hyperion* Moneta is as patriarchal as she is womanly.

A solution is to consider both romance and epic—or the high-visionary style in general—as belonging to an older, "epiphanic" structuring of consciousness. Against it can be put a nonepiphanic structuring; and if the older type is primarily associated with the East, the modern would be with the West or, at its broadest, Hesperia.[16] It is possible to treat this distinction formally as one between two types of structuring rather than two types of consciousness. Eventually, however, Keats's charge of superstition or obsolescence against the earlier mode will move us into ideology and beyond formalism. A man who says, like Keats, that life to Milton is death to him is concerned with more than formal options.

Epiphanic structure implies, first of all, the possibility of categorical shifts: of crossing into *allo genere,* and even, I suppose, out of ordinary human consciousness into something else. Apotheosis (as at the end of *Hyperion*), metamorphosis, and transformation scenes are type instances of such a crossing. It is accompanied by a doctrine of states, a philosophy of transcendence, and a formulary for the "translation" of states. Epiphanic structure can bear as much sophistication as an author is capable of. Take the sequence, based on *Paradise Lost,* Book VIII, which haunted Keats: "The Imagination may be compared to Adam's Dream: He awoke and found it truth." [17] This refers chiefly to Adam seeing Eve first in dream and, upon waking, in the flesh. Keats will often use it ironically rather than not use it at all. So in the "Eve of St. Agnes" Madeline wakes into Imagination's truth and finds it—how pale, how diminished! She melts the reality— Porphyro—back into her dream in a moment of, presumably, sexual union.

A more complex instance is the dark epiphany in "La Belle Dame sans Merci" where the enchanted knight wakes, as it were, into the arms of the wrong dream and cannot find his way back to the right one. Whereas, in Milton, one cunning enjambment expresses the intensity of the quest springing from imaginative loss,

> She [Eve] disappear'd, and left me dark, I wak'd
> To find her

a moment Keats repeats faintly in the Autumn ode,

> Sometimes whoever seeks abroad may find
> Thee

in "La Belle Dame" there is nothing—no natural food—can satisfy the knight. He starves for his drug, like Keats so often for the heightened consciousness of epiphanic style.

In *Paradise Lost,* Adam's dream prepares him for the truth he is to meet. Truth is conceived of as a fuller, perhaps more difficult, dream; and God seeks to strengthen Adam's visionary powers by engaging him in these dream-corridors. Instead of a single dramatic or traumatic change there is to be a gradual tempering of the mind. This modification of epiphanic structure may have inspired a favorite speculation of Keats, that happiness on earth would be enjoyed hereafter "repeated in a finer tone and so repeated." Miltonic tenderness, by allowing Adam's consciousness to develop, by giving it time for growth, lightens the all-or-nothing (sometimes, all-and-nothing) character of epiphanic vision.[18] Though the end remains transport and deification, the means are based, at least in part, on a respect for natural process.

The naturalization of epiphanic form is less effective in "La Belle Dame" than in this prototypal sequence from Milton. The reason lies perhaps in the genre as much as in Keats himself. Quest-romance is a particularly resistant example of epiphanic form. Though Spenser helps to detumesce it he also throws its archaic lineaments into relief: his faërie remains a montage, a learned if light superposition. The dominant feature of quest-romance (as of fairy-tale) is the ever-present danger of trespass: of stepping all at once or unconsciously into a daemonic field of force. Often the quest is motivated by redeeming such a prior trespass; but even when it starts unburdened it cannot gain its diviner end without the danger of *allo genere* crossings. Keats's knight steps ritually, if unknowingly, into demonry. So also Coleridge's mariner, whose act of trespass is clear but who before it and after crosses also invisible demarcations. From this perspective the exile of Adam and Eve and the wanderings of Odysseus are both the result of a trespass against the divine, or of stepping willy-nilly into a daemonic sphere.[19]

This is not the place to work out the formal variations of quest-romance. But when a poet does succeed in subduing the form, the result is both remarkable and mistakable. In "Strange Fits of Passion" Wordsworth's rider is a becalmed knight from Romance whose rhythm parodies the chivalric gallop and who is always approaching yet never crossing a fatal border. The moon that drops and deflates the dreaming into a mortal thought is a pale metonymy of itself when considered against the backdrop of epiphanic romance. It alone belongs to the sphere of "strange fits"; and while it still divides before and after and even suggests that an imaginative or unconscious trespass has occurred, it cannot be drawn fully into the lunatic symbolism of romance. Keats, I think, did not manage to humanize this form: he feared too much that leaving Romance behind meant being exiled from great poetry. He was unable to "translate" the inherited code either into the Miltonic Extreme or into Wordsworth's fulfillment of Miltonic tenderness.

And yet: did he not humanize epiphanic form in the special case of the ode? Recent scholarship by Kurt Schlüter and others has established the basic form of the ancient cult-hymn as it impinged on European poetry.[20] The easiest division of the form is, as you might expect, into three: invocation, narrative or mythic portion, and renewed invocation. Sappho's "Ode to Aphrodite" is a clear example, so is Shelley's "Ode to the West Wind." Basically, however, the structure consists simply of a series of apostrophes or turns petitioning an absent god or attesting his presence. To the modern reader it may all seem somewhat hysterical: a succession of cries modulated by narrative or reflective interludes.

The sublime or greater or Pindaric ode flourished in the eighteenth century like a turgid weed, all pseudo-epiphany and point, bloat and prickles, feeding off an obsolescent style. Dr. Johnson vilified Gray's Pindaric experiments as "cucumbers." The best that can be said for the genre is that like contemporary opera it became a refuge for visionary themes: an exotic and irrational entertainment which reminded the indulgent consumer of the polite good sense of his society, and sent him back, all afflatus spent, to trifle with the lesser ode. It is not till Collins that a dialogue begins within the genre between its sublime origins and the English ground to which it is transplanted.

A brief notice of this dialogue in Collins's "Ode to Evening" prepares us for Keats. Collins uses all the features characterizing the sublime ode except one. His extended apostrophe suggests the hieratic distance between votary and the invoked power, anticipates at the same time its presence, and leads into a narrative second half describing in greater detail the coming of the divinity and its effect on the poet. This is followed by a renewed invocation which acts as the poem's coda. The one feature conspicuously absent is the epiphany proper. The invoked personification, evening, is a transitional state, a season of the day, whose advent is its presence. By addressing in epiphanic terms a subject intrinsically nonepiphanic, and adjusting his style subtly to it, Collins opens the way to a new, if still uneasy, nature-poetry.

What adjustments of style are there? The movement of the ode is highly mimetic, as Collins, suiting his numbers to the nature of evening, slows and draws out his musings.

> If aught of oaten stop, or pastoral song,
> May hope, chaste Eve, to soothe thy modest ear,
> Like thy own solemn springs
> Thy springs and dying gales
> O nymph reserved, while now . . .

Instead of hastening some eclipsing power, or leaping into a fuller present, his verse becomes a programmatic accompaniment to the gradual fall of night. The form, in other words, is self-fulfilling: as the processional verse blends with processual nature, and an expanding shadow (a "gradual, dusky veil") is all of relevation there is, the poet's prayer results in what it asks for: "Now teach me, *Maid* compos'd / To breathe some soften'd Strain." This "now" is only in echo that of an ecstatic, annihilative present: it refers to an actual time of day, and perhaps to a belated cultural moment. With this drawn-out "now" nature-poetry is born:

> and now with treble soft
> The red-breast whistles from the garden-croft;
> And gathering swallows twitter in the skies.

Collins's "soften'd strain," his conversion of epiphanic style, will find its culminating instance in Keats's poetry of process.

That Collins represents Evening as a god is more than a naturalized archaism. Evening, invoked as the source of a new music, stands for Hesperia, the evening-star land; and what the poet asks for, in these prelusive strains, is a genuinely western verse, an *Abendlandpoesie*. Like Keats's Psyche, Evening is a new goddess:

the poetic pantheon of the East contained only Sun and Night, but Evening is peculiar to the Western hemisphere. In the courts of the East, as Coleridge noted in his *Ancient Mariner,* "At one stride comes the dark." The East, in its sudden dawn and sudden darkness, is epiphanic country. But the English climate, in weather or weather of the mind, has a more temperate, even, evening effect. Collins embraces the idea that his native country, or the cultural region to which it belonged, has a style and vision of its own.[21] He shows spirit of place as a felt influence, and gothic eeriness as eariness. That is, he uncovers a new sense for nature by uncovering a new sense: the natural ear. What the sublime ode had attempted by overwhelming the eye—or the "descriptive and allegoric style" which dominates the age—Collins achieves through this finer sense. The eye, as in Wordsworth's "Tintern Abbey," and in the last stanza of "To Autumn," is made quiet by "the power of harmony."

In the "Ode to Evening" the concept of a Hesperian poetry conditions even sensory mimesis or impels it into a new region. It is no accident that the last stanza of "To Autumn" contains an evening ode in small. That "Evening Ear," which Collins else-where attributes to Milton, is, to use a rare Wordsworthian pun, an *organ of vision:* responsive to a particular climate or "spiritual air" (*Endymion,* IV) in which poets feel themselves part of a belated and burdened culture yet find their own relation to the life of things. As the landscape darkens gently, the blind and distant ear notices tones—finer tones—that had escaped a domi-nant and picture-ridden eye: a weak-eyed bat flits by, curious em-blem, and the beetle emerges winding its horn, as if even pastoral had its epic notes. There is still, in Collins, this airy faërie which has often dissolved in Keats—who, however, is never very far from it. What matters is that creatures jargon, like "To Au-tumn"'s parliament of birds; that the sounds are real sounds, a produce of the air; that the heard is not exclusively divine or human; and that within the sheltering dark of the ear other senses emerge: "I cannot see what flowers are at my feet, / Nor what soft incense hangs upon the boughs, / But in embalmed darkness guess each sweet." Here absence is presence, though not by way of mystical or epiphanic reversal. In every temperate zone the air is full of noises.

This sensory ideology, if I may call it such,[22] must have affected Keats one early autumn day looking at stubble fields:

How beautiful the season is now—How fine the air. A temperate sharpness about it. Really, without joking, chaste weather—Dian skies—I never lik'd stubble fields so much as now—Aye better than the chilly green of the spring. Somehow a stubble plain looks warm— in the same way that some pictures look warm—this struck me so much in my sunday's walk that I composed upon it.

That ideology is in the air is proven by what follows:

I always somehow associate Chatterton with Autumn. He is the purest writer in the English language. [Chatterton's language is entirely northern.] He has no French idiom, or particles like Chaucer—'tis genuine English idiom in English words. I have given up Hyperion. . . . English ought to be kept up.[23]

We have already commented on the northernisms in "To Autumn" 's last stanza: even romance language (let alone romance) is gently shunned. Nothing but "home-bred glory."

Can we see the gods die in "To Autumn," the epiphanic forms dissolve, as it were, before our eyes? Autumn is, by tradition, the right season for this dissolution, or dis-illusion.

> Let Phoebus lie in umber harvest

Stevens writes in "Notes toward a Supreme Fiction,"

> Let Phoebus slumber and die in autumn umber
> Phoebus is dead, ephebe.

But, in tradition also, a new god treads on the heels of the old, and loss figures forth a stronger presence. In Hesperian poetry, from Collins to Keats to Stevens, this entire absence/presence vacillation does no more than manure the ground of the poem, its "sensible ecstasy."

Consider the invocation "Season of mists and mellow fruitfulness." The odic O is hardly felt though the verses immediately fill one's mouth with rich labials extended in a kind of chiastic middle between "Season" and "sun." Nothing remains of the cultic distance between votary and personified power: we have instead two such powers, autumn and sun, whose closeness is emphasized, while the moment of hailing or petitioning is replaced by a presumptive question ("Who hath not seen thee") suggesting availability rather than remoteness. The most interesting dissolve, however, comes with the grammatical shift, in the opening line, from mythic-genealogical to descriptive-partitive "of," which effectively diffuses autumn into its attributes. Compare "Season of mists and mellow fruitfulness" with the following apostrophes:

> Thou foster-child of silence and slow time.

Here the poet uses clearly and finely a formula which alludes to the high descent of the apostrophized object. In our next example

> Nymph of the downward smile, and side-long glance

the grammatical form is analogous but the "of" has moved from genealogical toward partitive. The nymph is eminently characterized by these two attributes: they *are* her in this statuesque moment. The opening of "To the Nile":

> Son of the old moon-mountains African
> Stream of the pyramid and crocodile

actually brings mythic-genealogical and partitive-descriptive together. Against this background we see how beautifully dissolved into the ground of description is the mythical formula of "To Autumn" 's first line.

We do, of course, by what appears to be a regressive technique, meet Autumn personified in the second stanza. If the poem approaches a noon-point of stasis—of arrest or centered revelation—it is here. The emergence of myth serves, however, to ripen the pictorial quality of the poem rather than to evoke astonishment. The emphasis is on self-forgetful relaxation (at most on "forget thyself to marble") not on saturnine fixation. No more than in "To Evening" is nature epiphanic: Keats's autumn is not a specter but a spirit, one who steals over the landscape, or "amid her store" swellingly imbues it.[24] The poet's mind is not rapt or astonished and so forced back on itself by a sublime apparition.

It is essential, in fact, to note what happens to mind. In the cult hymn the invocation merges with, or is followed by, the god's *comos:* an enumeration of his acts and attributes.[25] But Keats's first stanza becomes simply the filling up of a form, a golden chain of infinitives hovering between prospect and fulfillment, until every syntactical space is loaded and the poet's mind, like the bees', loses itself in the richness. The stanza, in fact, though full, and with its eleven lines, more than full, is not a grammatical whole but a drunk sentence. The poet's mind, one is tempted to say, has entered the imagined picture so thoroughly that when the apostrophe proper is sprung at the opening of stanza 2, and the grammatical looseness corrected, it simultaneously opens a new speculative movement. And when the generative figure of Autumn appears in the second stanza, it is self-harvesting like the poet's own thoughts. The last stanza, then, leaves us in a "luxury of twilight" rather than dropping us into a void where "no birds sing."

The demise of epiphanic forms in "To Autumn" raises a last question: is not the sequential movement of the whole poem inspired by a progressive idea with Enlightenment roots? There seems to be, on the level of sensation, something that parallels the first *Hyperion*'s progress from heavier to lighter, from Hyperion to Apollo, and from fixed burdens to a softer oppression. Several key phrases in Keats's letters suggest an "enlightenment" of this kind. The poet talks of "widening speculation," of "the regular stepping of Imagination toward a Truth," and of easing the "Burden of the Mystery." Magical moments like the fourth stanza of "Ode on a Grecian Urn"

> Who are these coming to the sacrifice?
> To what green altar, O mysterious priest

are surely related to this lightening. Mystery survives, but in a purged, airy, speculative form. The "overwrought" questions of the ode's beginning, which sought to penetrate or fix a symbol-esssence, are purified into surmise and evoke a scene of "wide quietness" rather than bacchic enthusiasm.

There is a progress then; but is it toward a truth? We know what the conclusion to the Grecian Urn ode suggests. "Beauty is Truth, Truth Beauty" is a chiastic phrase, as self-rounding as the urn. No ultimate turn or final step toward a truth occurs. Though there are turns in the poem, they are more musical than epiphanic, and the very notion of "the turn" merges with that of the art-object: Keats turns the urn in his imagination until the urn is its turnings. The poet's speculation is circular.

Keats's rondure, his counterprogression, subverts without rejecting the received idea of "enlightenment." Poetry clearly has its own progress, its own lights. Formalistic or art-centered terms have, therefore, a certain propriety. But they cannot suffice for Keats any more than for Wordsworth, who also seeks to ease the "burthen of the mystery" ("Tintern Abbey," line 39). Consider the profound difference between these poets, who both believe in a dispersion of older—poetical or religious—superstitions. Such qualities as decorum, impersonality, symbolic adequacy are a function mainly of the concenteredness of "To Autumn": the poem turns around one image like a "leaf-fring'd legend." Though Wordsworth's poems may also have a center of this kind (Lucy's death, a peculiar landscape, a remembered scene), it rarely appears as picturesque symbol or image. Wordsworth's kernels are mysteries: charged spiritual places which confront and confuse a mental traveler who circles their enchanted ground—or who, like a policeman, tries to cordon off the disturbance. This too is an important "enlightenment" form, delimiting a romance apparition or sublime feelings—yet how different from Keats! In Wordsworth the spirit must find its own containment, and never quite finds it; those "spots of time" erupt from their hiding-places like the Hebraic God; the structure of his poems expresses various attempts at containment which accrete with difficulty into a personal history ("Tintern Abbey") or an eschatological and cultural one ("Hart-Leap Well"). But

Keats's experience is limited from the outset by Greek or picturesque example. What perplexes his imagination is a mysterious picture rather than a mystery.

Keats's formal a priori takes us back to Greece and where, according to Hegel, modern consciousness began. Formal beauty mediates "between the loss of individuality . . . as in Asia, where spiritual and divine are totally subsumed under a natural form, and infinite subjectivity." Greek character is "individuality conditioned by beauty" and in its respect for divine images modern and free, rather than Asiatic and superstitious. "He [the human being] is the womb that conceived them, he the breast that suckled them, he the spiritual to which their grandeur and purity is owing. Thus he feels himself calm in contemplating them, and not only free in himself, but possessing the consciousness of his freedom." [26]

That Hegel's description can fit Keats makes one cautious about the whole enterprise of dividing consciousness into historically localized phases. All the more so as Hölderlin has his own myth of the Hesperian character, which is said to begin when Homer moderates oriental pathos or "fire from heaven." [27] I make no claim for the historical exactness of either Hegel or Hölderlin. Historical speculation and criticism stand, as Professor Wimsatt has observed, in a highly problematic relationship.[28]

Yet there is something like "Hesperian" freedom in "To Autumn," a poem which becomes—in Hegel's words—the womb for the rebirth of an astral or divine image. Such a divine image is certainly there; we should not exaggerate the absence of poetical superstition in Keats. Though his central figure is picturesque its star quality glimmers through.

Much has been written on Autumn's affinities to Demeter or other harvest deities.[29] The divinity, however, that haunts Keats early and late is Apollo: sun-god, god of song, and "fore-seeing god." [30] The difference between Hyperion and Apollo is, in good part, that the former is now doomed to live under "the burden of the mystery." Hyperion cannot dawn any more; he remains darkling. But Apollo in *Hyperion,* even though that poem breaks off and leaves the young god's metamorphosis incomplete—even though he too must shoulder the mystery—should break forth like the sun to "shape his actions" like "a fore-seeing god." [31] In the Autumn ode the major theme of clairvoyance—at once fore-seeing and deep-seeing (deep into the heart or maw of life)—is tempered.[32] Yet it is far from absent.

For Autumn's "conspiring" function is comparable to that of the guardian genius, the *natale comes qui temperat astrum*.[33] An idea of poetic or personal destiny enters, in however veiled a form. The poet who writes this ode stands under the pressure of an omen. As summer passes into autumn (season of the year or human season), his dreaming deepens into foresight:

> When I have fears that I may cease to be
> Before my pen has glean'd my teeming brain,
> Before high-piled books, in charact'ry,
> Hold like rich garners the full-ripen'd grain . . .

Herr es ist Zeit. Der Sommer war sehr gross [34]

In fear of early death, and sensing riches his pen might never glean, Keats evokes a figure of genial harvests. Three times he renews his surmise of fruitfulness, three times he grasps the shadow without self-defeating empathy. Even fruitfulness is not a burden in "To Autumn." This, at last, is true impersonality.

NOTES

1. Jonathan Wordsworth, *Cornell Library Journal,* 11 (1970), 22. Cf. Allen Tate, *Collected Essays* (Denver, 1959), p. 168: "'Ode to Autumn' is a very nearly perfect piece of style but it has little to say."

2. *John Keats* (Cambridge, Mass., 1963), pp. 581 ff.

3. Theodor Adorno, "Rede über Lyrik und Gesellschaft," *Noten zur Literatur I* (Frankfort, 1958). The debate that took place in the thirties and forties, under the influence of T. S. Eliot, concerned literature and belief—where "belief" referred primarily to religious dogma, or political and moral positions inspired by it.

4. See Kurt Schlüter, *Die Englische Ode* (Bonn, 1964), chap. 2.

5. On "climate" theory in Milton, cf. Zera Fink, *The Classical Republicans,* 2d ed. (Evanston, 1962), pp. 91–94.

6. Wallace Stevens, "The Westwardness of Everything."

7. W. J. Bate, *John Keats,* pp. 581 ff.

8. My italics. "Dying" is qualified by "soft" but also perhaps by the pictorial sense of the word continued in "rosy hue."

9. On *templum* and its suggestive context in Renaissance poetry, cf. Angus Fletcher, *The Prophetic Moment* (Chicago, 1971), pp. 14 ff. Cf. also Northrop Frye on *tenemos* in Keats, *A Study of English Romanticism* (New York, 1969).

10. *Wordsworth's Poetry* (New Haven, 1964), pp. 9–13.

11. See John Hollander, "The Metrical Emblem," *Kenyon Review,* 21 (1959), 290.

12. "Always the goal is his mastery of infelt space." John Jones, *Keats's Dream of Truth* (London, 1969), p. 11 and passim.

13. Wallace Stevens, "The Course of a Particular."

14. John Jones, *Keats's Dream of Truth,* p. 269. Jones has fine and inward remarks on the ode's "antiphonal whisper," on "gathering" as "the last of the poem's harvesting and perfecting words" and on the poem's objectivity.

15. The presence of nonmigrating robins as well as migrating swallows increases the tension between staying and departure. Some have felt that the swallows are not gathering, at this point, for longer flight; but if the impression is, as I think, that night comes before winter, the precise nature of the gathering is not that important. The word "bourn" (1.30) is from the French only if it means "boundary"; if "stream" it comes from an Anglo-Saxon root.

16. Hesperia belongs to what Vico calls "poetical geography" (*Scienza Nuova,* bk. 2, sec. 11, chap. 1). It referred originally to the western part of Greece, and extended into Italy (Hesperia magna) and Spain (Hesperia ultima). England seems excluded except from a visionary point of view. And although the extension is partly of my own making (a visionary concept of this kind being needed to clarify the geospiritual sense of writers like Milton and Collins), the Tudor myth encouraged it by its linking of James and Elizabeth to the Hesperus-Hesperides-Atlas complex. See, e.g., Ben Jonson, *Pleasure Reconciled to Virtue* (1619). Hesperia, as Lemprière also defines it, is basically the region of the setting sun.

17. Letter to Benjamin Bailey, 22 Nov. 1817.

18. Wordsworth was highly impressed by Milton's "Union of Tenderness and Imagination." Cf. *Wordsworth's Poetry,* p. 266, and pp. 51–53 (on *Paradise Lost* VIII).

19. See Charles I. Patterson, Jr., *The Daemonic in the Poetry of John Keats* (Chicago, 1970), for an interesting but very different approach. His chap. 7 on "The Triumph of the Anti-Daemonic" emphasizes the distinctiveness of the Autumn ode in Keats's work, and anticipates the tenor of the interpretation given here.

20. *Die Englische Ode,* chap. 2.

21. On the development of "Hesperianism," see "Romantic Poetry and the Genius Loci" in *Beyond Formalism* (New Haven, 1970). See also pp. 287–89, for

remarks on the ideology of temperateness. There is no study of the relation between poetics and politics (or national ethos) centering on the "frame of Temperance," but important indications can be found passim in Angus Fletcher's book on Spenser, *The Prophetic Moment* (Chicago, 1971). Fletcher's interest in the encyclopedic (and cyropedic) qualities of *The Faerie Queene* lead him to weigh the interactions of law, culture, national ideals, and poetry. Leo Spitzer's study, *Classical and Christian Ideas of World Harmony* (Baltimore, 1963), contains information and speculation galore on the semantic field of *temperare*.

22. Marx and Engels would doubtless interpret Hesperianism, as I have described it, as the penetration of a mystifying ideology into the poetical domain. "We do not set out from what men say, imagine, conceive, nor from men as narrated, thought of, imagined, conceived, in order to arrive at men in the flesh. We set out from real, active men, and on the basis of their real life-process we demonstrate the development of the ideological reflexes and echoes of this life-process. The phantoms formed in the human brain are also, necessarily, sublimates of their material life-process, which is empirically verifiable and bound to material premises. . . . Life is not determined by consciousness, but consciousness by life" (*The German Ideology*, trans. by Roy Pascal [New York, 1947], pp. 14–15). It is important to acknowledge, therefore, that I do indeed set out from "what men say, imagine, conceive . . . from men as narrated"—in short, from literature. The question is whether this starting point is as inauthentic as the authors of *The German Ideology* believe. Is literature, as treated here, the *English* ideology, or is it in its own way a "material premise"?

23. Letter to J. H. Reynolds, 21 Sept. 1819. I have inserted the sentence in brackets, which comes from a journal-letter of the same date to George and Georgiana Keats, and which goes on to the famous statement that "Life to him [Milton] would be death to me."

24. Cf. what W. K. Wimsatt says about latent design in "The Structure of Romantic Nature Imagery." He refers, inter alia, to Keats's ode (*The Verbal Icon* [New York, 1958], p. 110).

25. See Schlüter, *Die Englische Ode*, chap. 2. His important, specific analysis of the Autumn ode (pp. 218–35) recognizes the muting of epiphanic structure but fails to understand its structural or ideological context.

26. *Philosophy of History*, trans. J. Sibree (New York, 1901), pp. 317–19. This book was compiled posthumously from a series of lectures given by Hegel between 1822 and 1831. Sibree's translation is not always very literal but it catches well enough the spirit of the original. "Individuality conditioned by beauty" renders a conception of the Greek aesthetic character introduced by Winckelmann but which Lessing associated specifically with Classicism's understanding of the limits of the picturesque.

27. See Peter Szondi, "Überwindung des Klassizismus. Der Brief an Böhlendorff vom 4. Dezember 1801" in *Hölderlin-Studien* (Frankfurt, 1967). It is interesting that, as Szondi points out, Hölderlin should use the word "Geschik" to suggest both "destiny" and "(poetic) skill." To be a poet, yet a national poet, is always a com-

plex fate. See also Hölderlin's remarks on Weather, Light, and the natural scenery of his native country in the second letter to Böhlendorff (2 Dec. 1802): "das Licht in seinem Wirken, nationell und als Prinzip und Schicksalsweise bildend . . . das philosophische Licht um mein Fenster."

28. "History and Criticism: A Problematic Relationship," in *The Verbal Icon* (Lexington, Ky., 1954).

29. The best treatment is in Schlüter, *Die Englische Ode,* pp. 223–35.

30. For Keats's "Imitatio Apollinis," see esp. Walter H. Evert, *Aesthetic and Myth in the Poetry of Keats* (Princeton, 1965).

31. Letter to B. J. Haydon, 23 Jan. 1818.

32. "Temper my lonely hours / And let me see thy bow'rs / More unalarm'd," Keats wrote in his poem to Apollo ("God of the Meridian") of January 1818. The poem breaks off at that point and in the letter to J. H. Reynolds which quotes it, is followed by "When I have fears that I may cease to be."

To emphasize Apollo is not to discount Demeter but to suggest a trans-mythologic merging in the poem of "conspiring" (foreseeing) and "maturing" functions. The poem to Apollo breaks off, like *Hyperion,* when "bearing" becomes "overbearing," when maturing, instead of strengthening the prophetic or fore-seeing character, leads to an overload destructive of it.

33. Horace, *Epistle* 2.2.187.

34. The first quotation comes from Keats's sonnet of late January 1818; the second is the opening line of Rilke's sonnet "Herbsttag."

James and the "Man of Imagination"

CHARLES FEIDELSON

In his preface to *The Ambassadors* James makes much of the artistic assurance with which he undertook and wrote this book, which he came to regard as "the best, 'all round,' of my productions." As on so many other occasions, a friend had told him an anecdote, here about an encounter with a certain "man of distinction" whom James identifies in his notebooks as his own friend William Dean Howells. He knew at once, he says, that he had a perfect subject—"for I think," he goes on, "that there are degrees of merit in subjects." The situation described to him could be taken over almost without modification, though with some new factors added, in the book that he proposed to write. Like the Howells of the anecdote, Lambert Strether of *The Ambassadors* would find himself in Paris, at a gathering of "persons of great interest," and "in a charming old garden attached to a house of art," and there he would make an impassioned appeal to a young acquaintance to "live" while he yet has time, even if the freedom to "live" should amount to no more than a benign illusion. Strether would feel that time has run out for him, except for the fact, as James puts it in his preface, "that he now at all events *sees*." What he sees, as the book itself makes clear, is an actual life behind him in which he has failed to "live" precisely in the degree that he has failed to "see," and a possible life of seeing before him, or at least a life in which he will see what a life of seeing consists in. That, in fact, is what he believes he is already seeing in the Paris garden of the sculptor Gloriani.

The situation was especially promising, from James's standpoint, because he thought he could detect in Howells's speech what he calls "the voice of . . . [a] false position," an expression of conflicting yet mutually relevant concepts and values, the "ironic . . . accent" of a "felt predicament." Strether's "false position," as the book develops, is constantly being defined and redefined, but the crux is always some new variation on the themes of "living" and "seeing"—or, more broadly, existence and vision—which he first attempts to formulate, appropriately enough, in a "garden attached to a house of art." The "ironic . . . accent" of his great speech reflects more than a personal embarrassment at finding himself adrift from his New England moorings. For New England itself, when one is in Paris, must be envisaged and lived out as a different combination of the two variables, living and seeing. Strether, one might say, is divided between his visionary apprehension of what he takes to be the unity of life and vision in the aesthetic life of Paris and his vital, existential commitment to the moral vision dogmatically prescribed by the life of Woollett, Massachusetts. And his position is made more complicated, not set on a firmer footing, by his increasingly sophisticated awareness of the limits of New England moral insight. What he wants from "aesthetic" Paris is nothing less than a rehabilitation of his moral being—paradoxically, he feels his long years of deprivation, in James's phrase, as an "injury done his *character*"—even while he secretly hopes that he will be somewhat liberated from his bondage to moral "character" by his visionary participation in the Parisian life of seeing.

What I intend to take up, however, is not Strether's story in itself; I have gone into it partly to recall the kind of abstract theme which is typical of James's later novels and partly because the preface to *The Ambassadors* can give us a lead to James's general cast of mind, which is what I mainly want to talk about. James's confidence in his scheme, his immunity from any "alarms as for a suspected hollow beneath one's feet," was founded, the preface implies, on the very untenability of his hero's position. In effect, his perfect subject was a situation in which his hero was vainly endeavoring to make full sense of himself in relation to the world in which he was cast—*vainly* endeavoring, always in a "false position," because the basic terms (vision and existence) in which he was obliged to define himself and the world yielded different worlds and correspondingly different selves. But James's preface also calls attention, obliquely but unmistakably, to a kind of hollow beneath his own feet, and one that he intimates in terms not very far removed from those that he applies to Strether and works out thematically in the book. One reason why he was artistically confident, he says, was that his hero would be full of "character," would be "quite naturally and handsomely possessed of it." Furthermore, Strether would have "character" in the particular sense that he "would have, and would always have felt that he had, imagination galore." But then James adds an odd proviso: Strether's gift, the "imagination" that would lend great density to his character, "yet wouldn't have wrecked him." As to what imagination *is,* or *why* it might have wrecked Strether's character, no hint is offered. Instead, James widens the issue, proceeding to talk in a very ambiguous fashion about the whole relation between "imagination" and "character" in his fiction. "It was immeasurable," he says, "the opportunity to 'do' a man of imagination." Still, Lambert Strether, "so enriched, wouldn't give me, for his type, imagination in *predominance* or as his prime faculty, nor should I, in view of other matters, have found that convenient." Without pausing to suggest how "other matters" might have been endangered by "imagination in predominance," James goes on invoking and at the same time backing away from the image of a fully "imaginative" man: "So particular a luxury—some occasion, that is, for study of the high gift in *supreme* command of a case or of a career—would doubtless come on the day I should be ready to pay for it; and till then might, as from far back, remain hung up well in view and just out of reach. The comparative case meanwhile would serve—it was only on the minor scale that I had treated myself even to comparative cases."

Strether, at any rate, was to be a "comparative case" on the major scale—perhaps the very most that one could expect to make of William Dean Howells. But we are left with an author foredoomed to "pay for" any depiction of a "supreme" case of imaginative power, just as Strether himself, as James has already informed us, might personally have had to pay too much—might have been personally "wrecked"—because he had "imagination galore." James is revealing a profoundly ambivalent attitude toward the idea of a "man of imagination," a feeling that "imagination" in a fictional character is at once an infinitely valuable quality and somehow a threat to the inner stability of his fiction. His authorial confidence, it seems, has nothing to do with an immunity from awkward questions. On the contrary, if there is no dangerous hollow beneath his feet, it is because he is conversant with questions, flourishes on "false positions," his own as well as those of his heroes.

In general, James displays, and knows that he is displaying, the sort of mind that cannot think for very long without creating an issue, which functions best and says most precisely when it is formulating issues rather than arguing theses. It is as though the question rather than the proposition is his natural medium of expression, as though the truth that he really has in view can emerge only through the interstices of his statements. This interrogative habit of mind became more pronounced instead of diminishing as he grew more certain of his artistic and intellectual distinction. He regarded his notorious "ambiguity" as his strong point. In a late collection of essays like *Notes on Novelists,* for example, the writers discussed are consistently presented as "part[ies] to the critical question"—that is, they serve to define an overriding question, not to illustrate a critical contention—and the essays are full of references to artistic "riddles," "puzzles," "enigmas," "dilemmas," "anomalies," and "prodigies," the "confounding," the "curious," the "strange," and the "monstrous." James's prefaces to his own fiction are no less pervasively problematic in conception. In the first paragraph of the preface to *Roderick Hudson,* the first of the series, we are introduced to the "admirable immensity" of an intellectual universe which "bristles with questions the very terms of which are difficult to apply and to appreciate." The artist's experience, his "whole operative consciousness," is personified as an "explorer" turning round upon an indeterminate realm which he has found and made. By formulating the constitutive questions of his art in these prefaces, seeking "to measure, for guidance, as many aspects and distances as possible," he would encounter a little more closely the ultimate question that propels him, "that veiled face of his Muse which he is condemned forever and all anxiously to study."

The veiled face of the Muse. Though James does not pursue the matter very far in the preface to *The Ambassadors,* what he says there suggests that questions surrounding the "man of imagination" were quite near to the center of his problematic artistic universe. He pictures himself as engrossed "from far back" with the figure of imaginative man, yet compelled, even at the height of his career, except in "comparative cases" like Lambert Strether, to leave this subject "hung up well in view and just out of reach." In a remarkable passage (chapter 11) of *Notes of a Son and Brother,* the second volume of his autobiography, he develops the problem in more detail and at greater length. Here, instead of putting the question in terms of the artistic costliness of any attempt to represent a "supreme" case of imaginative man, he intimates that this figure may be intrinsically unrepresentable in fiction. He does not mention the possibility of "comparative cases" at all. But the more difficult the problem is made to seem, the more momentous it becomes. "The personal history, as it were, of an imagination" had always struck him, James says, as "a task that a teller of tales might rejoice in." He had always been on the alert for an occasion to broach the subject even though no practicable "pretext" had ever been vouchsafed. In his mind's eye, "the man of imagination . . . showed, as the creature of that force or the sport of that fate or the wielder of that arm, for the hero of a hundred possible fields." He was convinced that the "imaginative passion" of the fully imaginative hero, "fed by every contact and every apprehension, and feeding in turn every motion and every act," would put the "whole scene of life" in a light that would be "as fine a thing as possible to represent." And it was nothing less than this ultimate hero whom he was forever unable to "catch," this archetypal man who remained unrepresented while he fell back on "other subjects" that he was more able to bring into focus.

Now this putative hero is, after all, quite recognizable, though it is a bit surprising to find a novelist invoking him so fervently.

He is the epic hero of the Romantic poets, from Blake's "Real Man, the Imagination," to the "major man," the "giant on the horizon," of Wallace Stevens. Most immediately, he is the Wordsworthian Poetic Everyman, whom Wordsworth undertook to "represent"—at once to depict and himself to *be*—by means of his long poetic journey into himself in *The Prelude.* In *Notes of a Son and Brother,* when James speaks of "the personal history . . . of an imagination" or describes his longing "to make trial of the recording and figuring act on behalf of some case of the imaginative faculty under cultivation," his language has a strong Wordsworthian resonance. Certainly the "imaginative passion" by which James defines his heroic man—an imagination "fed by every contact and every apprehension, and feeding in turn every motion and every act"—must be understood in the large sense that Wordsworth and the other major Romantics confer on this key term. Like them, James is conceiving of "imagination" as the total activity of the mind, not as a special psychological state, whether essentially reflective or essentially projective. For it is not even essentially *mental* in any way that would imply a basic antinomy between the imaginative faculty in general and the functions of living man or between the imaginative self and an "objective" world. "Imagination," on this view, is essentially the coming-into-being of the significant forms of consciousness and life, self and world—the ontological *image*-ination, as it were, of reality—so that "the creature of that force or the sport of that fate or the wielder of that arm" may well seem to be the potential "hero of a hundred . . . fields." The hero's imagination, in "every contact and every apprehension," does not supervene upon, but coincides with, his life in the human world; his humanity, in "every motion and every act," is identical with the exercise of his imaginative being.

What James seems to be dramatizing, both in the preface to *The Ambassadors* and in the passage from *Notes of a Son and Brother* that I have mentioned, is a problematic interplay between these Romantic premises and the premises of a "realistic" social novelist. In the end, he tells us in *Notes of a Son and Brother,* he found his long-sought hero where Wordsworth had found him—

in himself. "What was *I* thus, within and essentially, what had I ever been and could I ever be but a man of imagination at the active pitch?" But instead of rejoicing wholeheartedly at the discovery of a subjective avenue through which he might render the metaphysical reality of imaginative life, James wonders whether "objectivity, the prize to be won," won't "be frightened away by the odd terms of the affair." Instead of dwelling, like Wordsworth, on the literary autobiographer's peculiar opportunity, the chance to create an image of imaginative humanity by subjectifying the history of his objectively imposed experiences, James emphasizes precisely the opposite aspect of the autobiographical situation. His task, he says, is somehow to objectify the subjectively given "man of imagination" within him; in order to do so, he must "turn . . . [himself] inside out"; and in fact he would have much preferred to meet his hero "in the world . . . , the more convenient sphere of the objective." His discussion of the character of Lambert Strether is in a similar vein. Strether, a character drawn from the world, has "imagination galore," but both the character and James himself as author have reason to be glad that Strether is not blessed with "imagination in predominance," presumably because that would have prevented fidelity to any objective human type—would have required some sacrifice of "character" as a set of externally defined human attributes. Turning the question around, in *Notes of a Son and Brother* James implies that the reason for his inability to "catch" a predominantly imaginative man in his fiction was his insistence on looking for this paragon, as he puts it, "in the market as an exhibited or *offered* value." Having postulated a man "of *imagination*," he tried to discover him by means of "*other* signs and conditions," the characterizing marks of an objectively determined social "man."

Of course, James's fiction makes it obvious enough that he was in some respects committed to "romantic" consciousness and in other respects to socially "real" experience, both as elements of his novelistic method and as fictional themes. Perhaps I overestimate the significance of theoretical passages like those I have been citing, in which James acts out his statement of the complex problem that actuates him. Yet I think that these dramas of theory are fascinating in themselves and provide an important interpretive context for the fiction they accompany. In a kind of deliberate self-phenomenologizing, they trace the logic of the mind that made the fiction, anticipating (and partially forestalling) the phenomenological critics of the future. No writing could be more systematically self-exhibitory and self-explicatory. Thus the discussion of the "man of imagination" in *Notes of a Son and Brother* begins this way:

> I am fully aware while I go, I should mention, of all that flows from the principle governing, by my measure, these recoveries and reflections, even to the effect, hoped for at least, of stringing their apparently dispersed and disordered parts upon a fine silver thread; none other than the principle of response to a long-sought occasion, now gratefully recognized, for making trial of the recording and figuring act on behalf of some case of the imaginative faculty under cultivation.

Here, in a thoroughly Romantic fashion, the "recording and figuring act" is being exerted to record and figure itself at the present moment ("while I go"), the very latest stage of its own cultivation; but the autobiographical "principle" which James has discovered at this stage emerges out of a long quest for some objective vehicle, some externally given "occasion" for imagination to portray itself, and it culminates in the search for an objective man even in the James whose imagination has reached this dizzy height of self-awareness.

Conversely, in the fictional "case" of Lambert Strether, to return to him for a moment, as in all James's major fiction, an "objective" man is the necessary point of departure. Even when James comes closest to achieving "personal histor[ies] of . . . imagination," he is always dealing at the same time with "other subjects," relatively more "objective." But the other subjects are all, to a greater or lesser extent, translated into this one. For the central character as well as the author of such books as *The Ambassadors*, the problem is to shadow forth the Romantic hero within the weird disguise of a late-nineteenth-century social type and, moreover, through the given terms of that type. The character does not simply want to shuffle off the objective self he has always been; he wants to remain a "character"—for Strether, a rigidly "moral" character. But he seeks to live out this "real" life as an imaginative life, achieving the full measure of his actual identity by the promptings of a virtually metaphysical being within him. If he is predestined to failure, that is in the nature of his problem, the best expression of his problem, and his problem is what gives him his stature. His author also claims no more than to have created a "comparative case." And in the autobiography itself James is not disposed to argue that he has attained success by reversing the field and trying to objectify himself. All he claims, he says, is "the interest . . . of certain sorts of failure." That, one gathers, is the only kind of success he has much confidence in.

James's problematic logic runs through the whole body both of his fiction and of his devious discourse about himself and his art. The implicit scheme, the very signature of his mind, is a circular pattern, moving between his visionary awareness of the Romantic "man of imagination" and his existential conviction of the prior reality of the socially "real." On the one hand, he is a Romantic without any foothold in the world of physical nature, which the imaginative hero of Romantic poetry at once redeems and is redeemed by. The "objective" world, for him, is wholly social, historical, artificial to its deepest foundations—precisely the world that the Romantic vision was originally designed to transcend or undercut, to acknowledge only in the course of striving to evoke something quite different. On the other hand, James is a social realist without any governing rationale of contemporary society, any strictly historical concepts beyond the most commonplace working assumptions, even (in my opinion) any deeply felt class loyalties. The main source of social meaning, for him, is the Romantic life of imaginative consciousness, which he must somehow either presuppose or invest in the manners and morals he observes. What he does, in fact—the dynamic of his circular logic—is to presuppose and invest and presuppose once again; the trail he leaves behind him is a kind of hermeneutic circle. It is a record of his ever incomplete, ever renewed attempt to encompass the impossible ground on which the "man of imagination" would prove to be a "real" man, and "real" men would be Romantic heroes, men of imagination.

To the end of his career, he clung to the social data that from the outset had made him a "realist" of sorts—had even made him a novelist—what he describes in his early essay on "The Art of Fiction" as "the look of things, the look that conveys their meaning, . . . the color, the relief, the expression, the surface, the substance of the human spectacle." These given things-of-the-world are the occasion of the "experience"—the particular kind of *artistic* experience—that he glorifies in the same essay. It is an experience that comes only to a consciousness immersed in the social existence of the artist and eager to register the intrinsic "implications of things." Whatever doubts he already had or eventually came to harbor about the inherent meaningfulness of the "human spectacle" of his time, his presupposition always was that some objective significance in the human scene—" 'subject,' . . . 'character,' . . . a saving sense in things" [1]—awaited and invited his fictional "rendering." The "real," when he pointedly contrasts it with the "romantic" in a long disquisition in the preface to *The American,* not only presents the novelist with ingrained patterns of significance but also imposes salutary limits upon him. The "experience" attributed to a fictional person, James here says, must either be confined by the "real" conditions that delimit the novelist's own experience or must be extended deliberately and playfully—that is, "romantically"—beyond the known conditions of the real. In either case, the ultimate criterion of fictional truth is a given world of "real" things—"the things we cannot possibly *not* know, sooner or later, in one way or another"—by reference to which we can always "know where we are," test a work of fiction against the actual "way things happen," and judge just how much "romance" the writer has smuggled in for our entertainment.

In proportion as James exalts the "real," he accepts a rather debased notion of "romance." But at the same time, precisely because of his devotion to the "saving sense in things," he is acutely aware of *lapses* of sense in the contemporary world, a thinning-out of those ways of happening—definitive patterns of event, of behavior, of language—in which he can recognize a "meaning" and therefore a "subject." Despite his enormous productivity, he was often troubled, even visited by a kind of anguish, at what seemed to him a de-signification of the people and situations presented to him: "The great question of *subject* surges in grey dimness about me. It is everything—it is everything." [2] In effect, the "real," which had given him his working concept of a "subject," had betrayed him.

Of course, there is always an element of mere genteel fastidiousness in James's manner when he speaks most directly about his relation to the modern world—notably in his perplexity or dismay at the irruption of alien hordes into "Anglo-Saxon" culture —but his basic point is always larger and more compelling. His point is aesthetic; he speaks as an artist; and he is testifying that the art of fiction cannot remain the same when the very attempt to record the meaningful "look of things" reveals a look of nonmeaning. That the barbarian invaders are socially unacceptable is a minor matter beside the discovery that they are artistically unrepresentable on the familiar ground of James's "realism." They give "no account of themselves in any terms already consecrated by human use; . . . abysmal the mystery of what they think, what they feel, what they want, what they suppose themselves to be saying" (P, p. 209). And they are only the most flagrant instance of a state of affairs which the artist finds almost as evident in America at large as on the East Side and almost as far advanced in London as in New York. Therefore the novelist, as the prefaces picture him, cannot depend on the resources and the discipline of the "real" to see him through. Instead of simply rendering the "saving sense in things," he is in the position of trying to save the very concept of "sense." Confronting the "fatal futility of Fact," the sheer senselessness of "clumsy Life at her stupid work," he takes it upon himself to rescue hidden nuggets of "latent *value*" from the flux and to lend them the significant shapes that they somehow suggest but would surely never have attained in actuality (P, pp. 120–22). The "work of the intelligent painter of life" is a counterblow to the stupid work of life, an "aid given to true meanings to be born" (P, p. 224). It is the cultural midwifery of a world in which people no longer present any coherent "account of themselves."

The imaginative initiative required for the salvation of the "real" is probably James's underlying justification for the extreme formalism in which he often seems to be indulging. Engaged in a "high and helpful public and, as it were, civic use of the imagination" (*P*, p. 223), what better can he do than create formal exemplars, wholly artificial worlds that have far more "sense" than any actual world can ever show? Less purely formalistic, though it leads him to his most distinctive fictional form, is the intellectual method that he calls the "art of reflection." It is by "reflecting," actively responding to some fugitive sign of "latent value," that the writer is still able to conjure up "a strong, large, important human episode," full of "character and sincerity and passion." Even if he is not writing, as he wishes he could, out of the midst of life and at the immediate dictate of swarming "impressions," he assures himself that through "reflection" he can "feel again the multitudinous presence of all human situations and pictures" (*N*, p. 135).

Fully developed, the art of reflection proceeds through "reflectors" or "vessel[s] of consciousness," personages who have been invested with some of their author's reflective capacity. As the savior of public sense, James reasons, the novelist is not only the "teller of a story" but also, and most signally, "the reader of it," for he has been obliged "to make it out . . . on the crabbed page of life, to disengage it from the rude human character and the more or less Gothic text in which it has been packed away." And such a reading of an almost unintelligible world necessarily involves a certain element of hypothesis, an *"imputing* of intelligence" to someone, if any "story'" worthy of the name is to be found (*P*, p. 63). Mediated by the imputed intelligence of the hero, both the novelistic situation and the hero himself will manifest themselves to the storyteller, summoned up out of an inchoate world by the constructive mind that he assumes to be at work within them. The individual consciousness of such a character (or, in Jamesian language, his "imagination") will be a principle informing all that he *is* as a social man, all that he says and does as well as all that he thinks and feels, so that his "objective" existence—his "real" identity as a creature of the world—will have a weight and depth of intention that would otherwise remain hidden in the Gothic text. Similarly, the hero's objective situation, including the characters of all the people who impinge on him, will come into view largely through terms that his imagination proposes for them; this apparent subjectification, by putting the situation in its most intelligible form, will "serv[e] in the highest degree to record it . . . objectively" (*P*, p. 67).

James would like to claim that the central consciousnesses of his major fiction, like the "supersubtle fry" of his tales of writers and artists, are "in *essence* an observed reality." Even if they are linked to the actual world only by their "operative irony"—that is, by their ironic representation of what the world is *not* able to produce on its own—to some extent they remain functions of a given world (*P*, pp. 221–24). This roundabout realism, however, is almost indistinguishable from a roundabout romanticism, the representation of a kind of literary figure who is "in essence" not an "observed reality" at all. There is only a short step, and one that James often takes in the prefaces, between the idea of imputing imagination to someone in order to reveal his intelligible character and story and the idea of devising a character and story in order to display the dynamics of a totally imaginative life. It is difficult to maintain that the central consciousness can virtually create the significant existence of himself and others without implying that his existence is swallowed up by his subjective consciousness of existence. As James follows out his theory, he is always turning the canons of social realism upside down; even while insisting that the role of consciousness in his fiction is to evoke an objective reality, he repeatedly states that for him the "interest of . . . [an] attitude and act" does not inhere in *them* but in what lies behind them, in "the actor's imagination and vision of them, together with the nature and degree of their felt return upon him" (*P*, p. 63).

Pushed far enough, this inverted emphasis would lead to the strange sort of "vivid individual" that James tells us he found in Isabel Archer, the heroine of *The Portrait of a Lady*, when he first began to "reflect" upon her. She was "vivid" for him, he says, "in spite of being . . . at large, not confined by the conditions, not engaged in the tangle, to which we look for much of the impress that constitutes an identity." Though he could not conceive of a story or a character without *any* reference to the identifying "conditions" of the "real," his account of the genesis of the *Portrait* leans heavily on the notion of an autonomous, self-defining imaginative power both in his heroine and in her author. Instead of emphasizing the objective existence, of Isabel Archer and of those around her, which her intelligent consciousness enables him to represent, he gives us to understand that the prime aim of his book is to subjectify her existence, to convert her "life" into an "inward life" and the "impress" of external circumstances into "her sense of them, her sense *for* them." Just so, though James himself has necessarily "take[n] over straight from life . . . [her] constituted, animated figure or form," he suggests that such a figure attains its true locus only when it has been "placed" within his artistic consciousness, "the imagination that detains it, preserves, protects, enjoys it."

In sum, the "romantic" is in the ascendant, and it is not the mere artistic game that James pictures when he is most intent on affirming his "realistic" premises—a mere trick by which the novelist, "for the fun of it," cuts the rope that ties the "balloon of experience" to the earth (*P*, p. 34). The "romantic" is "experience liberated," but in a very positive way, which opens up a genuine alternative to the "real" experience of "conditions." As opposed to "real" things, the "things we cannot possibly *not* know," and even to the things that become knowable by an "imputing of intelligence" to the "real," there are purely "romantic" things—"things that . . . we never *can* directly know," but nevertheless "things that . . . reach us . . . through the beautiful circuit and subterfuge of our thought and our desire" (*P*, pp. 31–33).

The more prestige and autonomy James gives to "romantic" experience, the more problematic his concept of fiction becomes. If his campaign to save the significance of the "real" brings him to the verge of the "romantic" circuit of thought and desire, he also feels an obligation to humanize his own "romantic" impulse, to save himself and his heroes from the inhuman bliss of pure consciousness. One of his major concerns as a novelist is to deprive himself of the authority of transcendent vision, "the mere muffled majesty of irresponsible 'authorship.' " Having invented "vessel[s] of consciousness" by divinely conferring some of his own consciousness upon his characters, he reverses himself and wants to take on the limits of the human vessel. Instead of speaking primarily *ab extra,* he holds, the novelist should "get down into the arena," enter into the conflicting visions and voices of "the real, the deeply involved and immersed and more or less bleeding participants" (*P,* p. 328). These persons, in turn, must be preserved from the consequences of their own visionary powers, which would otherwise make them as "superhuman" as an omniscient author pretends to be. They must be endowed with sufficient "intelligence" that "the appearances reflected in it, . . . constituting there the situation and the 'story,' should become . . . intelligible," but they can acquire a *story* only by suffering the fate of human ignorance, a consciousness "bedimmed and befooled and bewildered, anxious, restless, fallible" (*P,* p. 16). For "it seems probable that if we were never bewildered there would never be a story to tell about us; we should partake of the superior nature of the all-knowing immortals . . ." (*P,* pp. 63–64). Though it is only by an imputing of intelligence that a *significant* story can be made to emerge out of the bewildering contemporary world, it is only by the bewilderment of intelligence that a human *story,* a sequence of "happenings," can be made to emerge out of the stuff of "romantic" dream.

That dream is always very present to James even as he repudiates it: "the dream of an intenser experience . . . [the] vision of a sublime security like that enjoyed on the flowery plains of heaven, where we may conceive ourselves proceeding in ecstasy from one prodigious phase and form of it to another" (*P,* p. 32). For the Romantic poets some such vision of total consciousness is the most precious of hopes, but they have their own kind of truthfulness to the human condition, their own way of acknowledging "bewilderment": for them, the longed-for state of visionary being, the completion of their anticipatory vision, is the most fleeting and fragile of achievements, if achieved at all. For James, on the other hand, the flowery plains of heaven are all-too-accessible, at least in his own experience: "What was *I* thus, within and essentially, what had I ever been and could I ever be, but a man of imagination at the active pitch?" If we take him at his word, that is surely more than any Romantic poet ever claimed. James's notebooks are full of passages in which he dramatizes his ascension, by the mere act of writing the passage, into a realm where his human limits are shed yet his humanity is miraculously restored in the life of imagination:

Thus just these first little wavings of the oh so tremulously passionate little old wand (now!) make for me, I feel, a sort of promise of richness and beauty and variety; a sort of portent of the happy presence of the elements. . . . I seem to emerge from these recent bad days—the fruit of blind accident . . .—and the prospect clears and flushes, and my poor blest old Genius pats me so admirably and lovingly on the back that I turn, I screw round, and bend my lips to passionately, in my gratitude, kiss its hand. [*N*, p. 357]

Embracing and embraced by his genius, he triumphantly exists, but literally out of this world. Throughout James's autobiography he frequently calls attention to a similar communion, here between his living past and his artistic present; his "imaginative faculty," turned round, is forever informing and informed by a small boy and youth in whom that faculty itself is "under cultivation":

The "first" then—since I retrace our steps to the start, for the pleasure, strangely mixed though it be, of feeling our small feet plant themselves afresh and artlessly stumble forward again—the first began long ago, far off, and yet glimmers at me there as out of a thin golden haze, with all the charm, for imagination and memory, of pressing pursuit rewarded, of distinctness in the dimness, of the flush of life in the grey, of the wonder of consciousness in everything; everything having naturally been all the while but the abject little matter of course.[3]

Given these propensities, it is quite understandable that James should permit himself only an oblique autobiography, under the cover of family memoirs, and should consider even this a perilous undertaking, in which "objectivity, the prize to be won," may easily be "frightened away." The "abject little matter of course" is hard to keep in view when the nascent consciousness of his early life and the present life of his masterful consciousness are continually merging into a single moment of imaginative humanity.

In the prefaces, some years earlier, as if foreseeing where he might be led, James positively disowns doing anything so "subtle," or perhaps "monstrous," as to "write the history of the growth of . . . [his] imagination" (*P*, p. 47). He chooses to think of a preface not as strictly autobiographical but as "the story of . . . [a] *story*," and he is ready to argue that, so regarded, a preface is even "more objective" than "the story of one's hero." The prefaces, his "licentious record" of his authorial adventures, are permissible because his work, not he, is always the true hero of the tale (*P*, p. 313). In part, the kind of "objectivity" that James hopes to preserve in this way is cognate to the "bewilderment" that he visits upon the heroes of his stories. A preface, the "story of . . . [a] story," is usually the tale of a work that has gotten itself written against the odds. Likewise, his own personal story, when he deals with it more directly in his autobiography, is the tale of a man who is at best confusedly striving to become the genius that indites the tale. But in larger part James falls back upon the objective meaningfulness of the "real," rather than its bewilderments, to contain his Romantic afflatus. We are back at our starting point, his need to assume significant objective "conditions," a "saving sense in things." The "real" in the autobiography is a vast network of personal and social relations, external determinants which have made the Master what he is. The "real" in the prefaces is the objective work, the "thing done," which is the ineluctable condition of any renewed vision of it.

When James is on this tack, the "real" returns to fiction as a set of "exhibitional conditions" which are imposed upon the imaginative hero by an author who proudly claims the title of "historian." And the most elaborate statement of this "realistic" imperative is in the preface to *The Ambassadors*, precisely where the "man of imagination" is most explicitly adduced as James's ideal fictional subject. Strether, the central consciousness of the book, must be at once "encaged and provided for" by being placed in a world of *others,* and he must reckon with them not merely as shadows in a self-centered story that he tells about himself but also as auditors and spectators, figures in the external story of his storytelling, which he himself cannot tell. The one who does tell it, the "historian," is not a writer who plunges into the arena in order to save himself from "the mere muffled majesty of . . . authorship," though here too he surrenders the greatest "privilege of the artist," the romantic entrancement of his own "constructive, . . . creative passion" with itself (*P,* p. 29). He does so now by becoming a detached objectifier and with the purpose of saving his hero and his story from "the darkest abyss of romance." That abyss, he maintains—the other side, I take it, of the "flowery plains of heaven"—will swallow up any story, or at least any "long piece," in which the hero is allowed to be "at once hero and historian." If the artist's own autobiography is suspect, a valid story certainly cannot be the autobiography of its protagonist. What James calls "the romantic privilege of the 'first person,' " or "the double privilege of subject and object," makes for dangers even greater than the illusory "golden glow" of self-involvement. It makes for—dreaded word!—"looseness," the "terrible *fluidity* of self-revelation," because the historian in such fiction has abdicated, and the hero cannot produce "exhibitional conditions" for himself. The story can assume determinate form only insofar as the writer is moved by and invokes the determining forms of social circumstance. Through those objective determinants, moreover, he comes back again to the objective "variety" of the "real"—"the color, the relief, the expression, the surface, the substance of the human spectacle."

These twists and turns of Jamesian argument, forever circling back to their point of departure, are all addressed to the general question of the status and meaning of meaning; taken as a whole, they articulate or "represent" that question. What is more, the prefaces are designed to emphasize a similar function performed by James's fictional works. The individual work of art, in the perspective of the prefaces, becomes essentially a conductor of the questions that have attended every stage of its conception and composition. For we are given very little else to connect it with. A Jamesian preface, as the "story of . . . [a] story," not only pushes the "personal history" of James himself largely into the background but also excludes any central discussion of the specific subject-matter of his books. Though he holds that "everything counts, nothing is superfluous," in his survey of his career (P, p. 3), and he makes gestures toward a self-portrait as well as an analysis of his materials, in the end he has told us even less about his subjects per se than about himself. Both consistently appear as factors in a highly abstract "compositional problem," hinging on the author's "relation to a given subject" (P, pp. 121, 319), in which the personal attributes of the author and the specific qualities of the subject tend to fade from view. Throughout the prefaces, the writer, regarded as the practitioner of an "absolutely premeditated art" by which he strives to extend "the very terms and possibilities of representation and figuration," is engaged with a subject-matter that half assists and half obstructs him as it "struggles . . . fully and completely to express itself" (P, pp. 84, 278, 319). What the completed work of art mainly records, then, and what the reader trained by the prefaces will know how to find in it, is the problematic process that has gone into its advent, epitomized in the opposition and the mutual need, the latent incongruities and the achieved congruence, of "subject" and "treatment," as revealed by "the logic of the particular case" (P, p. 121). Fiction, on this showing, gives an "aid . . . to true meanings to be born" chiefly by evincing the ambiguous birth of artistic meaning out of disparate factors which at once seek and deny their common ground.

This extraordinarily abstract function that James attributes to his work is a kind of significance which a story may presumably have even when its subject falls rather low on his scale of intrinsic "merit." But at the same time it provides an important clue to his way of judging concrete "degrees of merit in subjects." A perfect subject like that of The Ambassadors, we must suppose, was one in which the world itself had presented him with a potential instance of the same problematics of meaning that he wished all his works to display in their purely "compositional" aspect. The anecdote behind *The Ambassadors* struck James as made to his hand because he foresaw that the experience of Lambert Strether might unfold along much the same lines as his own complex experience of writing, of which the book would be a "recording scroll or engraved commemorative tablet" (*P*, p. 4).

It was not only that the voice of Howells, which was to become the voice of Strether, already had the ring of "intense reflexion," the saving grace of the Jamesian central consciousness. Nor was it simply that Howells's reported speech combined the tone of imaginative intelligence with the tone of "character," of New England, of "a moral scheme of the most approved pattern"—though this combination already placed Strether in a problematic position between the expressive claims of his given character and the figurative claims of his reflective consciousness. What James says that he treasured in his *donnée,* over and above the kind of hero it offered him, was "the gift of the old Paris garden," a "token" in which "were sealed up values infinitely precious." The Paris garden of the anecdote betokened what the Strether of the book sees in it when he arrives there, a world *of* "signs and tokens, a whole range of expression, . . . [an] assault of images." It stood for an imaginative world which would awaken Strether's inborn imagination by its "real" diversity of meaning and at the same time "encage" his increasingly "romantic" flights within "exhibitional conditions" far more stringent than anything found in the world of Woollett. Paris would raise the level of Strether's life and thought, his character and his vision, by allowing them to interpenetrate on the plane of imaginative life, a plane from which the moralism of Woollett would often seem no more than a makeshift alliance between vulgar "practices" and arbitrary "ideals." But Paris, within the higher terms that it proposed, would also spell out an insoluble question. Paris would eventually demonstrate something that the unregenerate man of Woollett within Strether has suspected all along—that the "real" conjunction of existence and vision can only be in large part a "romantic" imputation. Paris itself would prove that the actual world can begin "fully and completely to express itself" only under the ministrations of an "absolutely premeditated art," while such an art, on the other hand, presupposes a fully expressive world. Indeed, the final lesson of Paris would be that the "subject" Strether has most at heart, the affair of Chad Newsome and Mme de Vionnet which he desperately labors to "treat," is in itself another version of his own problematic predicament—an inconclusive encounter between a "real" life which is prone to verge off into impenetrable senselessness and a "romantic" vision which cannot be satisfied by anything less than a supreme case of imaginative man.

Undoubtedly, an author like this is enough to drive his characters crazy. They have very good reason to turn on him and tell him that *he* is crazy, as one of them virtually does in *The Sacred Flount*. For he lets them live out their particular lives and find their personal "sense" only in a universe formally shaped and thematically pervaded by his obsessive quest for sense-in-general. The "real" can concretely exist for them, whether in themselves or in others, only insofar as it is also a factor in his abstract problem of the "real" and the "romantic." In James's effort to invest the "real" with the "romantic" significance that he must simultaneously presuppose in it in order to write at all, he ends by investing it mainly with the unanswerable question of "real" and "romantic" meaning. And this outcome, one is tempted to say, suggests that his ultimate motive all along has been a militant romanticism, an underlying animus against that "real" which he professes to revere.

If so, however, James's problematics also involve a more profound realism than any fictional "character" is likely to evince on his own. It is the nature of "characters" to take most things for granted, especially themselves. That is their strength. But what is now most real in the "real," as James understands it, is the fact that the "sense in things" can no longer be taken for granted—the fact that people, willy-nilly, must be engaged in a quest for meaning, and for the meaning of meaning. James's major figures seem to perceive that their insoluble predicament, though it is a more exasperatingly "false position" than any other writer of their time would have visited upon them, makes them *more* "real" rather than less. Strether at least, the one of whom James felt surest, fully enters into the moment when he is called upon to recognize the riddling principles by which his author intends to make him a "comparative" hero. Face to face with Gloriani in the artist's garden, and "held by the sculptor's eyes," he welcomes the "deepest intellectual sounding to which he [has] ever been exposed." The positive value of the moment, as he continues to contemplate it for long after, lies in the inherent "mystery" of this sounding, its problematic essence:

Was what it had told him or what it had asked him the greater of the mysteries? Was it the most special flare, unequalled, supreme, of the aesthetic torch, lighting that wondrous world forever, or was it above all the long, straight shaft sunk by a personal acuteness that life had seasoned to steel?

Gloriani's vision, penetrating his, must be conceived by turns as either a question or a message; as either the manifestation of a worldly life grown wholly imaginative or the expression of an imaginative self in a consummate man of the world; but most of all as a scrutiny which is searching him for something correlative to itself. It is a "test of his stuff" which he has already passed insofar as he understands that its purpose is to bring him into the uneasy truth of his eternal "falsehood," the reality of his precarious position between the "real" and the "romantic."

NOTES

1. Henry James, *The Art of the Novel: Critical Prefaces,* ed. R. P. Blackmur (New York: Scribner's, 1953), p. 334. Hereafter cited as *P.*

2. *The Notebooks of Henry James,* ed. F. O. Matthiessen and K. B. Murdock (New York: Oxford University Press, 1947), p. 135. Hereafter cited as *N.*

3. Henry James, *A Small Boy and Others* (New York: Scribner's, 1913), p. 3.

T. S. Eliot as a "Modernist" Poet

CLEANTH BROOKS

A look backward to the earlier decades of our century reveals how urgent had become the need to unify man's experience, to bring together "scientific" description with human valuation or—to use the old-fashioned term—to reconcile the head with the heart. In varying forms the necessity to do so is stated over and over again in the work of W. B. Yeats and T. S. Eliot. Yeats, for example, defined the tragic generation, of which he considered himself a member, as composed of men who passionately required unity of being but who had been born in an age radically divided, in which the split between science on the one hand and poetry and religion on the other could not be healed. Yeats comments on his dilemma, not only in his poetry, but in many passages in his essays and his *Autobiographies*. One remembers too his minuscule history of English literature: first, there is Chaucer's company of Canterbury pilgrims, men and women of varying rank and degree, but all united by a common belief and moving in company toward a common shrine; then comes the breakdown of this company into the members of a Shakespeare's dramatis personae, the community beginning to dissolve but the individuals gaining dramatic force thereby; and finally, there is the isolated individual, driven in on himself, typically the *poète maudit,* the divine madman such as appears in Coleridge's "Kubla Khan," to his fellow men at once an object of veneration and an outcast and pariah.

> Beware! Beware!
> His flashing eyes, his floating hair!
> Weave a circle round him thrice,

> And close your eyes with holy dread,
> For he on honey-dew hath fed,
> And drunk the milk of Paradise.

Eliot's concern with the divided psyche is to be found everywhere in his poetry and essays, but in its most easily recognizable form, in his earlier work. It is with Eliot's treatment of the problem that I shall be principally concerned in this essay; but before taking up instances, it may be well to review briefly what might be called the history of the question.

The split between the realm of fact and the realm of value in Western culture is most often traced back to René Descartes. In separating the world internal to man, the world of attitudes and emotions, value judgments and affections, from the world of the objects and forces outside man, Descartes, it has been said, cut the throat of poetry.[1] Science was thereby freed to begin its triumphal progress. But was not the poet condemned to subjectivity? Traditionally, the poet had been the supreme truth-teller, bard, and seer; now his truth had no necessary reference to "fact."

The full implications of the Cartesian severance were not felt for some time. But by the end of the eighteenth century Wordsworth and Coleridge had become aware of the seriousness of the plight of poetry and took their own measures in an attempt to deal with it. In 1802 Coleridge, in a letter to William Sotheby, argued that "a Poet's *Heart & Intellect* should be *combined, intimately* combined & *unified* with the great appearances in Nature —& not merely held in solution & loose mixture with them." In this statement Coleridge takes for granted that the heart and intellect should be combined; his stress is on the means to be used for combining them, and even more emphatically on a genuine unification. It does not suffice for the poet to use some feature of nature as an occasion for moral reflections. Coleridge believed that in the greatest poetry the appearances in nature become living symbols of human values and emotions. By making imaginative use of natural appearances, Wordsworth and Coleridge wrote some very great poetry. In fact, their best poetry tended to be of this kind, and William K. Wimsatt has shown us in precise detail how their method characteristically worked to produce poetry that, for all its greatness, was a poetry that restricted itself to a particular subject matter and stressed particular themes.[2]

Coleridge's penchant for "the great appearances in Nature" is easily understood. Because the wilder and more remote aspects of nature had been least affected by the encroachments of applied science, head and heart could find common ground there. For primitive man living close to nature, the separation between mind and heart had scarcely occurred. Nor would it ordinarily have occurred for the peasant, whose life was still controlled largely by the rhythms of the seasons and who, as Wordsworth describes his Old Cumberland Beggar, had always lived "in the eye of Nature." Least of all in the child had the head challenged the heart. Wordsworth's own childhood was associated with the countryside, and Coleridge regretted that his childhood had not been closer to nature. In one of his finest poems he expresses the wish that his children might grow up under nature's tutelage.

We must be careful not to oversimplify the role of nature for the Romantic poet, a role much more complicated than this brief reference can suggest. But it is obvious—whatever the various reasons that account for it—that the heart can most easily be united with the head in a poetry that evokes the natural scene and that reflects the world of the child, the shepherd, or the peasant.

Because the rift between heart and head had become deeper and wider in the twentieth century, it was more difficult to write nature poems, and the attempt to write such poetry began to seem escapist. Very early in his career Eliot resolved to accept the challenge of industrialism and the urban scene. In a remarkable passage in the essay entitled "What Dante Means to Me," Eliot tells us that he learned first from Baudelaire a "precedent for the poetical possibilities, never developed by any poet writing in my own language, of the more sordid aspects of the modern metropolis, of the possibility of fusion between the sordidly realistic and the phantasmagoric, the possibility of the juxtaposition of the matter-of-fact and the fantastic." [3]

Eliot goes on to say that it was from Baudelaire that he also learned that the sort of experience he had had as an adolescent "in an industrial city in America"—something obviously very different from the experience of Wordsworth and Coleridge—could constitute the material for poetry. From Baudelaire he learned further that "the business of the poet was to make poetry out of the unexplored resources of the unpoetical; that the poet, in fact, was committed by his profession to turn the unpoetical into poetry." [4]

When Eliot speaks of a "fusion between the sordidly realistic and the phantasmagoric," his stress is on the rejection of any notion of intrinsically "poetic" materials, but he is also talking about the kind of union of disparate elements that Coleridge believed poetry must achieve. Conversely, when Coleridge says that what he applauds most in Wordsworth is "the union of deep feelings with profound thought," he acknowledges a separation between an objective world of matter-of-fact and a world of the fantastic and the phantasmagoric. For there is no need to talk about union unless a prior separation has occurred.

At the time that Eliot was writing his early poetry, in his critical essays he was writing about "transmuting ideas into sensations" and of the possibility of "transforming an observation into a state of mind." [5] Thus, the theoretic problem was very much on Eliot's mind during the time that he was trying to achieve such transmutations of ideas into sensations in specific poems.

If we are right in perceiving certain common elements in the way in which Eliot analyzed his cultural situation and the way in which Wordsworth and Coleridge analyzed theirs, and if a unification of ideas and sensations such as Eliot demands has affinities with Coleridge's vision of a poetry that unites head and heart, then why did Eliot, in looking for masters who might help him solve his problem as a twentieth-century poet, pass over the great English Romantics? We have already implied an answer: Eliot's commitment to make poetry out of the city put him off Romantic nature poetry as an evasion of the crucial issue. Romantic poetry must have seemed to him to offer no promise of the unification of sensibility that he sought. He could discern a struggle to achieve wholeness of experience in Shelley's "Triumph of Life" and in Keats's "The Fall of Hyperion," but he allowed no more than that to these late unfinished poems by the younger Romantic poets.

Today many of us who admire the poetry of Eliot and his masters, Donne and Baudelaire, can find in Romantic poetry instances of the unification of sensibility that Eliot required. But it is only fair to reflect that if we can do so now, we may owe our discernment in part to Eliot himself. For his achievement in poetry and in criticism was important in helping us to see that Coleridge's *Rime of the Ancient Mariner* is a remarkably complex poem on the very subject of division and reunification. It is a poem about the violation of nature and the deadening powers of abstraction, and even perhaps a poem about the Industrial Revolution. Again, though Eliot failed to see the greatness of Keats's Odes, and indeed in his comments on them is almost blunderingly clumsy, yet he may have put us up to asking the questions that we need to ask of the Odes if we are to see how truly great and even "modern" they are.[6]

Be that as it may, Eliot did not find in the Romantic poets what answered to his own needs. For English examples of what he needed, he went back to a period earlier than the Victorians and earlier than the Romantics, on back to the poets of the seventeenth century. Significantly, his most striking ideas about what poetry should be are to be found in his essays on the Elizabethan and Jacobean poets.

In his essay on *Hamlet,* Eliot defines the poet's characteristic method as that of the "objective correlative." That is, poets do not write with ideas or emotions but with words. Moreover, the essential element in poetry is not statement but concrete representation. A poem does not state an abstract truth but intimates it symbolically or embodies it in a drama. Consequently, it becomes a matter of real consequence when poetry begins to break down into more simple elements, its concrete details reduced to mere illustration or ornament and its meaning to an abstract proposition.

In his essay "The Metaphysical Poets" Eliot applies a special descriptive term to such a separation. He calls it a "dissociation of sensibility." As we shall see, he regarded it as a feature of our

modern culture generally, and he saw it as the characteristic defect of much of the poetry that came out of that culture. The dissociation of sensibility reflects the poet's having "thought and
felt" not simultaneously, but "by fits, unbalanced." [7] In the most
flagrant instances, the poet has simply abandoned thinking altogether in favor of indulgence in pure emotion.

As critical formulations, both the objective correlative and the
dissociation of sensibility have been attacked, but they are, I believe, defensible. I grant that Eliot's way of defining the objective
correlative invites misconceptions. Incidentally, his definition is
curiously like a passage in Wordsworth's famous Preface to the
second edition of *Lyrical Ballads*. Eliot defines the objective correlative as "a set of objects, a situation, a chain of events which
shall be the formula of that *particular* emotion; such that when
the external facts, which must terminate in sensory experience,
are given, the emotion is immediately evoked." [8] Wordsworth,
having said that poetry "is the spontaneous overflow of powerful
feelings," goes on to say that "it takes its origin from emotion
recollected in tranquillity: the emotion is contemplated till, by a
species of re-action the tranquillity gradually disappears, and *an
emotion, kindred to that which was before the subject of contemplation, is gradually produced, and does itself actually exist in the
mind"* (italics mine). [9] Eliot and Wordsworth here seem to imply
that the emotion is of a rather specific kind which can be transferred, more or less intact, from the poet's mind to that of his
reader or hearer. Both claim more for their theory of poetic
composition than they are entitled to claim—and more than in
fact their legitimate purposes require.

Eliot puts what is true and valuable in his notion of an objective correlative more persuasively in his essay on the metaphysical poets, where he writes that these poets at their best were
"engaged in the task of trying to find the verbal equivalent for
states of mind and feeling." [10] The phrase "states of mind and
feeling," of course, implies a totality of experience—the requisite
union of head and heart.

Frank Kermode has argued that no special dissociation of sensibility occurred in the seventeenth century; that it occurred only

in Eliot's own imagination; and that Eliot then projected his notion of such dissociation back onto an earlier historical period. But Eliot's thesis has recently been vigorously defended by Monroe Spears in his study of modernism entitled *Dionysus and the City*.[11] Spears's defense of Eliot's concept carries the more weight in that he admires Kermode's work and seems to understand what Kermode, as well as Eliot, was trying to say.

When Eliot writes that the "sentimental age began early in the eighteenth century," [12] he is certainly historically correct, and his use of the term "sentimentality" makes quite clear the kind of split that he is talking about: on the one side of the fissure one finds a poetry dangerously tilted over toward mere feeling; and on the other, an undramatic exposition of, or rumination on, ideas as such. The dissociation of sensibility clearly has affinities with the Cartesian duality; in fact, one is tempted to say that it is simply that very duality re-expressed. Eliot's essay on Andrew Marvell substantiates such an interpretation. In praising Marvell for having achieved "a tough reasonableness beneath the slight lyric grace," [13] Eliot celebrates poetry that is more than an emotional indulgence. The poet has been able to feel without bypassing the intellect and to think without having to suppress his feelings. There is a wholeness in the experience from which neither intellect nor emotion is excluded.

I have suggested earlier that no dissociation of sensibility had occurred for children and peasants and primitive men, types that appealed to the Romantic poets, for primitive men and children lived in a semi-animistic world and their thinking had not reached any notable pitch of abstraction. But what about Marvell and Donne, those poets to whose work Eliot appeals for models of wholeness in poetry? They were not guileless primitives, but men of keen intellect, capable of abstract thought as well as delicate feelings and passionate involvement. There is plenty of evidence that they were quite aware of the strains and tensions of the age as new ideas challenged the inherited world view and threatened to rend it apart. Yet they had somehow found the means to keep their experience whole without having to suppress or exclude its various and sometimes competing elements.[14]

The metaphysical poets of the Jacobean period, no less than the Elizabethan dramatists, were for Eliot that giant race before the flood. Slavish imitation, of course, was not to be thought of, though a modern poet might hope to learn something from their example. That a modern poet might possibly recover their unified sensibility was suggested by the achievement of poets born two centuries or more later in time, men like Baudelaire, Laforgue, and Corbière, who, though living in the modern divided world, had nevertheless managed a fusion of thought and feeling.

All of this is familiar material: Eliot's discovery of a likeness between these two schools, a discovery that enabled him to develop his own style. But there is one element which stands in need of more examination. It has to do with the crucial matter of precisely what elements Baudelaire and Laforgue really shared with Donne and Marvell. For there are at least two features of their poetry that hardly appear in the French poets. The first is the kind of logic by which Donne and Marvell organize their poems. Though their reasoning is sometimes no more than a show of logic—mock logic, as it were—they do, by and large, make use of a consecutive and even syllogistic structure. As W. H. Auden has pointed out, the English Romantic poets discarded such a structure.[15] So did Baudelaire and Laforgue, who in an important sense represent a continuation and further development of the Romantic tradition.

A second feature of the poetry of Marvell and Donne that is not characteristic of that of Baudelaire and Laforgue is the elaborated analogy, usually worked out through an extended simile. Though acknowledging that this feature of metaphysical poetry is often taken to be its special hallmark, Eliot—significantly, in view of what he is to say later in his essay—stresses other devices used by the metaphysicals: the "forcing" of new connections on a figure of speech as opposed to merely developing the implicit meaning; the use of "sudden contrasts"; the "telescoping of images." Through the use of such devices the contexts of their poems become alive with what Eliot calls "multiplied associations." It is this feature of their work, Eliot tells us, that allies them with dramatists like Shakespeare, Middleton, Webster, and Tourneur.

In general, we may say, Eliot stresses in the Elizabethan and Jacobean poets the elements of disparity and tension, the new and startling developments of an idea, and the sense of a "heterogeneity of material compelled into unity." This sense of contrast and shock, of reconciled heterogeneity, provides the complexity of tone that Eliot desiderates as necessary for the poet who is to deal with a complicated world—and specifically the modern world.

In discussing the wit of Andrew Marvell, Eliot does make reference to the English Romantics—but to their critical prose, not to their poetry. Evidently having in mind the distinction drawn by Wordsworth and Coleridge between poems of the fancy and poems of the imagination, Eliot remarks that the difference between imagination and fancy, in view of this poetry of wit, is a very narrow one. The elder Romantics' association of fancy with mere playfulness, brittle ingenuity, and triviality is misleading. The shock of bold analogies, the play of the mind, and intellectual sophistication are not necessarily opposed to the seriousness and profundity that Wordsworth and Coleridge regarded as the properties of the imagination. For there is no necessary incompatibility between mental activity and depth of emotion. Then Eliot goes on to invoke Coleridge's famous account of the imagination (in chapter 14 of the *Biographia Literaria*) as a reconciling and unifying force.

In discussing this matter of Eliot's stance with reference to the English Romantic poets, the work of Wimsatt can be particularly helpful. His most succinct statement of the difference between the structure of metaphysical poetry and that of Romantic poetry occurs in *Literary Criticism: A Short History*. There (p. 401) he points out that the structure of romantic poetry

makes only a restrained use of the central overt statement of similitude which had been so important in all poetry up to that time. . . . In such a structure, . . . the element of tension in disparity may not be prominent. The interest derives not from our being aware of disparity in stated likeness [as in Donne and Marvell], but in the opposite activity of our discerning the design and the unity latent in a multiform sensuous picture. This is no doubt a form of "reconciliation." At the same time, there are certain clear anti-"metaphysical" tendencies here—the absence of overt definition, the reduction of disparity, the play of phenomena on the one hand and of "spirit" on the other, rather than of entities conceived substantially.

How thoroughly the "statement of similitude" and the elements of "disparity" may be concealed in Romantic poetry comes out clearly in some of Wordsworth's Lucy poems. Thus, in "She Dwelt among Untrodden Ways," Lucy is compared to a modest violet "Half hidden from the eye," and yet she is also "Fair as a star, when only one / Is shining in the sky." [16] It is significant that Wordsworth leaves out the normally expected "yet." Another poet might well have written "Though in the eyes of the world Lucy was as little noticed as a humble flower blooming in the shadow of a great stone, yet for me, who loved her, she was the nonpareil, the single star in my firmament." Wordsworth does not want the poem to smack of rhetoric, and certainly he wants no hint of witty paradox. The reader is left to make out for himself the unity "latent in [this] multiform sensuous picture." [17] Or, we can put matters in this way: the meaning is meant to rise like an exhalation from the natural objects presented. Violets and fair evening stars have for Wordsworth a felt "natural" likeness, not only to the girl but to each other, and both are evoked from the same rural setting: look down into the shadow of the stone, and there is the violet; look up at the evening sky, and there is the star.[18]

We may sum up the relations between metaphysical poetry, Romantic poetry, and the French poets that Eliot praises in this way: in general structure, the French poets are much closer to the Romantics than they are to the metaphysicals. What they do share with the metaphysicals—or at least what Eliot believed they shared—are striking instances of heterogeneity, a powerful sense of disparity, and obscure and sometimes far-fetched analogies. These are the special features of the fragment of the Laforgue poem with which Eliot would clinch his point in "The Metaphysical Poets." As we have seen, Wordsworth makes Lucy at one moment a violet and at another, a star, leaving it to his reader to work out her relationship to each of these two dissimilar phenomena and of the two to each other. But as we have remarked, flower and star are not shockingly different in their associations.

When, on the other hand, Laforgue tells us that his geraniums are at once "sortilèges," "sacrilèges," and "emballages," not to mention "douches" and "layettes aux abois," the collision among usual associations may be so shocking as to baffle the reader.

Eliot tells us that in poetry like Laforgue's we get "something which looks very much like the conceit—we get, in fact, a method curiously similar to that of the 'metaphysical poets,' similar also in its use of obscure words and of simple phrasing." [19] So we do: simple phrases, but abounding in obscure words; and as for the implied analogies, they are indeed merely implied, not stated, and they are often deeply buried in the context. They are in fact "symbols"—that is, not "stated similitudes" but concrete particulars, the point and meaning of which are the more difficult to grasp because the reader must infer them from the context alone.

What we have just said is not meant to question Eliot's discernment of a real similarity between the methods of Laforgue and of Donne, but rather to particularize a little further what Eliot took to be the common ground they shared. But we are not, of course, introducing a new concept in suggesting that the context is important. As a matter of fact, the context is always important when the poet is thinking through his images, even when he is using metaphor rather than symbol. This, Wimsatt points out in his *Verbal Icon* (p. 128), when he quotes from W. B. Stanford's *Greek Metaphor: Studies in Theory and Practice*. Stanford says that metaphor is

the process and result of using a term (X) normally signifying an object or concept (A) in such a context that it must refer to another object or concept (B) which is distinct enough in characteristics from A to ensure that in the composite idea formed by the synthesis of the concepts A and B and now symbolized in the word X, the factors A and B retain their conceptual independence even while they merge in the unity symbolized by X.

Wimsatt goes on to add his own refinement.

A poem itself, I shall venture to add, is the *context* of Stanford's description. It is a structure of verbal meaning which keeps a metaphor alive, that is, which holds the focal terms A and B in such a way that they remain distinct and illuminate each other, instead of collapsing into literalness. . . .[20] It is just when metaphors are carelessly repeated out of context that they most readily become simplified, literal, and cliché.

Just so. The "eye of a needle" and "the bed of a river" are, in the contexts in which we ordinarily use them, literal terms: the original metaphor has collapsed.

If, however, the poet suppresses the tenor of a metaphor and makes explicit only the vehicle, trusting that it will function as a "symbol," then the context in which he places it becomes even more important. Lacking a proper context, such images will remain inert, mere surfaces which can generate at best only a very vague emotional quality and consequently lack any specific symbolic force.

There is an additional difficulty in reading symbolist poetry: we need, as in Romantic nature poetry, to make out the latent unity in the sensuous images, but whereas most Romantic imagery is drawn from nature and has close emotional associations, the images in a symbolist poem may have such sharply different associations as to raise difficult problems of tone. In Wordsworth, for example, we do not ordinarily have rapid shifts in tone; in Laforgue, just as in Donne, we do.

This perhaps tedious discourse on Eliot's conception of the relation of symbolist to metaphysical poetry takes on more significance when one asks: How does Eliot structure his own poems?

Wimsatt concludes his essay on "The Structure of Romantic Nature Imagery" by remarking that as "a structure which favors implication rather than overt statement, the romantic is far closer than the metaphysical to symbolist poetry and the varieties of postsymbolist poetry most in vogue today." [21] This is true, and it is true of Eliot's own poems. For in spite of his admiration for Donne and Marvell, since the ground plan of most of Eliot's poetry is symbolist, his is closer to that of the Romantic poets than to the metaphysicals.[22]

Thus, Eliot's "The Love Song of J. Alfred Prufrock" opens with a thorough-going Donne-like conceit: "When the evening is spread out against the sky / Like a patient etherised upon a table." But this and other such witty comparisons become discrete items floating in a kind of stream-of-consciousness. One can make out in "The Love Song" a vague narrative, but the structure is so loose that, almost in defiance of logic and apparently apropos of nothing, occur lines like "I should have been a pair of ragged claws / Scuttling across the floors of silent seas."

"Rhapsody on a Windy Night" shows much the same structure, and even a poem like "Whispers of Immortality," which makes specific references to Donne and imitates some of his verbal devices, pretty well dispenses with a logical skeleton. Thus, the first four quatrains beginning "Webster was much possessed by death / And saw the skull beneath the skin," and ending

> He knew the anguish of the marrow
> The ague of the skeleton;
> No contact possible to flesh
> Allayed the fever of the bone [23]

are played off against a concluding set of four quatrains which are all about Grishkin and her friendly bust and the feline aura that surrounds her. The poem does not lack unity, but the unity is of a special sort. It does not arise from an obviously logical structure, though the connections can be made out and spelled out if the reader wants to do so.

Here follows an attempt to spell out the meaning resulting from the juxtaposition of the two halves of the poem. The poem is specifically "modern": it comments on a contemporary situation. Webster and Donne express in their writings an overwhelming consciousness of death. Yet though their obsession with death contains an ingredient of terror, it also forces on them a heightened awareness of sensuous experience. ("Luxuries" in line 8 carries something of its original meaning of "lecheries.") This intensification of the sensual was not at the expense of thought; rather, thought with Webster and Donne took on a sensuous character. (One remembers Eliot's stated belief that the metaphysical poets achieved in their work "a direct sensuous apprehension of thought, or a recreation of thought into feeling. . . .") [24] A vivid sense of one's mortality can make life more intense through one's consciousness of its brevity. That is one of the matters suggested. But there is another: the intimate union of thought and feeling reflects something that a great many other people have found in Shakespeare and the other Elizabethans: there, men had inherited a language brought to maturity and they knew how to use it, so that even their theological and philosophical statements find concrete embodiment in appropriate metaphor and symbol.

The last four quatrains present a different world—our world—the world as we know it, now that the Cartesian split has occurred. The man who speaks the poem pays due respect to Grishkin's magnetic attraction. But he is no Donne or Webster. Thought has now separated from feeling—and this is a serious loss. The Abstract Entities, such as goodness, truth, beatitude, etc., still yearn toward concrete embodiment, but they walk warily around —the poet has said "circumambulate"—Grishkin's charms, much like aging men, now more or less impotent, though they still make some response to her sensuous invitation.

We have been told that Webster knew that "thought clings. round dead limbs" and that for Donne the bones possessed marrow and even suffered fever as if, in Donne's day, even the most nearly mineral part of man seemed alive with a deep passion and yearning. But the ribs between which it is the lot of the modern to crawl are dry, and the implication of the last line is that the metaphysics that we entertain are not really kept very warm: they —and we—have to be satisfied with a rather chilly comfort.

The poem "Sweeney among the Nightingales" shows a generally similar pattern. One can find a rather wispy narrative line running through the poem. Sweeney is in some kind of joint and the bar girls are making advances to him, presumably to get him drunk and roll him for his wallet. But Sweeney is suspicious and he "declines the gambit," pretends to be tired, leaves the room, and then looks in the window. What happens to Sweeney is never made plain; perhaps nothing at all happens to him. The poem simply ends with the sound of the nightingales singing near the Convent of the Sacred Heart, and with some reflections on other occasions on which their songs were heard.

It is not, of course, to the poet's purpose here to give us a well-defined plot in which something "happens." In fact, it might be more accurate to say that the poem is really about something that has happened, not to Sweeney, but to the twentieth century. This is why the poet has set Sweeney against a backdrop of the great myths and legends of the past.

Perhaps the most important part of the poem is the Greek epigraph that Eliot has prefixed to it, the cry of Agamemnon struck down within his own house by his estranged wife, Clytemnestra. Agamemnon's cry is referred to specifically in the last stanza, the cry and the epigraph thus framing Sweeney's experience—or rather, our perspective on Sweeney's experience.

It is significant that Sweeney is described in almost purely animal terms, with allusions to the ape, the zebra, and the giraffe. He is aggressively physical; so are his gestures. The silent man in mocha brown (unless he is Sweeney himself) is also described in biological terms: he is a vertebrate, a classification which includes everything from men to mammoths and marmosets. The woman named Rachel has "paws." Her companion, "The person in the Spanish cape," is described as if she were nonhuman, though the variation the poet uses here is to treat her not as animal but as purely mechanical, a brainless automaton.

Yet if this is the stress intended by the poet, why all the literary folderol? Why the epigraph from Agamemnon? And why the references to Death and the Raven? Why the luridly Poe-esque atmosphere?

In view of what follows, the Raven must be the constellation Corvo, for Orion, two lines further on, is the constellation of that name, and the Dog is presumably the constellation of Canis Major. Eliot is obviously providing a mock epic background for his antihero Sweeney. Agamemnon's world, a world of gods and demigods and heroes, has in this poem been completely canceled. Apeneck Sweeney, of course, has never heard of that world. Even the reader, who has, must now relegate it to obsolete literary "bricabrac." The modern seas are indeed "shrunken," though Eliot wrote this poem long before the advent of the jet plane. To describe the plot against Sweeney in the exalted terminology of an older mythical world is one way of sharpening our sense of the difference between that world and our own.

The second stanza provides a good example of this. The first two lines describe the moon with a ring around it (foretelling bad weather) moving on its natural course from east to west, toward the River Plate in South America—though the Mississippi or the Mekong would have pointed the westward direction just as well. To say that "Death and the Raven drift above" is a highfalutin way of expressing foreboding. "And Sweeney guards the hornèd gate" is a mockingly grandiose way of saying that Sweeney himself is suspicious. One remembers that in the *Odyssey* we are told that when dreams are released from the underworld, the false ones come through the gates of ivory, but the dreams that foretell what is really going to happen make their way out through the gates of horn. Sweeney presumably does not know anything about the *Odyssey,* but he is here properly suspicious of the women. He is on his guard and stationed at the proper gate—the one through which the true intimations of the future issue forth.

To sum up, the poem presents modern man, the most intelligent of the mammals (but merely that), operating in a mechanistic world. The poet has pointed up his modernity by providing as background the archaic mytho-poetic world.

One may ask what the nightingales are doing in this poem. They represent nature, which in the past mankind invested with all sorts of spiritual qualities and which a Romantic poet like Wordsworth, a century and a half ago, wanted to believe actually sympathized with man. But modern man faces a neutralized nature—pure mechanism—beautiful but in fact pitiless and indifferent to man. The nightingales sing as sweet an obligato to the intrigue against Sweeney, the antihero, as they sang thousands of years ago at the assassination of the hero Agamemnon. In fact, they neither know nor care about the human world: they let their "liquid siftings fall" as impartially on the murdered king's shroud as they formerly let their melodious songs fall on his living ears.

F. O. Matthiesson writes that Eliot once remarked to him that what he consciously set out to create in this poem was "a sense of foreboding," and there is no reason to reject the notion that this was all that Eliot consciously was trying to do: that is, this is a mood piece, and considerations of plot are subordinated to evoking the mood. But consciously or unconsciously, a great deal more has got into the poem, and we don't have to read Eliot's conscious or unconscious mind to see that it is there. But though the "logic" of the structure is vague and almost nonexistent, the sharp contrasts, the rapid association of thought, the rich texture of heterogeneous material that Eliot associates with the poetry of Donne and of Laforgue is present. The poem is audacious and even witty, as when in the fourth stanza the person in the Spanish cape is turned into a mechanical doll:

> Slips and pulls the table cloth
> Overturns a coffee-cup
> Reorganized upon the floor
> She yawns and draws a stocking up.

But in spite of what this poem owes to Donne and Marvell, it "works" like a Romantic poem, where the reader's principal activity will lie in "discerning the design which is latent in the multiform sensuous picture." [25] The similitudes and contrasts—Sweeney as the trousered ape, man without his myths—are merely implied. A seventeenth-century metaphysical poet would have spelled them out for us with appropriate ironies and paradoxes.

Does the poem succeed in "transforming an observation into a state of mind"? That question the reader will have to answer for himself, but whether or not this poem manages to bridge the chasm between thought and feeling, it may be remarked that its theme is the fact of that chasm and the consequences for our culture.

The poem that most strikingly displays Eliot's use of disparate and even antithetical materials and that employs practically no logical connective tissue is, of course, *The Waste Land*. Now that the original manuscript has been published, it is apparent to what lengths Eliot was willing to go in this mode of assembling a poem out of apparently unconnected and anomalous blocks of material. The cooperation demanded of the reader in "organizing" the poem—in making out the underlying pattern—is formidable, but it does not differ in essentials from that demanded by Wordsworth's "She Dwelt among the Untrodden Ways." As with that poem, the reader must make sense of the contrasts and abrupt juxtapositions.

Monroe Spears calls Eliot's method one of "rhetorical discontinuity," and quotes Eliot's own description and justification of it. In his introduction to his translation of St. John Perse's *Anabase,* Eliot argues that any obscurity in *Anabase* is "due to the suppression of 'links in the chain,' of explanatory and connecting matter," and goes on to say that "such selection of a sequence of images and ideas has nothing chaotic about it. There is a logic of the imagination as well as a logic of concepts." [26]

Rhetorical discontinuity, however, is only one of a series of discontinuities that Spears discovers as underlying the modernism that Eliot exemplifies. There is, for instance, metaphysical discontinuity. A theoretician of art and culture like T. E. Hulme carefully distinguishes the natural from the human and both from the supernatural. There is also aesthetic discontinuity: art is not continuous with life but has its own realm. A fourth discontinuity noted by Spears is temporal discontinuity, by which he apparently means to refer to the ways in which temporal sequences in modern art can be converted into spatial arrangements by juxtaposition, by montage, or by face-to-face confrontations. I find it hard to differentiate this category—as I believe Spears himself does—from the general category of rhetorical discontinuity. In fact, I find his basic relevance to the modern artist lies in his felt need to locate the present scene by specific reference to the past, for no longer can the essential continuity of the human being be taken for granted. This, I believe, is the real point involved in Eliot's saluting Joyce's discovery of the "mythical method" employed in *Ulysses*—that is, as Eliot described it, Joyce's manipulation of "a continuous parallel between contemporaneity and antiquity." [27]

More is involved here than the discovery of a new literary technique. The new technique was actually compelled by the modern's heightening sense of history. A writer of Shakespeare's time did not need to pay much attention to the qualitative differences between historical epochs. Shakespeare found no great difficulty in identifying himself with the Greeks and the Romans of the classical age. He could interpret the Ulysses of his *Troilus* and the Antony of his Roman plays as good contemporary Elizabethans. But with the rediscovery, in the eighteenth century, of the values of the medieval world, men began to notice that there are radically different states of mind to be found in history. Modern man has now become thoroughly aware of the differences between historical epochs and aware of himself as aware of those differences. In Joyce's *Ulysses,* Leopold Bloom is not simply another Ulysses trying to get home to a Penelope who is faithful after her own fashion. Bloom has no real home to which to return. There is, to be sure, shabby-genteel 7 Eccles Street, where he conducts his mundane living of dressing and undressing, eating and sleeping; and there is Bloom Cottage, or perhaps he will prefer to call it St. Leopold's or even Flowerville, the ideal home of which he dreams; but dream and materiality do not coalesce. Homer's Ulysses was prevented from getting home by purely external reasons. Throughout most of Bloom's day he can't go home for very different reasons. Joyce can make the situation yield a rather obvious irony by suggesting that we regard Bloom as a latter-day Ulysses. But, for an audience thoroughly aware of the shocking discrepancy between the Greek hero and the cuckolded canvasser of ads, Joyce can deliver an ironic jolt from the opposite quarter by revealing that the two men do resemble each other after all.

After reading Joyce's *Ulysses,* Eliot predicted that other writers after Joyce would have to adopt this method. Yet it seems clear that Eliot had already made the discovery independently. I have mentioned above "Sweeney among the Nightingales," where Sweeney and Agamemnon share a basic human kinship, though Sweeney is a sort of anti-Agamemnon. The same point, though in a very different tonality, was made by Joyce in the brothel scene in *Ulysses.* There Stephen Dedalus, Dublin-, not Boston-Irish, an artist and aesthete, who does not have an ape neck but one that is in fact surmounted by a head full of Ibsen and Aquinas, is deliberately cut down to a mere anthropoid. Joyce introduces him as "His Eminence, Simon Stephen Cardinal Dedalus, Primate of all Ireland, . . . dressed in a red soutane, sandals and socks" followed by "Seven dwarf simian acolytes, also in red, cardinal sins," who uphold Stephen's train.[28] That is, the emancipated Stephen Dedalus, in his new knowledge, has to confess that he is merely a special sort of vertebrate of the mammalian order, the wisest of the beasts, but a beast nevertheless.

"Sweeney among the Nightingales" was written in 1918, before Joyce had published or even completed the Circe chapter of *Ulysses*. Small wonder that Eliot was prepared to perceive the importance of Joyce's "new" method. He had been moving into it on his own power.

Whatever may be true of modernism in general, Eliot's own sense of the "discontinuities" was clearly important. I think that the most concise and most dramatic way in which to make this point is to examine Eliot's criticism of Matthew Arnold's program for culture and the arts. This procedure is worth undertaking for an additional reason: since many people have tended to see Eliot as the Arnold of our own epoch, they have sometimes been surprised at the sharpness of some of his thrusts at the great Victorian proconsul of culture. Yet in the light of what has been said earlier in this essay, I think it is easy to see why his criticism of Arnold is harsh.

Arnold in his own day, like Eliot in his, was thoroughly aware of the effect of science on culture and of its specific impact on religion and art, and he adopted his own solution of the problem presented. But neither Arnold's analysis of the situation nor the program that he urged could satisfy Eliot. In brief, Arnold envisaged an arrangement in which science would henceforth serve as technician-in-chief to civilization. It would supply far more powerful and effective means by which man's wants could be supplied. But what of the realm of value? In Arnold's estimate, the findings of science had rendered religion obsolete. If so, where could one now turn for values—for a definition of the ends that men should seek? Though religion (and Arnold was thinking particularly of Christianity) could no longer be believed, Arnold apparently felt no disposition to go beyond its value system. As Eliot puts it in his 1930 essay on "Arnold and Pater," Arnold's writings amount to an affirmation "that the emotions of Christianity can and must be preserved without the belief. . . . The effect of Arnold's religious campaign [thus was] to divorce Religion from thought." [29] Though Eliot does not call this separation of religion from thought a "dissociation of sensibility," clearly it is another aspect of such a dissociation.

In Eliot's view, Arnold was essentially a moralist; and religion, having been cut loose from thought, becomes for Arnold "morality touched by emotion." Walter Pater, on the other hand, was essentially an artist, and the appeal religion held for him was essentially aesthetic. But these two stances are responses to the same split down the middle of the culture. Thus, Eliot remarks that Pater continued the "degradation of philosophy and religion [which had been] skilfully initiated by Arnold." [30]

Eliot then provides a sort of summary of what he evidently regards as the wrong kind of discontinuity and of some of the abortive attempts to reinstate a superficial continuity. In the last paragraph of the essay Eliot tells us that

the dissolution of thought in [the nineteenth century], the isolation of art, philosophy, religion, ethics, and literature, [was] interrupted by various chimerical attempts to effect imperfect syntheses. Religion became morals, religion became art, religion became science or philosophy; various blundering attempts were made at alliances between various branches of thought. Each half-prophet believed that he had the whole truth.[31]

But, Eliot argues, these "alliances were as detrimental all round as the separations." That is, if I may interject my own comment at this point, because the fundamental split in Western culture was not fully understood, certain necessary distinctions were ignored, and so religion became art—that is, was reduced to art—morality proceeded to devour religion, and so on.

Eliot's insistence on what he regarded as the needful discontinuities is put forthrightly in his chapter on Arnold in *The Use of Poetry*, published three years after the essay from which I have been quoting. There Eliot asserts

that nothing in this world or the next is a substitute for anything else; and if you find that you must do without something, such as religious faith or philosophic belief, then you must just do without it.

I can persuade myself, I find, that some of the things that I can hope to get are better worth having than some of the things I cannot get; or I may hope to alter myself so as to want different things; but I cannot persuade myself that it is the same desires that are satisfied, or that I have in effect the same thing under a different name.[32]

Eliot cites the comment by a friend of York Powell's to the effect that Powell was just as serene in his loss of faith as the mystic is in his firm belief, and adds: "You could not say that of Arnold; his charm and his interest are largely due to the paniful position that he occupied between faith and disbelief." [33]

This is surely the charm of Arnold's characteristic poetry—the poems in which he expressed his cultural situation—poems like "Dover Beach" and "The Scholar Gypsy." How different such poetry is from Eliot's poetry—though it treats the same basic situation. Eliot's poetry is not gently melancholy, the ruminations of a refined Victorian Stoic. It is dramatic, ironic, and, at times, even approaches the apocalyptic. In Eliot's verse we do not hear the melancholy long withdrawing roar of the ebbing tide, but the thunder of waters pouring over the precipice just ahead. I have in mind here Eliot's sense of the crisis in Western culture—the predominant mood of the fifth section of *The Waste Land*. If, however, we were thinking of the actual human beings described in Eliot's early poetry, the comparison would have to be of a very different kind—to the stagnant, breathless calm of Gerontion's Sargasso Sea, the "sleepy corner" to which this old man has been "driven by the Trades." In short, the people of Eliot's earlier poetry rarely make apocalyptic gestures and almost no outcry. They are too numbed for that.

As for the intimations of the supernatural: instead of Arnold's legendary scholar-gypsy, half glimpsed as he walks over the hills around Oxford, Eliot gives us Baudelaire's specter who in broad daylight reaches out to grasp the passerby—that is, instead of a dream of the past, we have hallucinations bred of the city in its inhuman unreality. The scene is the present, not the past, and in Eliot's early poems, at least, it is urban, not rural; yet the present day for Eliot is never mere surface. It is the product of the past, everywhere proclaiming the past, mocked by the past or else mocking it. In the world of Eliot's poetry, one cannot be fully human unless he sees his present world in the perspective of history. Man lives in the present, but he cannot disavow the past, though he is not in absolute bondage to it and may be able to redeem it.

To sum up: just in proportion as the culture is seen to lack unity, unity is demanded of poetry. The present fact of cultural fragmentation and multiplicity has to be acknowledged and must not be evaded; yet merely to record disunity would be to give in to it. If the disunity comes from the splitting apart of thought and feeling, whether from some failure in philosophy or from the increasing complexity of the human enterprise, in either case authentic poetry must attempt to bring thought and feeling together once more—not that one can expect poetry to heal the break in the culture (Eliot insists that art is not religion or philosophy)—but for the sounder and more honest reason that its own health and wholeness demands that it embody a total state of mind. The protagonist in *The Waste Land* did not shore the fragments of past cultures against his ruins in order to erect a memorial cairn to a dead past or to collect interesting cultural bits and pieces for a museum. The action undertaken was evidently related to his resolution to set his lands in order. For Eliot, poetry was order.

NOTES

1. Yeats also traces the split back as early as Descartes, but he uses a different metaphor to describe what Descartes and his followers did. In "Pages from a Diary in 1930" he writes: "Descartes, Locke, and Newton took away the world and gave us its excrement instead. . . ." Yeats praises Bishop Berkeley for having rescued from this abstract abomination "the world that only exists because it shines and sounds."

2. See his "The Structure of Romantic Nature Imagery," in *The Verbal Icon* (Lexington, Ky., 1954), pp. 103–16, and the chapter on "Imagination: Wordsworth and Coleridge," in *Literary Criticism: A Short History* (New York, 1957), pp. 384–409.

3. In *To Criticize the Critic* (London, 1965), p. 126.

4. Ibid.

5. "The Metaphysical Poets," in *Selected Essays, 1917–1932* (New York, 1932), p. 249.

6. If these comments seem extravagant, the reader might try reading the prevailing criticism of the Romantics from, say, 1880 to 1920.

7. *Selected Essays,* p. 248.

8. "Hamlet," in *Selected Essays,* pp. 124–25.

9. *The Poetical Works of William Wordsworth,* ed. E. de Selincourt, 2d ed., 5 vols. (Oxford, 1952), II, 400–01.

10. "The Metaphysical Poets," p. 248.

11. (New York, 1970), pp. 18–20.

12. "The Metaphysical Poets," p. 248.

13. "Andrew Marvell," in *Selected Essays,* p. 252.

14. Eliot regards this power as "a quality of a civilization, of a traditional habit of life." Marvell's best verse, he writes, "is the product of European, that is to say Latin, culture" (ibid., pp. 251–52). It was the quality of culture that later intellectual events of the century were to disturb and partially destroy.

15. "The real novelty in Romantic poetry is not its diction but its structure. If the Romantic poets, after rejecting Pope and Dryden, did not rediscover Donne and the metaphysical poets, this was because the latter, no less than the former, organized their poems logically" (W. H. Auden and N. H. Pearson, eds., *Poets of the English Language,* 5 vols. [New York, 1950], IV, xviii).

16. *Poetical Works,* II, 30.

17. See p. 361 above and also Wimsatt's discussion of this issue in "Romantic Nature Imagery," p. 110.

18. I have commented on this and other such poems by Wordsworth at some length in *A Shaping Joy* (New York, 1972), pp. 55–57.

19. "The Metaphysical Poets," pp. 248–49.

20. Wimsatt, *The Verbal Icon,* p. 128. Wimsatt has in another essay put it thus: "Metaphor is the holding together of differences" ("Poetic Tension: A Summary," *New Scholasticism,* 32 [January 1958], 82).

21. P. 116.

22. One of Wimsatt's most interesting studies of Eliot is that entitled *"Prufrock and Maud:* From Plot to Symbol," in *Hateful Contraries* (Lexington, Ky., 1965). In this essay Wimsatt is concerned principally with parallels of theme, mood, and imagery between Tennyson's monodrama and "The Love Song of J. Alfred Prufrock," which is also a kind of monodrama. Yet though Wimsatt's stress is not on organization as such, he makes it abundantly clear that the organization of "Prufrock" is in essentials that of Tennyson's poem. In this, then, as in other ways, Prufrock is a poem that "typifies the symbolist and postsymbolist era in poetry" (p. 212). We shall argue in the pages that follow that even Eliot's "metaphysical" poems in ironic quatrains are also essentially postsymbolist in structure.

23. In T. S. Eliot, *The Complete Poems and Plays* (New York, 1952), pp. 32–33, ll. 1–16. All poems by Eliot quoted here are from this edition.

24. "The Metaphysical Poets," p. 246.

25. Wimsatt, "Romantic Nature Imagery," p. 110.

26. *Ambasis* (New York, 1938), p. 8.

27. "Ulysses, Order, and Myth," *Dial* (November 1923), reprinted in *James Joyce: Two Decades of Criticism,* ed. Sean Givens (New York, 1948), p. 201.

28. Corrected and reset edition (New York, 1961), pp. 523–24.

29. In *Selected Essays,* p. 349.

30. Ibid., p. 352.

31. Ibid., pp. 356–57.

32. (Cambridge, Mass., 1933), p. 106.

33. Ibid.

Some Post-Symbolist Structures

HUGH KENNER

Part of the discovery of Language that was going on in the early nineteenth century was the discovery of Anglo-Saxon, which fascinated the young Lewis Carroll by being not-quite-English. People were exclaiming over the "epic" qualities of *The Battle of Brunanburh* as though it were a fragment of the *Iliad,* and citing, in that Romantic-vernacular heyday, bits from which you could extract a kind of sense without knowing except in the most general way what any of the words might denote. Lewis Carroll's imitation of this effect is better known than any of the Anglo-Saxon models he had in mind—

> And, as in uffish thought he stood,
>   The Jabberwock, with eyes of flame,
> Came whiffling through the tulgey wood,
>   And burbled as it came!

"Somehow it seems to fill my head with ideas," said Alice, "— only I don't exactly know what they are!" This gets cited in books on linguistics nowadays, with careful demonstrations of how much we can actually know without knowing the words.

The Romantic enthusiasts had discovered how thoroughly reader and writer can rely on the structural pattern of English. "Structure," so understood, corresponds to a higher level of generalization than "grammar" and "syntax." It is thanks to our understanding of structural patterns that we can enjoy a feeling of inwardness with such an utterance as "All mimsy were the borogoves," connecting the verb-form "were" with the -s termination on "borogoves," divining (how?) an inverted construction, assigning adverbial rather than adjectival force to "all," and concluding, faster than thought, that the borogoves, whatever they may be, are in a state of total mimsiness of which we can form no idea.

To state in detail and in order of application the exceedingly intricate rules by which we make structural sense of any utterance that may confront us has been the work of a generation of linguists, the most recent of whom are suggesting that the job is barely begun. Though this work has nearly all been done in the twentieth century its field of operation was discovered in the nineteenth, and largely by poets confronting the baffling fact, much later formulated by Eliot, that poetry can communicate before it is understood. Elizabeth Sewell in her pioneering work *The Field of Nonsense* has pointed to the analogy between the work of Mallarmé in France and the work of the English nonsense-writers Lear and Carroll. Nonsense-verse builds intelligible structures without intelligible words; thus Lear discovered you could create Coleridgean or Tennysonian effects with a minimum of reliance on words that are in the dictionary—

> . . . over the stark Grumboolian plain.

And Tennyson, as though returning the compliment, dedicated to Edward Lear a poem whose first five lines feature three adjectives and two nouns of which hardly anyone is likely to know the exact significance:

> Illyrian woodlands, echoing falls
>   Of water, sheets of summer glass,
>   The long divine Peneïan pass,
> The vast Akrokeraunian walls,
>
> Tomohrit, Athos, all things fair . . .

This is very likely the only appearance anywhere of the word *Akrokeraunian;* one understands that these are very splendid and ancient walls without examining that word's credentials. Tennyson seems to have remembered *infames scopulos Acroceraunia* from Horace (i.iii.20) and inserted his pseudo-kappas to point up the derivation from Greek words meaning high-thundering. We are no doubt to imagine the sheer sides of mountains from which thunderbolts are hurled, and Acroceraunia, for that matter, is the Latin name of a rocky promontory in Epirus. Yet, prompted as we are to think of walls, not of mountains, we feel curiously little need of such information. Akrokeraunian walls rise, it may be, from a Grumboolian plain, in a landscape made wholly of linguistic structures, and once this possibility was under control poetry could never be the same. By 1853, the date of Tennyson's poem, acute eyes might have sighted on the furthest horizon, slouching toward Dublin to be born, the rough beast *Finnegans Wake*.

If we look at Tennyson's line more carefully we discover that the structural and the rhetorical principles can be separated. Our sense of linguistic structures can establish with perfect exactness the relationship between words; thus anyone reasonably familiar with English knows at once that *Akrokeraunian* is an adjective: that it denotes some quality of those walls. We are drawing on a different order of knowledge when we divine from its formidable length and sound that the quality it denotes has to do with exotic impressiveness, and we are really doing more than the poem asks us to do when we poke into its etymology, assign it a meaning, and find that its meaning turns the meaning of *walls* into a metaphor for cliffs. From the structural point of view, *Akrokeraunian* is a six-syllable phenomenon that comes between *vast* and *walls* and has the same kind of syntactic function that *vast* has. It is clear that Tennyson could have drafted the line with a blank in it, to be filled up later by six appropriate syllables, and seeing the line in his work-sheet with that blank in it we should know at once that the missing six syllables would constitute one or more adjectives. In fact a prose draft of the whole poem is quite conceivable, a floor-plan of its syntax, with blanks where all the interesting words were to be installed. The plan would be of no interest whatever; it would run,

[A lot of things] you describe so well I felt I was there; and as I read I felt I was in the golden age; and for me [a lot of exotic images] seemed realities.

This is the substance of Tennyson's compliment to Lear; we can probably agree that it is as banal as that of a thank-you note, and

that the handsomeness of the compliment will depend on his success with the parts in square brackets. Such a draft, in fact, is so
trivial we may feel fairly sure Tennyson never wrote one, but
rather devised his clots of gorgeous words and then cobbled together the connective matter in the middle. This is no more than
most of us would expect. We have been taught to ask scornfully
what poetry may have to do with prose drafts, and are unsurprised
when paraphrase, which is like an attempt to recover a prose
original, yields little of interest.

But not always. At Westminster School, late in the sixteenth
century, the young Ben Jonson acquired from his famous master
William Camden a precept he never forgot, that before writing
verse he should work out his sense in prose, and knowing this we
may often be astonished at how little alteration the prose draft
seems to have undergone in the course of being transmuted.
When he makes the stone speak to passersby over the grave of the
lady named Elizabeth, what it has to say defies paraphrase because
it is already identical in structure and diction with any paraphrase we might venture to make:

> Would'st thou heare, what man can say
> In a little? Reader, stay.
> Under-neath this stone doth lye
> As much beautie, as could dye:
> Which in life did harbour give
> To more vertue, than doth live.
> If, at all, shee had a fault,
> Leave it buryed in this vault.
> One name was Elizabeth,
> Th'other let it sleepe with death:
> Fitter, where it dyed, to tell,
> Than that it liv'd at all. Farewell.

The stone has three statements to make about Elizabeth, three
ceremonious sentences, the middle one short. Before entering on
these statements it asks if we want to hear them, and bids us pause
if so. At the end it bids us, in one word, Farewell. That is all;
and in working out the structure of those three central sentences
Jonson worked out his poem also. This defeats the Romantic dis-

tinctions between prose and verse; it becomes verse only in becoming decorously neat, and in being neat and quiet it imitates
the qualities of the neat quiet lady whose virtue is reticence now
as it was when she lived.

> Would'st thou heare, what man can say
> In a little?

means both, observe the virtues of this poem, small as this stone,
and still more, be instructed in the qualities of this lady, whose
life was a statement here completed by death, a statement the
poem rephrases.

We can scarcely think about this poem except syntactically, nor
is it easy to imagine Jonson thinking his way into it, while it was
unwritten, by any but a syntactic route. Neither are the words
bright jewels to justify the structures, nor are the structures, as
they were for Tennyson, an unobtrusive mounting for the words.
We may find it profitable to adduce another pre-Romantic poem
for which no one would claim decorous neatness, yet for which,
as much as for Jonson, the structures that hold the words in relation are exactly as indispensable as the words they hold. That
great baroque structure the opening sentence of *Paradise Lost* is
grown from a kernel sentence Milton seems to have imitated from
the beginning of the *Iliad. Menin aiede thea,* Homer commences,
"Wrath sing, goddess . . . ," and Homer goes on to explain what
he means by the wrath of Achilles and the mischief it did. "Disobedience sing, Muse," commences Milton, placing the key words
in the same order as Homer's but appending his explanations
directly to the words they amplify. Having specified "Man's first
disobedience" he elaborates on it at once, summarizing the whole
drama of loss and redemption in a circular structure which begins
with "the fruit of that forbidden tree" and ends ("one greater
man" having negated the disobedient man) with "regain that
blissful seat," thirty-eight words occupying in the sentence the
place of one word in Homer. Then comes, just where it comes in
Homer, the imperative "sing"; then, as in Homer, the vocative,
"Heavenly Muse," which he proceeds to elaborate just as he had
elaborated the word "disobedience," by way of establishing to

what Muse a Christian poet may address himself. The verb stands unadorned in the middle, "sing"; the words before it and after it, "disobedience" and "Muse," receive parallel amplification.

Whether from the custom of diagramming sentences in classrooms or from the writings of Noam Chomsky, we are all familiar with the notion of a long sentence elaborated from a kernel sentence, and with the principle that there is no other way to arrive at syntactic English. We may be less familiar with the fact that the kernel sentence, after it has generated the elaborate sentence, may or may not prove to be of any rhetorical salience. For Milton the kernel sentence is clearly salient. As he elaborates, he releases the latent energies of his predicate and his subject, showing us all that may be implicit, since Adam, in *disobedience,* all that may be implicit, since the Holy Spirit revealed himself, in *Muse:* two words which, he allows us to feel, are expanding across his page their own inherent orderly energies. The kernel sentence does not simply permit all this, it contains all this, and if, as we read on in *Paradise Lost,* we chance to forget those majestic elaborations, it will remain true that the Muse singing of disobedience comprises the poem's business.

But this is not an invariable practice; in particular, it is not Symbolist practice. In the minor Tennyson poem we have looked at, the kernel sentence, far from mapping the poem's business, reduces to nothing but "I felt . . . and I felt . . . ," the merest excuse for the rest of the poem to assemble its sonorities and exoticisms. And we may say that Tennyson was working toward a new poetic which he never succeeded in formulating, and that it got formulated instead in France. About ten years after Tennyson's homage to Lear, we find the very young Stéphane Mallarmé composing in ten Alexandrine couplets a poem called "Soupir," a single long sinuous sentence whose subject and verb are not huddled inconspicuously away, but so disposed as to command a maximum of evocative detail. Its kernel sentence appears to be "Mon âme monte vers l'Azur," my soul mounts toward the azure, the azure of the infinite pale sky being already for Mallarmé, it would seem, an ultimate and a word of great power.

Arthur Symons's translation is faithful to the features we are interested in:

Sigh

My soul, calm sister, towards thy brow, whereon scarce grieves
An autumn strewn already with its russet leaves,
And towards the wandering sky of thine angelic eyes,
Mounts, as in melancholy gardens may arise
Some faithful fountain sighing whitely towards the blue!
—Towards the pale blue and pure that sad October knew,
When, in those depths, it mirrored languors infinite,
And agonizing leaves upon the waters white,
Windily drifting, traced a furrow cold and dun,
Where, in one long last ray, lingered the yellow sun.

This is a subtle piece of syntactic engineering. Symons remarks that "a delicate emotion, a figure vaguely defined, a landscape magically evoked, blend in a single effect." So they do; they are present like overlayered transparencies, not sorted out as the first sentence of *Paradise Lost* sorts things out. But Mallarmé does not huddle these elements together and allow us to associate them; he makes use of the remarkable sentence he is constructing, a sentence the progress of which uncoils like a plot. "My soul," he commences, both beginning the poem and giving the sentence its subject; then "towards," so that we know we are to expect a verb of motion, and for three lines the poem relies on that expectation to assimilate details we would not have expected:

My soul, calm sister, towards thy brow, whereon scarce grieves
An autumn strewn already with its russet leaves,
And towards the wandering sky of thine angelic eyes,
Mounts . . .

Already we have the woman and the landscape, and the qualities felt in the woman have given rise to the landscape. We also have, it would seem, a sentence completed. And yet two-thirds of the poem is still to be produced, and produced not by tacking more things on but by generating a new syntactic necessity. He does this economically, in plain sight, with such assurance we hardly see it done, and are apt to wonder where the rest of the poem came from. Yet if we watch closely it is easy to see what he does: he effects a mutation in the kernel sentence.

We have said that the kernel sentence seems to be, "My soul mounts towards the azure." This is not strictly true. The kernel sentence is complete in the opening lines, before the azure has been mentioned. It is, "My soul mounts toward your brow and toward the sky of your eyes." That mention of "sky" prepares for the mutation; the mutation itself occurs immediately after the verb. For the line that begins with the poem's main verb goes on,

> Mounts, as in melancholy gardens may arise
> Some faithful fountain sighing whitely towards the blue!

—all very orderly, an adverbial clause telling how the soul mounts and comparing its aspiration to a fountain's. The fountain mounts toward the sky but never gets there: its energy goes into striving. But instead of leaving us with this trim analogy, Mallarmé commences a new line by reduplicating the phrase with which the last line ended: "—Towards the blue pale and pure that sad October knew . . . ," and since we cannot help connecting the energy of *towards* with *mounts,* we connect, without noticing, the subject of *mounts* and that aspiration toward blueness. And there is the soul, mounting toward the azure sky, the kernel sentence mutated by a fountain's intervention. This works because each of its key elements, *My soul, mounts, towards the blue,* occupies a rhetorical strong point where a line commences, while the previous constructions in "towards" have expended themselves in less prominent niches. And with the soul mounting toward the azure and the fountain playing, he can allow the rest of the poem to concern itself with the still water in the fountain's basin:

> —Towards the blue pale and pure that sad October knew,
> When, in those depths, it mirrored languors infinite,
> And agonizing leaves upon the waters white,
> Windily drifting, traced a furrow cold and dun,
> Where, in one long last ray, lingered the yellow sun.

Since *it* may refer to the blue or to October, there is some blurring of the relative pronoun, less evident in Symons's translation than in the French, where it governs not one verb but two. It appears to be a calculated blurring; Mallarmé shows every sign of interest in the sentence he is putting together, and of awareness that such linguistic chemistries as he aspires to need shaped vessels to contain them. His syntactic arrangements, unlike Tennyson's, are like the interconnected glass vessels on a laboratory bench, of virtually sculptural interest in themselves, yet functional and everywhere transparent, to let us watch the colors change within them. Yet they are unlike Milton's too, not to mention Jonson's, in being strangely devoid of independent interest. Confronted by "My soul mounts toward your brow and toward the sky of your eyes," we may legitimately ask what it may mean. Unlike Tennyson's kernel sentence, it contains words vital to the poem's chemistry as well as to its syntactic legitimacy. Yet it is already sufficiently a piece of opportunism to be saying, in itself, nothing very forceful: nothing of the order of "Disobedience sing, Muse."

We have seen that Mallarmé's formal kernel sentence is supplanted by a mutant version composed of words that open lines. Many of his poems exploit that order of nearly geometrical coherence. He will make of the first and the last words of a poem a thematic phrase which the intervening words fill in like a chord. His most famous sonnet begins "Le vierge . . ." and ends ". . . Cygne": "the virgin swan." His *Toast Funèbre* to the memory of Gautier is enclosed within the words "O . . . nuit": "O night." His memorial sonnet to Edgar Allan Poe not only announces in its first line that eternity will change Poe's mere self into what he was meant to be, but has for its first word "tel" and its last "futur." The Poe sonnet moreover is made of Poe-words, dark Gothicisms, sortilege and hydra and a black flood and a tomb and blasphemy; it does not fail to capitalize *Poète* in its second line to anticipate the *Poe* of its twelfth; it manages to resonate with basement metaphysics like *Eureka* itself; and amid its controlled semi-penetrabilities three isolated strong lines like bars of steel assert the aphoristic weight of the French Alexandrine. These may be the most important facts about the sonnet, and all of them except the presence of the three strong lines may be gathered by a scanning eye that does not actually *read* it. So far are we on the way toward *la poésie concrète,* and Mallarmé as we know from his last work was to carry that possibility still further, and dispose clusters of words in pure spatial contingency on a page otherwise white.

Such instances may help us describe Mallarmé's syntactic structures: they are ways, among other ways, of governing the exact relationship of the poem's elements, and all his ways, including his syntactic ones, have something of the geometer's economy about them. This is in part because the French language contains more syntactic orthodoxies than does the English. When the French writer does something so simple as place the adjective before the noun instead of after, he can anticipate a seismic dislocation in the sensibility of the French reader.

English usage being less rigid, the poet who attempts comparable effects in English must go to greater extremes. In 1896, after some years of hearing from Symons and others about what was going on in France, W. B. Yeats attempted some syntactic legerdemain of his own: a twenty-four-line poem that consists of one sentence, and like so many poems of Mallarmé's proceeds by systematic digression from its formal structure. Indeed the importance of the kernel sentence is vanishingly small. It is simply "I press my heart . . . and I hear. . . ." And so little are we likely to ask what it means, that we are even unlikely to notice it, amid Yeats's exploitation of the pliancy of English subordinate structures.

He Remembers Forgotten Beauty

When my arms wrap you round I press
My heart upon the loveliness
That has long faded from the world;
The jewelled crowns that kings have hurled
In shadowy pools, when armies fled;
The love-tales wrought with silken thread
By dreaming ladies upon cloth
That has made fat the murderous moth;
The roses that of old time were

Woven by ladies in their hair,
The dew-cold lilies ladies bore
Through many a sacred corridor
Where such grey clouds of incense rose
That only God's eyes did not close:
For that pale breast and lingering hand
Come from a more dream-heavy land,
A more dream-heavy hour than this;
And when you sigh from kiss to kiss
I hear white Beauty sighing, too,
For hours when all must fade like dew,
But flame on flame, and deep on deep,
Throne over throne, where in half sleep,
Their swords upon their iron knees,
Brood her high lonely mysteries.

Are we prepared to say without hesitation where those flames come from, and those swords and those thrones? Their ring is Miltonic (pre-Raphaelite Miltonic), but we are far from Milton, whose effort in his long sentences is to keep clear whereabouts we are from moment to moment as the sentence works itself out. Yeats's effort is nearly the opposite, as we can tell from the way he revised this ending. The version he published in 1896 heard white Beauty sighing, too

For hours when all must fade like dew
Till there be naught but throne on throne
Of seraphs, brooding each alone,
A sword upon his iron knees,
On her most lonely mysteries.

This is clear enough, at least in structure: Beauty sighs for those hours when everything will fade except the seraphs who brood on Beauty's mysteries. "Till there be naught but . . . ," runs the governing structure: we cannot mistake it. But he seems to have disliked a structure we could not mistake, and three years later the ending was revised to run as it now does in the definitive edition:

I hear white Beauty sighing, too,
For hours when all must fade like dew
But flame on flame, and deep on deep,

> Throne over throne where in half sleep,
> Their swords upon their iron knees,
> Brood her high lonely mysteries.

This not only substitutes "high lonely mysteries" for "seraphs," it makes everything turn on an "all but" construction which we are almost certain not to notice. The phrase "when all must fade like dew" has such a ring of completeness that only by nearly scholastic effort, and with a printed text to pore over, can we force the "But" that opens the next line to give up its air of magisterial disjunction and link itself with "all."

Yeats is willing to dissolve one strong effect into another, leaving us with no clear idea how they are supposed to be related, though structural relations are specified in the text if we choose to undertake the work of recovering them. Thus we can determine that eleven successive lines develop from four nouns (*crowns, tales, roses, lilies*) that are all in apposition to the noun *loveliness;* that three lines about the pale breast and the lingering hand return us to a person we had quite forgotten, the *you* of the poem's opening; and that a new kernel sentence in parallel with the first one, *when you sigh I hear . . .* , paralleling *when my arms wrap you round I press . . .* , presides over the second lobe of the poem. Yet the way these kernel sentences preside is curiously oblique. Each serves to introduce an abstract noun, the first one *loveliness* and the second one *Beauty,* which nouns are the real seeds from which the enchanted thickets grow. And these nouns are not the objects of the main verbs in the kernel sentences, but abstractions produced within subordinate clauses which those verbs have produced. The effect is to move our attention as far as may be from the thrust of subject–verb–object. The structure is formal, elaborate, symmetrical, and syntactically faultless; and yet only by a very great effort of attention is the reader likely to discover what it is.

Tennyson's structures, which are equally unassertive, turn out when we disengage them to be informal, asymmetrical, and unimportant. They enable him, while he deploys his sumptuousness of diction, to fulfill the schoolmarm's requirement that the sentence shall parse, and they tend to comprise its least effectual words.

The Yeatsian structure, though elaboration encumbers and conceals it, has been an object of the poet's careful attention, and though it may never chance to attract our notice its presence does matter, and not merely to the schoolmarm in us. Its presence underwrites the feel of ceremony and formality Yeats's poems of the 1890s characteristically yield. Those were the years when Yeats was being a Symbolist, meeting people familiar with what was going on in Paris, listening during the year he roomed with Symons while Symons talked out the still-unwritten *Symbolist Movement in Literature,* or expounded the translations he was then making, which Yeats called "the most accomplished metrical translations of our time," adding that the ones from Mallarmé "may have given elaborate form to my verses of those years, to the latter poems of *The Wind Among the Reeds,* to *The Shadowy Waters.*" In 1937, looking again at Mallarmé in a translation, Roger Fry's this time, he called that way of working "the road I and others of my time went for certain furlongs. It is not the way I go now, but one of the legitimate roads."

Yeats did not abandon the intricate long sentence; each stanza of *Byzantium* is one sentence, each stanza of *Coole Park, 1929,* each stanza of *Ancestral Houses,* each but three of the twelve stanzas *In Memory of Major Robert Gregory.* What he abandoned was the Mallarméan way of proceeding by digressions from the sentence's main business. By transposing this particular method into English, and discovering its possibilities and limitations, he may have saved other poets time. Other poets, certainly, whose later work is quite unlike Yeats's later work because they did not adopt Yeats's final attitude to syntax, display in their early as well as their later work a debt to Symbolist syntax which is less than obvious if only because Yeats had already explored the obvious.

Thus instead of progress by digressions we encounter progress by ellipses. In Mallarmé's "Soupir," we may remember, Arthur Symons discovered a delicate emotion, a figure vaguely divined, a landscape magically evoked, three things that would seem not to be related but are blended into a single effect. The trick of the blending was to make the elements digress from a kernel sentence which holds them firmly in relation to one another and allows the reader's mind to overlay them. But if they can be held firmly by some other means, the kernel sentence may simply be omitted.

One way of holding them, giving each element in the poem its identity and still persuading the mind that they relate, is by metrical definition, as in Ezra Pound's 1912 poem "The Return," in which a strong metrical figure—

> Góds ŏf thĕ wíngèd shóe!
> Wíth thĕm thĕ sílvĕr hóunds,
>   sníffĭng thĕ tráce ŏf aír

—dominates the part characterized by verbs in the past tense, enforcing the contrast between the emphatic way the gods once *were,* and

>   the tentative
> Movements, and the slow feet,
> The trouble in the pace and the uncertain
> Wavering

that expresses their unstable way of returning *now.* The poem encompasses a long historical span, from Sappho's time, say, to H. D.'s, but no kernel sentence makes a statement to that effect. The sentences of which the poem is made are very simple: "See, they return"; "These were the souls of blood"; while no syntax specifies the coherence of the poem as a whole. We may feel that a statement of some length has been made but that important syntactic members of this statement have dropped out. And yet nothing has dropped out; we have, thanks to the rhythmic definition, every necessary element, held in place in the poem's continuum so exactly that alterations of tense will specify everything.

Or we encounter progress by incantation, as in Eliot's "Marina." Some parts of "Marina" can be treated as sentences and some parts cannot; nor can "Marina" as a whole be treated as though it were a long statement, even a statement of which parts are missing. Its organization is not syntactic at all. One probably wants to call it "musical," based on associations and recurrences, among them the Shakespearean associations aroused by the title. It is as far as Eliot ever went in that particular direction, but the direction is implicit in most of his work, and confirmed as well by work of Valéry's: the poem faced toward a domain of waking dream, so certain of its diction that we concede it a coherence it need not find means of specifying. It has no paraphrasable structure at all, and yet seems to affirm its elusive substance as authoritatively as Mozart.

Eliot admired Tennyson when Tennyson was out of fashion, and now that Eliot too is out of fashion it is pertinent to recall his great indebtedness to Symons's *Symbolist Movement in Literature*. Everyone remembers how he discovered Laforgue in that book; we tend to forget how quickly he dropped Laforgue, and also tend not to notice how tenaciously he developed hints from Mallarmé, of whom he and Valéry are the principal heirs. I think Donald Davie has been alone in insisting that Eliot's sensibility is post-Symbolist. Yet surely he imitated the unseen eye-beam that falls in *Burnt Norton* on flowers that seem looked at, from "le regard diaphane" which in *Toast Funèbre* rests on unfading because verbal flowers; surely the intent insistence on a silence into which "words, after speech, reach" (for "that which is only living / Can only die") reflects Mallarmé's best-known preoccupation. *Burnt Norton,* by intention a counter-poem to *The Waste Land,* is also a sustained homage to Mallarmé, the austere codifier of its difficult art. The art is in touch with Tennyson's as well, and with Edward Lear's. The inventory of its structures remains to be made, so long, ironically, despite all Eliot's warnings, was criticism preoccupied with his "ideas." What Mallarmé wrote darkly of Poe, that the dipsomaniac who went by that name would be transformed by the operations of Eternity not into some myth but precisely into himself, we may see exemplified, more convincingly than in Poe's case, when Eliot is sufficiently forgotten to be rediscovered. His work may then seem a compendium of examples for such a survey of post-Symbolist structures as this paper has hinted at.

Wallace Stevens and the Variation Form

NORTHROP FRYE

We cannot read far in Wallace Stevens's poetry without finding examples of a form that reminds us of the variation form in music, in which a theme is presented in a sequence of analogous but differing settings. Thus in "Sea Surface Full of Clouds" the same type of stanza is repeated five times, each with just enough variation to indicate that the same landscape is being seen through five different emotional moods. Another type of variation form appears in "Thirteen Ways of Looking at a Blackbird," where a series of thirteen little imagist poems are related by the common theme of the blackbird, and which, to pursue the musical analogy perhaps further than it will go, gives more the effect of a chaconne or passacaglia. Sometimes the explicit theme is missing and only the variations appear, as in "Like Decorations in a Nigger Cemetery."

We notice also that in the titles of Stevens's poems the image of variation frequently turns up, either literally, as in "Variations on a Summer Day," or metaphorically, as in "Nuances of a Theme by Williams," "Analysis of a Theme," and, perhaps, "Repetitions of a Young Captain." "The Man with the Blue Guitar" also gives us a strong sense of reading through a set of thirty-three variations, or related imaginative presentations, of a single theme. Then again, the long meditative theoretical poems written in a blank tercet form, "Notes toward a Supreme Fiction," "The Auroras of Autumn," "An Ordinary Evening in New Haven," "The Pure Good of Theory," are all divided into sections of the same length. "An Ordinary Evening" has thirty-one sections of six tercets each; the "Supreme Fiction," three parts of ten sections each, thirty sections in all, each of seven tercets; and similarly with the others. This curious formal symmetry, which cannot be an accident, also reminds us of the classical variation form in which each variation has the same periodic structure and harmonic sequence. Even the numbers that often turn up remind us of the thirty Goldberg variations, the thirty-three Diabelli waltz variations, and so on.

The variation form in Stevens is a generic application of the principle that every image in a poem is a variation of the theme or subject of that poem. This principle is the first of three "effects of analogy" mentioned in Stevens's essay of that title. There are two other "effects." One is that "every image is a restatement of the subject of the image in the terms of an attitude" (NA, 128).[1] This is practically the same thing as Eliot's objective correlative, and is illustrated in "Sea Surface Full of Clouds," where five different moods are unified by the fact that they all have the same correlative. Stevens also says, "In order to avoid abstractness, in writing, I search out instinctively things that express the abstract and yet are not in themselves abstractions" (L, 290). His example is the statue in "Owl's Clover," which he also calls a "variable" symbol (L, 311). The implication is that such images are variations on the idea of the poem which is within the poem of words, the true as distinct from the nominal subject or theme (OP, 223). We note that the correlative in Stevens may pair with a concept as well as with an emotion, which helps to explain why his commentaries on his own poems in the letters are so often woodenly allegorical.

The third "effect of analogy" is that "every image is an intervention on the part of the image-maker" (NA, 128). This principle takes us deep into Stevens's central notion of poetry as the result of a struggle, or balance, or compromise, or tension, between the two forces that he calls imagination and reality. We notice that in the musical theme with variations, the theme is frequently a composition by someone else or comes from a different musical context. Similarly the poet works with imagination, which is what he has, and reality, which is given him. So, from Stevens's point of view, poems could be described as the variations that imagination makes on the theme of reality. In "Sea Surface Full of Clouds" a question is asked in each variation about who or what created the picture in front of us, and the answer, given each time in French, defines a distinctive mood of the imagination.

In a letter Stevens says, "Sometimes I believe most in the imagination for a long time, and then, without reasoning about it, turn to reality and believe in that and that alone. But both of these things project themselves endlessly and I want them to do just that" (L, 710). This somewhat helpless remark indicates the strength of the sense of polarity in his poetic world. Stevens often speaks of the intense pressure that the sense of external reality exerts on the modern mind. One of the "Adagia" says, "In the presence of extraordinary actuality, consciousness takes the place of imagination" (OP, 165). Consciousness, by itself, is simple awareness of the external world. It sees; it may even select what it sees, but it does not fight back. The consciousness fighting back, with a subjective violence corresponding to the objective violence of external pressure (cf. NA, 36), is the consciousness rising to imagination.

The imagination confronts a reality which reflects itself but is not itself. If it is weak, it may either surrender to reality or run away from it. If it surrenders, we have what is usually called realism, which, as Stevens often makes clear, is almost the opposite of what he means by reality. He says, for instance, in connection with the painting of Jack Yeats, that "the purely realistic mind never experiences any passion for reality" (L, 597). This maxim would also apply to the "social realism" demanded in Marxist countries, for which Stevens never expresses anything but contempt. The imagination that runs away retreats from the genuinely imaginative world into a merely imaginary one, for, Stevens says, "If poetry is limited to the vaticinations of the imagination, it soon becomes worthless" (L, 500). Certain recurring symbols in Stevens represent the kind of facile pseudoconquest of reality which the imagination pretends to make whenever reality is not there: one of them is the moon. Such imaginary triumphs take place in a self-contained world of words which is one of the things that Stevens means by false rhetoric, or "Rodomontade" (NA, 61).

The world of false rhetoric is a world where the imagination encounters no resistance from anything material, where the loneliness and alienation of the mind, about which Stevens speaks so eloquently, has consoled itself with pure solipsism.

Stevens says that it is a fundamental principle about the imagination that "it does not create except as it transforms" (*L*, 364). It is the function of reality to set free the imagination and not to inhibit it. Reality is at its most inhibiting when it is most externalized, as it is in our own time. In "Two or Three Ideas" Stevens speaks of the way in which the pressure of externality today has created a culture of what he calls "detached styles," and which he characterizes as "the unsuccessful, the ineffective, the arbitrary, the literary, the non-umbilical, that which in its highest degree would still be words" (*OP*, 212). In one prophetic flash, which sums up the essence of the world we have been living through for the past few years, he speaks of this world of false imagination as the product of "irrationality provoked by prayer, whiskey, fasting, opium, or the hope of publicity" (*OP*, 218). It follows that Stevens does not accept the mystique of the unconscious and has nothing of Yeats's or Joyce's feeling for the dreamworld as having a peculiarly close relation to the creative process. He always associates creativity with cognition, with consciousness, even with calculation. "Writing poetry is a conscious activity. While poems may very well occur, they had very much better be caused" (*L*, 274).

Stevens associates his word "reality" with the phrase "things as they are," which implies that for him reality has a close relation to the external physical world as we perceive it. The imagination contemplates "things as they are," seeing its own unreality mirrored in them, and its principle of contemplation Stevens calls resemblance or analogy. He also calls it, quite logically, "Narcissism" (*NA*, 80). This word points to the danger of uncontrolled imagination and the ease with which it can assume that there is another reality on the other side of things as they are. Traditional religious poetry, for instance, projects heavens and hells as objective and hidden realities, though it can construct them only out of the material of things as they are. Crispin, the hero of one of Stevens's most elaborate variation poems, soon comes to a point at which he can say, "Here was the veritable ding an sich, at last" (*CP*, 29). But this is a Kantian phrase, and Stevens is not Kantian: reality for him is always phenomenal, something that "seems" as well as is (cf. *CP*, 339), and there is no alternative version of it that the poet should be trying to reach. Hidden realities always turn out to be unreal, and therefore simply mirrors of the imagination itself. Similarly, "poetry will always be a phenomenal thing" (*L*, 300).

Stevens's arguments are poetic and not philosophical, and like many poetic arguments they turn on a verbal trick. The trick in this case consists in using the special-pleading term "reality" for the external physical world, which means that conceptions set over against this "reality" have to be called, or associated with, the unreal. Stevens is not unaware of this by any means, but his use of the word "reality," which becomes almost obsessive in the letters, indicates that, like his spiritual sister Emily Dickinson, he has a Puritanic distrust of all self-transcending mental efforts, especially mysticism. More particularly, he feels that, as the poet's language is the language of sense experience and concrete imagery, any poet who bypasses things as they are, however subtly, is dodging the central difficulty of poetry. Such poets, who look for some shortcut or secret passage through reality to something else, and regard poetry as a kind of verbal magic, have what Stevens calls a "marginal" imagination, and he associates this marginal imagination, which explores itself to find its own analogue in reality, with, among others, Valéry, Eliot, and Mallarmé.

Stevens goes even further in suggesting that the conquest of reality made by the reason is also somewhat facile compared to that of the imagination, because it is possible for reason, in some degree, to live in a self-contained world and shut its gates in the face of reality. One of the products of reason is the theological belief in reality as a creation, a product of the infinite imagination of God. Such a belief is repugnant to Stevens: this would mean that reality is analogous to the imagination. The poet is a Jacob who has to wrestle with the necessary angel of reality, and if reality is itself ultimately a "supreme fiction," or something made out of nothing, then all his agonized efforts and struggles are a put-up job, something fixed or rigged, as so many wrestling matches are. Stevens says:

> The arrangement contains the desire of
> The artist. But one confides in what has no
> Concealed creator. One walks easily
>
> The unpainted shore, accepts the world
> As anything but sculpture.
>
> [CP, 296]

So whatever the imagination may do to reality, reality continues to present something residually external, some donkey's carrot pulling us on, something sticking through everything we construct within it. Even in the moment of death (or what appears to be death, on the last page of the *Collected Poems*), we confront something "outside" giving us the sense of "a new knowledge of reality." Or, as Stevens says in prose, "Poetry has to do with reality in that concrete and individual aspect of it which the mind can never tackle altogether on its own terms, with matter that is foreign and alien in a way in which abstract systems, ideas in which we detect an inherent pattern, a structure that belongs to the ideas themselves, can never be" (*OP*, 236). The imagination is driven by a "rage for order" (*CP*, 130), but it works toward, not the complete ordering of existence, but rather a sense of equipoise or balance between itself and what is not itself.

We soon come to understand that for Stevens there are different levels or degrees of reality (*NA*, 7), arranged in a ladder or mountain or winding stair in which the poet has to undertake what he calls an "ascent through illusion" (*NA*, 81). In his essay "A Collect of Philosophy" Stevens attempts to list a few philosophical conceptions which seem to him to be inherently poetic, meaning by that, presumably, conceptions that particularly appeal to him as a poet. Among these, the theme of anabasis or ascent, the theme of Dante, looms up prominently (*OP*, 193). At the bottom of the ladder is the sense of reality as an undifferentiated external world, or what Stevens calls a *Lumpenwelt* (*NA*, 174). Such a world, Stevens says, is "all one color" (*NA*, 26), a "basic slate" (*CP*, 15), a sinister or scowling "pediment of appearance" (*CP*, 361). As such, it forces the imagination to define itself as its opposite, or nothingness. At this point a construct emerges which is rather similar to the construct of being and nothingness in Sartre. The *Lumpenwelt* is reality on the minimum imaginative basis; the imagination on the same basis is merely the unreal: reality is everything; the imagination is nothing. The imagination never brings anything into the world, Stevens says in an unconscious echo of the burial service (*NA*, 59), though it is not quite so true for him that it can take nothing out. This confrontation of being and nothingness, the starting point of imaginative energy, is the vision of the listener in "The Snow Man," who,

> nothing himself, beholds
> Nothing that is not there and the nothing that is.
>
> [*CP*, 9]

Traditionally, the world of becoming has always been regarded as the product of being and nothingness. For Stevens there is no reality of being in the traditional sense of something that does not change. Whenever we try to imagine an unchanging ideal, we get involved in the hopeless paradox of Keats's Grecian urn, where the little town on the hidden side of the urn will never be inhabited to all eternity. The woman in "Sunday Morning" asks resentfully, "Why should she give her bounty to the dead?" but soon comes to realize that she cannot have any alternative without change, and therefore death, at the heart of it. Reality is phenomenal and belongs to the world of becoming. In the very late poem "Of Mere Being" (*OP*, 117) the only unchanging thing about being is that it remains external, "at the end of the mind," "beyond the last thought."

Two of the requirements of the "supreme fiction" are that it must change and that it must give pleasure, and it is clear that for Stevens these two things are much the same thing, change being the only real source of pleasure. Over and over Stevens returns to what he calls "the motive for metaphor," the fact that what is change in reality is also pleasure in the imagination. The imagination, the principle of the unreal, breaks up and breaks down the tyranny of what is there by unifying itself with what is not there, and so suggesting the principle of variety in its existence. This is the point of identity on which all art is founded: in the imaginations of Cézanne and Klee, Stevens says, reality is transmuted from substance into subtlety (*NA*, 174). We get the idea of unchanging being from the thereness of the physical world, the fact that it doesn't go away. What does go away, and is to that extent unreal, is what the unreality of the imagination builds on. The imagination, in short, "skims the real for its unreal" (*CP*, 272).

This kind of activity gives us a relatively simple type of variation form, the kind represented by the "Blackbird" poem. Here the variations are what Stevens calls the "casual exfoliations" (*NA*, 86) of an imagination contemplating a real thing. The recipe for this type of variation form is given in the poem "Someone Puts a Pineapple Together," one of "Three Academic Pieces" in *The Necessary Angel*:

> Divest reality
> Of its propriety. Admit the shaft
> Of that third planet to the table and then:

The third planet, he has explained, is the imagination, and there follow a series of twelve numbered variations on the pineapple. It is clear that such a conception of imagination and reality has much to do with the affinity to the pictorial in Stevens, with his fondness for subjects analogous to still life or landscape painting, where the real object and the imaginative variation of it are most dramatically exhibited. Such variation poems are fanciful in Coleridge's sense of the term: Stevens was familiar with Coleridge's distinction, which he acquired through his reading of I. A. Richards (*NA*, 10). They are, so to speak, cyclical poems, where the variations simply surround the theme. As such, they are not the most serious kind of writing. Stevens speaks of the almost total exclusion of "thinking" from such a poem as "Variations on a Summer Day" (*L*, 346) and says also, "I have no doubt that supreme poetry can be produced only on the highest possible level of the cognitive" (*L*, 500). Again one thinks of the musical parallel. The greatest examples of the variation form, such as the last movement of Beethoven's Opus 111, do not merely diversify the theme: they are sequential and progressive forms as well, and we feel at the end that they have, so to speak, exhausted the theme, done what there is to be done with it. We have now to see if we can discover a sequential and progressive aspect to Stevens's variation form also.

We began with a confrontation between imagination and reality, in which the former is a negation, the opposite of reality. Then we found that the imagination can intensify reality by seizing on the "unreal" aspect of it, the aspect that changes and therefore gives pleasure. Stevens says, "A sense of reality keen enough to be in excess of the normal sense of reality creates a reality of its own" (NA, 79). As he goes on to say, this is a somewhat circular statement, and one would expect it to lead to some such principle as Blake's "As the Eye, such the Object," the principle that the degree of reality depends on the energy of the imagination. Stevens resists this implication, because of his constant fear that the imagination will simply replace reality and thereby deprive itself of its own material cause. For him the imagination is rather an informing principle of reality, transmuting its uniformity into variety, its "heavy scowl" (CP, 362) into lightness and pleasure. Still, it seems clear that we cannot go on indefinitely thinking of the imagination merely as a negation or nothingness.

The fact that the imagination seizes on the changing aspect of reality means that it lives in a continuous present. This means not only that "the imperfect is our paradise" (CP, 194), but that the imagination is always beginning. The only reason for finishing anything is that we can then be rid of it and can come around to the point at which we can begin again. The shoddiness of being fixated on the past, of refusing to discard what he calls the "hieratic" (NA, 58) meets us everywhere in Stevens. The imagination in the sunlit world of reality is like food in hot weather: whatever is kept spoils. Hence "one of the motives in writing is renewal" (NA, 220). This emphasis on constant fresh beginnings is connected, naturally, with the steadfast resistance to anything resembling an echo or an influence from other poets in Stevens, in striking contrast to the absorption of echoes and influences that we find in, for instance, Eliot.

What is true of the past is also true of the future, the desire to use the imagination to make over reality that we find in so many romantics, revolutionaries, and spokesmen of the irrational. Stevens speaks of this desire with a good deal of sympathy and understanding, for instance, in his essay on the irrational in poetry (*OP*, 216), where he links the irrational, once again, with the pressure of external fact on the modern poet and his consequent sense of claustrophobia and desire for freedom. "Owl's Clover" is a carefully considered effort to come to terms with the revolutionary desire for freedom and equality on a vast social scale. But when the imagination is used as part of an attempt to make over reality, it imposes its own unreality on it. The result is that perversion of belief which we see in all religions, including the contemporary atheistic ones. Belief derives from the imaginative unreal: what we really believe in is a fiction, something we have made up ourselves. But all beliefs, when they become institutionalized, tend to ascribe some hidden reality to themselves, a projection of the imagination which can end only in disillusionment or self-hypnotism. The "romantic" of this type (Stevens uses the word romantic in several senses, but this one is pejorative: cf. *L*, 277) is "incapable of abstraction" (*NA*, 139), abstraction being among other things the ability to hold a belief as a "supreme fiction" without projecting it to the other side of reality.

At the same time Stevens holds to an intensely social conception of poetry and its function, though a deeply conservative one. The poet, he says, should try to reach the "centre," and by this he means first of all a social center. The poet expresses among other things "that ultimate good sense which we term civilization" (*NA*, 116). For him reality includes human society as well. As such, the imagination defines the style of a culture or civilization: it is whatever it is that makes everything in Spain look Spanish, and makes every cultural product of Spain a variation on a Spanish theme. Stevens uses the phrase "variations on a theme" in connection with a closely related aspect of culture: the predominance and persistence of a convention, as in medieval or Chinese painting (*NA*, 73).

If we ask what the characteristics of such imaginative penetration of reality are in human life, the words "nobility" and "elegance" come fairly close, though Stevens admits that they are dangerous words. The quality in literature that we recognize as heroic, the power of the imagination to make things look more intensely real, is a quality of illusion in reality that is at the same time a growth in reality. The imagination is thus socially aristocratic, though not necessarily in a class sense. The more power it gains, the more freedom and privilege it enjoys, and the more confident society becomes about its culture. In a time like ours the imagination is more preoccupied in fighting its environment, which presses in on it much harder. In the poem "Mrs. Alfred Uruguay," Mrs. Uruguay herself rides up a mountain in the state of the snow man, looking at her world honestly but reductively, as totally without illusion. She meets going down the mountain a "capable man" who recalls the noble rider of Stevens's earliest prose essay, whose imagination is of the same kind as her own, but is more emancipated, and hence to some extent its fulfillment. It is he who creates

> out of the martyrs' bones,
> The ultimate elegance: the imagined land.
>
> [*CP*, 250]

So our confrontation between a negative imagination and a positive reality has reached the point where this negation has informed human civilization and produced a style of living. This process, considered in an individual context, is the theme of the sequential variation form "The Comedian as the Letter C." Crispin, the hero of the poem, begins with the principle: "Nota: Man is the intelligence of his soil," a strictly Cartesian principle in which man is the "sovereign ghost." This first variation is headed "The World without Imagination." The fourth variation brings us to "The Idea of a Colony," which begins:

Nota: his soil is man's intelligence.
That's better. That's worth crossing seas to find.

[CP, 36]

Stevens calls Crispin a "profitless philosopher," says that he never discovers the meaning of life (L, 293), that social contact would have been a catastrophe for him (L, 295), that he is an everyday man whose life has not the slightest adventure (L, 778), and symbolizes him by the one letter of the alphabet which has no distinctive sound of its own. Nevertheless, Crispin works very hard to achieve his own kind of reality, and if he is not a poet he is at least a colonizer, someone who achieves a life-style out of a pilgrimage and a settlement in new surroundings. The poem as a whole goes around in an ironic circle, and Crispin ends much where he began, using his imagination as so many people do, to select and exclude rather than create, a realist who rejects reality. Hence the final line of the poem, "So may the relation of each man be clipped." Stevens may also have Crispin partly in mind when he says, "The man who has been brought up in an artificial school becomes intemperately real. The Mallarmiste becomes the proletarian novelist" (OP, 221). Still, Crispin represents something of the historical process that produced the culture and the tradition out of which Stevens himself developed, moving from baroque Europe to realistic New England.

We have next to see how a negation can be an informing principle in reality. This brings us to Stevens's conception of the "supreme fiction." The imagination informs reality through fictions or myths (the word "fictive" in Stevens means mythical), which are the elements of a model world. This model world is not "reality," because it does not exist, it is not "there"; but it is an unborn or, perhaps, potential reality which becomes a growth out of reality itself. Stevens quotes Simone Weil, obviously with approval, on the subject of "decreation," a moving from the created to the uncreated, going in the opposite direction from destruction, which moves from the created to nothingness (NA, 174). The conception is Stevens's, though the terms are not. The first law of the supreme fiction is that it must be abstract. It is abstract for the same reason that a god is not reducible to his image. The supreme fiction is not a thing, something to be pointed to or contemplated or thought of as achieved. In its totality, the supreme fiction is poetry or the work of the imagination as a whole, but this totality never separates from the perceiving subject or becomes external. Stevens says, "The abstract does not exist, but . . . the fictive abstract is as immanent in the mind of the poet, as the idea of God is immanent in the mind of the theologian" (L, 434). This last indicates that God is one of the supreme fictions. God for Stevens, whatever he may be in himself, must be for man an unreality of the imagination, not a reality, and his creative power can manifest itself only in the creations of man. The explicit statement that God and the imagination are one is made by the "interior paramour," an anima-figure working under the direction of the imagination.

According to Stevens, "The wonder and mystery of art, as indeed of religion in the last resort, is the revelation of something 'wholly other' by which the inexpressible loneliness of thinking is broken and enriched" (OP, 237). The phrase "wholly other," which is in quotation marks, suggests the existential theology of Karl Barth, as relayed through a poet who calls himself a "dried-up Presbyterian" (L, 792). In Barth, of course, the otherness of God and the alienation of man are conditions of man's unregenerate state. God does not remain wholly other for two reasons: first, he has created and redeemed man; and second, he has revealed himself. Let us see what reality in Stevens can do along parallel lines.

When Crispin discovers that the Cartesian principle "Man is the intelligence of his soil" is less true than its reverse, that "his soil is man's intelligence," Stevens is saying that the antithesis of imagination and reality did not begin as such. Man grew out of "reality," and the consciousness which enables him also to draw away from it is a recent development. The human is "alien," but it is also "the non-human making choice of a human self" (NA, 89). The imagination is a product of reality, its Adam, so to speak, or exiled son. Just as, in Dante's Purgatorio, the poet makes his way back to the Eden which is his own original home, so the imagination contemplates the "rock," the dead inert reality before it, and realizes that it is itself the rock come to life. "I am what is around me" (*CP*, 86), the poet says, and he continually returns to the sense of the "wholly other" as not only the object but the origin of the sense of identity.

The rock is not dead, because it has never died; death is a process, not a condition. It represents rather the unconscious and undifferentiated external world at the bottom of the imaginative ladder, where the sense of thereness is overpowering and the imagination is simply its negation. In the course of time leaves cover the rock: life emerges from the inanimate, breaks up and diversifies the heavy *Lumpenwelt*. Life, then, if Stevens's general argument still applies, is the negation of the inanimate, the unreal at work in the real. The imagination does with "things as they are" what life does with the rock, and the poet's imagination is inseparably attached to the articulating of life in the rest of the world. The "howl" of the doves (*OP*, 97), the "cry" of the leaves (*OP*, 96), the sea in "The Idea of Order at Key West," the "Bantams in Pine-Woods," who are praising themselves and not a divine bantam in the rising sun, are all part of the symphony of life in which the poet has his own voice. We speak of a will to live, and similarly "imagination is the will of things" (*CP*, 84).

The poem "Oak Leaves Are Hands" describes a "Lady Lowzen," who is also the goddess Flora, and who continues to "skim the real for its unreal" in human imagination as formerly in the vegetable world. Lady Lowzen is "chromatic," and the delight of vegetable nature in color supplies Stevens with his chief image for the imagination, which he thinks of as, so to speak, the coloring principle of reality. The basis of nature is metamorphosis, the basis of poetry is metaphor, and metaphor and metamorphosis are for Stevens interchangeable terms. Stevens completes the identification by saying "in metaphor the imagination is life" (*NA*, 73). In this context the variations which the imagination makes on reality join the Darwinian theme with variations in which every variety is a mutation thrown out toward the environment, the "reality" it has to struggle with, until a successful mutation blends and identifies with that reality.

The limit of poetry, as Stevens himself frequently remarks, has always been the imaginatively conceivable, not what is or "things as they are," and any poet deeply impressed by things as they are is apt to suffer from imaginative claustrophobia. Stevens has relegated God to the imaginative unreal, a fiction the human mind creates. He has made an uncompromising bourgeois rejection of all politically revolutionary values. He dismisses Nietzsche and his doctrine of the self-transcendence of man as being "as perfect a means of getting out of focus as a little bit too much to drink" (L, 432). What is left? How much further can a "harmonious skeptic" (CP, 122) carry his rage for order? Even things as they are present themes which the poet cannot avoid and yet can hardly deal with on their terms. For instance, a surprising number of Stevens's poems are about death, and death is one subject where the imagination, like Good Deeds in *Everyman*, may be prevailed on to accompany the poet as his guide, while "reality," in whatever form or disguise, will always mutter some excuse and slope off. When Stevens gets to the point of saying that "Life and Nature are one" (L, 533), he has left very little room for any reality which he has not in some other context called unreal.

In Stevens's cultural situation about the only consistent "position" left is that of a secular humanism. But, he says, the more he sees of humanism the less he likes it, and, more briefly and explicitly, "humanism is not enough" (L, 489). He also says, "Between humanism and something else, it might be possible to create an acceptable fiction" (L, 449) and that "there are fictions that are extensions of reality" (L, 430). This last concession means that Stevens is capable, at least in his poetry, of sweeping "reality" out of the way as a superego symbol and of reducing it to its proper role as the material cause of poetry.

In reality, man is a social being, and society is partly an aggregate, a mass of men, often dominated by, and expressing their will through, some kind of hero or leader. The hero in this sense is a fiction which has been, like so many other fictions, misapplied and misunderstood by society. In two poems particularly, "Examination of the Hero in a Time of War" and "Life on a Battleship," Stevens shows us how the dictatorial hero or charismatic leader is a false projection of the imagination, like the heavens and hells that are created by the imagination and are then asserted to be actual places in the world which is there. The genuine form of this fiction is the conception of all men as a single man, where the difference between the individual and the mass has ceased to exist. Or, as Stevens puts it, in commenting on a passage in "Notes toward a Supreme Fiction" which contains the phrase "leaner being" (*CP,* 387), "The trouble with humanism is that man as God remains man, but there is an extension of man, the leaner being, in fiction, a possibly more than human human, a composite human. The act of recognizing him is the act of this leaner being moving in on us" (*L,* 434). This "leaner being" is the "central man" or "man of glass" (*CP,* 250) who is all men, and whom Stevens portrays as a titanic being striding the skies (*CP,* 212). Even Crispin reaches an apotheosis of identity with this being (*OP,* 24).

In this conception of a "general being or human universe" (*CP,* 378), we are still in the area of fictions, but by now we understand that the poet "gives to life the supreme fictions without which we are unable to conceive of it" (*NA,* 31). Whatever unreal grows out of reality becomes real, like the graft of art on nature which Polixenes urges on Perdita in *The Winter's Tale.* The human universe is still a fiction and to that extent is not strictly true, but, as Abraham Cowley said of the philosophy of Thomas Hobbes, " 'Tis so like Truth 'twill serve our turn as well." In any case, on this level of fiction we can understand how poetry can be called "a transcendent analogue composed of the particulars of reality" (*NA,* 130), the word "transcendent" here being used, I think, quite carefully in its philosophical sense as going beyond sense experience but not beyond the mental organization of that experience. Certain sentences in *The Necessary Angel* which Stevens mutters out of the corner of his mouth when he thinks his censor is not listening take on a new and illuminating significance. One such sentence is this one from "Imagination as Value": "The imagination that is satisfied by politics, whatever the nature of the politics, has not the same value as the imagination that seeks to satisfy, say, the universal mind, which, in the case of a poet, would be the imagination that tries to penetrate to basic images, basic emotions, and so to compose a fundamental poetry even older than the ancient world" (*NA,* 145). This universal mind is the mind that has produced "the essential poem at the centre of things" (*CP,* 440), which is *the* supreme fiction as such. In this perspective, "reality" becomes the stabilizing principle which enables us, even as we outgrow our gods, to recognize, even in the act of coming around to the beginning again, that the creative faculties are always the same faculties and that "the things created are always the same things" (*OP,* 211). In all the variations of what might be we can still hear the theme of what is there.

The supreme fiction of the "central," which is the total form of both man and the human imagination, takes us into a very different context of variability, a context less Darwinian than Thomist. It would be easy, but simplistic, to say that ultimately what is real in Stevens is the universal, the universal being the theme of which the individual is the variation. Easy, because one could quote a good many passages from the later poems, at least, in support of it; but simplistic, because the traditional context of the real universal is a kind of essential world that Stevens never at any point accepts. "Logically," says Stevens, "I ought to believe in essential imagination, but that has its difficulties" (*L,* 370). In the early "Peter Quince at the Clavier" we have the line "The body dies; the body's beauty lives." Considering the number of poets, in English literature and elsewhere, who would have drawn a Platonic inference from that statement, it comes as a deliberate and calculated shock for Stevens to say:

> Beauty is momentary in the mind,
> The fitful tracing of a portal,
> But in the flesh it is immortal.

"A Collect of Philosophy" has nothing of medieval realism, though it reflects Stevens's fascination with Plato, but it does express a keen interest in such conceptions as Alexander's "compresence" of mind and existence, and, more particularly, in the great passage in Whitehead's *Science and the Modern World* in which Whitehead rejects the conception of "simple location" in space and announces the doctrine of interpenetration, the doctrine that everything is everywhere at once. Stevens's comment on this passage is, "These words are pretty obviously words from a level where everything is poetic, as if the statement that every location involves an aspect of itself in every other location produced in the imagination a universal iridescence, a dithering of presences and, say, a complex of differences" (*OP*, 192). This last phrase shows that Stevens is still thinking within the metaphor of a theme and variations.

Stevens often refers to Eliot as a poet who represents the exact opposite of everything he stood for himself, and perhaps we are now beginning to understand why. The fifth way of looking at a blackbird, for example, is a way that Eliot constantly refuses to look at it:

> I do not know which to prefer,
> The beauty of inflections
> Or the beauty of innuendoes,
> The blackbird whistling
> Or just after.

"A Collect for Philosophy" assumes in passing that all knowledge is knowledge after the experience of the knowledge (*OP*, 190). For Eliot, the fact that there is a split second between an experience and the awareness of having had the experience is a memento of the Fall of Man. All three dimensions of time for Eliot are categories of unreality: the no longer, the not yet, and the never quite. Our ordinary existence in this time is the fallen shadow of the life we might have lived if there had been no Fall, in which experience and consciousness would be the same thing, and in which the present moment would be a real moment, an eternal now. Eliot's imagination revolves around the figure of Percival in the Grail castle, who, in the words of "The Dry Salvages," "had the experience but missed the meaning," because he was afraid to put the question that would have unified experience and meaning. In this sense we are all Prufrocks, vaguely aware that there is an "overwhelming question" to be asked, and wasting our lives in various devices for not asking it.

Stevens has nothing of Eliot's sense of the phenomenal world as a riddle, to be solved by some kind of conscious experience that annihilates it. When we start climbing the Ash-Wednesday staircase, we have to regard such things as "a slotted window bellied like the fig's fruit" as a distraction. This is because at the top of Eliot's staircase is a total unification and an absorption of reality into the infinite being of God. Like Dante whom he is following, Eliot wants his pilgrimage to pass beyond the categories of time and space and the cycle of nature that revolves within these categories. The slotted window is an image of that cycle, the vegetable cycle of flower and fruit, the cycle of human life that begins with birth from a womb. Stevens does not resemble Yeats any more closely than he resembles Eliot, but, like Yeats, he sides with the "self" in the "Dialogue of Self and Soul." For his Mrs. Uruguay, as for Yeats, the top of the mountain or staircase or whatever has to be climbed is the top of the natural cycle, and the fulfillment of climbing it is in coming down again. In Stevens, the imagination is life, and the only way to kill it is to take it outside nature, into a world where it has swallowed nature and become a total periphery or circumference, instead of remaining "central." So for Stevens, as in a very different way for Joyce in *Finnegans Wake*, the cycle of nature is the only possible image of whatever is beyond the cycle, "the same anew."

There is an elaborate imagery of the seasons of the year in Stevens, where summer represents the expanded and fulfilled imagination, autumn the more restricted and realistic imagination, and winter the reduction to a black-and-white world where reality is "there" and the imagination set over against it is simply unreal. The emotional focus of this imagery comes at the moment in spring when the first blush of color enters the world with "an access of color, a new and unobserved, slight dithering" (*CP,* 517: the last word echoes the comment on Whitehead already quoted), or when a bird's cry "at the earliest ending of winter" signals "a new knowledge of reality" (*CP,* 534), or at Easter. "On Easter," says Stevens, "the great ghost of what we call the next world invades and vivifies this present world, so that Easter seems like a day of two lights, one the sunlight of the bare and physical end of winter, the other the double light" (*OP,* 239). What Easter symbolizes to Stevens is that we are constantly trying to close up our world on the model of our own death, to become an "owl in the sarcophagus." As long as some reality is still outside us we are still alive, and what is still external in that reality is what has a renewing power for us. This vision is the point at which "dazzle yields to a clarity and we observe" (*CP*, 341), when we see the world as total process, extending over both death and life, always new, always just beginning, always full of hope, and possessed by the innocence of an uncreated world which is unreal only because it has never been fixed in death. This is also the point at which the paradox of reality and imagination comes into focus for the poet and he understands that

> We make, although inside an egg,
> Variations on the words spread sail.

>   [*CP*, 490]

NOTE

1. The following abbreviations for works by Wallace Stevens are used in this paper:

CP   *The Collected Poems of Wallace Stevens* (New York: Knopf, 1954).

L   *Letters of Wallace Stevens,* selected and edited by Holly Stevens (New York: Knopf, 1967).

NA   *The Necessary Angel: Essays on Reality and the Imagination* (New York: Knopf, 1951).

OP   *Opus Posthumous,* edited by Samuel French Morse (New York: Knopf, 1957).

Selected Bibliography of William K. Wimsatt

BOOKS

The Prose Style of Samuel Johnson. New Haven: Yale University Press, 1941.

Philosophic Words: A Study of Style and Meaning in the "Rambler" and "Dictionary" of Samuel Johnson. New Haven: Yale University Press, 1948.

(Ed.) *Alexander Pope: Selected Poetry and Prose.* New York: Rinehart, 1951; rev. ed., 1972.

The Verbal Icon: Studies in the Meaning of Poetry. Two preliminary essays written in collaboration with M. C. Beardsley. Lexington: University of Kentucky Press, 1954.

(Ed.) *English Stage Comedy: Six Essays.* New York: Columbia University Press, 1955.

(With Cleanth Brooks) *Literary Criticism: A Short History.* New York: Alfred A. Knopf, 1957.

(Ed. with F. A. Pottle) *Boswell for the Defence, 1769–1774.* New York: McGraw-Hill, 1959; London: William Heinemann, 1959.

(Ed.) *Samuel Johnson on Shakespeare.* New York: Hill and Wang, 1960.

CEA Chap Book: What to Say about a Poem. With comments by seven other critics and responses by WKW. Ed. D. A. Sears. Supplement to *The CEA Critic,* 26, no. 3, December 1963.

(Ed.) *Explication as Criticism: Selected Papers from the English Institute, 1941–1952.* New York: Columbia University Press, 1963.

Hateful Contraries. With an essay on English meter written in collaboration with M. C. Beardsley. Lexington: University of Kentucky Press, 1965.

The Portraits of Alexander Pope. New Haven: Yale University Press, 1965.

How to Compose Chess Problems and Why. New Haven: Privately printed, 1966.

(Ed.) *The Idea of Comedy: Essays in Prose and Verse, Ben Jonson to George Meredith.* Englewood Cliffs, New Jersey: Prentice-Hall, 1969.

UNCOLLECTED ARTICLES AND NOTES

"Poe and the Chess Automaton," *American Literature,* 11 (1939), 138–51.

"Poe and the Mystery of Mary Rogers," *PMLA,* 56 (1941), 230–48.

"Comment on 'Two Essays in Practical Criticism,'" *The University Review,* 9 (1942), 139–43.

Articles in *Dictionary of World Literature.* Ed. Joseph T. Shipley. New York: McLeod, 1943: "Antithesis," "Elegant Variation"; with M. C. Beardsley, "Abstract," "Intention."

"What Poe Knew about Cryptography," *PMLA,* 58 (1943), 754–79.

Analysis of W. H. Auden's "Sir, No Man's Enemy," *The Explicator,* 3 (1945), no. 51.

"Further Comment on Constable and Collier," *PQ,* 24 (1945), 119–22.

"Johnson and Scots," *TLS,* 9 March 1946, p. 115.

"Johnson on Electricity," *RES,* 23 (1947), 257–60.

"Johnson's Treatment of Bolingbroke in the Dictionary," *MLR,* 43 (1948), 78–80.

(With Margaret H. Wimsatt) "Self-Quotations and Anonymous Quotations in Johnson's *Dictionary.*" *ELH,* 15 (1948), 60–68.

"Mary Rogers, John Anderson, and Others," *American Literature,* 21 (1950), 482–84.

"Philosophic Words," *PQ,* 29 (1950), 84–88.

"The Game of Ombre in *The Rape of the Lock,*" *RES,* n.s. 1 (1950), 136–43.

"Samuel Johnson and Dryden's *DuFresnoy,*" *SP,* 48 (1951), 26–39.

"A Further Note on Poe's 'Balloon Hoax,'" *American Literature,* 22 (1951), 491–92.

"The Bodleian Portrait of Alexander Pope," *The Bodleian Library Record,* 7 (1963), 87–91.

"'Amicitiae Causa': A Birthday Present from Curll to Pope." In *Restoration and Eighteenth-Century Literature: Essays in Honor of Alan Dugald McKillop.* Ed. Carroll Camden. Chicago: University of Chicago Press, 1963, pp. 341–50.

Le Moyne College Commencement Address. *The Heights, The Le Moyne College Magazine,* 3 (1965), 47–51.

"Northrop Frye: Criticism as Myth." In *Northrop Frye in Modern Criticism.* Ed. Murray Krieger. New York: Columbia University Press, 1966, pp. 75–107.

"History of Literary Criticism." In *The New Catholic Encyclopedia.*
New York: McGraw-Hill, 1967, VIII, 794–803.

"Genesis: A Fallacy Revisited." In *The Disciplines of Criticism.*
Ed. Peter Demetz et al. New Haven: Yale University Press, 1968,
pp. 193–225.

"In Praise of *Rasselas:* Four Notes Converging." In *Imagined Worlds:
Essays in Memory of John Butt.* Ed. Maynard Mack and Ian Gregor.
London: Methuen & Co. Ltd., 1968, pp. 111–36.

"Day of the Leopards," *Ventures, Magazine of the Yale Graduate School,*
9 (1969), 46–52. Reprinted in *College English,* 33 (1972), 877–82.

"Laokoön: An Oracle Reconsulted." *In Eighteenth-Century Studies in
Honor of Donald F. Hyde.* Ed. W. H. Bond. New York: Grolier
Club, 1970, pp. 347–63.

"Imitation as Freedom, 1717–1798." In *Forms of Lyric: Selected Papers
from the English Institute.* Ed. R. A. Brower. New York: Columbia
University Press, 1970, pp. 47–74.

"Battering the Object: The Ontological Approach." In *Contemporary
Criticism: Stratford-upon-Avon Studies,* no. 12. Ed. Malcolm Brad-
bury and David Palmer. London: Edward Arnold, 1970, pp. 60–81.

"The Rule and the Norm: Halle and Keyser on Chaucer's Meter,"
College English, 31 (1970), 774–88.

LONG REVIEWS

Jacques Barzun, *Teacher in America.* In *The Yale Law Journal,* 54
(1945), 733–37.

Charles Morris, *Signs, Language and Behavior.* In *Quarterly Review
of Literature,* 3 (1946), 180–85.

Perspectives of Criticism, ed. Harry Levin. In *Comparative Literature,*
3 (1951), 368–72.

"Exhuming the Recent Past." Review article on William Van O'Con-
nor, *An Age of Criticism, 1900–1950.* In *Sewanee Review,* 62 (1954),
348–53.

The Kenyon Critics, ed. J. C. Ransom. In *Comparative Literature,*
6 (1954), 265–71.

John Thompson, *The Founding of English Meter.* In *Renaissance
News,* 16 (1963), 130–33.

Eliseo Vivas, *The Aesthetic Transaction.* In *Criticism,* 8 (1966),
196–202.

"Eliot's Weary Gestures of Dismissal." Review article on T. S. Eliot,
To Criticize the Critic and Other Writings. In *The Massachusetts
Review,* 7 (1966), 584–90.

Murray Krieger, *A Window to Criticism: Shakespeare's "Sonnets" and Modern Poetics.* In *MP,* 64 (1966), 71–74.

"Sparshott on Aesthetics: A *Guided* Tour." Review article on F. E. Sparshott, *The Structure of Aesthetics.* In *The Review of Metaphysics,* 20 (1966), 71–87.

"On Scanning English Meters." Review article on Harvey Gross, *Sound and Form in Modern Poetry: A Study of Prosody from Thomas Hardy to Robert Lowell.* In *Michigan Quarterly Review,* 5 (1966), 291–95.

Robert Marsh, *Four Dialectical Theories of Poetry: An Aspect of English Neoclassical Criticism.* In *JEGP,* 65 (1966), 727–30.

Index

419